Overview

Contents

About the Authors

PAUL CASSEL has been working with small computers since the late 1970s. His interest in Microsoft Windows dates back to the first release in the mid-1980s. By 1991, he was developing programs for Windows and consulting with clients about the then revolutionary operating system. He has worked with Microsoft's development teams on many projects since then, including Windows for Workgroups, Windows 95, Windows 98, Windows NT, and many application programs. He has won numerous MVP awards from Microsoft and similar awards and recognition from other software companies.

MICHAEL HART is a consultant with over twenty years of computer experience. He has served in all sizes of Information Systems departments—from as small as one member to as large as a multinational organization of hundreds. Michael has held positions ranging from field engineer to client/server systems developer to systems manager. Michael has been involved with the deployment and management of Windows-based systems since the release of Windows/386. He also participated in the beta testing programs for Windows 3.0, Windows 3.1, Windows for Workgroups, Windows 95, and Windows 98. In his spare time, Michael enjoys traveling and spending time with his wife Diana, daughter Jaimie, and their two dogs Aladdin and Mitzvah.

Dedications

I'd like to dedicate this book to my daughter Tirilee Cassel. By solving the networking problems on the Zuni Nation, she freed up the time I needed to write this book.

—Paul Cassel

To Diana, my loving and beautiful wife of many years, without whom I would not be who or where I am today.

To Jaimie, my beloved daughter, the joy of my life. Honey, I don't have to write tonight!

To my sons Ira and David—thank you for your support.

—Michael Hart

Acknowledgments

I'd like to express my deepest thanks to my coauthor, Michael Hart. I also thank the people at Macmillan Publishing. I cite them using first names only to protect the bone weary: Dean, Grace, Dana, Philip, Brian, Sunthar, Fran, Jeff, Craig, Maureen, Kate, Kate, Mandie, and Tracy. I also want to acknowledge a non-Macmillan person: Carolyn Linn, the ever patient, who as usual cleaned up whatever messes we others left behind.

—Paul Cassel

A book is no more a single person's effort than a car is. Any number of bright, skilled people contribute to the content between the covers. The authors of a book rely on so many others to do what they do best, yet the authors get the credit.

Many, many thanks to Paul Cassel for the encouragement when I needed encouragement, for the advice when advice was needed, for the cheerleading, the thought-provoking discussions on computer technology and trends, and for just being there when needed.

The fine team of people at Sams Publishing deserve so much credit for all they do. Much thanks to our Executive Editor Grace Buechlein, who kept us all on track (and in line) with the patience of a saint. Thanks to Jeff Perkins and Craig Arnush for keeping us honest with their superb technical editing. Thanks to Philip Wescott, Brian Proffitt, Sunthar Visuvalingam, Fran Hatton, and Craig Arnush for their development input. Thanks to Mandie Rowell for making our words look like a book should look. Thanks to Dana Lesh, Maureen McDaniel, Kate Talbot, Kate Givens, Carolyn Linn, and all the editors who contributed their efforts to this book.

—Michael Hart

Introduction

What's new in Windows 98? A number of great new features that will make your Windows operating system faster, easier, and more enjoyable to use. A short time with the product quickly taught us that this operating system isn't a rehashed Windows 95, but an entirely new product. What you hold in your hands is a completely new book written exclusively for Windows 98.

If you're familiar with Windows 95 or Windows NT 4, you can see some superficial resemblance between them and Windows 98. It's true that Microsoft didn't start utterly fresh when designing Windows 98, but built on the foundation laid by its predecessors. However, the result is that little in Windows 98 is the same as Windows 95.

Many of the changes in Windows 98 are of the structural kind. This isn't a book about operating system theory, but a hands-on book about how to use Windows 98. In other words, this is a user's book. Because of this we tend to skip over, or treat lightly, the pro-
'mming aspects of Windows 98.

'ser standpoint, there are enormous differences in Windows 98 when you com-
'at has come before. Here are a few of the new features:

Desktop—A new feature included in Windows 98 (and of Windows 95
'n with Internet Explorer 4), the Active Desktop enables you to dis-
'ktop Web pages and other objects that have live connections to the
'net. The desktop becomes "active" in that such objects automati-
'es to reflect new or changed content at the remote source.
'Classic Desktop, the Active Desktop offers a uniform
'l, network, and Internet resources.

there's a way to really back up your system, so if
'ou have to replace your hard drive, you can fully

'l to tell you much more about your comput-
'ntil you really *need* to know something
's information without buying an

'en you're connected to the
'f there are newer or better versions
', you'll be notified and given the option

can
'r on

USB?
's—from
'all without
'stuff.

'he new
'l and news
'ut but never
'dozen or more
'le display adapters
'plays. If you think
'o the same thing, but

- Optimization—Again Microsoft provides the utility you used to have to pay more for. Windows 98 contains not only a real disk defragmenter, but also another utility that cleans unneeded files from your disk, bogus entries within your Registry, and broken links within your folder structure. Previously, these services required expensive utilities that often broke more than they fixed.

- The System File Checker—This is a utility to make sure the system files haven't been erased, moved, or corrupted. These types of problems will cause odd behavior or even system failures. Now all you need to do is to run this simple service, and Windows 98 will not only check to see if the files are all right, but will also offer to fix any that aren't.

- The System Configuration utility: At long last, Microsoft has given us a way to 100% control the profile of an operating system at startup. No longer will you have to choose between full startup and the old "safe" boot, but you'll be able to add or remove any aspect of Windows 98's startup profile. This is ultimate tool for troubleshooting! This program pays for the upgrade cost to Windows 98 the first time you use it.

- Improved Dr. Watson—The doctor has been around a long time. He has now been updated to help support personnel (which might be you) diagnose an application crash after the fact to prevent its recurrence.

- Vastly improved power management—Microsoft has been talking about the desi ability of the legendary "instant on" computers. We finally have this in Windov 98. You will need some of the latest hardware, but if you are so equipped, you choose from a large array of power saving settings. Somewhere between nev and never off is the setting just right for you.

- Support for USB (Universal Serial Bus) hardware—Have you heard abou This is the new standard allowing you to daisy chain dozens of periphera mouse devices to scanners to keyboards to modems (and much more)— worrying about I/O addresses, IRQs (Interrupt Requests), or other nast Windows 98 is the *only* operating system that fully supports USB.

- Internet integration—Windows 98 is made for interconnections. All Internet options—from WebTV to a fully integrated browser, a ma client, NetMeeting, and many other items you might have read ab tried—are all in this operating system. There's no need to buy a add-ons to get fully connected—it's all there in Windows 98.

- Multiple monitor support—Windows 98 has support for multi and monitors. You can run different programs in different di multitasking two or more programs is neat, wait until you d running each program on its own display!

- More efficient use of disk space—FAT32 and the converter alter your current outmoded file system to a new one capable of not only greater efficiency, but also vastly greater capacity (no more 2GB limit or huge cluster sizes). FAT32 is the new way to store data on your hard disk.

- Hosting capabilities—With Windows 98, you can set up your computer to act as a Dial-Up Server for not only TCP/IP, but also IPX/SFX and NetBEUI networks.

- Improved connections to the Internet—Have you ever had trouble figuring out what all those mysterious Internet settings mean? If so, the new wizards that step you through the configuration process are tailor-made for you. The mystery of connecting to the Internet (or various sources such as CompuServe or America Online) is now gone.

- Virtual private networks—By using the new PPTP (Point-to-Point Tunneling Protocol) within Windows 98, you'll provide a high-level of security (privacy) when communicating over public lines such as the Internet. This is almost as good as having your own cables!

- The Win32 Driver Model (WDM)—A new universal driver model for much of the new hardware coming out. Using WDM, you can easily configure a vast array of hardware. In fact, because of PnP (Plug and Play), you don't need to do anything other than watch the system configure itself. WDM is the new model for both Windows 98 and future versions of Windows NT.

And there's more, but you get the idea. Windows 98 beckons, so let's jump right in and start computing!

Conventions Used in This Book

Special design features enhance the text material:

- Notes
- Tips
- Cautions
- Tasks
- Workshops

Note

Notes explain interesting or important points that can help you understand Windows 98 concepts and techniques.

Tips are little pieces of information that help you in real-world situations. Tips often offer shortcuts or information to make a task easier or faster.

Cautions provide information about detrimental performance issues or dangerous errors. Pay careful attention to Cautions.

Tasks walk you through the actual steps of various Windows 98 activities that you will undertake as you use and maintain your Windows 98 system.

Each chapter ends with a Workshop. Each Workshop includes a Terminology Review section, a Q&A section, and Exercises so that you can review terms from the chapter, see the answers to some commonly asked questions, and practice what you've learned.

WEEK 1

At a Glance: Getting Started with Windows 98

1

2

3

4

5

6

7

WEEK 1

DAY 1

Welcome

by Michael Hart

Welcome to Windows 98! Windows 98 is the next step in the evolution of the Microsoft Windows operating system. This product release, probably the most popular piece of software ever written, is newly revised and updated with a boatload of enhancements and improvements designed to make using your computer easier than ever.

This chapter covers

- What's new in Windows 98
- Getting started in Windows 98
- Windows 98 basics
- How to get the most out of your computer using this book

For instant gratification, Figure 1.1 shows the Welcome to Windows 98 dialog box. From the Welcome, you can register your copy of Windows 98, take a tour, and so on.

FIGURE 1.1.

The opening screen of Windows 98.

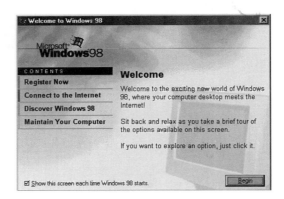

Windows 1.0. Windows 2.0. Windows 386. Windows 3.0. Windows 3.1. Windows for Workgroups. Windows 95. Now, Windows 98. Although the name continues to be unexciting, the product is better than ever. This evolutionary step of the Windows operating system offers more enhancements, more usability features, and more behind-the-scenes improvements than any other in the history of the product.

What's New in Windows 98

Let's take a brief look at what is new and updated in Windows 98. A large number of enhancements and additions to the product bear mentioning. I have divided the highlights into the following five categories:

- Usability
- Multimedia
- Communications
- System tools
- Hardware support

You will undoubtedly notice that several features can easily fit into more than one category. That's okay; in a product as broad as this one, it's hard to nail down a particular feature to a single category. As an example, take Dial-Up Networking, used to make a connection between your PC and another computer or the Internet. Dial-Up Networking is improved and easier to use than in Windows 95—for communications, to facilitate the retrieval of multimedia content from the Internet, and to keep your system up to date in conjunction with the System Update facility. Now, would Dial-Up Networking fall under *usability*, *multimedia*, *communications*, or *system tools*?

Note

> If you're like me, you're probably more interested in seeing it and doing it than reading about it. If you like, bookmark this section for later.
>
> If you're new to Windows or upgrading from MS-DOS, I recommend reading the "Getting Started in Windows 98" section later in the chapter.
>
> If you're upgrading from Windows 3.x or Windows 95, you might skip the Windows introduction and read the section "How to Get the Most out of Your Computer Using This Book."
>
> In any case, be sure to read the Workshop material at the end of this (and each) chapter.

Usability

Microsoft spends a lot of time and money making its software easier for the average PC user to work with. Software that might be technically the best available is of no value if no one can figure out how to use it. The usability features and enhancements in Windows 98 increase its ease of use.

A Single-Click Interface

One problem that many Windows users have always had is remembering when to click and when to double-click. Windows 98 provides an option for configuring the user interface to act as either the classic Windows style interface or a single-click Web browser style interface. Whether you prefer the classic style or the single-click Web browser style, Windows 98 will keep you happy.

Web Viewing of Local Folders

You can now add HTML—World Wide Web (WWW) style—content to any (or all) folders. You can create a Web page that will be displayed in the folder, complete with links, images, sounds, or whatever, or you can just put a nice background image into the folder. Each and every folder can share the same HTML content or background, or you can create a unique look for each folder.

The Active Desktop

The Windows desktop used to be about as exciting as a desk blotter (even if it was a desk blotter with a picture), but now the desktop can actually do something productive. Making your desktop active, you can place ActiveX controls or Java applets directly on the desktop, and they will work in the background. For example, you might download a stock ticker control from the Internet, configure it to watch the stocks in your portfolio, and always have current stock prices available right on your desktop. You might have your desktop also display the latest weather reports for your area.

Part of the Windows 98 Active Desktop is the channel bar, a sort of TV tuner for Internet content. The channel bar enables you to select which information channels you want your desktop to receive.

Built-in Internet Explorer

The single-click interface and the Active Desktop are usability enhancements that spring straight from the latest incarnation of Internet Explorer. With Internet Explorer built in, Microsoft has blurred the distinction between the Web browser and the operating system. To the average user, this simply means that using and viewing information, whether stored on the Web or on your computer, are simpler and easier.

With Internet Explorer comes the ability to navigate Web pages that are stored on your computer. This is called offline browsing and means that you don't even have to be connected to the Internet to view Web pages. For those favorite sites or pages that you always want to keep tabs on (I mean, who could live without a daily Dilbert fix?), you can subscribe to your favorite sites and be notified when they change or even automatically download them for offline viewing.

An Online Services Folder

As an aid to connecting the average user to other content providers, Microsoft has arranged to include the applications from major online service providers such as America Online, CompuServe, AT&T, and The Microsoft Network. This makes it very easy for you to choose a service provider and hook up quickly and easily without having to search for the required software.

A Mail and News Client—Outlook Express

Besides the browser for surfing the World Wide Web, the most popular applications for the Internet are email and Internet newsgroups. Outlook Express, a scaled-down version of the full Outlook product, provides a capable, integrated email client and newsgroup reader. You can now use the same program to access both your email and your favorite newsgroups, saving you the time it would take to learn separate programs.

A Common Address Book

Another convenience included in Windows 98 is the Windows Address Book. Microsoft has created a standard format for storing address information that all kinds of different programs can use. This will cut down on the annoying duplication of having different address books for your email, fax, and contact management programs.

Public Directory Support

The Lightweight Directory Access Protocol (LDAP) is a protocol that makes searching for people on the Internet a lot easier. In fact, Windows now offers an enhancement to the Find command, Find | People, which uses LDAP to search a number of public directory services for contact information.

Multiple Display Support

For those of you who have never been happy using a single monitor and have envied your Macintosh friends' ability to use multiple monitors, envy no more. Windows 98 supports up to nine—count 'em, nine—display adapters and monitors. This is an especially useful feature for certain applications such as financial market monitoring, desktop publishing, and engineering applications.

I believe that even the average user will find that using two or more moderately sized monitors, as opposed to a single large monitor, provides superior usability and flexibility. Picture having two monitors, the first set up to do your normal stuff and the second monitor to display some ActiveX controls, such as the stock ticker and weather watch mentioned previously, and you watching CNN in another window.

An Improved Setup Program

For most users, the usefulness of the Setup program ends after the program is installed, but that doesn't lessen its importance. The new Setup offers improved device detection, better Plug and Play configuration and detection, and automatic reboots as needed. Whether upgrading from a previous Windows installation or installing from scratch, Windows 98 Setup is almost completely hands-off, making your transition to Windows 98 almost effortless.

The My Documents Folder

Continuing its goal of assisting the user in performing everyday tasks, Windows now creates a folder on the desktop, named My Documents. This is intended as a storage place for all your documents. The standard File Open and File Save dialogs have been modified to default to the My Documents folder, also.

This modification not only makes it easier to keep track of where your documents are located but also makes it easier to back up your documents because they are stored in one folder.

Display Enhancements

Besides multiple monitor support, additional enhancements have been added to the display system, giving you better control over almost all aspects of your video system.

Start Menu and Taskbar Customization

The Start menu, introduced in Windows 95, has always been customizable to some extent; that is, you could create your own folders of icons or place icons directly on the Start menu itself. In Windows 98, you can now customize the Start menu even further, giving you the opportunity to mold Windows 98 exactly the way you want it. The taskbar can scroll and contain multiple rows of icons; you can drag nearly anything onto it. Repositioning icons on toolbars is also drag-and-drop simple.

Improved Accessibility Options

For users with visual, aural, or motion disabilities, the Accessibility options provide enhanced feedback. Additional audible feedback, enhanced visibility settings, and alternative multiple keystroke activation sequences are configurable.

Microsoft also includes a Magnifier application that configures a user-definable section of the screen to display a magnified image of the display.

User Interface Effects

Some enhancements to the user interface are for show, as in the case of the new zooming menus—cute, but they don't really enhance usability. Another, the colorized taskbar icons, does add some utility. With this feature, an application needing attention has a blinking task button on the taskbar.

An Improved Help System

The Windows Help system has been completely rewritten and expanded. The Help window now also includes a button to take you directly to the Microsoft Web site, should you need additional technical help.

Multimedia

Windows 98 offers the capability to use data stored in any number of new formats on a variety of storage media. It also offers the capability to send your own content out to others, using new tools, and opens new avenues for your acquisition and sharing of multimedia materials.

Web Publishing Tools

Included with Windows 98 is a scaled-down version of the Microsoft FrontPage 98 program called *FrontPage Express*. Although not as full-featured as its full-package cousin, it nevertheless has a large range of capabilities and is an excellent vehicle for learning about Web page creation.

Digital Versatile Disc Support

The Digital Versatile Disc (DVD) format, which just began appearing in 1997, is a multipurpose format for CD-style media that can contain a variety of data types, such as sound, video, and data. DVD players are supported by Windows 98 for movie playback; drivers are also included for using DVD devices as storage devices.

Video and Still Image Capture

Windows 98 supports multiple devices used for the capture of still images from devices such as digital cameras and scanners and for the capture of video from devices such as FireWire (IEEE1394) devices.

NetShow

Formerly called *ActiveMovie*, NetShow is a streaming media player, which means that the audio and video data is played back even as it streams down into your computer (rather than wait for the entire file to be downloaded before it is played back). This application enables you to view content streamed from the Internet in Active Streaming Format.

DirectX 5 and OpenGL Libraries

The DirectX 5 and OpenGL technologies are standard graphics libraries that enable Windows 98 to take advantage of their strengths for applications that support them; these provide extreme levels of realism and enhanced imagery for games.

Imaging by Kodak

Imaging by Kodak is an image viewer application by Kodak that enables you to open and view image files in many different formats.

TV Tuner and Broadcast Architecture Support

Windows 98 includes direct support for a number of TV tuner products. Beyond that, the tuner support also includes support for the broadcast architecture. Together, these promise to deliver amazing extra content along with traditional TV content. By utilizing unused portions of the television signal, computer content is broadcast at the same time. This enables broadcasts to contain not only the video and audio portions but also supplemental information. For example, the additional material broadcast during a sporting event could be player statistics, live links to teams' home pages, updates on other scores, and so on.

Support for MMX Programs

Although the multimedia extensions (MMX) in Intel chips are obviously a hardware addition, Windows 98 includes drivers necessary to provide application support for any applications that use the MMX features.

Communications

The tools built into Windows 98 for communicating with the outside world have been greatly enhanced over those previously available. Getting connected and communicating with others is now easier than ever.

The Internet Connection Wizard

For users who've not yet connected to the Internet, the Internet Connection Wizard guides you step-by-step through the entire process. The Internet Connection Wizard dials up the Microsoft Internet Referral Service via a toll-free 800 number, downloads a list of Internet service providers (ISPs) in your area, and then steers you through setting up an account.

Dial-Up Networking

First appearing in Windows 95, Dial-Up Networking eases the process of connecting via a modem to some other computer or the Internet. Microsoft has continued to improve Dial-Up Networking to make it easier and more powerful.

The Personal Web Server

Besides the Web page creation capabilities of FrontPage Express, Windows 98 also includes the capabilities to publish those pages via the Personal Web Server. Although not a commercial-grade server, its functionality serves small workgroups or home systems, and it's a great way to learn about creating your own Web site.

Internet NetMeeting

Making private telephone calls or video conferencing calls via the Internet is possible, using Microsoft NetMeeting. Included with Windows 98, NetMeeting enables you to video conference, chat, use a shared whiteboard, share an application, send files, or talk with others across the Internet.

Virtual Private Networking

For remote and mobile workers, obtaining a secure, private connection to the office can be not only difficult but also costly. Using Microsofts' implementation of Virtual Private

Networking, a secure network connection can be established over the Internet to your corporate systems. This enables you to use readily available dial-up Internet connections from nearly anywhere in the world to establish a private connection to the office.

Networking Protocol Enhancements

Microsoft has included enhancements to several networking protocols in this release of Windows. Whether you're connected to a corporate network or you dial in to the Internet, you'll experience better connectivity.

Multilink Channel Aggregation

Multilink channel aggregation is an excellent feature, originally intended for ISDN users. It enables combining multiple dial-up, ISDN, or regular modem connections into a single logical connection, thereby giving higher aggregate throughput. Your ISP must support the protocol before it will work, however.

System Tools

Besides all the enhancements that enable you to do new things, there are more tools included with Windows 98 that make it easier to keep your system running at its peak.

Windows Update

Windows users already know the...um...fun of finding and obtaining updates to the operating system in order to fix bugs. Using the new Windows Update tool, Windows itself can connect to the Microsoft Update site on the World Wide Web, analyze your system, make recommendations, and download the appropriate updates. Included in the process are listings of those updates you already have and the ability to remove updates, rolling back to previous versions.

FAT32 Utilities

All the disk utilities you might be familiar with from using Windows 95 have been updated to run with the new FAT32 file system. The FAT32 file system is an update of the older FAT16 file system. FAT32 provides greater efficiency of utilization for high-capacity disk drives. These include FORMAT, FDISK, ScanDisk, Defragmenter, and all the rest.

DriveSpace3

If you need to squeeze every possible byte of storage space out of your hard drives, you'll appreciate Microsoft including DriveSpace3 compression with Windows 98. DriveSpace3 provides a way to compress your drives, giving you more storage space for data and programs.

Backup and Restore

An improved Backup program with support for all kinds of storage devices makes it easier than ever to protect your data by making it easy to back it up. Never again suffer the frustration of losing valuable files to a hardware failure or accidental deletion.

The System Information Utility

Gathering information about your system and configuration used to require much digging and poking and occasionally such extreme measures as calling in the neighborhood whiz kid. Microsoft updated the MS Diagnostics program to produce the System Information utility, which generally tells you more than you would ever care to know about the hardware and software configuration of your computer.

The Maintenance Wizard

Users want the best performance possible from their computers. The new Windows Maintenance Wizard makes wringing every last drop of speed out of your computer as easy as answering a series of questions.

The Disk Defragmenter

The Disk Defragmenter is a utility that first debuted as part of Windows 95. It's been updated for Windows 98 and enhanced even further, now including an optimization portion. This utility observes which programs you use on a regular basis and rearranges them on your hard drive so that they load faster. This task can be run independently or as part of Windows Maintenance.

The System File Checker

Do you have a heavy hand on the Delete key? regularly rename the wrong file? receive frequent messages that a required system file is missing? If so (and even if not), the System File Checker (SFC) will save the day. This new utility checks that all the files Windows requires are present and correct. It also helps you restore any damaged or missing files from your CD-ROM, returning you to tiptop shape with a minimum of fuss.

Windows 98 Troubleshooters

It never seems to fail that, after installing or updating a piece of software, adding a new piece of hardware, or updating a hardware driver, something doesn't work. The Troubleshooters in the Help files make it easy to isolate what's causing your system problems.

The System Configuration Utility

Used in conjunction with the Help Troubleshooters, the System Configuration Utility enables you to specify exactly what Windows does as it's starting up, bypassing any trouble-causing configuration information.

The Automatic Skip Driver Agent

Similar to problems that the System Troubleshooter can help you resolve, device driver conflicts might occur that Windows determines to be severe. Under these conditions, the Automatic Skip Driver agent will kick in, automatically skipping the offending driver.

The Registry Checker

The Windows Registry, the very heart of your Windows configuration, is a vital repository of configuration information. The Registry has been updated for Windows 98 with some companion utilities that automatically check and repair the Registry on startup and create a backup.

Automatic ScanDisk on Startup

With the ever increasing complexity of computers, it's more and more important that file system integrity be maintained. Beginning in Windows 98, the ScanDisk utility runs automatically at system startup if it detects that the disk drives were not closed properly at the last shutdown.

The Task Scheduler

The Task Scheduler is used primarily for running system tasks in an unattended mode, such as those scheduled by the Maintenance Wizard. However, it can also be used to run programs at specified times.

Dr. Watson

For assistance in troubleshooting system or application problems, Dr. Watson is again available. Dr. Watson has been around since at least Windows 3.1; it's now greatly enhanced and is a valuable tool when reporting problems to support personnel.

Zero Administration Kit Support

For companies with hundreds, even thousands, of desktop and laptop computers to support, the magnitude of the task becomes monumental. Windows 98 includes built-in support for the Windows Zero Administration Kit, a package designed to ease the administrative burden of maintaining a large number of computers.

User Profiles

For those computers used by a number of people, User Profiles enables each user to maintain his own personalized settings for the computer. A user can set his own preferences for the desktop, colors, Start menu, and other things, as well as maintain his own My Documents folder.

The Windows Scripting Host

More experienced users will find the Windows Scripting Host a useful feature. Using a scripting language, you'll be able to automate tasks and actions that can then be played back in an unattended mode.

The Distributed Component Object Model

Also called DCOM, the Distributed Component Object Model is a method whereby "componentized" applications can communicate with each other over the network and different parts of an application can run on different computers.

Hardware Support

Just as software changes constantly, so does the hardware available to the personal computer market. Windows 98 includes improvements that enable you to not only better use existing hardware but also take advantage of the new and exciting hardware options available now and in the near future.

FAT32

The File Allocation Table file system has been with us since the days of DOS 1.0. The 16-bit FAT file system, which worked just fine (and still does), becomes very inefficient with today's large disk drives. The 32-bit FAT32 file system updates the FAT file system and improves its efficiency.

A FAT32 Converter

With the introduction of the FAT32 file system, a method of safely converting your FAT16 file systems was obviously needed. The Windows 98 FAT32 converter is up to the task, providing safe, efficient conversion from your existing FAT16 system to the newer FAT32 file system.

Power Management Support

Windows 95 introduced support for the APM (Advanced Power Management) 1.0 standard, a protocol for managing the power consumption of a computer. Windows 98 carries on this tradition by extending support for both APM 1.2 and the newer ACPI (Advanced Configuration and Power Interface). The ACPI standard is designed to make computers that are, in effect, *instant on*, that is, little or no boot time required, unlike the lengthy boot sequences we're used to now.

FireWire (IEEE1394) Device Support

The IEEE1394 hardware standard, usually known by the somewhat more exotic name *FireWire*, is quite exciting. FireWire devices are amazing. You can plug them in (up to 63 devices!), they'll automatically be recognized and added to the system, and you can use them without rebooting. What's even more awe-inspiring is what they do. With data transfer rates in the range of hundreds of megabits per second, they can do things such as real-time video transfers without any image loss. Very soon, possibly by the time you read this, you'll see FireWire devices like digital camcorders that plug into your PC!

Universal Serial Bus Device Support

A slower but less expensive bus than FireWire, Universal Serial Bus (USB) is intended primarily for devices with lower data transfer requirements. Already appearing are USB keyboards, mice, and trackballs. You'll also see joysticks or game controllers, digitizer tablets, digital cameras, and similar devices. Like FireWire, USB devices are hot plug-gable and Plug and Play.

IRQ Steering

An enhancement to the Plug and Play standard, IRQ steering makes it easier for your system to configure peripheral devices so that they'll all get along together.

PC Card and CardBus Support

Windows 98 expands on the very good PC card support in Windows 95 and extends it to the newer CardBus PC cards. Windows 98 also enhances the support available for the multifunction PC cards, such as those with a modem and network adapter on one card.

Accelerated Graphics Port Support

The Accelerated Graphics Port (AGP) is a technology developed by Intel to significantly increase graphics performance. Full utilization of an AGP display card requires a mother-board that supports it. An AGP-capable system significantly increases the graphics per-formance of the display subsystem by opening a high-performance port between system memory and the graphics card. The result is much better 3D graphics and modeling.

Improved InfraRed Device Support

Introduced with Windows 95 was a point-to-point transfer technology that used an infrared device for wireless transmission and reception of data. Windows 98 continues to build on this by implementing support for Fast InfraRed (FIR) devices and by providing not only point-to-point transfer capability but also networking over infrared.

Storage Device Support

With the popularity of nontraditional storage devices—such as parallel port hard drives like the Iomega Zip Drive and the Syquest Jet, the 120MB LS-120 floppy, CD-ROM changers, and bus-mastering IDE controllers—Microsoft has included device drivers for these popular peripherals.

ISDN Support

For those of you lucky enough to have an ISDN (Integrated Services Digital Network) connection, you'll be happy to know that Windows support of ISDN connections is now built into the operating system.

Microsoft Intellimouse Support

The latest version of the popular Microsoft mouse is the one with the scroll wheel built into it—the Intellimouse. Support for this mouse is included with the operating system.

The Win32 Driver Model

Another feature that the average user will probably not care about is the capability of Windows 98 to use device drivers written to the WDM (Windows32 Driver Model) standard. The WDM is designed to let hardware manufacturers write a single device driver that will work on both Windows NT and Windows 98. The idea is that the hardware manufacturer, by not having to support two different drivers, can offer the consumer more hardware options and better driver support.

Getting Started in Windows 98

You've seen the feature list, marveled at the enhancements, and waited patiently. Now what? If you're a seasoned Windows (any version of Windows) user or Macintosh user, you already possess the skills needed to successfully use the user interface: pointing, clicking, double-clicking, dragging, and using windowed applications. If these skills are new to you, stay tuned for an introduction to them.

If you're familiar with Windows 3.x or Windows 95, you can skip to the next section, "Windows 98 Basics." If not, take a minute to read through this section for an introduction to using a windowed interface.

Microsoft Windows, the Macintosh OS, and others have what used to be called *WIMP* user interfaces. *WIMP* doesn't mean *98-pound weakling*; it stands for windows, icons, menus, and pointers—the key tools for a user's interaction with the computer. Windows are the framed areas of the screen in which a program runs. Several windows can be open at any one time, and more than one window can be visible onscreen, or a single window can cover the entire screen, with the other windows hidden beneath it. Figure 1.2 shows several windows open at the same time, each running a different program.

In a windowed operating system, all programs run in a window. The visible area on your display monitor is referred to as the *desktop*. When a window is opened, it floats above the desktop.

FIGURE 1.2.

The Windows 98 user interface showing multiple program windows open at the same time.

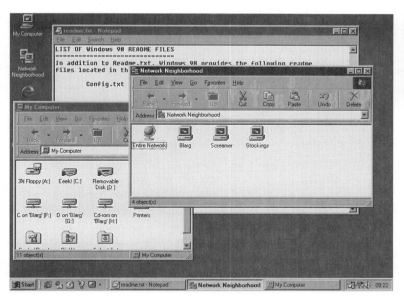

Objects, such as programs or files, are represented on the desktop and in windows by icons. An *icon* is a small picture that depicts something about the program or file. Usually each program has a unique icon, and each file created with a particular program has an icon similar to the program's icon.

Menus are groups of related program commands listed in a drop-down list from a menu bar, typically located at or near the top of the window. In Microsoft Windows, you'll always see a File menu, an Edit menu, and in the last menu position, a Help menu.

The pointers are driven by the mouse. You use the mouse (or another pointing device, such as a trackball) to move the point across your desktop or program window to select or point to items. The mouse can have one to three buttons on it, with Windows expecting a two-button mouse. Windows supports mice with different numbers of buttons, but two buttons are standard. The left button is the primary button. (For left-handed users, the button orientation is reversed.)

The mouse performs five main actions: pointing, clicking, double-clicking, dragging, and selecting. *Pointing* is the process of moving the mouse so that the mouse pointer onscreen is positioned on what you want to point to. *Clicking* means to point at something, press the left mouse button down, and then release it. This is also referred to as a *single click. Double-clicking* means to press and release the left mouse button twice in rapid succession.

Dragging and selecting are very similar actions. *Dragging* means to click the left mouse button and, while holding the button down, move the mouse. You can use the dragging motion to move something, such as an icon, from one location onscreen to another. It might be helpful to think of the left mouse button as holding what you're pointing at while moving the mouse. When you let up on the mouse button, the object you're dragging (holding) is dropped.

Selecting is very similar to dragging. In Windows, when something is selected, it is highlighted. When you click on an icon, it becomes highlighted, or selected. The selection is whatever is currently highlighted. The selection can be an icon, text, or a portion of a picture. Selecting is the process of highlighting a specific object or objects. For example, say you want to highlight some words in a text document. Using the mouse, position your pointer at the beginning of the text you want to select. Click the left mouse button and hold it down. While continuing to hold down the mouse button, drag the cursor to the end of the text you want to select. Now release the mouse button. As you move the mouse, the text, from the point where you clicked the mouse button to where the cursor is currently positioned, becomes highlighted, or selected.

Why would you want to select something? The commands on the menus are intended to act on either the entire document or on the current selection. Say you want to make some words boldface and italic. You'd select them and then use the menu commands to change them to bold italic. The commands act only on the text that is currently selected.

Program windows can be in one of several states at any time. They can be visible, either partially or completely. Windows can also be *maximized*, or full screen; in this case, the window completely fills the visible screen, obscuring any other program windows. A window can also be *minimized*; this means that the program window is still open, but it's been hidden away. The program itself is still open, but the window has been tucked away, set aside. Usually, when a program is minimized, you'll see a small icon of it on the bottom of the screen. In Windows 98, a minimized program window icon is visible on the taskbar.

Program windows are also usually resizable to whatever size you like. You can make them thinner, wider, taller, shorter, square, rectangular, or full screen. A window can be resized by grabbing the edge or corner of the window and dragging it.

With a number of program windows onscreen at any one time, how does the computer know which program your keystrokes and mouse commands apply to? At any one time, only one program window can have the *focus*, or be active. All the other windows are there, waiting to be activated again. You can tell which window is active, or has the focus, by looking at the title bar of the window. The one with the colored title bar is the one that's active.

Menus, as stated before, are lists of program commands. You'll find menus on windows and on objects. Generally, menus are located on a menu bar across the top of a program window. Figure 1.3 shows the menu bar in the Notepad application with the File menu displayed. The File, Edit, and Help menus are common to all Windows applications. Many applications also contain the Window menu, for switching between multiple windows open within the same application. To activate or display a menu, click once on the menu name. This causes the menu to display. To select a menu choice, just click it. The menu will disappear, and the choice that you made will be executed.

FIGURE 1.3.

The menu bar displays menus for the application, each containing specific commands.

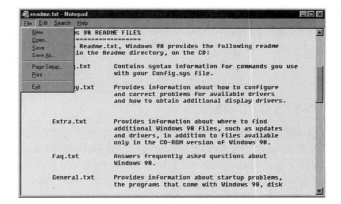

On some menu choices you'll see a triangle after the command name. This indicates that there is a submenu available. Moving the cursor over the triangle causes the submenu to display. On other menu choices you'll see an ellipsis (…) after the command name. This indicates that a dialog box will be presented, with additional options related to the selected command. Lastly, menus are *context sensitive*. That means that, depending on what you're doing in the program, some menu choices are not applicable. The invalid menu choices will be grayed out in the menu, and you won't be able to select them. When those menu choices are applicable, they'll be active again.

Dialog boxes are windows that pop up onscreen. These contain options or settings for a particular action, such as the File Open dialog box, shown in Figure 1.4. You'll see this dialog when opening files from within an application. The File Open box has a number of controls related to which file to open and from where. Most importantly, when a program has a dialog box open, you must finish with the dialog box before continuing with the program. Use the dialog box and click OK, Close, or Open to make it execute your commands, or click Cancel to abort what you're doing. Either way, you must finish with the dialog box before doing anything else with the program. There are some exceptions, but 99% of the time you must put the dialog box away before continuing.

FIGURE 1.4.

The File Open dialog box is a common dialog box in Windows.

Don't worry if you're not comfortable navigating Windows. Take the Windows 98 tour by clicking on it from the Welcome to Windows 98 box, displayed earlier in Figure 1.1. You can open the Welcome box by clicking Start I Programs I Accessories I Welcome to Windows.

Windows 98 Basics

A quick guided tour of the basics of Windows 98 is in order. Although you might already be familiar with many items that are pointed out on the tour, you might not know their names, or you might recognize them by other names; it's better to know the proper names for these objects.

Refer back to Figure 1.1 to see what your desktop will look like after Windows 98 is installed. The background, stretching top to bottom and left to right, is the desktop itself. Along the bottom of the screen is the taskbar. Every application that is currently running will have a button displayed on the taskbar. On the left end of the taskbar is the Start button. Clicking the Start button pops up the Start menu, which will be discussed shortly.

Just to the right of the Start button and also on the taskbar are four icons on a toolbar—in this case, the Quick Launch toolbar. The four icons are, left to right, Internet Explorer, Outlook Express mail, Show Desktop, and Show Channels. Clicking any of these icons will launch the associated program, except for Show Desktop. Clicking the Show Desktop icon minimizes all the open windows so that the desktop is once again visible, very handy if you have lots of windows open and must get to something on the desktop.

At the right end of the taskbar is the System Tray. Here you'll find, by default, a power indicator, a volume control if your computer has a sound card, and a clock. Other controls might also wind up here, as you enable them or install additional hardware or software. Double-clicking a System Tray icon brings up the related program.

1

The rest of the taskbar shown earlier in Figure 1.1 is blank. As mentioned before, each program currently running has a button on the taskbar. Clicking the button for any application will bring that application to the foreground, making it the active application. Clicking the taskbar button again for that application will minimize the application, hiding its window but leaving it running.

Throughout Windows 98, right-clicking an object brings up a context menu. This menu will be specific to the item you're clicking and will display some actions you can take on the item.

Right-clicking on the taskbar brings up the context menu for the taskbar. One context menu choice is Toolbars. Choosing Toolbars, you see Desktop, Quick Launch (which has a check mark next to it), and New Toolbar, as shown in Figure 1.5. The check mark indicates that the selected toolbar is being displayed. Selecting it again will turn off the toolbar. Selecting New Toolbar will enable you to create and display your own custom toolbar on the taskbar. By doing so, you can create a toolbar of your favorite applications and have them all just a single click away at any time.

FIGURE 1.5.

To add new toolbars to the taskbar, use the taskbar context menu.

In Windows 98, two choices control the click behavior of the interface—Web style or classic style. The setting is accessible by clicking the Start button and selecting Folders and Icons; you'll now be looking at the Folder Options dialog. In this dialog you'll see a setting titled Windows Desktop Update, and it will be set at Web Style, Classic Style, or Custom.

Web style means that to select an object, you hold the mouse pointer over it for a second and it will select. To open or launch the object, single-click it. Classic style is what you've experienced when using any other version of Windows. Click once on an object to select it, and double-click the object to open or launch it. Choosing Custom enables you to modify the behavior between these two styles.

I've just given you conflicting information. I said that on the taskbar, a single click on any icon on a toolbar will launch the application or open the document; that's true. I've also said that your system could be set to Classic Style, which requires a double click to launch an application; that's also true. Huh? This is an exception to the rule. On the taskbar, a single click always works. On the desktop or in program windows, Folder Options determines whether a single or double click is required.

Along the left side of the desktop, you'll find several icons displayed. Opening the My Computer icon or the Network Neighborhood icon displays an Explorer view of the chosen object. Figure 1.6 shows both My Computer and Network Neighborhood opened.

FIGURE **1.6.**

In Windows, there are always multiple ways to accomplish a task. Here are Network Neighborhood and My Computer.

Clicking the Internet Explorer icon launches the Microsoft Internet Explorer browser window. You'll use Internet Explorer to browse Web sites.

Clicking the Outlook Express icon launches the Outlook Express mail and news client. You can use Outlook Express (OE) to send and receive Internet email and to read and participate in Internet newsgroups.

If you haven't connected to the Internet before, the first time you open Internet Explorer or Outlook Express, the Internet Connection Wizard will guide you through getting connected to an Internet service provider.

Clicking the Set Up The Microsoft Network icon, or opening the Online Services folder and clicking any of those icons, will install, set up, and start the configuration of the programs to connect you to the Microsoft Network, CompuServe, America Online, Prodigy, or AT&T WorldNet.

The Recycle Bin is what it appears to be—a trash can. You can drag unwanted files here to delete them. Like a real trash can, which isn't emptied every time you throw away something, the Recycle Bin is emptied only when you manually empty it or when it becomes too full. In the meantime, you can always open up the Recycle Bin and restore something you've thrown away.

Clicking the Start menu button, you'll see the Start menu pop up from the taskbar, as shown in Figure 1.7. You can very easily customize the Start menu to suit your needs and tastes. At the top of the Start menu is Windows Update. In the bottom section are two choices, Log Off (*Username*) and Shut Down. The Log Off option shuts down any open programs you have running, closes your desktop, and leaves the computer at the logon screen. Shut Down gives you the option of restarting the PC, shutting it down, shutting down into MS-DOS mode, or if your machine supports it, going into standby mode.

FIGURE 1.7.

The Start menu is the starting point for most of your Windows tasks.

In the middle section of the Start menu, you'll see the choices Programs, Favorites, Documents, Settings, Find, Help, and Run. The Find choice is used to locate a computer on your network, a file on your computer, a Web site, or a person's name, using an Internet directory. Selecting Help launches the Windows Help file. The Run option enables you to type in a command line for execution.

Clicking the Settings choice will bring you to a submenu where you can change the settings for the taskbar and Start menu, Folder Options, or the Active Desktop. From the same submenu, you can open the Control Panel, where you control most of the configuration settings for all the hardware on your system, and you can also open the Printers folder.

The Favorites choice enables you to directly open any of your desktop channels, Web links, or documents.

The first menu item in the center section of the Start menu is Programs. Access to every other program on your computer is via the Programs choice. Selecting Programs gives you a submenu, itself with multiple submenus (and on and on), where you'll find program groups and program items. Selecting a group will open it up; selecting a program or document icon will start the application associated with the document and then display the document.

One important thing to remember when working in Windows 98 is that there are always multiple ways to do something and multiple ways to display information.

For example, there are at least three ways to run the Notepad application (a simple text editor). First, you can select Start | Programs | Accessories | Notepad. Second, you can click Start | Run, then type **notepad**, and click OK. For a third way, you can open a Windows Explorer window, view the contents of the Windows folder, find the file named Notepad.exe, and double-click it.

For displaying information, Windows also gives you a lot of choices. On the View menu in Windows Explorer, you can choose to display folder contents with large icons, small icons, in a list, or with all details. You can sort them by type, size, date, or name.

Note

> Throughout this book, I suggest ways to do things. Feel free to use any alternative methods that you're more comfortable with, as long as you wind up at the same place!

How to Get the Most out of Your Computer Using This Book

If you're like most readers, some of the topics covered in this book will be new to you, and others old hat. Some of the ideas and uses for Windows will not be of any interest or use to you; others might fulfill a need that's been frustrating you for a long time. It's not likely that everything in this book will be directly applicable to you, but that's to be expected.

As you work your way through the book, if you run across a topic that's particularly germane to your requirements, highlight it, make notes, bend the corner of the page. Do the Tasks. On your computer, re-create the book's screen shots. The best way to learn the subject is to practice it. You'll absorb the topic much more quickly and thoroughly if you take the read-and-do approach than if you treat this book as a textbook. By *read-and-do*, I mean that you read a bit and then do what you read about. When I refer to a particular menu item, program, or dialog box, open it on your computer. Hands-on activity rein-

1

Summary

This introduction to Windows 98 shows you the desktop, gives you a brief tour of its major features, and describes the basics of using Windows. You learned about the major enhancements to the product compared to its predecessor, Windows 95, and also about its new features.

Using this knowledge, you're now prepared to teach yourself everything else there is to know about Windows 98—in just 21 days!

Workshop

To wrap up the day, you can review terms from the chapter, see the answers to some commonly asked questions, and practice what you've learned. You can find the answers to the exercises in Appendix A, "Answers."

Terminology Review

Active Desktop—Your Windows desktop, with controls on it that are intelligent and perform their designated tasks autonomously.

ActiveX—A programming interface and specification for writing applications and controls.

applet—Generally, a small standalone program that performs a specific task.

clicking—Depressing a button on the mouse once.

context menu—A small menu, opened by right-clicking an object, that contains only those actions or commands that make sense for the selected object in its current context or state.

cursor—A small icon that moves in response to movement of the mouse, used to indicate where your actions are to be directed.

desktop—The entire viewable area displayed on your monitor.

dialog box—A window-like box that pops up to display or request information and usually must be acknowledged before you can continue.

double-clicking—Pressing a mouse button twice in rapid succession.

dragging—Moving an onscreen object by clicking it and keeping the mouse button depressed while moving the mouse to guide the object.

driver—A small piece of code that controls the operation of a particular piece of hardware.

dropping—The termination of dragging, when an object is dragged to its destination and the mouse button is released.

focus—Where your input (mouse or keyboard) will be directed. The active window, the one that will receive your keyboard or mouse input, is said to *have the focus*.

HTML (Hypertext Markup Language)—A layout language used to define the look and layout of World Wide Web pages.

icons—Small symbols or pictures used to represent programs, files, shortcuts, disks, or computers on the desktop and in other programs.

ISDN (Integrated Services Digital Network)—A digital communications line that enables voice and high-speed data access via the public telephone network.

Java—A platform-independent programming language used to create applications that run on any type of computer.

maximized—A window that is the largest size possible, as large as your desktop.

menus—Lists of program commands, usually accessible from the main menu bar near the top of each window but also found in other locations.

minimized—A window that is hidden.

pointer—See *cursor*.

push—A method of obtaining information from a provider, usually over the Internet, in which the provider pushes the data to the consumer instead of the consumer requesting it from the provider. An analogy is that your cable TV system is a push provider, as opposed to the video store, where you must go to find a movie.

Recycle Bin—The trash can where deleted files are held before being permanently erased.

selecting—Causing an object or text to be highlighted.

Start button—The button labeled Start on the taskbar, used to gain access to all other programs.

taskbar—The gray bar at the bottom (normally) of your desktop that displays buttons for all currently running tasks and can contain toolbars of icons for other applications.

window—A frame, displayed over the desktop, that contains a running program.

Q&A

Q What's the difference between Web style and classic folder options?

A The classic settings are what Windows users have been familiar with since way back. Selecting is done via a single click, and files or programs are opened with a double click. Using Web style settings, selecting is done by simply resting your pointer on top of an object for a second or two, no click necessary. To open a file or application, click it once. The easiest way to remember it is to think of how you use a browser; you use a single click to follow a link or open a file. That's Web style.

Q I'm a Windows 3.1 user, and I don't understand some of the references to the way Windows 95 works. Will I be able to learn Windows 98 from this book?

A Absolutely! Although much of this book discusses the differences between Windows 95 and Windows 98, you'll have no problems picking up Windows 98. In those few places where Windows 3.x users might have difficulty, I've specifically added extra help.

Q I don't have an Internet connection, although I'm considering getting one. Will I need one to use this book, and will I learn how to get an Internet connection?

A No, and yes. No, you don't need an Internet account to learn Windows 98 using this book. However, to fully use the power and capability of Windows 98 to bring Internet content to your computer, you'll want to have a connection at some point. And yes, you'll learn how to get an Internet connection, and it's easier than you think!

Exercises

1. Name three ways to display the contents of your C drive.
2. List three ways to run the Notepad program.

DAY 2

Installing Windows 98

by Michael Hart

Yesterday you took a tour of all the highlights of Windows 98; now, how do you get there? Today you'll discover how to install Windows 98 on your computer. You'll likely get Windows 98 in one of four main ways, each of which I'll talk about. In this chapter, I'll cover the following:

- Getting a new PC with Windows 98 preinstalled
- The Windows 98 installation requirements
- Installing Windows 98 from scratch
- Upgrading from Windows 3.*x*, Windows 95, or DOS
- Creating an Emergency Startup Disk
- Installing additional Windows components

Getting a New PC with Windows 98 Preinstalled

There's a certain list of the pleasures in life that have no equal—a new house, a new car, a new job, a new spouse, a new baby, a new computer. (Your list might be a little different, and if you already have a spouse, you should cross *new spouse* off the list!) Of all these, the new computer is probably the one you'll enjoy the most often. If you're fortunate enough to be enjoying that right now, you've probably received it with Windows 98 already installed.

When you receive a new computer with Windows preinstalled, the manufacturer has configured both the hardware and the software for optimum performance. There should be very little, if anything, for you to do in terms of installation.

Some computer vendors sell systems with dual or multiple operating systems installed, and the first time you start the system, you are asked to make a choice of which operating system you'd like to use. Remember that in cases like this, your license to use the operating system software is usually limited to one of the choices. More than likely, at the time that you make your initial OS choice, the alternatives will be deleted. Make sure to refer to any documentation accompanying your system to determine exactly what software licenses you are entitled to.

Your new computer might have shipped with a Windows 98 CD-ROM (or floppies) and a CD-ROM boot floppy. If so, you can then use the CD-ROM if you ever need to reinstall Windows 98. If you didn't receive a CD-ROM with your system, this means that the installation files for Windows are copied into a directory on your hard drive. If you lose or delete this directory, you won't be able to reinstall or reconfigure Windows. If you didn't receive either a Windows 98 CD-ROM or floppy set, your first task will be to make a backup copy of the Windows installation files. You can accomplish this in a number of ways. First, you can create a backup of the installation file directory by using a tape backup device or another storage device such as a Zip, Jaz, or Syquest disk. If you need to reinstall later, you recover the installation directory and use the files from it.

Your second option is to use a specific program created expressly for the purpose of backing up the installation files. As always, check your system documentation for specific instructions. A sure clue that this is an option for you is the inclusion with your system of a set of floppy disk labels titled Microsoft Windows 98 Setup Disks. You might find an icon for a program called Microsoft Disk Creator or something similar. When you launch this program, you'll be guided through the process of creating a set of Windows installation floppies that can be used again later if you need to recover a file, install additional Windows features, or reinstall Windows.

Because your preconfigured machine is all set up, you might want to consider another alternative—performing a complete backup of your system before changing anything. This preserves the software configuration of your new machine, allowing you to restore it to factory fresh condition if needed. Day 12, "Maintaining Your System," contains additional information on backing up your system. If you do decide to back up your entire system, create the backup tape, label it appropriately, and then set it aside. Don't use it or overwrite it. This tape is now a system backup—your master copy of your software. Safeguard it.

Windows 98 Installation Requirements

Before you attempt to install Windows 98 on an existing computer, you need to make sure that your machine meets the minimum requirements for running Windows 98. You'll also want to verify that your hardware is compatible. If you already have access to the World Wide Web, visit the Hardware Compatibility List at `http://www.microsoft.com/hwtest/hcl/`.

For installation, the following are the minimum requirements:

- A 486SX processor with a 66MHz, or higher, clock
- A minimum of 110MB of hard disk space
- 16MB of RAM
- A VGA or higher resolution display adapter and monitor
- A 3.5-inch high-density floppy drive
- A mouse or other pointing device
- Windows 95, Windows 3.*x*, or access to another command prompt

My list of preferred equipment also includes the following:

- A Pentium processor with a 100MHz, or higher, clock
- 32MB of RAM
- A CD-ROM drive

During setup, have a blank, formatted, high-density floppy disk available for the creation of an Emergency Startup Disk.

Installing Windows 98 from Scratch

Baking brownies from scratch means taking raw ingredients, combining them in a personalized way, and producing the finished goodies. Installing Windows from scratch means taking a computer with no operating system on it and a Windows CD-ROM, picking and choosing what features you want and how you want them, and making it so.

Most people will probably never do a Windows installation from scratch; the installation will almost always be an upgrade from an existing Windows system. In fact, unless you specifically want to learn about partitioning and formatting a hard disk drive, you can skip to the next section, "Upgrading from Windows 3.x, Windows 95, or DOS." Most users won't need to perform the steps described here or in Task 2.1 in this section.

If you are installing Windows on a new or blank drive, you still aren't required to know and perform these steps; Setup will guide you through them.

You might do this if you purchase a new disk drive that you want to use as your C: drive. You might want to use this method just to ensure a clean start for your installation. Some of us are frequent abusers—I mean, *users*—of software and systems, constantly adding, changing, and removing software from our systems. For this reason, I like to wipe out my drive occasionally, perhaps every 6–8 months, and start over.

Note

This is not to say that you should or even need to reinstall Windows every 6 months. If, however, you *frequently* install and remove software and hardware, test out new things, reconfigure your system, and generally push your system to the limit, you might want to periodically reinstall just to clean out old stuff that might be hanging around.

Caution

The procedures in the rest of this section could cause you to lose all your programs and data. Don't perform these procedures without having a full backup of your files.

If you're not *sure* you should do these, don't!

For the sake of discussion, I'll assume that you have purchased a new hard drive and want to install Windows 98 on it from the CD-ROM. Also, I'll assume that your drive has already been installed and configured into the machine's BIOS. For more information on adding drives and configuring your BIOS, see Day 9, "Managing Hardware."

Your hard disk needs to be prepared before you can use it to store information. To do this, you need to create one or more partitions on the drive. Then the partitions need to be prepared before you can copy information to them. This process is called *formatting*. Last, the operating system needs to be installed on the drive.

When you partition a drive, you determine how much of the physical hard disk will be used for a file system—that is, how much will actually be used to store data and program files. Normally, you'll want to use all the available area; you paid for it, so why waste it? On a larger hard drive, say 2GB and larger, you might want to configure a single physical drive as two or more logical drives. In other words, that 2GB drive can be made to appear as though it were two 1GB drives. There's no compelling reason, in general, to break a large drive into smaller drives; it's just an option. I prefer to have large drives; this gives me fewer drive letters to mess with, and I have to worry less often about managing the free space.

There are just as many good reasons to leave a large drive as a single large partition as there are good reasons to break it into smaller partitions. As I said, splitting a large drive into smaller partitions is an option, not a requirement. Which route you choose will be determined by your needs and preferences.

Task 2.1. Preparing to Install Windows from Scratch

Remember—only perform this Task if you're *sure* this is what you want to do. You could lose your data!

> **Caution**
>
> DO NOT DO THIS unless you have just installed a new hard disk and are preparing to put Windows on it!
>
> The following procedure will cause you to lose any and all data and programs on your disk drive!

Before starting, you'll need a DOS bootable floppy with the FDISK and FORMAT utilities on it, your Windows 98 CD-ROM, and your Windows 98 Setup floppy. If your Windows 98 distribution includes a Windows 98 Setup Boot floppy, you can use that.

To prepare your hard disk for Windows 98 installation, complete the following steps:

1. With your PC off, insert a bootable floppy and turn the machine on.

2. If you're using the Setup Boot floppy, press F3 twice to exit Setup, which leaves you at the DOS prompt. From the DOS prompt, type **FDISK**. If your disk drive is larger than 528MB, you'll be asked whether you want to enable support for large drives; answer Yes.

▼

Note

Enabling large disk support is covered in more detail on Day 9. For now, if you intend to run only Windows 98 from this disk, select Yes. If you plan on installing multiple operating systems on this disk (for example, Windows 98 and Windows NT), select No.

3. If you have more than one hard disk, you'll see an option number 5—Change Current Hard Disk. If you see this option, use it to ensure that you're operating on the correct hard disk—the one that you want to wipe clean and start over with.

4. Select option 3—Delete Partition Information to Delete Any Partitions or Logical DOS Drives. You need to delete any logical drives first and then the partitions on the physical drive.

5. After you've deleted all the partitions, you need to select option 1—Create DOS Partition to Partition the Drive. In general, I suggest creating a single large partition, unless you have specific reasons not to.

6. Make the partition active. If you created only a single partition, it will already have been made active, but it never hurts to verify.

7. Escape out, and you'll be told to reboot. Reboot your PC, booting again from the bootable floppy disk. Type **FORMAT C:** (or whatever drive you're preparing) and press Enter. Answer Yes when you're asked whether you're sure. The format will take some minutes, depending on the speed of your PC and the size of the hard disk.

8. When the formatting is finished, you will have a blank prepared hard disk ready for installation of Windows 98.

To continue with your Windows 98 installation, boot from a bootable floppy (or the Windows 98 Setup Boot floppy) and then run SETUP.EXE from your Setup floppy or from the CD-ROM drive.

Tip

If you're not booting from the Windows Setup floppy and you intend to install from your CD-ROM drive, remember that you must have a CD-ROM driver loaded in CONFIG.SYS and the MSCDEX driver loaded in the AUTOEXEC.BAT file on your bootable floppy.

If you're unsure what all that means, you should boot from the Setup floppy included with Windows.

> **Note**
> Your system might also support booting directly from your CD-ROM drive, so you could bypass the boot floppy altogether.

Upgrading from Windows 3.x, Windows 95, or DOS

2

The differences when upgrading from the Windows 3.1, Windows 95, and MS-DOS operating systems are so slight that I'll cover them all here. What's most important is what you need to do before you upgrade.

Before upgrading, the most crucial step is to back up your system. At the very least, you should back up any critical data files, such as documents, spreadsheets, or presentations. Next on the list for backup are configuration files such as AUTOEXEC.BAT, CONFIG.SYS, WIN.INI, or SYSTEM.INI. You might also have configuration files for some applications that you want to back up.

> **Note**
> Why are you always warned to back up before doing anything major to your computer? The answer, of course, is that Murphy has a tendency to poke his nose in where it doesn't belong. Things go wrong; mistakes happen. Perhaps you'll have a power glitch in the middle of the upgrade process; maybe the planets aren't in alignment—who knows?
>
> Backing up your system helps to make these accidents easier to recover from. When accidents happen, being prepared with a full backup allows you to easily get back to square one with a working system.
>
> Because you're performing an operating system upgrade, it's very possible that any errors you encounter might be *extremely hazardous to the operating capabilities of your computer*—possibly to the point where it won't run anymore, at least not without some major surgery!
>
> If you've never backed up before and never intend to again, please back up your system before upgrading.

Next, if your computer is on a network, you'll want to have handy your computer name, workgroup name, and computer description. Setup should automatically detect these items, but if not, it's nice to have them at hand.

To install Windows 98, you must run the Setup program from the distribution media, either the CD-ROM (preferred!) or floppy disks. Start the setup task in one of the following ways.

To start Setup from DOS, complete the following:

1. Insert your CD-ROM into the CD-ROM drive or insert Setup Floppy 1 into your floppy drive.

2. From the command prompt (DOS prompt), type **D (or your drive letter):\Setup** and press Enter.

To start Setup from Windows 3.*x* or Windows 95, complete the following:

1. Insert your CD-ROM into the CD-ROM drive or insert Setup Floppy 1 into your floppy drive.

2. Using File Manager (from Windows 3.*x*) or Windows Explorer (from Windows 95), launch SETUP.EXE from the CD-ROM or floppy.

In all cases, Setup will run, informing you first that the Setup Wizard is being prepared and then displaying the Setup screen. You will see the Setup screen, shown in Figure 2.1, throughout the setup process. The Windows 98 Setup screen shows you what stage of the setup process is currently running, gives an estimate of the time remaining, and displays informational messages as it does its work.

FIGURE 2.1.

The Windows 98 Setup screen.

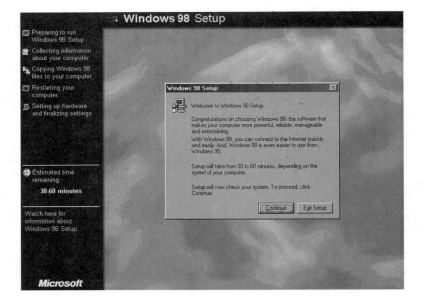

Table 2.1 lists the major steps of the setup process that require input from you, including what it's doing and what your options are.

TABLE 2.1. MAJOR SETUP SCREENS WITH CHOICES.

Screen	Purpose	Options
Select Folder	Determine where Windows will be installed.	By default, `C:\Windows`. If you're upgrading Windows 3.*x* or Windows 95, the default will be the directory Windows was previously installed in.
Setup Options	Determine the type of Windows installation.	You have four options: *Typical*—Installs the components for the average user. *Portable*—Installs the components normally desired by laptop or notebook users. *Compact*—Installs the minimum components required to run Windows 98. Use this when you don't have much disk space available. *Custom*—Use this when you want to choose exactly which Windows components are installed.
Windows Components	View or select which components are to be installed.	Add or remove any of the optional components. You can also add or remove these later.

2

The major configuration choice you have to make when installing Windows 98 is what type of installation you want: Typical, Portable, Compact, or Custom.

Regardless of what you choose, you can always add or remove Windows components later, so don't fret much over which type of installation you want. For the vast majority of users, selecting the Typical installation is fine.

I give you the overall flow of the setup process in the following list. During setup, you complete the following:

- Click Continue at the Welcome to Windows 98 Setup screen.
- Accept the license agreement.
- Select the directory in which to install Windows.
- Select the installation type (Typical, Portable, Compact, or Custom).
- Enter your name and company.
- Choose to add or change the components to be installed.
- Create the Emergency Startup Disk.
- Set up Plug and Play hardware.

- Set up non–Plug and Play hardware.
- Log on.

During the setup process, Windows reboots itself at least twice, possibly more, depending on your particular hardware configuration. Even the reboots are hands-off because if you wait long enough (about 15 seconds), the machine will reboot itself. The entire setup will take between 30 and 60 minutes, depending on the speed of your hardware, whether you install from CD-ROM or floppy, and what options you choose.

Near the end of the process, you'll be presented with a Windows Logon dialog box. After you enter a password (a password isn't required) and confirm it, you'll see the last few Setup dialogs flash by, and then you'll be left at the Welcome to Windows 98 screen, with some pretty snazzy music playing.

The Welcome application, shown in Figure 2.2, gives you the option of registering your copy of Windows, connecting to the Internet, taking the Discover Windows 98 tour, or running the Maintenance Wizard. You can rerun this Welcome whenever you like; it's located under Start | Programs | Accessories | System Tools | Welcome to Windows. The checkbox at the bottom of the dialog box controls whether or not you see the Welcome to Windows dialog every time you start Windows. Although the music is cool, you'll eventually want to uncheck this box.

FIGURE 2.2.

The Welcome to Windows 98 program allows you to register your copy of Windows, connect to the Internet, take a tour of Windows 98, or run the Maintenance Wizard.

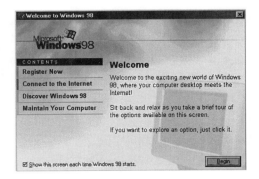

Creating an Emergency Startup Disk

One of the steps during the installation process is the creation of an *ESD*, or *Emergency Startup Disk* (also referred to as an *EBD*, or *Emergency Boot Disk*). This floppy can be used to boot Windows 98 when something has happened to your hard disk installation and it won't properly boot anymore. The ESD contains enough configuration information and system files to allow your computer to boot to a command line prompt and allow you to get back to a working system.

When you make changes to your system, such as installing drive compression or new hardware or even an update to Windows 98 (should there be one), you should be sure to create an updated ESD. The following procedure will assist you.

Task 2.2. Creating an Emergency Startup Disk

Before starting, you'll need a single floppy disk. The disk can be blank or not, but it will be overwritten. Follow these steps:

1. Open the Control Panel by clicking Start | Settings | Control Panel, and then open the Add/Remove Programs applet.

2. Click the Startup Disk tab, and then click the Create Disk button.

3. You'll be prompted to insert a floppy disk. A warning appears notifying you that any files on the floppy will be erased. Insert the disk, and then click OK.

4. When all the files have been copied to the floppy, you'll be left at the Startup Disk tab of the Add/Remove Programs applet. Click OK or Cancel to put it away.

5. Be sure to label your ESD as such, write the date of creation on it, and store it in a safe place.

When the time comes that you need the ESD floppy, you'll simply insert the floppy into the floppy drive and restart your computer. When the boot has finished, you'll be at a
▲ command prompt.

Installing Additional Windows Components

Regardless of which type of installation you choose when first installing Windows 98, you'll eventually want—or need—to install or remove a Windows component. The process is quite simple, and you shouldn't hesitate to do it as necessary.

Adding Windows components will be required as you progress through this book. Whenever necessary, refer back to Task 2.3 for help.

Task 2.3. Installing Additional Windows Components

You need to have your Windows 98 distribution media (either your CD-ROM or floppy set) handy before beginning the following steps:

1. Open the Windows Control Panel by clicking it in Windows Explorer or by clicking Start | Settings | Control Panel.

2. Find the applet Add/Remove Programs and open, or launch, it. Click the tab labeled Windows Setup. In a few moments, the dialog box will display a list of the
▼ installed Windows components (see Figure 2.3).

FIGURE 2.3.

The Add/Remove Programs Properties dialog displays which Windows software components are currently installed and enables you to choose which components to add or remove.

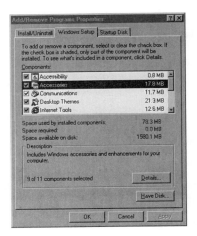

3. Click any component in the list, such as Accessories. When you click a component, the Description pane changes to display a description of the component. The Description pane also displays a message telling you how many subcomponents are currently installed. In the case of the Accessories component, 9 of 11 subcomponents are installed. If a Windows component has subcomponents, when you click it, the Details button will become active, as shown in Figure 2.3.

4. Clicking Details displays another dialog box listing each subcomponent. This secondary dialog box behaves just as the main dialog does, displaying a description for each subcomponent as you click it. For both dialog boxes, checking a component causes it to be installed, and unchecking a component causes it to be removed.

5. After selecting whatever components you want installed or removed, click OK until the Add/Remove Programs Properties dialog disappears. Depending on what components you've chosen to install or remove, you might see one or several progress boxes appear as the software components are added or removed. You'll also be prompted to install your Windows CD-ROM when needed.

6. In most cases, you'll be asked to reboot before the changes take effect. Go ahead and reboot.

7. After the reboot, you'll be able tell that your chosen changes have been made.

Remember that Windows components can be added, removed, or reinstalled at any time using this procedure.

Summary

In today's chapter, you learned how to install Windows 98 over an existing DOS, Windows 3.*x*, or Windows 95 system. You also learned about partitioning and formatting a new hard disk in preparation for use under Windows. You learned what to expect during the Windows 98 Setup process and what configuration choices you'll be faced with during installation. Finally, you learned how to add and remove optional Windows components at any time after initial installation.

Workshop

To wrap up the day, you can review terms from the chapter, test your knowledge of today's topics, and practice what you've learned.

Terminology Review

back up—To copy an existing disk drive onto a mass storage device, such as a tape drive, for later recovery, if needed.

backup device—A large capacity storage device such as a tape drive.

drive—Usually a hard disk drive. Used to store the operating system and programs.

FDISK—A low-level program used to partition a disk before formatting.

FORMAT—A low-level program used to prepare a disk to receive files by creating a file system on the drive.

install—For software: the process of installing a new program on a computer. For operating system software: to put the operating system on a disk that didn't previously have an operating system. For hardware: the physical placing of new hardware in or on a computer.

partition—A portion of a physical disk drive to be used as a single drive visible to the operating system. A physical disk drive can be used as a single partition or broken into two or more partitions, each of which might be visible to the operating system as a disk drive.

restore—The opposite of *back up*. To use the information previously backed up to a storage device to return a disk drive to its original state.

upgrade—For an operating system: to put a new version of an operating system on a disk drive that has an older version.

Q&A

Q I'm not sure what I need to do before upgrading my computer to use Windows 98. What should I do first?

A Yes, this is a trick question! Until and unless overridden by an act of Congress, the first thing you'll always do before upgrading your system is *back up*!

Q If I upgrade to Windows 98, can I revert back to my previous operating system?

A It depends. You must do two things to be able to uninstall Windows 98: *(a)* select the option (during setup) to allow the uninstalling of Windows 98 and *(b)* not compress your hard drive or convert it to FAT32.

Exercise

Because you like playing FreeCell so much, you've decided to remove the game from your system so that you can actually get some work done. Describe two ways to remove the FreeCell game.

DAY 3

Navigating Within Windows 98

by Paul Cassel

One of the primary design goals of Windows 98 was ease of use. Because there isn't a perfect consensus on what "easy" means, Windows 98 gives you many different ways to approach its graphical user interface (GUI). Combine the ways in which you can customize Windows 98 with the ways you can navigate in it, and no two users need to have identical setups.

Today's lesson shows you the various ways to navigate, or view resources, in Windows 98. You will gain the most from it by combining its information with Day 8, "Customizing Windows 98," because the topics are related in many aspects. Today's lesson covers the following:

- Active and default desktops
- Navigating the desktop
- Windows Explorer

- Creating and using file associations
- Manipulating files
- The taskbar and its toolbars
- Making a custom toolbar for inclusion on the taskbar
- The Recycle Bin

The Active Desktop

The *Active Desktop* is a user interface with elements connected to an outside source so that those elements can be regularly updated. Two examples of updated elements are stock tickers and weather maps.

The Active Desktop is the result of integrating Internet Explorer, a Web browser capable of using ActiveX components, into the GUI of Windows 98. If you've used any Web browser capable of using active components—either Java or ActiveX—you know about having your screen updated without any user intervention. For example, Figure 3.1 shows a weather map of the United States displayed in Internet Explorer. This map is updated regularly with no input from the user.

FIGURE 3.1.

This weather map, shown in Internet Explorer, is updated at regular intervals as the data changes.

In a similar way, you can set up your desktop with an embedded weather map. Updating this map, like the map shown in Figure 3.1, requires no user action. Microsoft's term for a desktop with embedded objects is an *Active Desktop*. Think of an Active Desktop as viewing a piece of Internet Explorer as part of your desktop.

Figure 3.2 shows a desktop with a weather map included as one of its elements. This map, like the map in Figure 3.1, updates automatically.

FIGURE 3.2.

Including automatically updatable elements in the Windows 98 desktop converts it into an Active Desktop.

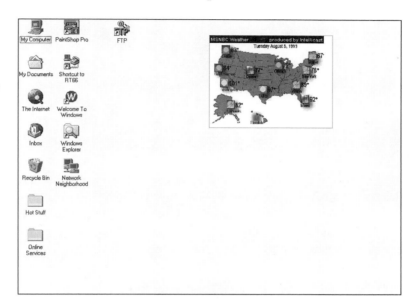

The secret to updating Active Desktop elements is to have an Internet connection. That's all you need to include this feature in your Windows 98 installation.

Task 3.1. The Active Desktop

The following steps will configure your desktop to accept active elements and then go on to show how to include these elements as part of your working setup:

1. You will need an Internet or intranet connection. Any kind will do. If you use a dial-up connection, this is the time to log on to your dial-up server. If you connect through your LAN, you should be all set without further ado.

2. Windows 98 enables you to view Web-type content on your desktop. Because Web content is the heart of an Active Desktop, you'll have to make sure this option is in place. Right-click on your desktop, choose Properties from the context menu, and choose the Web tab. Locate the View My Active Desktop as a Web Page check box and make sure that it's checked (see Figure 3.3). The check box in question is just below the graphic depiction of a monitor.

FIGURE 3.3.

This check box enables Web content on the Active Desktop.

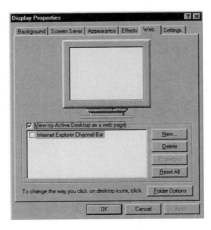

3. Click OK to return to your desktop. Right-click on the desktop and note the first entry on the context menu, Active Desktop. Figure 3.4 shows the context menu with the Active Desktop entry and its fly-out (submenu) selections. Note that you can easily manipulate the setting from step 2 by selecting the View as Web Page menu item.

FIGURE 3.4.

Now that you've enabled Web content, the desktop context menu has an Active Desktop entry with several options.

4. Choose the second entry from the fly-out shown in Figure 3.4, Customize my Desktop. This brings up a familiar screen with the Web tab already selected.

Note

> Keep in mind that the contents of your Web tab, as shown in Figure 3.3, will vary, depending on your registered components. The next few steps will show how to locate and register new components for your desktop.

5. To add a new active element (usually a control), click the New button at the right of the Web tab shown in Figure 3.3. Windows 98 will bring up the dialog shown in Figure 3.5. This will let you go directly to the Microsoft Gallery. If you choose No in the dialog box shown in Figure 3.5 or have previously tried this and checked the

▼ In the Future, Do Not Show Me This Dialog Box check box, your screen will look like Figure 3.6.

FIGURE 3.5.

You browse for new active elements either by visiting the Gallery or by the usual browse routines identical to Web surfing.

FIGURE 3.6.

If you choose not to visit the Microsoft Gallery, you still have the entire Web to choose from.

3

6. This Task will use the Microsoft Gallery. Click Yes in the dialog box shown in Figure 3.5. If you jumped to the dialog box shown in Figure 3.6, enter the URL `http://www.microsoft.com/ie/ie40/gallery/`, the location of the Gallery. Your screen will resemble Figure 3.7 (but not exactly, because Microsoft regularly updates this site).

Note

This example installs a weather map and a stock ticker. You can choose those elements or any others if you're following along. The only difference will be the final appearance of the desktop.

7. To install any active element, click on its hyperlink and follow the prompts on the screen. Figure 3.8 shows the screen after choosing the MSNBC Weather Map.

8. After adding the elements you want for your computer, return to the desktop, right-click on it, and again choose Active Desktop. Make sure the Web View choice from the fly-out is checked. Then choose Active Desktop|Customize My Desktop ▼ and note the additions in the Web tab. Figure 3.9 shows these changes.

FIGURE 3.7.

The Gallery is where Microsoft gathers interesting Active Desktop themes for easy installation on your machine.

FIGURE 3.8.

After selecting the elements you want to add, click on the hyperlink and follow the prompts.

9. After you choose the two downloaded elements and then select them in the Web tab, the previously static desktop transforms into an Active Desktop, complete with an updating weather map and a scrolling stock ticker, as you can see in Figure 3.10.

▼
FIGURE 3.9.

After downloading ele-ments for an Active Desktop, you can pick and choose what you display on the Web tab of the Display Properties dialog box.

FIGURE 3.10.

A few simple clicks have transformed this static desktop into an active one, complete with an automatically updated weather map and a scrolling stock ticker.

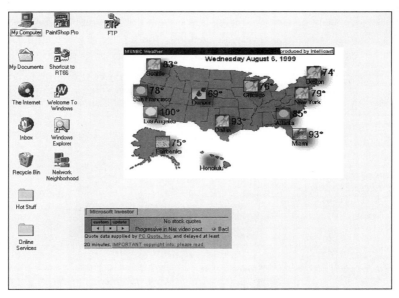

3

That's all there is to transforming your desktop from a static one to one that incorporates
▲ active elements.

Navigating the Desktops

Mouse and key actions vary, depending on what type of desktop you have active. The Active Desktop is designed to have the same feel as a browser on the Web, whereas the classic desktop acts like the user interfaces of Windows 95 or Windows NT 4. Table 3.1 outlines these differences.

TABLE 3.1. NAVIGATING THE ACTIVE DESKTOP AND DEFAULT DESKTOPS.

Action	Default Desktop	Active Desktop
Selection	Click	Move pointer over
Open, launch, or run	Double-click	Click
Select more objects	Ctrl+click or Shift+click	Ctrl+Move pointer over or Shift+Move pointer over

Unfortunately, the Active Desktop metaphor isn't perfectly consistent. If you choose it, Windows objects such as dialog and message boxes will still remain operationally the same as with the standard desktop. On the other hand, Windows Help is generally configured for navigation using the active method.

This can be a bit confusing if you want to base your Windows 98 navigation within a rules-based system of your making. You'll have to make a rule and then create many exceptions. A better way to track what system or metaphor you're in is to watch for the changing window. If moving your mouse over a window or object changes that window or object, you're in or partly in an object adhering to the Active Desktop system. Figure 3.11 shows part of an Active Desktop.

FIGURE 3.11.

Moving the mouse cursor over the stock ticker Active Desktop component selects the component.

Tip

The easiest way to see whether you're in an Active Desktop object is to see whether it's selected when you move the mouse pointer over it. However, active elements, such as hyperlinks, can also occur within non–Active Desktop schemes. You can identify these elements because the mouse cursor changes into a hand when you move over them. In these cases, a single rather than a double click is all it takes to launch them.

Windows Explorer

The primary navigation tool for disks and directories is Windows Explorer. Actually, the entire desktop is the Explorer, but for most people, the name Windows Explorer means the view of files and directory listings. Figure 3.12 shows the default view of Windows Explorer. To see this view, choose Start | Programs | Windows Explorer.

FIGURE 3.12.

Windows Explorer is a files and directory view of the desktop.

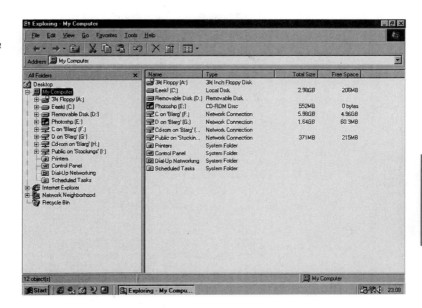

The default view of Windows Explorer is two panes. On the left is a list of folders or directories, along with some handy shortcuts to often-needed components such as the Control Panel. Within the right pane are the contents of whatever is selected in the left pane.

Task 3.2. Opening the Control Panel from Windows Explorer

The following steps will show you how to open the Sounds applet within the Control Panel from Windows Explorer:

1. Open Windows Explorer by choosing Start | Programs | Windows Explorer.

2. Locate the Control Panel entry in the left pane and click it (see Figure 3.13).

Note

Your Windows Explorer will surely have different entries than those in Figure 3.13 because the contents of Windows Explorer depend on your particular setup. However, your screen's basic layout should resemble the figure.

▼

▼

FIGURE 3.13.

The Control Panel is part of the Windows Explorer view of your computer.

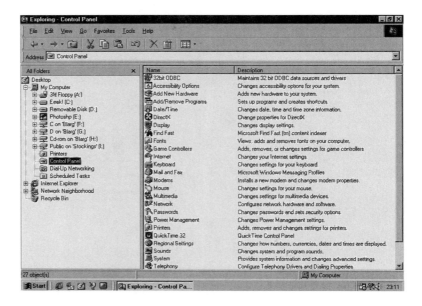

3. Locate the Sounds applet on the right panel. Double-click it to launch the Sounds dialog box. Your screen should resemble Figure 3.14.

FIGURE 3.14.

You can get at the Control Panel's applets using the express route through Windows Explorer.

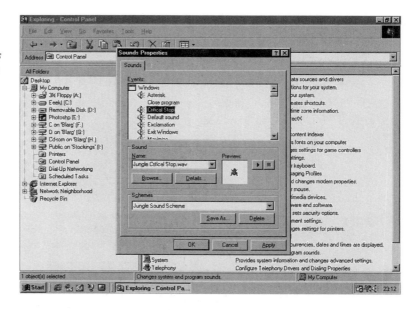

▲

You can also add items from Windows Explorer to the desktop by dragging them there.

Task 3.3. Handy Desktop Shortcuts

The following steps will show you how to add a shortcut for launching a Control Panel applet onto the desktop:

1. Follow steps 1 and 2 from Task 3.2.

2. Locate the Mouse applet within the right pane of the display. This is easier if you're in List or Details view. To change views, click the View menu choice and make a choice from the drop-down list.

3. Right-click and drag the Mouse applet from Windows Explorer to the desktop. Release the mouse button. Choose Create Shortcut(s) Here from the pop-up menu, as shown in Figure 3.15.

FIGURE 3.15.

Adding shortcuts from Windows Explorer objects to the desktop is as simple as dragging them there.

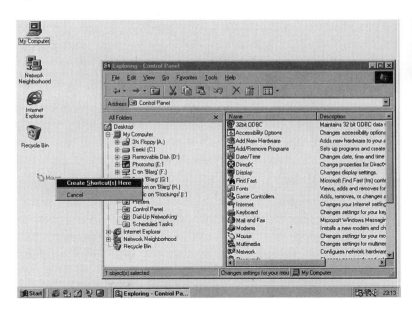

3

This will leave a shortcut to the mouse configuration applet on your desktop. Similar drag-and-drop actions will place shortcuts for most Windows Explorer objects just about anywhere you might want them.

Configuring Windows Explorer

Windows Explorer in Windows 98 has greatly expanded configuration options when compared to the Explorers and File Managers found in older Windows versions. How you set up Windows Explorer will depend on your tastes and what tasks you have at hand.

The basic setup for Windows Explorer is the Folder Options dialog box, found under the menu choices View|Folder Options. Figure 3.16 shows this dialog box open.

FIGURE 3.16.

The Folder Options dialog box sets global options for Windows Explorer.

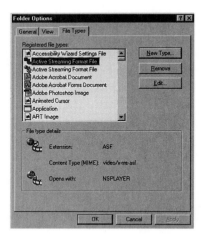

The three tabs of this dialog box are General, View, and File Types. The General tab has several display options. To customize these settings, click the General tab and click the Settings button. The meat of how Windows Explorer acts is in the View tab. Click this tab to see a series of check boxes with behavioral and display options for the Explorer.

By default, Windows hides files having system type extensions or those with the hidden attribute set. Most people have no need to see these files, so their appearance only clutters up a screen. Advanced users will, from time to time, need to see or even manipulate these files, so Windows Explorer gives them the option to turn on this view. This is through the View tab under the Hide File Extensions For Known File Types and the Hidden Files choices. Feel free to experiment with all the options under the View tab. You can always return to the installation defaults by clicking the Restore Defaults button on this tab.

File Associations

For better or worse, Windows 98 continues the Windows tradition of associating files with their applications by means of a three alphanumeric extension of the filename. When an application installs itself, it usually will set those associations by directly manipulating the registration database.

In some cases you might want to change those associations or add some new ones of your own. For example, suppose you have Paint Shop Pro installed with the file extension .bmp associated with it. *Association* in this context means that double-clicking a file with the `.bmp` extension (visible or not in Windows Explorer) will launch Paint Shop Pro with the file loaded.

Now you load a new application, BrushMaster Pro. Its installation alters the Registry to associate those `.bmp` files with it, and you want to change the association back to Paint Shop Pro. You must use the File Types tab in the Folder Options dialog box shown earlier in Figure 3.16. Task 3.4 will show you how to associate a file type with an application so that the file type will load in the associated application when you double-click the file in Windows Explorer.

Task 3.4. Creating a File Association

These steps will show you how to associate a file extension with an application. By following along, you'll learn how to delete and edit associations as well. This Task uses the extension `.log` and associates it with Notepad. Practically speaking, you can just add the `.log` extension to the entry for Notepad's `.txt` extension, but this exercise uses a longer, more detailed method for illustration purposes.

1. Open the File Types tab by choosing View | Folder Options | File Types from Windows Explorer. Your screen should resemble Figure 3.17. Your screen won't be identical to the figure because what appears in this dialog box depends on what your current associations are.

FIGURE 3.17.

The File Types tab is where you associate files and their applications.

2. Click the New Type button. This will bring up the dialog box shown in Figure 3.18, but with the text boxes unpopulated.

3. Fill in the top three text boxes as shown in Table 3.2.

FIGURE 3.18.

The Add New File Type dialog box.

TABLE 3.2. INFORMATION FOR THE FILE ASSOCIATION EXAMPLE.

Text Box	Data
Description of Type	Example
Associated Extension	.log
Content Type (MIME)	text/plain

4. You can choose the text/plain content type from a pull-down list. After you finish, Windows will fill in the Default Extension for Content Type box with what's already associated with the content type. Use the pull-down list to change it to .log.

5. Click in the Actions text box and click the New button to add a new action for this file type. Fill in Open for the action and Notepad.exe for the application. Click OK to close the New Actions dialog box. Your screen will now completely resemble Figure 3.18.

6. Click Close to exit the File Types tab.

This operation is a bit clunky the first few times you run through it. Windows has a shortcut to accomplish the same thing. If you double-click a file with an unknown extension in Windows Explorer, Windows 98 will ask if you want to associate this unknown file type with an application. From there you can either fill in the blanks for the application or browse for it. You should become familiar with the File Types tab because it's the only way to delete or edit file types, their associated applications, and their actions.

Manipulating Files and Directories

Windows Explorer is the most used view to move, copy, and delete files and directories or folders. The DOS term *directories* has now been supplanted by the Macintosh-inspired word *folder*, and this chapter will refer to them as such. Old DOS hands need only think *directory* when reading *folder*.

The computer industry analogy of file organization is one of a file cabinet. Think of your entire disk, or disk and network if you're part of a LAN, as a file cabinet. Inside the cabinet are folders and inside the folders are documents. Think of all disks or other data storage sources you can access as your file cabinet. Inside the cabinet are folders for collections of usually related files. You can have folders within folders, too.

Figure 3.19 shows Windows Explorer. The currently selected folder, selected by clicking it with the mouse, is on a CD-ROM.

3

FIGURE 3.19.

Windows Explorer displays a graphical representation of your computer's layout.

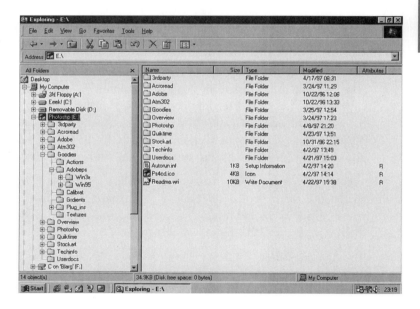

Let's take a tour of all the information shown in this view. If your Windows Explorer doesn't look like the one shown in Figure 3.19, you might have its properties set differently from the book's example. Try pulling down the View menu and choosing Toolbar. Click Standard Buttons and Address Bar, the first two choices from the fly-out menu, if they're not already selected. That will configure your Windows Explorer to look like the one in the book, but with contents specific to your machine.

The label for the selected CD-ROM in drive E: is Photoshp. You can see it as the high-lighted selection in the left pane. The Photoshp disc contains several folders. You can see those folders both underneath the Photoshp label in the left pane and also in the right pane.

The plus and minus signs in the left pane indicate whether a tree, or hierarchy of folders, exists and whether it's expanded. A minus sign indicates an expanded branch, that is, one showing folders and files contained in another folder. A plus sign indicates a branch that's not expanded.

To expand a branch, click on the plus sign. To collapse or condense an expanded branch, click on the minus sign.

> **Tip**
>
> As with many things in Windows, you can work in various ways to achieve identical outcomes. Double-clicking on folders in the left pane of Windows Explorer toggles them from the expanded state to the collapsed state.

The pull-down box in the toolbar containing the text Photoshp (E:) contains a list of resources you can access from Windows Explorer. It's essentially a duplicate of what's shown in the left pane. The drop-down list is condensed. If you have a large or complex list in the left pane, navigating to other disks or sections is usually faster using the drop-down box than scrolling through the left pane. To see the drop-down list, click the down arrow at the right of the list box or click in the list box and press F4.

Windows Explorer is fully loaded with ToolTips, as is most of Windows 98. To see what each button on the toolbar does, move your mouse over a particular button. After a little pause, Windows 98 will bring up a small black-on-yellow tip explaining the function of the button. Figure 3.20 shows one of these ToolTips in action.

The standard buttons on the toolbar in Windows Explorer have these functions, from left to right:

- Back—Returns to previous selection.
- Forward—Moves to subsequent selection after you've already moved back. (Windows Explorer can't see the future.)
- Up—Moves up one level through the folder hierarchy.
- Cut—Cuts the selected object.
- Copy—Copies the selected object.
- Paste—Pastes a previously cut or copied object.

- Undo—Undoes, or rescinds, previous action.
- Delete—Moves the selected object to the Recycle Bin.
- Properties—Brings up the properties sheet for the selected object.
- Views—Alters the view of the right pane.

FIGURE 3.20.

ToolTips hint as to the use of Windows 98 objects. Here a ToolTip hint indicates that the button under the cursor deletes highlighted objects.

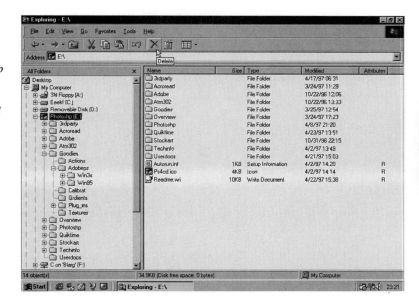

You can also right-click on objects to bring up a context menu loaded with many of the same choices found in the toolbar or in the menus. Figure 3.21 shows the context menu for a file in Windows Explorer.

Note As with many other Windows features, what you see in the context menu depends on what you have installed on your system. Don't be alarmed if your menu doesn't look exactly like what's shown in Figure 3.21.

If you choose Open for a program, the program will launch. If you choose Open for a document, the document's associated program will open with that document loaded.

An interesting option on the context menu is Send To. This is an express train to send a file, usually a document, to a set of customizable destinations. Figure 3.21 shows the Send To menu open to show the destinations available for one computer. The objects you can send to depend on the entries in the SendTo directory, which is contained within the main Windows 98 folder. Usually the main folder for Windows is on the C: drive and is called Windows.

FIGURE 3.21.

Right-clicking on Windows Explorer objects brings up a heavily optioned context menu.

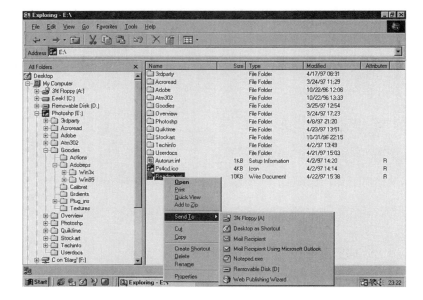

Figure 3.22 shows the SendTo folder opened. As you can see by comparing the contents of this folder with the context menu in Figure 3.21, whatever's in this folder appears on the context menu.

If you want to add things to the context menu, add a shortcut (right-click and then drag and drop) to the SendTo folder.

To use the context menu, choose an object, right-click it, and then choose an action from the Send To menu choice. For example, to mail a document on the machine shown in Figures 3.22 and 3.23, locate the document, right-click it, and choose Mail Recipient.

Selecting Files or Objects

Windows Explorer will act upon selected objects. To select a single object, click it. To select a series of contiguous objects, click one at the top or the bottom of the list; then Shift+click the one at the other end of the list. To select noncontiguous objects, click the first one and then Ctrl+click the others.

FIGURE 3.22.

The SendTo folder contains objects that appear in the right-click Windows Explorer context menu.

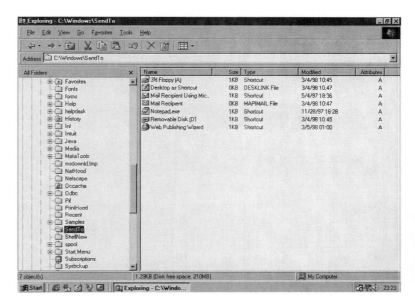

Copying and Moving

You have three common Windows Explorer ways to copy or move a file or a group of files from one place to another. Here is the basic way to do this:

1. Locate the file or files you want to move or copy.

2. Select one or more of the files.

3. Choose Copy or Cut from the Edit menu, the toolbar, or the right-click context menu.

4. Locate the place to which you want to move or copy the objects. Click on it.

5. Choose Paste from the toolbar, the Edit menu, or the right-click context menu.

You can also drag files from one location to another. If you drag a file to a subfolder (or anywhere in the same volume), you'll move it from where it is to that subfolder. If you drag a file to a folder on a different volume, you'll copy it to that folder. *Move* means that there is no copy left in the original location. *Copy* means there is. To make sure you're copying a file, hold down the Ctrl key while dragging. If you don't like to drag files, you can always highlight them and choose the appropriate commands from the Edit menu or from the right-click context menu.

If you want to drag files and want to make sure that you know whether you're moving or copying them, you can drag them with the right mouse button. When you drop the files, a context menu will appear, giving you the choice of moving, copying, creating a shortcut, or canceling the whole operation altogether.

Tip
If you find you're copying or moving to the same place, make a shortcut in the SendTo folder so that it appears on the context menu for Windows Explorer. The time you save can be significant.

Changing the View

Windows Explorer is one view of your computer's resources. That view can have different views or presentations. Figure 3.23 shows the Views button of the Windows Explorer toolbar clicked open.

FIGURE 3.23.

Windows Explorer has four views. One is just right for you.

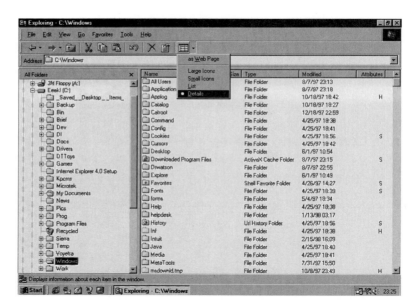

This list is duplicated in the View menu choice of Windows Explorer. The choices are

- Large Icons—Shows objects with large icons—good for the visually oriented (see Figure 3.24).
- Small Icons—Similar to the Large Icons view, only with smaller icons (see Figure 3.25).
- List—Shows objects as a list with small icons to the left (see Figure 3.26).
- Details—Shows the file list with details such as file date and properties (see Figure 3.27).

FIGURE 3.24.

The Large Icons view works well for artistic visual types.

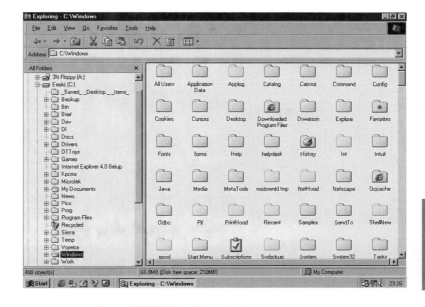

FIGURE 3.25.

The Small Icons view is horizontally oriented.

FIGURE 3.26.

The List view is similar to the Small Icon view but vertically oriented.

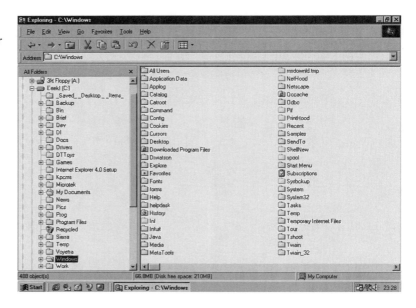

FIGURE 3.27.

The Details view includes size, type, time and date, and file attribute information.

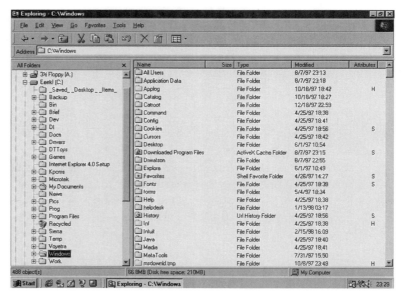

Customizing the Taskbar in Windows 98

The *taskbar* is the bar at the bottom of the screen by default. Introduced with Windows 95 and then continued with Windows NT 4, the taskbar is the heart of navigating around running programs.

Microsoft has materially improved the taskbar in Windows 98. Rather than just one bar with a Start button and a tray, as in previous iterations of Windows, the new taskbar has more capabilities added with nothing material left off. The most important aspect of the new taskbar is its capability to be divided into a bar with specialized functions. Figure 3.28 shows the default taskbar at the bottom of the desktop. The post-Setup layout of the taskbar will vary from machine to machine, but the elements will all be the same.

FIGURE 3.28.

The default taskbar looks just like the ones in Windows 95 and Windows NT 4.

At the far left is the Start button. The Start button, and its related menu entries, is part of the Taskbar view of your Windows 98 objects. To its right is the Quick Launch toolbar with icons that will quickly launch programs at a single click. The next entries are representations of open programs. Windows Explorer is first on the left, WordPad is next, and Paint is third. The cursor is over the WordPad entry to show that a ToolTip-like box will open, showing a complete entry on those open items that are too large to fit in the displayed area. In this case it shows the truncated entry RunOnceEx Log.txt - Wor..., which is truncated from RunOnceEx Log.txt - WordPad. This indicates that WordPad is running the current document RunOnceEx Log.txt.

The farthest right area of the taskbar is the *tray*. This holds entries that enable you to quickly navigate to programs or system settings. For example, double-clicking the time, shown in Figure 3.28, jumps you to the time and date settings dialog box, whereas double-clicking on the speaker icon jumps you to volume settings for multimedia audio components. Other icons in the tray shown in Figure 3.28 are specific for the particular display used in this computer. The one farthest to the left within the tray is a jump to the Task Scheduler. To see what the icons (if any) do in your tray, move your mouse over them and a ToolTip will pop up with the information.

To customize the taskbar settings, right-click an empty spot on it and choose Properties from the context menu. Figure 3.29 shows the resulting dialog box.

FIGURE 3.29.

The Taskbar Properties dialog box.

The following are the meanings of the four check boxes on the Taskbar Options tab:

- Always on Top—Floats the taskbar over all other objects on the desktop.
- Auto Hide—Moves the taskbar off the desktop unless the mouse hovers over its location.
- Show Small Icons in Start Menu—Shows icons like List view in Windows Explorer in the Start menu.
- Show Clock—Displays time in the tray.

The Start Menu Programs tab has four very useful buttons (see Figure 3.30).

Here are the purposes of these four buttons:

- Add—Adds an item to the Start Menu by using a wizard.
- Remove—Removes an item from the Start menu by browsing through a list for it.
- Advanced—Changes the Start menu view into an Explorer view, allowing you to do any and all file manipulations to the Start menu entries.
- Clear—Clears the Documents menu item from the Start menu. Good if you don't want others to see what documents you've been working on.

FIGURE 3.30.

Many people search all through Windows to find a way to clear their Documents menu. The Start Menu Programs tab is where to find the Clear button for this task.

The context menu (right-click) of the taskbar also has several powerful entries. Figure 3.31 shows the context menu with the Toolbars entry fly-out displayed.

FIGURE 3.31.

The context menu for the taskbar is a hotbed of customizing options.

Here is what these options do:

- Toolbars—Adds or removes standard or custom areas to or from the taskbar.
- Cascade Windows—Stacks windows like a slightly spread deck of cards.
- Tile Windows (Horizontally or Vertically)—Spreads windows across the desktop like bathroom tiles.
- Minimize All Windows—Minimizes all windows at the same time.
- Undo Minimize All (appears only after Minimize All Windows is selected)—Restores windows to their former state.
- Properties—Opens the Taskbar Properties dialog box.

The Quick Launch toolbar is a customizable area like the tray where you can stack programs or documents you want to have always available from the taskbar. The Desktop toolbar creates an area on your taskbar with entries for all your entries on the desktop.

Figure 3.32 shows the taskbar with both the Desktop and Quick Launch toolbars.

FIGURE 3.32.

Adding toolbars to the taskbar soon makes it crowded.

As you can see, the taskbar is now so crowded it is less convenient than not having these entries. However, you can change the look of the new toolbars by right-clicking them and choosing to suppress text displays. You can also adjust the horizontal size of any taskbar toolbar by clicking on its double line and dragging to a new size. If that isn't enough flexibility, you can also "grab" a toolbar by its adjuster and drag it to the desktop, where you can set it to float.

 Tip

> Moving your cursor over the top part of the taskbar will change the cursor to a double arrow. Dragging this double arrow will enlarge or decrease the width of the taskbar.

Figure 3.33 shows the same taskbar as Figure 3.32, but the Show Text property has been removed from the Desktop toolbar and added to the Quick Launch one. Although the taskbar is more spacious, the unlabeled folders in the Desktop toolbar aren't very informative.

FIGURE 3.33.

Changing the display of the taskbar toolbars adds space but can reduce function.

The Quick Launch toolbar on the taskbar is user customizable. To add programs, documents, or shortcuts to this area, just drag and drop them there. To remove them, drag them off either to the desktop or to the Recycle Bin.

The final toolbar entry for the taskbar is a user-customizable toolbar. To add a custom toolbar to the taskbar, click the New Toolbar entry from the Toolbar fly-out on the taskbar context menu. This brings up a browsing box, as shown in Figure 3.34.

You can add as many custom toolbars to the taskbar as you choose. Figure 3.35 shows the results of including a folder holding the Adobe program Photoshop in a toolbar and placing it on the taskbar. Note that the Desktop toolbar has been deleted from the taskbar and the relative sizes of the other taskbar areas have been adjusted for optimal display.

FIGURE 3.34.

You can browse for entries on a custom toolbar for inclusion in the standard taskbar.

FIGURE 3.35.

Here is a folder containing many subfolders relating to the Adobe program Photoshop, an image-editing program.

3

To remove a custom toolbar, right-click on the taskbar, choose Toolbars, and uncheck its entry.

There are more ways to customize the Start menu part of the taskbar. Those are covered on Day 8.

The Recycle Bin

The Recycle Bin is an area that holds discarded items, usually files, until it reaches a user-configurable percentage of a disk's capacity. At that point it discards them for good.

In the old DOS and Windows 3.*x* days, deleted files were gone. This created a demand for utilities such as Norton's to restore erased files. The often-used but ungrammatical term for restoring erased files is *unerasing*. The Windows 98 system moves files to the Recycle Bin for potential subsequent restoration. Today Norton Utilities remains in place for enhanced protection against accidental erasure (better than Windows' native), but for many, the Recycle Bin is good enough.

Normally, erasing (deleting) files in Windows Explorer will move them to the Recycle Bin. How long they remain there depends on the bin's properties. Right-click the bin on the desktop to bring up its Properties dialog box (see Figure 3.36).

FIGURE 3.36.

*Most of the Recycle
Bin's properties are
user configurable.*

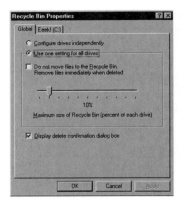

Here are the entries on the dialog box for the Recycle Bin:

- Configure Drives Independently—Sets the percentage the bin can hold for each drive, independent of other drives.
- Use One Setting for All Drives—Sets the percentage globally.
- Do Not Move Files to the Recycle Bin. Remove Files Immediately When Deleted—A security measure to bypass the Recycle Bin.
- Display Delete Confirmation Dialog Box—Shows the nuisance Confirm Delete dialog box in Windows Explorer whenever you delete a file.

In the dialog box shown in Figure 3.36, as soon as the Recycle Bin's contents reach 10% of the drive capacity, Windows 98 will start throwing away items, starting with the oldest.

Tip

You can bypass the Recycle Bin by holding Shift as you drag items from Windows Explorer to the bin. Items deleted in the MS-DOS command-line interface (CLI) aren't moved to the bin. They are just gone. Norton Utilities for Windows can recover some of these files, however.

Sorting Through the Recycle Bin

To recover items from the Recycle Bin, double-click its desktop icon to open it, or right-click it and choose Open or Explore, depending on the view you want. The bin is like any other folder. To remove items from it, just drag them out. You can also open Windows Explorer and explore the bin (it's in the left pane), dragging items out that way or using the copy/paste routine common to Windows Explorer.

To remove all items from the bin, right-click the icon on the desktop and choose Empty Recycle Bin from the context menu. Remember that items emptied from the bin can't be recovered using standard Windows 98 tools.

Summary

Windows 98's user interface is made up mostly of different views of the same information. The desktop can be similar to that in Windows 95 and Windows NT 4: the default view. You can also change your view to an Active Desktop, which will allow the inclusion of dynamic objects in your user interface.

Windows Explorer is the chief tool for viewing and manipulating objects on your local computer and LAN. Using it, you can move, copy, and delete files and make shortcuts to programs and documents. The File Types tab on the View | Options menu enables you to create, edit, and delete file associations.

Windows Explorer has four basic views of files and folders: Large Icon, Small Icon, List, and Details. Windows Explorer remains operationally identical no matter which view you choose.

The taskbar is much more configurable than in past Windows versions. You can add several predefined toolbars to it or make up a toolbar from one of your folders.

The Recycle Bin is a folder in which deleted items reside until the folder exceeds a user-defined capacity. At that point Windows 98 starts to delete the oldest items first. You can move items from the bin just as you can any other folder.

Workshop

To wrap up the day, you can review terms from the chapter, see the answers to some commonly asked questions, and practice what you've learned. You can find the answers to the exercises in Appendix A, "Answers."

Terminology Review

context menu—The menu that appears when you right-click the mouse. It's called a *context* menu because its contents change depending on the context of where you right-click.

fly-out menu—A submenu that flies out from a main menu entry.

volume—A logical drive. For example, a physical hard drive might be divided into more than one logical drive. Each logical drive or volume has a letter assigned by Windows 98.

3

taskbar—The specialized toolbar that contains buttons to switch to running tasks, the tray, and the Start button.

tray—An area of the taskbar that contains icons for running services such as the volume control and the modem connection status.

shortcut—A link to a file or program. You can locate shortcuts anywhere you choose without affecting the logical (physical) location of the file referred to.

Q&A

Q If you drag a file from one folder to another on the same volume, will you move or copy that file?

A Move it.

Q How can you copy a file when dragging from one location to another on the same volume?

A Hold down the Ctrl key while dragging, or use the right mouse button for dragging and then select Copy from the context menu that appears at the drop location.

Q How can I move toolbars within the taskbar to another location such as the desktop?

A Click when your pointer is over the adjuster bar (the raised bar at the far left of any toolbar) and then drag.

Q How can I tell Windows 98 to show the entire names of all files, including those with known extensions?

A From Windows Explorer, choose View | Folder Options | View and uncheck Hide File Extensions for Known File Types.

Q How can I restore display defaults for Windows Explorer?

A From Windows Explorer, choose View | Folder Options | View and click the Restore Defaults button.

Exercises

1. Earlier in this chapter, you learned that the Control Panel uses Windows Explorer to present the tools that allow you to change the settings for your computer. The Control Panel is also included in the Windows Explorer that you launch from the Start menu. Use Windows Explorer to show the Control Panel.

2. Create a new toolbar that allows you to run the Windows Paintbrush program with one click. (Hint: First create a directory, put a shortcut in the directory, and then add the toolbar.)

DAY 4

Working with Files and Folders

by Paul Cassel

All versions of Windows, from the earliest versions back in the middle 1980s, swap the abstract file organization of MS-DOS with a graphical one. Actually, the file organization remained the same, but the presentation to the end user of the PC changed.

In the first days of IBM-style PCs, all files existed on one place—a floppy disk. That arrangement became impractical when, in 1983, hard disks, with their greater capacities for storing information, arrived on the scene as part of the standard factory computer in the guise of the IBM XT.

Microsoft responded to the need of a more flexible file organization with the then standard (from other operating systems) hierarchical file system. In such a system, files exist as part of a chain. Microsoft gave these chains the name *directory trees* after their organizational structure. *Directory* is the original name for what Windows 98 calls a folder.

Today's lesson covers the following:

- The difference between logical and physical drives
- What a disk volume is
- Common types of storage media
- Strategies for disk volume organization
- Implementing the strategy of your choice
- Creating and deleting folder structures
- Selecting and acting on files and folders
- Copying, moving, and deleting files or folders
- Renaming files or folders
- Mass actions on files and folders
- Creating a practice folder structure

The Arrangement of Files and Folders

The structure of files and folders logically within a volume of your hard disk is easier to understand with an illustration. Figure 4.1 shows a very simple file and folder tree.

FIGURE 4.1.

A simple file and folder structure.

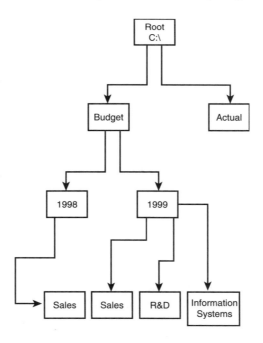

The root folder or directory is the disk volume C:. Disk volumes are always letters followed by a colon. There are two folders under the root, Budget and Actual. There are two folders under Budget, 1998 and 1999, and so forth.

ARE YOU LOGICAL OR PHYSICAL?

When talking about files and folders, people use the two terms *logical* and *physical*. The logical layout of a storage system is how it appears to a user. The physical layout refers to the actual physical location of the magnetic signals making up a file or folder. For this chapter, consider all drive and directory notations to be logical.

The analogy Microsoft likes to use for files and folders is the following: A file is like a document, a folder like a manila folder in a filing cabinet, while the volume or disk itself is a filing cabinet. It follows that many files can fit in a folder, many folders in another folder (such as a hanging folder), and many hanging folders in a file cabinet.

ZIP, JAZ, OR DISK?

This chapter refers to hard disks and floppy disks as if they are the only possible storage media. This saves space by eliminating almost endless qualifications. If your system has different or additional devices than these, substitute them for the term *disk*. There are many DOS-addressable random access devices currently on the market or soon to arrive on the market. This chapter is equally relevant to them all.

4

Figure 4.2 shows the file and folder structure of a typical volume as shown in Windows Explorer. To see a view similar to this, open Windows Explorer by choosing it from the desktop, the Quick Launch area of the taskbar, or from the menu choices Start|Programs|Windows Explorer.

If your display, especially the right pane, looks different from Figure 4.2, choose View|Details in Explorer. Your exact display will differ in details from the one shown in Figure 4.2.

As you can see from your display, the entries in Explorer are of several types. The majority are files and folders. You can tell a folder at a glance by two keys—the folder icon to the left of the folder name and the File Folder entry under the Type column in the right pane of Explorer. These two items are circled in Figure 4.2.

Files are the actual documents you create, save, edit, and work on with your computer and its application programs.

FIGURE 4.2.

An actual file and folder display as shown in Windows Explorer.

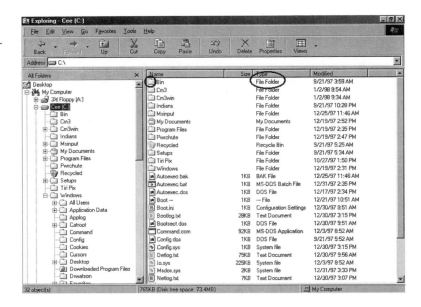

Deciding on a Strategy

Before organizing your files and folders into a structure that makes sense to the way you work, you must decide on a strategy. Some people like leaving the details to Windows 98, which will, if you let it, dump everything into My Documents, located on the same volume as Windows itself.

Although better than randomly scattered files, the "leave it to Windows" approach isn't optimal for the following reasons:

- Unless you only have a few files, you don't want them all in the same folder. When your files grow beyond roughly 50 in number, you'll encounter difficulty locating them if all of them are in the same folder.
- There is no logic to an unorganized dump. Look at Figure 4.1 again; you have a good idea where files relating to budgets for 1998 should be located, at a glance.
- Windows has limitations as to how many files it can handle in a folder. A good rule of thumb is to avoid having more than 500.
- Unless your entire storage space is on one volume (such as C:), you will likely end up wasting disk space by placing all your documents in My Documents.

Windows users have worked out several general strategies for storing documents. Here are a few:

- Store documents in folders under their application. Using such a strategy, one would store all WordPerfect documents in folders starting under the main WordPerfect folder. Lawyers and accountants seem to favor this approach.

- Store documents on their own volume. To do this you must have a disk or disks partitioned in more than one volume (such as C: and D:). C: would store Windows and the application programs such as Excel and Microsoft Access, whereas D: would hold all the documents. This strategy is very effective for backup purposes.

- Create a Documents folder and then place classified folders under that. This is the basic strategy of Microsoft when it created the My Documents folder.

Within those strategies (and there are many others), you can choose to classify documents by any of these common means or one of your choosing:

- By document type (such as WordPerfect) and then by purpose or client.

- By client (or customer) and then by classification (such as correspondence or invoice).

- By year or month and then by client or customer.

- By classification (such as invoice) and then by customer.

The variations are endless. You need to decide what makes sense to you based on the function of your computing and your inclination. For example, if you only do invoicing, bunching all invoices together doesn't do much to organize them because all your documents are invoices. In that case, you'd probably want to classify first by customer and then by date or service.

Decide on a strategy and then give it a try for a while. You can always reorganize your folder and file structure by manipulating these objects using Windows Explorer. The balance of today's lesson deals with this and related topics.

Changing the Location of My Documents

Remember, you can move My Documents from its installation location to any other place of your choosing. Too many people leave My Documents in the root of the same volume as their Windows 98 installation and then run out of space in that location while having loads of space elsewhere.

To change the location of My Documents and by extension the default location where your applications store files, right-click My Documents and choose Properties. Fill in a new location for the folder in the ensuing dialog box. You can see this dialog box as it appears on a typical desktop in Figure 4.3.

FIGURE 4.3.

You can alter where My Documents resides.

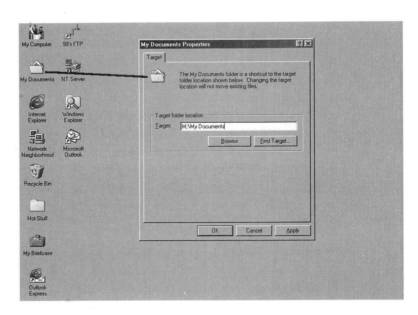

For more information about manipulating files and folders, see the section "Manipulating Files and Directories" on Day 3, "Navigating Within Windows 98."

Creating New and Renaming Old Folders

The standard Windows 98 File Save As dialog enables you to create new folders on-the-fly. Figure 4.4 shows this dialog box with a square drawn around the New Folder button.

Creating New Folders

You can also create new folders using Windows Explorer. To do this, right-click in the right pane of Explorer and choose New|Folder from the context menu. Explorer responds by creating a new folder with the words *New Folder* active; you then rename this folder by typing in the actual name of your choice. Figure 4.5 shows a newly created folder in Explorer.

When you have renamed your folder, press Enter to leave edit mode, and you're done creating your new folder. Remember that you can cut, copy, delete, or move this folder along with its contents just as you can any file.

You can also create a new folder by choosing File|New|Folder from the Explorer main menu.

FIGURE 4.4.

The standard Windows 98 File Save As dialog box.

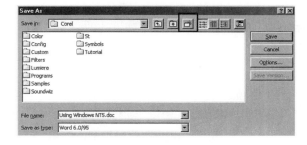

FIGURE 4.5.

You're only a right-click away from as many new folders as you want to create.

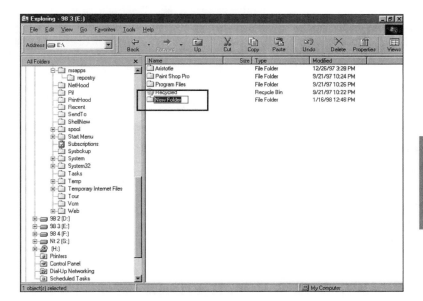

Renaming Files and Folders

Renaming folders is fairly simple. If you're very dexterous, you can click once, pause, and then click again on a file or folder. This puts you in edit mode for the name. In this mode the file or folder name looks like the New Folder name after you've created a new folder.

Most people find clicking into edit mode to be quite difficult. An easier way is to just right-click the target file or folder and then choose Rename from the context menu. This puts you directly into edit mode. After changing the name, press Enter to leave edit mode. Pressing Esc during edit mode will exit edit mode and return the original name to the file or folder.

Windows 98 allows you to rename some system folders such as local Recycle Bins, but doing so might confuse Windows and its applications.

Deleting Files and Folders

To delete a file or folder (along with its subfolders and all contents) using Explorer, highlight the file or folder on your hit list by clicking it. Press the Delete key on your keyboard or click the Delete button on Explorer's toolbar.

If you're deleting a large number of files or folders with files at one shot, Explorer might respond that the deletions are too great for storage within the Recycle Bin and any deletions will be permanent. This isn't a joke message. Proceed with mass deletions (or any deletions) with care. If in doubt, you can always increase the capacity of your Recycle Bin by right-clicking it, choosing Properties, and then sliding the Maximum Size slider to the right.

Marquee Highlighting

You can drag a box around multiple files to select them; this is known as *marquee selection*. To do this, click the right pane of Explorer anywhere away from filenames. While holding the mouse button down, drag a rectangle around the files you want to select. You don't need to surround the entire filename with the rectangle—any part will do.

As you drag, Explorer creates a "rubber band" box and highlights the filenames. You can select multiple marquees by first selecting one and then pressing Ctrl as you drag around subsequent ones. Marquee selection works in other places in Windows 98 such as the desktop.

Putting It All Together

The best way to get used to manipulating files and folders is with practice. The problem is that if you practice on real files and folders, you might end up losing data or leaving your computer in a less than fully functional state. Task 4.1 shows a safe way to practice.

Task 4.1. Manipulating Files and Folders

▼ TASK

The following demonstration is a practice session for manipulating files and folders without any danger of data loss or computer malfunction:

1. Open Windows Explorer. If possible, move to a volume other than the one that hosts Windows 98, preferably an empty volume. For example, if Windows 98 is in `C:\Windows` (it usually is), move to volume D: if you have one. If not, use the Windows host volume. Figure 4.6 shows Explorer moving to a different volume than the one hosting Windows 98.

▼

FIGURE 4.6.

This exercise is most safely done on an unused volume or one away from Windows 98 itself.

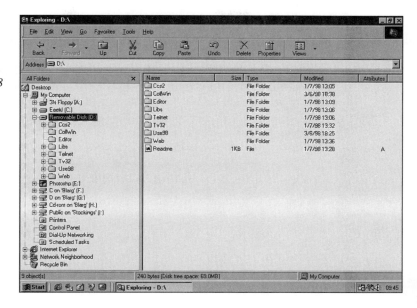

2. Right-click in the right pane and choose New|Folder from the context menu. When Explorer creates the new folder, name it Practice by typing in that name and pressing Enter when done. Figure 4.7 shows this operation in progress.

FIGURE 4.7.

The Practice folder is a good place to, well, practice.

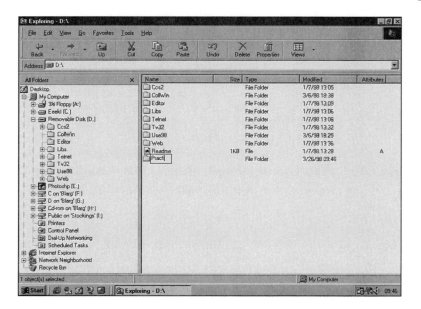

4

▼ 3. Open up the tree in the left pane of your practice drive if necessary. Click the Practice folder to highlight it; then click in the right pane of Explorer and choose New|Folder from the context menu. Create a subfolder called First. Repeat this process to create another folder named Second. Your screen should resemble Figure 4.8 when you're done. If your screen doesn't visually resemble Figure 4.8, you probably have a different set of Windows Explorer options set. The visual aspect of your screen isn't important as long as you can do a "mental" translation between the book and your computer. This example uses a standard Web page look with the Explorer view set to Details.

FIGURE 4.8.

A complete folder structure to practice on.

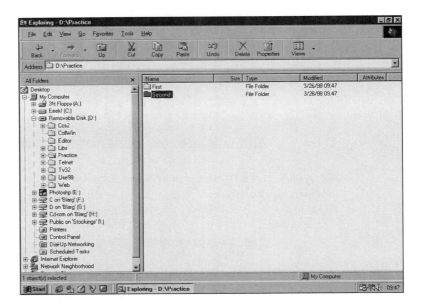

4. The only thing left in the exercise setup is to populate the folders with some files. Locate the Windows host folder (usually C:\Windows) and then locate the Command subfolder. Highlight the first file in the folder, hold down the Shift key, and click another file roughly ten files down. You can also drag to highlight files. Right-click on the series of highlighted files and choose Copy from the context menu. Your screen should resemble Figure 4.9. Be sure to choose Copy and not Cut!

5. Return to the First folder under Practice. Open the folder by clicking it, right-click in the right pane of Explorer, and choose Paste from the context menu. You now ▼ have about ten disposable files (copies of the needed files) to practice on.

▼

FIGURE 4.9.

And now to find some innocent files to practice on!

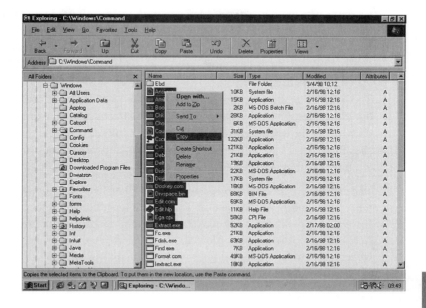

▲

4

From here, what you do is up to you. Here are some ideas:

- Drag some files up and down the folder tree.

- Try cutting, copying, and pasting files from one folder to another.

- Manipulate Explorer so that you can see it and the Recycle Bin. Drag some files from a folder to the Recycle Bin. Open the bin by double-clicking it, locate the files, and drag them back out again to their original location.

- Do the same as above, but try dragging deleted files or folders to a new location. Does Windows 98 let you?

- Highlight a folder with some files in it. Press the Delete key or click Delete on the toolbar. Open the Recycle Bin. Locate the folder you just deleted. Highlight it by clicking it. Choose File|Restore from the Recycle Bin's menu. Return to the folder in Explorer. Does it contain its original files or are they still in the Recycle Bin?

- Hold down Shift while dragging a file to the Recycle Bin. Can you now find that file in the bin?

- Copy a file. Try to paste it back into the location where you copied it from to have two files with the same name in the same folder. Did Explorer let you do this?

- Practice holding down the Ctrl key while dragging files up and down the folder tree. What effect does that have on the files' behavior? Does Explorer give you any visual clue as to what it's doing in that case?

This is just a start, but it gives you some ideas of what you can do with Windows Explorer. When you're done practicing with the practice folder structure, you can highlight it and click Delete in Explorer's toolbar to remove the unnecessary folder tree.

Summary

The heart of a current technology computer is its files. Once you've mastered manipulating these files, you've mastered roughly 95 percent of what experienced computer users do when in the operating system. Windows Explorer is the chief tool for manipulating files in Windows 98, although you can do some manipulations in the Open and Save dialog boxes within applications.

The chief file operations are Copy, Move, Delete, and Rename. After you figure out these procedures, you're well on your way to operating system mastery. The best way to learn these operations using techniques of your choosing is to create a practice folder tree, populate it with a few files, and start practicing away. Just make sure you use a folder structure containing copies—not originals—of needed files.

Workshop

To wrap up the day, you can review terms from the chapter, see the answers to some commonly asked questions, and practice what you've learned. You can find the answers to the exercises in Appendix A, "Answers."

Terminology Review

copy file—To make an exact duplicate of a file in a different place. When you choose Copy within Windows Explorer, you are really copying a command to later copy (after Paste) the file to a new location. Using the command line, you can also copy a file to a new name within the same folder.

cut file—Remove a file from its current location after the Paste command is executed.

delete file—Move a file to the Recycle Bin unless you override the move by holding down Shift. In that case, the file is permanently deleted. Third-party utilities and services can often retrieve "permanently" deleted files.

folder—A holding place for a group of files.

move file—To copy a file to a new location and delete the file from its current location at the same time.

paste file—To finish the cut or copy operation in the target location.

volume—A logical disk such as C: or D:. A partition made using FDISK or a similar utility.

Q&A

Q If I keep moving files into the Recycle Bin, won't that eventually fill up and take over my entire disk?

A The Recycle Bin has a property (right-click it and choose Properties) that restricts the size of the bin to a percentage of your disk space.

Q Am I restricted to single word folder names?

A No, you can use long filenames such as My New Folder for folders you create. Keep in mind that the few old MS-DOS and Windows 3.1 programs still around can't see long filenames. Instead they see truncated versions of the names.

Q If I cut or move a file from one folder to another, does the cut part of it move to the Recycle Bin?

A No.

Q Can I drag a subfolder from one folder to another?

A Yes, you can drag and drop folders to just about anywhere your heart desires.

Q Can I drag the Control Panel from Windows Explorer to live on the desktop?

A You can drag it there, but Windows Explorer will only create a shortcut to it on the desktop rather than actually moving it. This has the same effect as having the Control Panel handy on the desktop without the functional problems that would crop up if Windows 98 actually allowed a move there.

4

Exercises

1. Having a folder named My Documents is useful, but there will probably be occasions when you waste time looking through all those files. You need a way to instantly locate your key documents. Create a new folder named Key Documents at the same directory level as My Documents and place a few files in it.

2. Now that you've mastered file manipulation, take a good look at the way your files are organized. Are you happy with them? Is there a more intuitive way to organize things? Take a shot at a new organization method.

DAY **5**

Fonts and Printing in Windows 98

by Paul Cassel

All versions of Windows, including Windows 98, extend the concept of what an operating system does beyond their DOS predecessors. In those old DOS days (and with some non-Microsoft operating systems today), you had to add and configure a printer for each application you installed on your system. Each printer had a separate driver (interface program) for each application.

Installing and configuring printers were major issues confronting those early computer systems. Windows has made the job of printing much easier by associating the configuration of a printer, or printers, with the operating system itself rather than with each application. This means that you set up a printer once and all native Windows applications will know how to use it. Actually the application programs don't know a thing. They only know to ask the operating system, Windows 98, for printing services. Windows handles all the down-and-dirty details for the application programs. This means that you need to set up and configure a printer only once and all your programs can use it without fuss or muss.

Similarly, Windows 98 handles fonts in a central manner. After you install a font or a series of fonts, it becomes available for use to all Windows programs.

This chapter covers the following:

- Font types
- Advantages and uses for different font types
- Font locations
- Instantly inspecting fonts by similarity
- Deleting fonts
- Installing new fonts
- Setting up a printer and installing drivers
- The Properties dialog box for printers
- Examining printer options
- Paper handling
- Printer woes and solutions
- Locating and using a network printer

What Is a Font?

A *font* is the summation of all elements contributing to how characters appear. These characters are all the letters, symbols, numbers, and other items that might appear on your screen or from your printer. The following list contains the elements that contribute to making up a font:

- Typeface—The shape of the characters. Do the characters have a serif? How much above and below the line of text do the characters protrude?
- Style—Is the typeface presented in italics, bold, or with other special stylistic attributes? Some definitions of fonts exclude style.
- Effects—These include underline, double underline, and strikeout.
- Size—How much physical space does each character occupy? This part of a font is usually given in points, where 72 points equal an inch.
- Pitch—The horizontal space for monospace fonts.
- X height—The vertical height of lowercase characters.

- Width—If a font has been compressed horizontally.

- Bounding box or spacing—Does each character have the same allotment of space (*monospace*), or does the room each character is allotted depend upon the character's attributes (*proportional*)?

Figure 5.1 shows Microsoft Word 97 with two fonts onscreen. These fonts show the various font characteristics listed above.

FIGURE 5.1.

A font is the sum of a character's appearance.

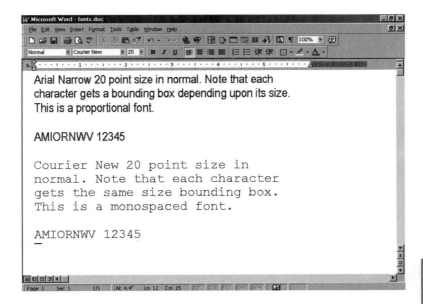

Font Differences

There are several types of fonts. Some fonts, called *screen fonts*, are designed mainly for use on display screens (monitors). Some fonts are strictly for use with a printer. Some fonts are flexible enough to be used for both purposes.

Fonts also differ in how they're treated by your computer. Here is a summary of font differences. Each of these systems varies in how the glyph, or font shape, is stored within your computer.

- TrueType fonts—Actually a font subsystem within Windows that uses outlining technology rather than the literal of raster or the line of vector. This system uses commands along with "hints" (a system to optimize the look of a font, depending on a series of variables) to generate a font. TrueType fonts, and their similar counterparts such as Adobe Type 1 fonts, can be scaled, rotated, and varied in almost all of their characteristics while maintaining their intended look.

- Raster fonts—Bitmaps, or an array of dots literally outlining and then filling in the outline of a font. A literal representation or picture of a font.

- Vector fonts—Fonts rendered from mathematical expressions. Vector fonts are generated based on instructions rather than a stored image.

Most output within modern versions of Windows, including Windows 98, uses TrueType. However, other type technologies are quite important to your computer. For example, Windows comes with several specific raster fonts for use in different screen resolutions. You can use these fonts for printing, but they don't scale very well because Windows is at a bit of a loss as to how to interpret the spaces left between the dots as you expand these fonts.

Figure 5.2 shows a raster font used for screen displays. Raster fonts scale very poorly. Note that as the font gets larger, it looks more jagged.

FIGURE 5.2.

This font is designed for use up to about 12-point size. By the time it reaches 36 points, it looks quite ragged.

Vector fonts scale better than raster fonts, but a vector font usually doesn't look as good as a raster when compared to the raster's intended size. They're also time-consuming to generate because they're stored as font description calls (little programs) without the font management subsystem of TrueType fonts.

Vector fonts look fine as they scale. Their primary use in today's systems is with plotters. Figure 5.3 shows a vector font.

FIGURE 5.3.

A vector font.

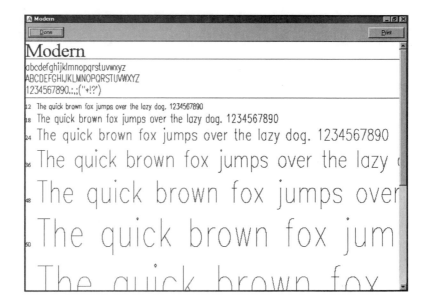

Figure 5.4 shows one of several TrueType fonts. These fonts are fast to generate yet scale quite well.

FIGURE 5.4.

A TrueType font.

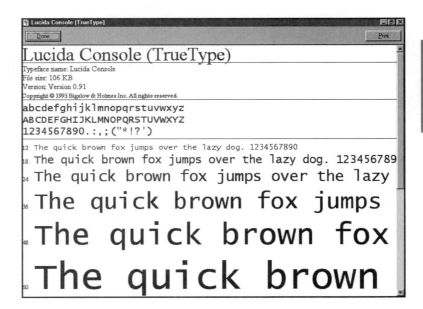

5

By far the best font type to use for your documents, either onscreen or for output, is TrueType or its Postscript Adobe counterpart, Type 1. Here are a few reasons for using TrueType outlining technology above others, including Type 1:

- TrueType is WYSIWYG (what you see is what you get). The image on your screen is the same as what you see coming out of your printer. In pre-WYSIWYG days, you could spend hours fooling around with minor adjustments to make sure that your screen rendering was the same as your printed rendering. In some cases, they could never be the same, and the hapless user had to make some serious design compromises in output.
- TrueType is portable. As you move your documents to other systems, you can be assured that their appearance won't vary.
- If a specific TrueType font isn't available, Windows 98 substitutes a close match from its selection of supplied TrueType fonts.
- Any printer using a Windows 98 driver (or another Windows TrueType driver) outputs your documents identically to all other such equipped printers.
- You can rotate and scale TrueType fonts to your heart's desire without bogging down your system with onerous font calculations.
- TrueType looks the same on Postscript and non-Postscript printers.
- TrueType fonts are very common and often come bundled with applications. Other comparable fonts often cost you dearly.

Installing, Inspecting, and Deleting Fonts

Many application programs and printer setup programs install fonts automatically or semi-automatically. Windows 98 creates the fonts you see by interpreting information supplied by files bearing the font names.

By default, Windows 98 installs its fonts in the Fonts folder within the main Windows folder, usually `C:\Windows`. Figure 5.5 shows a Windows Explorer view of the Fonts folder. The figure uses a Details view of the font files.

Windows Explorer's flexibility and knowledge about what type of object it displays are no better demonstrated than with fonts.

Viewing Your Fonts

You can manage your fonts either directly through the Windows Explorer or by launching the Fonts applet within Control Panel. Either method takes you to the same place.

FIGURE 5.5.

The usual place for font files is the Fonts folder contained within the Windows folder.

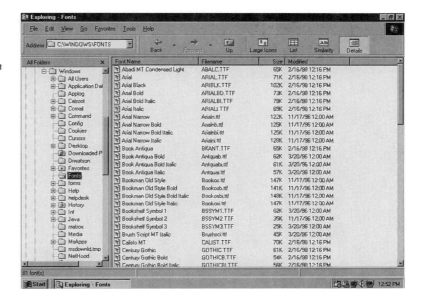

Task 5.1. Exploring and Comparing Fonts

The following example uses Windows Explorer's special abilities to examine the fonts loaded on your computer:

1. Launch Windows Explorer if necessary. Locate the Fonts folder within the Windows folder and click to open it. This example uses the List view; if you want your screens to look substantially like this example, choose View | List. Your screen should resemble Figure 5.6, although the specific fonts you have installed will very likely differ. Unless you have no optional fonts or are part of a unified setup plan, your Fonts folder files will vary from others even in the same organization. To see any font in a view window, double-click it or right-click and then choose Open from the context menu.

2. The computer used for screens in this example has a fairly large selection of fonts. However, the selection shown isn't by any means as large as some computers used for work such as page layout.

3. Pull down the View menu selection in Explorer. Note that there is a new entry not available in other folders—List Fonts by Similarity. This is an example of Explorer's context intelligence. It knows you're looking at font files, so it offers this extra service. Choose the view for your Fonts folder. Your screen should resemble Figure 5.7.

5

FIGURE 5.6.

Most computers have a variety of fonts.

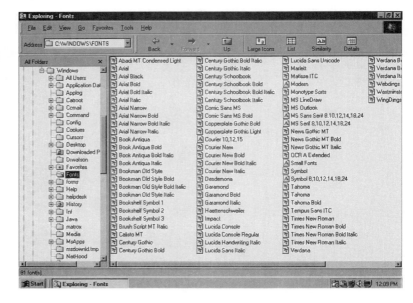

FIGURE 5.7.

Listing fonts by similarity adds a combo box to Explorer for easy selection of a font to use for comparison.

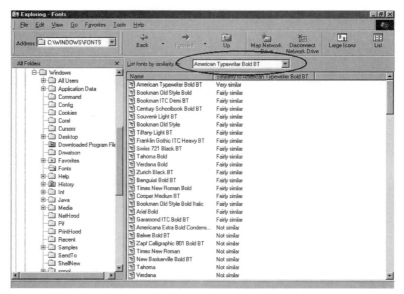

4. To see how any font compares with another installed font, you can click the Similarity icon shown in the toolbar in Figure 5.6 or select View | List Fonts by Similarity from the menu to bring up the the combo box circled in Figure 5.7.

▼ Select another font from the drop-down list and watch the fonts list re-sort by similarity. Figure 5.8 shows the results for one computer after choosing Arial for a comparison.

FIGURE 5.8.

Arial, a descendent of the popular Swiss or Helvetica, has many similar fonts. Two others exist on this machine.

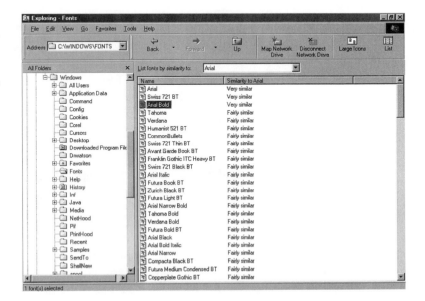

SIMILAR FONTS—WASTED DISK SPACE

Many programs insist rather strongly (some don't even give you the option of declining) on installing a set of fonts for them to use. In many cases these fonts are similar or even almost identical to fonts already installed on your machine. The problem is that setup programs don't have the intelligence to determine whether a usable font already exists on your computer; to play it safe, they tend to load you up with their own fonts. If this seems like a waste of disk space to you, you're right. However, you can't freely discard similar fonts because many application programs use fonts based on their names, not on their characteristics.

---

5. Open the compared file (Arial in this case) and another shown to be Very Similar on your machine by double-clicking them or right-clicking and choosing the Open command from the context menu. Also open a file called Fairly Similar and one ▼ Not Similar (if possible). Figure 5.9 shows these files opened.

5

FIGURE 5.9.

Even fonts that are Fairly Similar to the compared Arial will likely serve well in its stead.

6. Examine the fonts carefully. Usually you'll see little or no difference between fonts that are Very Similar and little functional difference between fonts that are Fairly Similar to each other. In Figure 5.9, Arial is Very Similar to Swiss 721 BT and Fairly Similar to Futura Light BT. However, fonts that aren't similar (Not Similar in the list) usually are quite different. In Figure 5.9, the Not Similar font is MicrogrammaDBolExt.

Installing or Deleting Fonts

You can add or delete fonts yourself either through Windows Explorer or by using the Fonts applet in the Control Panel. This section uses the Control Panel.

If you prefer to use Explorer, it's just as easy. To delete a font or fonts, highlight the ones you want to rid your system of in Explorer and then press Delete or choose the Delete icon on the toolbar. Windows 98 asks you to confirm the elimination of this font. If you agree to delete the font, Explorer erases the file or files making up that font set. These font files are recoverable through the Recycle Bin for as long as they reside there.

To install a new font from Explorer, navigate to the Fonts folder, choose File | Install New Fonts, and follow the dialog boxes. This routine is identical to the one launched from the Control Panel applet. Figure 5.10 shows the Add Fonts dialog box launched from Explorer.

FIGURE 5.10.

You can install new fonts directly from Windows Explorer.

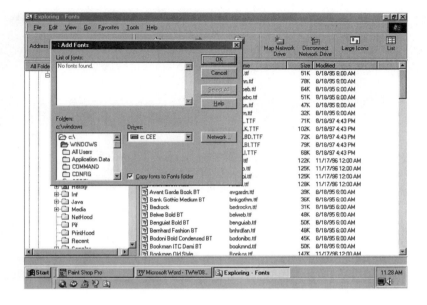

Task 5.2. Using the Applet to Install a New Font

This example uses the Control Panel Fonts applet to install a new font. You need a font not currently on your system to follow these steps precisely, but even if you don't have any new fonts, you can get a good idea of what the procedure is like by reading along:

1. Open the Control Panel. Open the Fonts applet by double-clicking it or using your preferred way to launch a program or applet. The default view for the Fonts applet is Large Icons. As you can see, launching the Fonts applet leaves you in the same place as using Windows Explorer to navigate to the Fonts folder. The only difference might be the view. Your screen should resemble Figure 5.11.

2. Choose File | Install New Font. The Add Fonts dialog appears, as shown in Figure 5.12. This example uses a font on drive A:. If you want to install a new font yourself, you'll have to locate the font file on either your local computer or your network.

3. Note a few peculiarities here. The Add Fonts dialog box won't allow you to browse the Fonts folder because that would serve no purpose and could confuse things with the resulting circular references. Also, the font file (on drive A: in this case) shows up with the full name of the font—Park Avenue BT and its type, TrueType.

FIGURE 5.11.

The Control Panel applet launches an Explorer view of the Fonts folder.

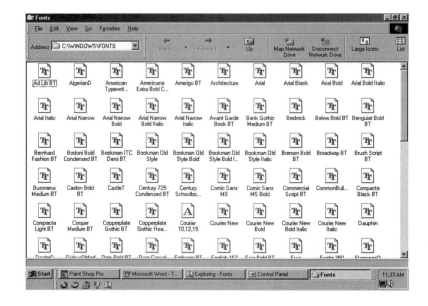

FIGURE 5.12.

The Add Fonts dialog box enables you to browse for new font files to add to your system.

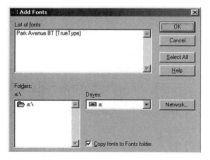

4. Click OK after finding the font or fonts you want to install. Windows 98 prefers that all fonts reside in the Fonts folder, so unless you have an overriding reason not to, make sure that the Copy Fonts to Fonts Folder check box is checked.

That's it. You've just had the grand fonts tour. Consider yourself educated in fonts or "fontucated."

The next section deals with printers and is strongly related to the fonts, section because printers use font technology to represent the characters they output.

DUPLICATE FONTS

It's just a waste of disk space to have fonts located in more than one place on your computer. Duplicate font files serve no purpose other than eating up disk space. After you've installed a font from one place on your hard disk to your Fonts folder, you can delete the file from its original place, unless you have a good reason to keep it as a backup.

Printers

Today, the dream of a paperless office, once predicted for a few years ago, seems farther away than ever. We've come far with email, Web pages, paperless fax, and other forms of electronic distribution of previously printed information, but we're still swimming in a sea of paper. Much of this paper comes from the printers attached to our computers. This section details how to install, use, and manage printers attached to your computer or on your network. Day 20, "Windows 98 Networking," describes how to share a printer with others on your network.

Printers interface with Windows 98 through a driver, like most other hardware. In the case of most printers, you need to manually tell Windows that it has a new printer and direct a setup-like program to install and configure that new printer.

Adding a Printer

Accessing and manipulating printers is similar to fonts. You can access the Printers applet either from Start | Settings, Windows Explorer, or the Control Panel's Printers applet. Any approach will lead to the same place, but the transitory views will differ.

Figure 5.13 shows the result of selecting Settings | Printers from the Start menu. Your screen should resemble Figure 5.13, although you probably have a different printer or printers installed than the Kodak shown.

To install a new printer, you'll need the driver. Windows 98 comes with a wide variety of printer drivers, most of which are regularly updated by the printer manufacturers. In some cases you might have a specialty printer with a driver not supplied with the Windows 98 distribution media. In those cases, you'll need the driver supplied by the manufacturer of the printer.

5

FIGURE 5.13.

Many paths lead to the Printers folder. What you do there remains the same, no matter which path you take.

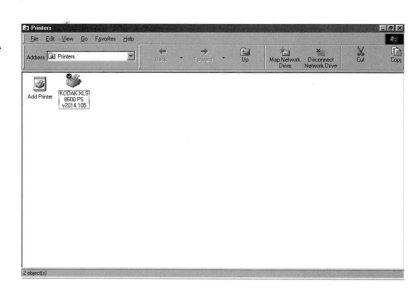

AUTOMATED SETUPS

Some printers come with distribution media (disks or CD-ROMs) that have automated setup routines. These routines either bypass the Add Printer applet or automatically activate it. If your printer uses one of these automated setups, you don't need to—and sometimes can't—use the Add Printer applet described in this section.

Task 5.3. Adding a Printer

To use the Add Printer applet to install an HP 870 printer to an existing Windows 98 installation, complete the following steps:

1. Launch the Printers applet from the Control Panel or Windows Explorer or by choosing Start | Settings | Printers. Your screen should resemble Figure 5.13, although the printer or printers installed might vary.

2. Double-click the Add Printer applet shown in Figure 5.13. The first screen of the Add Printer Wizard appears, as shown in Figure 5.14. Click the Next button to move on to the next screen of this wizard.

3. The next dialog box asks you whether the printer you are adding is part of your network or is physically attached to your computer. This example uses a computer physically attached (local printer) to the computer via the first parallel port called LPT1:. You might have a printer attached to this port, the network, or a USB or SCSI chain. If so, you'll have to make the appropriate choices from the wizard when they vary from the book's example.

FIGURE 5.14.

The first screen of the Add Printer Wizard.

Note

The term for parallel ports in PC type computers, LPTX, stems from the term *line printer*—a printer found in mainframe shops. The usage has remained, although the term is now lost in obscurity.

4. The next dialog box is the most critical. You need to select a make and model for the printer driver to be installed in Windows 98. This box has the printer manufacturers in the left list box, whereas their printers (the ones Windows knows about) are in the right panel. Locate your printer manufacturer first in the left panel; then choose the correct printer from the right one. In the case of an updated printer driver for an HP 870 CSE, the printer isn't listed, so to install the new driver, choose the Have Disk button and then choose Browse in the resulting dialog box to browse for a new driver (see Figure 5.15). After you do so, the wizard brings up a browsing dialog box.

5. After locating the new driver set from your hard drive, network, floppy distribution disk, or CD-ROM, your screen should resemble Figure 5.16. Note that unless you've previously installed a particular printer, you'll need either the Windows 98 distribution CD-ROM or driver files from your printer's manufacturer to install any printer.

5

Note

Windows 98 needs an.inf file (information file) to "know" what drivers it has available to it. When browsing for a so-called driver file, what you're really browsing for is the.inf file that contains information and pointers to the correct files needed by Windows 98 for proper setup of peripherals.

FIGURE 5.15.

The Add Printer Wizard comes complete with a way for you to browse to a new printer driver.

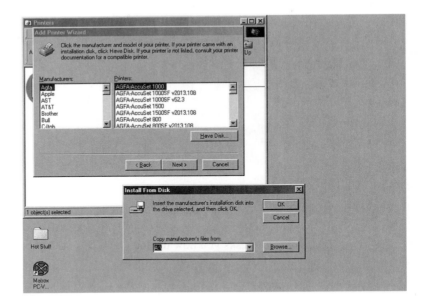

FIGURE 5.16.

Browsing for a printer driver means locating the information (.inf) file along with the accompanying driver support files.

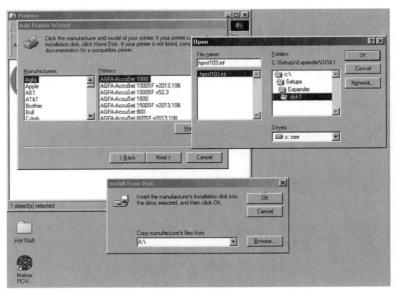

6. Some .inf files contain multiple drivers, although most don't. Choose the .inf file from your driver set. In this example, the .inf file does contain two drivers, one for the target printer for this Task and one for an HP 850. After you click OK

▼   twice, the `.inf` file opens, showing its driver selection. You can see one such screen in Figure 5.17, with the 850C entry highlighted. Click Next to move on.

FIGURE 5.17.

This `.inf` file contains information about two printers, the HP 850 and 870.

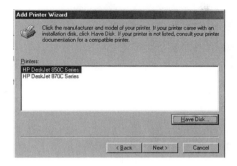

7. The next screen asks you how the local printer is attached to your computer. In this example, you use the last entry on the list, the ECP Parallel Port called LPT1:. If you choose this port, your screen should resemble Figure 5.18.

FIGURE 5.18.

You're almost finished installing a new printer when you see the Available Ports list in the Add Printer Wizard.

5

8. The final step is to tell Windows 98 the name you want to give your printer and whether you want it to be the default printer. In the example shown in Figure 5.19, you use the default name and set it as the default printer.

9. Click Finish, and you have set up a new printer manually.

Windows 98 then copies and installs the printer drivers.

What happens next depends on your printer driver routine, but usually the procedure ends with an offer to print a test page to make sure everything is all right.

If your printer setup program, or Windows 98's wizard, offers you a chance to print a text page, take it. This is the final proof of the pudding and the best assurance that you

▼   are set up properly.

FIGURE 5.19.

You can set up your printer as the default printer and give it an interesting name if you want.

Examining Printing Options

The Windows 98 printing subsystem has a large variety of options you can use to customize the printing process for yourself personally or your organization.

The specific options for any printer depend on the printer make and model, as well as the complexity of the options provided with the driver. For example, a color printer usually has options to set the quality of the color output from quick and cheap to presentation quality. An inkjet-type printer might have settings to align the printer cartridges.

Some of these options are changeable at printing time, and some are not. To see the options for a particular printer, right-click the printer's icon in the Printers group; then choose Properties from the context menu. Figure 5.20 shows the Properties sheet for the HP 870C printer installed in Task 5.3. The Properties sheet for Printers is like many other Properties sheets, although the contents of each tab relate specifically to printer issues.

FIGURE 5.20.

The Properties sheet for the HP 870C printer.

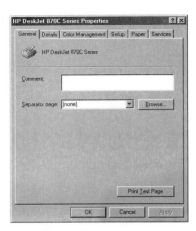

The Pause Printing entry on the context menu for a particular printer pauses but still allows spooling up of print jobs. Use this if you want your system to accept print jobs, but you don't want to actually produce them. To see paused print jobs, right-click the paused printer; then choose Open from the context menu. Figure 5.21 shows the HP printer with a paused job.

FIGURE 5.21.

Opening a printer shows whether its jobs are in progress or paused.

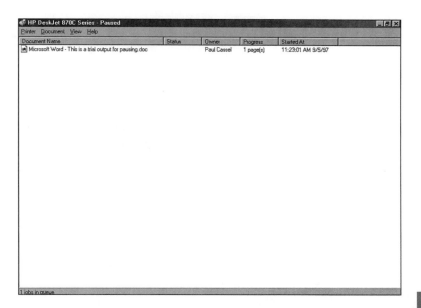

When you want to output any paused jobs, highlight them and choose Printer | Pause Printing to uncheck the entry. You can also access the Properties sheet from the Printer menu, purge (erase) print jobs, and use the Document menu to control individual document output.

Most of the tabs shown in Figure 5.20 have settings exclusive to this printer or are self-explanatory or both. The Details tab has settings that aren't obvious and are common to most if not all printers you might use in Windows 98. Figure 5.22 shows the Details tab of the HP 870C printer, but you will see this tab and its entries for other printers as well.

As you can see from Figure 5.22, many buttons allow customization for this printer. The Details tab gives you the following options:

- Add Port—Tells Windows 98 that your computer has a new port that you want to use for this printer.
- Delete Port—Removes a port from this printer's use.

5

Figure 5.22.

The Details tab is the control center for general printer and port settings.

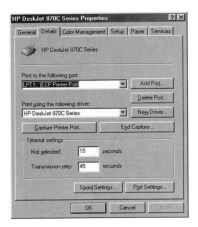

- New Driver—A quick way to update the driver for this printer. The alternative is to remove the current printer from Printers and then use the Add Printer Wizard to add it back with the new driver.
- Capture Printer Port—Redirects or maps a port to a network resource. This is a similar procedure to mapping a network drive. *Mapping* means you make a network resource, in this case a printer, appear as a local printer port on your computer.
- End Capture—Ends network mapping.
- Timeout Settings—Tells Windows 98 how long to keep trying to establish a connection with this printer.
- Spool Settings—Sets whether jobs for this printer spool (buffer) to disk or go to the printer directly. Spooling a print job enables the job to be output faster, but it also eats up some disk space. A spooled print job is "printed" to disk and then fed out to the printer at whatever rate the printer can take it. This frees up the printing application (such as Word) faster because application programs can send print jobs faster than printers can produce them.
- Port Settings—Alters the default settings for the chosen output port.

Spool and Port Settings

The Spool and Port settings in the Windows 98 print facility aren't self-explanatory, as are some settings. Figure 5.23 shows the Spool Settings dialog box; the list following the figure describes the settings and their meanings.

FIGURE 5.23.

*The spool settings for
Windows 98 printing
are fairly complex.*

- Spool Print Jobs So Program Finishes Printing Faster—Activates the spooler. A spooler uses the hard disk (or other storage medium) to buffer print jobs and place them in a queue because application programs can almost always output a print job many times faster than a printer can produce them. In the case of a network printer, you might be far down in the queue, awaiting some print time.

- Start Printing After Last Page Is Spooled—If spooling is activated, the entire job is output from the application before sending any information to the printer. This is fast but uses more disk space because the entire job will be spooled. It also uses slightly fewer processor cycles.

- Start Printing After First Page Is Spooled—If spooling is activated, this creates a duplex mode for the spooler. As the job comes from the application, the spooler simultaneously accepts more input and outputs the job to the printer. This makes for smaller spool files but takes up a few more cycles. Slower than letting the spooler buffer the entire job.

- Print Directly to the Printer—Disables spooling for this printer. You can't print directly to a printer that is being shared on your network.

- Spool Data Format—A diagnostic tool. EMF is a fast common format for spooled jobs. RAW is a format specific to the printer itself. Use EMF for its speed, unless you're seeing bad spooled print jobs; if so, try RAW.

- Enable Bi-directional Support for This Printer—Enables the printer (if so equipped) to have a two-way dialog with your computer. This option is printer specific. Many printers don't have this capability.

- Disable Bi-directional Support for This Printer—Disallow the printer's capability (if equipped) to talk back to your computer.

There are fewer port settings, but in many ways, these settings are even less obvious than those found in the Spool Settings dialog box. They will vary with the type of port you have for printing. Figure 5.24 shows the port settings dialog box for the most common local port, a parallel one; the list following the figure describes the settings and their meanings.

5

FIGURE 5.24.

*This particular port
dialog box has two
critical settings.*

- Spool MS-DOS Print Jobs—This setting intercepts MS-DOS port output and sends it to the spooler. If unchecked, MS-DOS applications print directly to the printer as if they weren't running under Windows 98 at all.
- Check Port State Before Printing—This option has Windows 98 do a small diagnostic to determine the status of the port before trying to send a print job to it.

For reasons known only to Microsoft, other important port settings reside on the main tab of the Properties dialog box. Figure 5.22 shows the Details tab containing the timeout and retry settings for the port. The default settings are fine for most setups, but if you have a printer that is slow to respond or a busy connection, you might need to increase those settings significantly. If, for example, you get a timeout or communications error message when trying to print and you're sure everything is all right with your hardware, try increasing these settings. Figure 5.25 shows a type of communications error message for the HP 870C printer.

FIGURE 5.25.

*A Printer Error
message.*

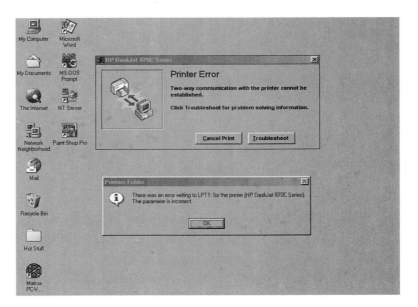

The rarely used serial (Communications or COM) port settings are much more complex than the common parallel port. Figure 5.26 shows a screen with these dialog boxes open. The default settings for serial printer ports usually work. If they don't, you'll need at least your printer documentation and perhaps your computer's specification sheet to troubleshoot problems with serial communications to a printer.

FIGURE 5.26.

COM advanced settings.

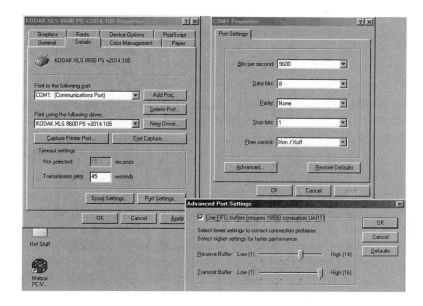

Printing to a File

Windows 98 enables you to print not only to an output device such as a paper printer or a fax machine but also to a disk file. In the Details tab, the combo box named Print to the Following Port offers a File option. Figure 5.27 shows the combo box pulled down to the File entry.

Most applications have a Print to File option on their Print or Printer Setup dialog boxes. When you print to a file, Windows 98 creates a file with the extension .prn. Today the chief use for printing to a file is to be able to output it to a device you can't connect to directly. For example, say you want color output and don't have a color printer, but you have the use of one at another site. You can print your job to a file and carry or transfer the file to the color printer's host computer. At that point, you can try to dump the file to the printer, even if the host computer doesn't have the output program. This isn't foolproof, but it's worth a try. Naturally, if the host computer has the program you used to create the print job, forget printing to a file. Instead, use the native file format and use the program to do the printing on the spot.

FIGURE 5.27.

One option for printer output is to print to a file for use as a file or for storage for much delayed printing.

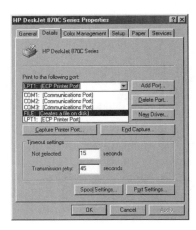

Paper Handling

The Paper tab is another tab in the printer Properties dialog box that has many options. Like so much in Windows 98's hardware, this tab's appearance and choices vary as widely as the driver and the facilities of the printers.

Figure 5.28 shows the Paper tab for two different printers, the HP 870C and the Kodak. Note that there is little in common here other than paper size choices. Even then, the format of choosing a paper size is different for the two printers. The Kodak uses a visual metaphor with the forbidden sizes circled out. The HP uses a combo box.

FIGURE 5.28.

The Paper tab of the Properties dialog box for a printer is where a printer manufacturer can really strut its stuff.

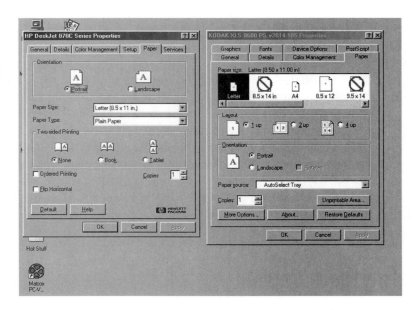

The variety of the Properties box Paper tab is as extensive as the features manufacturers add to their products. Be sure to check this tab for your printer's capabilities. If you're in doubt about any button, list, or combo box, right-click it and then choose What's This? from the context menu. If the manufacturer and Microsoft have done their work, this brings up a ToolTip-like message hinting at its function. Figure 5.29 shows one such message for the otherwise mysterious Unprintable Area button on the Kodak Paper tab.

FIGURE 5.29.

Right-click any object on a tab and then choose What's This? from the context menu to learn what it is.

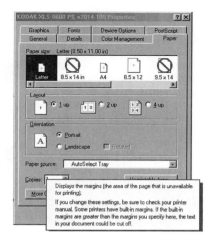

Printing Woes

Printers are static devices. Once set up, they stay set up unless something drastic occurs. When it does, or if you can't get an initial setup, you need to do some hands-on diagnostics to figure out what went awry. Here is where Windows 98's device independence works for or against you. Back in MS-DOS days, a printer might work for application A, but not B. When using Windows, a printer works for either all applications or none.

There are two troubleshooting walk-throughs—the regular Print Troubleshooter and the advanced Enhanced Print Troubleshooter (EPTS). Setup installs only the regular troubleshooter. You can find the Enhanced version on most distribution CD-ROMs (this can vary, depending on licensing agreements) under \other\misc\epts. The application comes with a readme.txt file containing its options and setup information.

If you have the Enhanced troubleshooter, you might as well use it rather than the standard one that comes with the Windows 98 Help system, which is available from Start | Help. Search under printers, troubleshooting.

Figure 5.30 shows the Enhanced troubleshooter in action. You can run this from the CD-ROM, if you choose.

5

FIGURE 5.30.

The Enhanced Print Troubleshooter is a comprehensive diagnostic tool for printing problems.

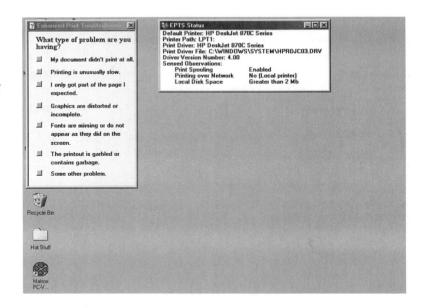

One huge advantage of the EPTS is its capability to use optional data files as data for error probability. This gives Microsoft and third parties the potential to customize the EPTS for organizations or printers. If you are part of a large organization, you might want to check with your administration to see whether you have one of these customized data files for your use.

Many printing problems are solvable without much ado. Before running any troubleshooter, check the things suggested in the following two sections.

If the Printer Never Responds to a Print Command

If your printer never responds to a Print command, check the following:

- Is the printer properly connected and online? If you have a way to directly print to a local printer from MS-DOS, fire up the old system and try a print job. If the printer responds, your problem isn't mechanical. You can always try Start | Shutdown | MS-DOS Mode. When in that mode, enter

  ```
  copy some text file prn
  ```

  at the command line, where *some text file* is a text file such as readme.txt. If you know the printer port you want to address, use it specifically rather than the generic PRN. For example,

  ```
  copy readme.txt lpt1:
  ```

copies a file, readme.txt, to the first system parallel port. If the printer responds, your problem is within Windows 98 or the driver configuration.

- Are you printing to the right printer and port? Make sure that the port you have attached to your printer is the one you have specified in your Details tab. Make sure that you're printing to the right printer in your application's Print dialog box. Figure 5.31 shows one such dialog box for Microsoft Word.

- Is there paper in your printer?

FIGURE 5.31.

The Print dialog box for applications has enough options to mess up any print job.

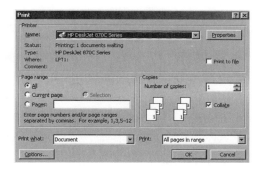

If the Printer Prints Poorly or Garbles Jobs

If your printer prints poorly or garbles jobs, check the following:

- Make sure that you're using the right driver. If you've recently upgraded or changed drivers, try changing back.

- Check the Properties dialog box for this printer to see whether any settings strike you as untoward. Experiment with suspect ones.

- Delete the printer from Printer and reinstall. This fixes a corrupt setup.

Finding and Using Network Printers

Windows 98 doesn't care if you print to a local or network printer, as long as you have the proper network privileges. There are several methods to locate a network printer. Here is one:

1. From the desktop or Windows Explorer, choose Network Neighborhood. Browse for the host computer and then the specific printer. Figure 5.32 shows the network browsed for a printer. The AGFA printer is hosted by the server \\Tirilee. You can also use the Find command from the Start menu to locate the server that you seek.

5

FIGURE 5.32.

Network Neighborhood is one way to find a networked (or shared) printer.

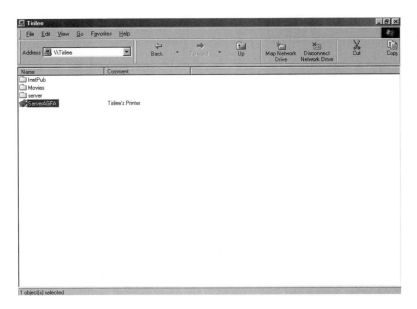

2. Right-clicking this printer enables you to use this device by setting up a port capture or installing the printer for use on your machine.

You can also direct a print job from your local machine to any printer you have the right to use from the application's Print dialog box. Figure 5.31 shows such a dialog box. Figure 5.33 shows that after you've installed the networked printer to your local machine, it appears in the combo box of applications such as Word. Assuming it's online, you can now use it like a local printer.

FIGURE 5.33.

When you have your drivers locally situated, using the network printer is no different than using a local printer.

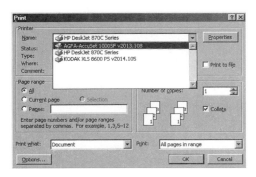

USB connections are still in flux, but you need to know whether your peripheral (printer in this case) needs a powered hub. If so, you must supply such a hub to enable it to function.

Additionally, current USB devices should *not* be attached when installing their driver software. This is a major deviation from all other hardware. Expect the USB to change to put it in tune with the rest of the industry.

Summary

This chapter covers printers and fonts in Windows 98. Printing actual jobs is part of your application programs. In many cases, the Print dialog box and related dialog boxes enable you to override Windows 98's default settings for a printer. For example, refer to Figure 5.31. There is a Print to File check box enabling you to create a print file from this application even if the printer is configured to print to a local or network port.

The entire fonts topic relates to the look of your character output. There are several types of fonts, with the two main characterizations being vector (outline) or raster (bitmap). TrueType, the most common and efficient font technology for Windows 98 output, is an outline technology. Raster fonts are usually applied to system chores, in which they appear in one optimized size.

You can set up and use as many printers as you want. These can be either local or network printers. Configuring the printers after setup is done through the printers' Properties dialog box. The tabs within this dialog box vary, depending on the printer technology and the printer itself. Even printers having the same tabs will have different tab entries, depending on the features of the specific printer.

To use a shared printer on your network, locate the printer by first locating the host computer and then the printer. Choose Start | Find | Computer to help you find a particular computer on your network. When you've located the printer, right-click it and then, if necessary, install it or use the Windows 98 Capture Printer Port facility to use the printer, just like any local printer.

5

Workshop

To wrap up the day, you can review terms from the chapter, see the answers to some commonly asked questions, and practice what you've learned. You can find the answers to the exercises in Appendix A, "Answers."

Terminology Review

monospaced font—A font in which every character takes up the same size bounding box.

proportional font—A font in which characters are assigned different size bounding boxes to accommodate each character's shape.

raster font—A font that's generated based on a stored image of the font.

spooling—Printing a job first to disk and from there feeding it to the printer. This speeds up the length of time it takes for an application (program) to print. It can dramatically decrease the time a program is tied up generating a print output.

TrueType—An advanced font technology created by an industrywide consortium in reaction to the high license fees demanded by Adobe for PostScript. TrueType is a font technology, whereas PostScript is a full page layout language.

vector font—A font that is generated based on stored commands to the operating system.

Q&A

Q Will a deleted font move to the Recycle Bin or fully disappear from my computer?

A Unless you use Explorer to truly delete it, it resides in the Bin for as long as your Recycle Bin settings allow it to.

Q Why should I permit very similar fonts to reside on my computer?

A Some application programs demand certain specific fonts in order to behave correctly. For example, Microsoft Word 97 uses the Tahoma font extensively and will complain pitifully if it's missing.

Q How do I install a new printer?

A One way is to choose Start | Settings | Printers and double-click the Add Printer icon. Then follow the standard Windows 98 wizard prompts.

Q How can I group a font list by similarity?

A Choose Start | Settings | Control Panel | Fonts. Click the Similarity button on the toolbar.

Exercises

1. Take advantage of the powerful font support in Windows 98 and use the standard WordPad program to make a simple birthday banner. Give the banner a bold Happy Birthday title in a large font, and then put a personal message underneath it in a smaller font.

2. Windows Explorer allows you to navigate to practically any part of your Windows system. Use it to quickly view the status of all your printers.

DAY 6

Multimedia in Windows 98

by Paul Cassel

Multimedia means the simultaneous use of more than one delivery medium. For example, radio uses only sound as a content-delivery medium. Television and movies use two: sound and moving pictures. Thus, television and movies are multimedia, while radio isn't. Although a static screen display is technically a way to deliver content, for most purposes, multimedia excludes static displays other than when used in presentations such as those made using Freelance or PowerPoint. To paraphrase a Supreme Court justice's comment, multimedia might be hard to define, but you'll know it when you see it.

Back in the old MS-DOS–only days, PCs could barely use any media. There were no real animations, and the only sounds made by those pre-1990 (roughly) computers were squeaks, pops, and burpy noises. Windows 3.0 (to a very small extent) and then Windows 3.1 (to a greater extent) added the ability to show animations, play or record decent sound, and generally enter the arena most would call multimedia. However, competitors such as Macintosh and to some extent Amiga were openly contemptuous of where Windows was in terms of multimedia.

Then Windows 95 roared onto the scene, giving PC users the multimedia equality they yearned for when compared to the Mac and even the now long obsolete Amiga. More importantly, the setup for multimedia devices in Windows 95 became something reasonable for most users, where it clearly wasn't under previous versions of Windows. Windows 98 continues the Microsoft march to multimedia mastery started by Windows 95.

Some of the salient features of Windows 98 multimedia over other—even other Microsoft—operating systems, are

- A built-in CD player.
- Built-in support for digital video.
- Improved Plug and Play, allowing for easy installation of new multimedia devices.
- Inherent support for digital standards such as `.avi`, `.wav`, `.midi`, and online digital video.
- Support of the latest DirectX API setup, allowing for the fastest display of sound and pictures for use especially in games. DirectX is a set of standards supporting 2D, 3D, sound, input such as joysticks, and connectivity. The latter is useful for Internet gaming and conferencing.
- Support for the new CD Plus CD-ROM standard.
- Support for DirectShow, an accelerated way to play back movies and sound, especially used for compressed content.
- Operating support for Intel MMX processors such as the Pentium MMX, the Pentium II, and their clones from AMD or Cyrix.
- The introduction of WinToon and Surround Video. Both these technologies will be incorporated into productivity, entertainment, and educational titles in the future.
- Support for voice command add-ons. This will enable both content and command dictation with personal computers.

Multimedia Control Center

The central applet for control of multimedia is the Multimedia applet in the Control Panel. Figure 6.1 shows this applet.

The tabs on the dialog box are

- Audio—Sets the preferred (default) audio device and sets volumes for this device. There are also two Advanced Properties buttons for fine-tuning your audio output devices.

FIGURE 6.1.

The Multimedia applet has the familiar tabbed format.

- Video—Sets video playback size. This can be either a window or full screen.

- MIDI—Specifies MIDI device and sets properties.

- CD Music—Settings for how Windows 98 treats music CDs that are inserted.

- Devices—Similar to the Devices tab of the System applet. Here is where you can set properties for multimedia hardware (see Figure 6.2).

FIGURE 6.2.

The Devices tab enables you to adjust the hardware settings for multimedia devices.

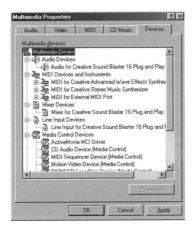

6

The Multimedia Player

Windows 98 has a versatile multimedia player program. Although it can play many types of multimedia files, it can't edit any. Some third-party player tools, such as those distributed with sound or video hardware, can both play and edit these files. The Windows 98 player program determines the type of multimedia file based on the extension of the file and then configures itself to play or display it.

You can use the Media Player either by opening it using the menu choices Start| Programs|Accessories|Multimedia|Media Player or by opening a multimedia file. Table 6.1 lists some multimedia file extensions and types.

TABLE 6.1. SOME WINDOWS 98 MULTIMEDIA FILE TYPES.

Extension	Description
`.fl(x)`	AutoDesk Animator
`.avi, .m3d, .prp, .lit, .cam,` `.mpg, .mpeg, .au(x), .aifc`	Windows video
`.m1v`	ActiveX or DirectX animations
`.wav, .snd`	Windows digitized sound files
`.asf, .asx`	Streaming active media
`.cda`	CD audio track
`.idf`	MIDI instrument identification
`.sbk, .sf2`	Sound fonts
`.qt, .mov`	QuickTime movie
`.rmi, .mid`	MIDI sound (music) files

Table 6.1 contains a partial list. As the multimedia capacity of Windows 98 expands through the efforts of Microsoft as well as third-party vendors, the complete list will grow. Microsoft openly publishes the hooks that programmers need to create multimedia applications for Windows 98. This costs Microsoft some control over the multimedia process but also makes for a very vigorous market in these applications. There is nothing preventing a vendor from creating a file standard, extension, and application program on its own.

The Media Player will also play CD music selections, although you'll probably want to use the CD Player that is part of Windows 98 instead. In many cases, your sound card or CD reader will come with excellent software programs superior to the Media Player or CD Player. As with other programs, Microsoft supplies bare-bones applets with the operating system that are often best replaced with more feature-filled programs offered by third-party suppliers.

Figure 6.3 shows the Media Player playing a small `.avi` file while the CD Player plays a music CD. To start the CD Player, choose Start|Programs|Accessories|Multimedia|CD Player. In this example, the CD Player is playing the music from the movie *Sleepless in*

Seattle (tough to hear in the book) while the Media Player shows a clip from the old *Star Trek* TV series. This effectively has *Sleepless* as the background music to *Star Trek*.

FIGURE 6.3.

Multimedia means mixing and combining media types; this can lead to some interesting combinations.

Multimedia File Associations

As with other Windows 98 files, the file extension of multimedia files indicates what the file contains and what application to associate it with for opening or playing. The associations for multimedia files are the usual type found on the File Types tab in Windows Explorer under View|Folder Options. These associations are handled automatically by Windows 98 or the installation programs for various multimedia applications. You can modify the associations, but do so with caution because multimedia is a complex topic. Unwise edits to multimedia file associations will have unintended and often confusing results.

The CD Player

There's little to do with the CD Player other than play music CDs. To play a music CD, insert it into your CD-ROM drive, launch the player applet by choosing Start|Programs| Accessories|Multimedia|CD Player, and then point to the drive letter that's your CD-ROM drive. You can select the track to play from the combo box at the bottom of the player dialog box. If you have a magazine CD-ROM drive, you can also choose the CD to play.

6

By choosing Disc | Edit Play List, you can add or remove tracks from the selected CD. Figure 6.4 shows the CD Player: Disc Settings dialog box, which comes up when you select Edit Play List. You can similarly change your play options to Continuous Play, Random Selections, or Introduction Only (the start of each track) from the Options menu. The Preferences entry in the Options menu enables you, among other things, to set how long the introduction period is. The default is 10 seconds. By default, the CD Player will play all tracks on an inserted CD. Remember, you can set a CD to launch automatically in the Control Panel by choosing System | Device Manager | CD ROM | Properties | Settings and enabling or disabling Auto Insert Notification.

FIGURE 6.4.

*You can edit the tracks
you want to play on
any CD.*

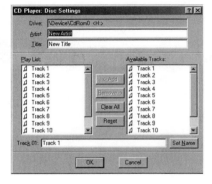

Volume Control

If you have a sound card installed, Windows 98 puts a Volume icon in your taskbar by default. This enables you to set the volume and balance for various sound-related devices, both input and output. This applet is also available by choosing Start | Programs | Accessories | Multimedia | Volume Control.

Many sound cards come with their own applets that have the same functions (usually a superset) as the Windows 98–supplied applets. You can use the controls that come with your sound card or the ones supplied with Windows 98. In most cases, the custom sound card controls have more features. Figure 6.5 shows the Windows 98 Volume Control at the top of the screen with a Creative Labs volume control, called a Mixer Control by the manufacturer, at the bottom of the screen.

The number and type of volume and balance controls on your sound control depend on the type of sound device you have installed. As you can see from Figure 6.5, you can adjust the overall sound and balance as well as individual settings. For example, you might want to set the .wav sound player low because this is the sound type played by Windows itself for alerts, while you make the CD sound louder for blasting away your favorite tunes as you work. Naturally, if you work in a crowded office, you will want to keep your sound at a reasonable level. Some speaker systems offer a headphone jack—a good option if you like a lot of noise and your coworkers don't.

FIGURE 6.5.

Volume controls for Windows 98 and a custom sound card.

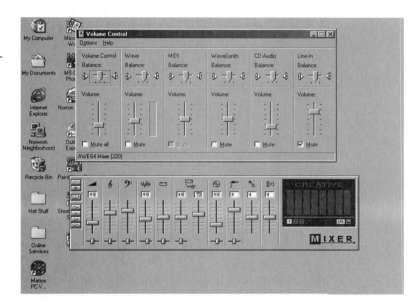

NetShow, Real Audio, and Real Video

Early on, Internet futurists realized that the Internet, and specifically the Web, would be a great alternative to broadcast such as conventional radio or TV for content distribution. However, the problems of delivering *streaming content*—content or a show that's viewed in real-time as it's downloaded from the Internet rather than downloaded for later viewing—are substantial.

The problems revolve around the uncertain delivery speed of the Internet, the uncertainty of the recipients' acceptance speed (modem speed, for example), and the loss of packets due to switch queues between the sender and receiver.

Several startup companies addressed these problems in trying to make their proprietary systems an Internet standard for online streaming content. Perhaps the most successful was RealNetworks, the makers and distributors of the Real line of audio and video clients and servers. Client software is what you run to receive the stream, whereas server software is the sending program. RealNetworks cleverly gave away a limited version of its client software while selling the full version as well as the server-side software. The

6

giveaway assured that the Real line became a success as the technology proved itself in the field.

Thus, prior to Windows 98 and Internet Explorer 4, the Real line of streaming content delivery was in wide use for both video and audio. People tuned in through their Real-enabled browsers to view online television shows and listen to radio broadcasts as they worked or played online. Microsoft has introduced its own Internet streaming technology, NetShow, prior to and with Windows 98.

Figure 6.6 shows a TV show playing on the Windows 98 desktop under NetShow. The content providers aren't trying to make a substitute for broadcast TV, so don't expect to see the latest episode of the *X-Files* or *King of the Hill* under NetShow—although either is technically feasible. Instead, the Real line as well as NetShow providers are both trying to supply a narrowly focused special interest type of broadcast (or just *'cast*) to attract targeted audiences.

This particular show is from Johns Hopkins Hospital, a teaching facility. It is broadcast weekly and covers current issues in geriatric care. The 'cast also has commercials just like ordinary TV, and it has production expenses as well. Figure 6.6 shows an ad for an adjustable bed. The ad is, contentwise, indistinguishable from the usual TV ads for this product.

FIGURE 6.6.

It's not the X-Files, *but this Johns Hopkins continuing medical education series has the usual commercials just the same.*

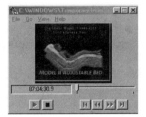

Installing and Configuring NetShow

Windows 98 will not install NetShow by default. If you've chosen (or had chosen for you) to install NetShow, it appears on your Start menu under Programs|Internet Explorer. If you don't see it, you can add it by choosing Add/Remove Software in the Control Panel and checking for its existence under the Windows Setup tab in the Multimedia section. Figure 6.7 shows the Multimedia dialog box.

After you have NetShow installed, launching it will bring up the player itself. Choose Go|NetShow Home Page to open up a page with various NetShow news items and links. You need to be online to use the Go menu choices.

FIGURE 6.7.

The NetShow Player is an optional part of Windows 98.

When you're at the NetShow home page, you can view the various introductory videos and audio 'casts here or find the usual Internet Explorer–type links to other sites having standing or scheduled content. When you start linking to sites, you'll find many regularly scheduled or one-off 'casts for your viewing or listening enjoyment.

Internet broadcasts vary from the usual drivel to the truly interesting and educational. You'll find not only common interest type 'casts but also special interest items not generally found even on cable TV or radio. For example, Figure 6.8 shows a NetShow series teaching American Sign Language (ASL). This particular series deals with how to form certain letters in ASL.

FIGURE 6.8.

A lesson in American Sign Language. This screen demonstrates how to make an A.

6

Configuring NetShow isn't terribly technical. The configuration dialog box is the usual tabbed type found under File|Properties. Figure 6.9 shows this dialog box open with a show running. If you choose File|Properties with no show running, the dialog box pertains to only universal properties, or defaults—a subset of what you see in the figure.

FIGURE 6.9.

The NetShow Player has some properties unique to itself due to its specialized functions.

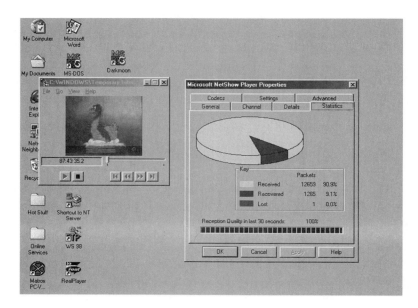

There is nothing you need to configure other than the Settings tab. Here you can adjust the size of the player screen, if the show loops, and the complexity of the controls shown. If you're configuring the player for others and you don't want them to be able to adjust the program, visit this tab and choose No Controls, as shown in Figure 6.10.

FIGURE 6.10.

You can disable the control display in NetShow.

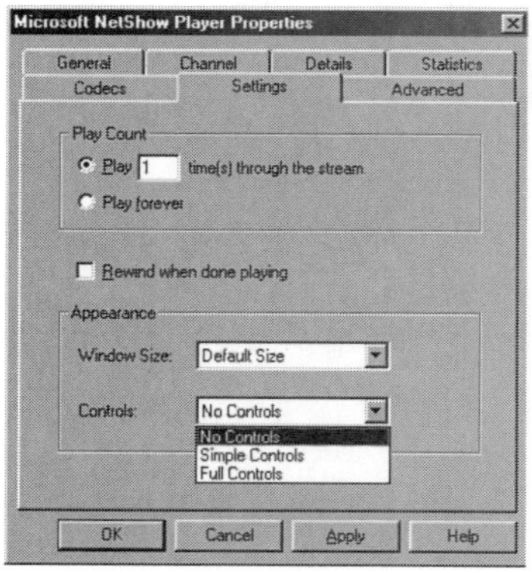

This won't stop determined fiddlers because they can always reset the controls to be displayed, but this does eliminate unintentional setting changes.

The Statistics tab primarily shows how successful your reception has been. Figure 6.9 shows this tab. As you can see, there has been only one lost packet in almost 13,000 sent, demonstrating that NetShow is running optimally. There has been roughly a 10 percent recovered packet rate, however. This is usually due to heavy server loads between the 'cast server and client.

You can always jump to the NetShow home page by choosing the entry NetShow Home Page under the Go menu. This grounds you, enabling you to download the latest drivers and see the current links to content providers.

Although the NetShow Player is mostly automatic, Microsoft has included a troubleshooter as part of its help system. If you're having problems with NetShow, you can step through this guide, shown in Figure 6.11. It works just like other Windows 98 troubleshooters.

FIGURE 6.11.

Nothing is truly foolproof, including NetShow, but you can usually solve your problems using the troubleshooter.

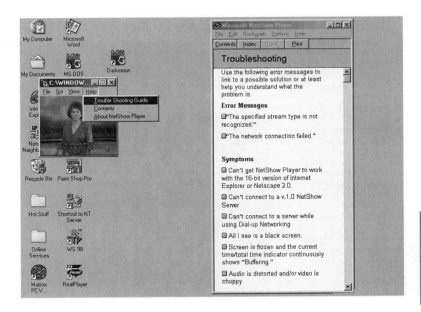

The RealNetworks player is an alternative to the Microsoft product. You can download the player from the RealNetworks Web site (www.real.com) or link to it from Microsoft's Web site. Like NetShow, the RealPlayer plays both audio and video and can be configured by choosing View|Preferences. Figure 6.12 shows version 5 of the RealPlayer. It's playing a streaming video show about literary criticism.

6

FIGURE 6.12.

The RealNetworks player has easily accessible channels for finding streaming content online.

The video and audio with either the RealNetworks player or the Microsoft one are roughly on a par with antenna reception of a TV or radio signal when the Internet stream's squeezed through a 28.8 modem. Faster connections such as ISDN or T1 enable much better reception. Figure 6.13 shows the Preferences dialog box for the RealNetworks player. Like NetShow, the configuration is mostly automatic and needs no user intervention in normal conditions. The Bandwidth setting on the Connection tab is what you adjust most often if you should change the speed of your Internet (or intranet or extranet) connections.

FIGURE 6.13.

The RealNetworks player has user-configurable options, but most people never have to fiddle with them.

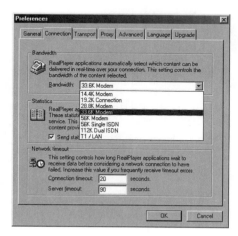

The other possible change in the RealPlayer is adjusting the quality of playback and thus the processor time used. That is, reducing the quality of the playback will free up some CPU time. Most modern machines have the excess CPU capacity to run the RealPlayer at full quality. Figure 6.14 shows the Advanced tab with the Playback Performance box circled.

FIGURE 6.14.

The Advanced tab has troubleshooting and diagnostic tools on it.

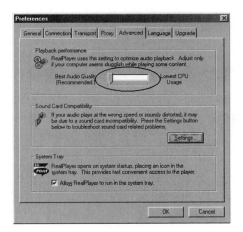

If you're having trouble with sound synch, the Settings button on the Advanced tab has a few useful options.

Drivers and the WDM

One of the most frequently voiced criticisms of the entire Windows family is its confusing need for different drivers for many different hardware components. The idea of drivers goes back to the very earliest days of the IBM PC.

Drivers are extensions to a basic operating system that enable nonstandard hardware. For example, there is no standard video adapter for PCs. One person might use a Matrox brand, another an ATI, another a Number Nine. Each brand has lines of adapters. Each adapter or at least adapter family must use a discrete driver custom made just for it. The driver for a Matrox card won't work with a Number Nine.

The drivers extend the operating system, in this case Windows 98, to use that card. This prevents the need for Windows 98 to be so extensive that it can accommodate all possible cards, which cuts down on its size. It also means third-party manufacturers can create cards having features never envisioned or approved by Microsoft because they can write drivers to make Windows work with their cards.

The downside of all this flexibility is the need to identify and install the correct drivers for every piece of hardware in your computer that is in any way unforeseen or unplanned

6

by Microsoft. Windows 98 does come with a large set of installable device drivers, but because new hardware and new drivers for existing hardware appear all the time, there is no way for the distribution media to have all the drivers you need.

The two branches of Microsoft operating systems further muddy the waters. The Windows 95 family uses one model driver while the Windows NT family uses another. With Windows 98 and Windows NT 5, Microsoft has made a large step in unifying the drivers into one model.

This one-size-fits-all generic driver model is the *Win32 Driver Model* (WDM). A WDM will work with many different devices and within either Windows 98 or Windows NT 5 or later. This greatly simplifies administration and configuration for both systems but does so at some cost. The WDMs will drive many different devices and drive them the same in either Windows 98 or Windows NT. However, they won't necessarily drive them optimally. For example, the very popular Creative Labs SoundBlaster AWE64 card will work with the WDM, but it won't exhibit as many features as when driven by the Creative Labs brand driver specifically made for the AWE64.

Windows 98 will tend to install the WDM for any devices it can, especially when installing *clean versions*, or not over an existing version, of Windows 98, Windows 95, or Windows 3.1 (Windows 3.11 too). If you find your multimedia devices aren't working as you expect them to, especially if you can't see certain features, check the properties by choosing Control Panel|System|Device Manager|Properties to see the type of driver the device in question is running. If you want, you can use the Update Driver button to custom-install a driver in place of the existing driver, including the WDM.

Sometimes Windows 98 will be stubborn about replacing the WDM drivers with those of your choosing. In those cases, delete the device from the Device Manager and then restart Windows 98. The operating system will detect a new device and enable you to specify the drivers, or it will hunt up some of its own. This is the time to direct Windows 98 to use the driver of your choice rather than the WDM. This is a somewhat tedious process, but when done, it's done for good. Here is a list of the types of devices that might find themselves hooked to the WDM:

- Busses—The USB and Firewire (IEEE 1394). Unless you're very sure of yourself, don't change these WDM drivers.

- Modems—Many come with their own drivers, but the WDM ones work well. Keep them unless something is seriously awry.

- Human-to-computer devices—Keyboards, trackballs, mouse devices, joysticks, and so on. Leave these alone unless you have an input device that's not fully functional due to the WDM.

- Imaging devices—Video cameras, scanners, digitizers of all sorts. The WDM is usually the right way to go with these devices.

- Sound and fury—DVD, sound cards, amps. Leave these alone if they're working well.

Using and Troubleshooting Multimedia

Most multimedia applications diagnose and troubleshoot themselves on installation. The more complex the software, hardware, or combination of the two, the more care the manufacturer should take when it comes to setup.

Take video editing as an example. Disk speed is extremely important when capturing (digitizing) a video stream from an analog source such as a VCR, a TV broadcast, or a Camcorder. To assure a computer is fast enough to capture input without lost frames, one video capture board manufacturer, Matrox, includes a hard disk benchmark program as part of its setup routine. Figure 6.15 shows this benchmark after a run.

FIGURE 6.15.

The manufacturer of this video capture board includes a benchmarking utility as part of setup.

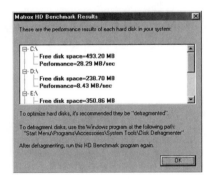

Matrox has determined that a hard disk needs a throughput of at least 5 megabytes/second to run well. The benchmark tells the computer operator if the machine is up to this standard. Including this benchmark informs the user and avoids calls to technical support.

Similarly, other multimedia setup programs should evaluate the computer they're being set up on. Some programs require certain color depths or resolutions, sound cards having certain compliance standards, or lately, MMX (Intel's Multimedia Extensions standard) operation, or some other feature.

In some cases, the setup program will diagnose what's wrong but can't or won't fix it. For example, if a setup program tells you that you need a different color depth or resolution, you need to go to Control Panel and choose Display|Settings to adjust these. The

6

setup program can't do it for you. You can also adjust the display by right-clicking the desktop and choosing Properties|Settings from the context menu.

Most if not all multimedia hardware is now PnP (Plug and Play) compliant. This should eliminate all hardware conflicts, but it doesn't. The tools to diagnose and fix hardware conflicts in Windows 98 multimedia are the same as with any hardware.

The first step is to open the Control Panel and choose System|Device Manager to examine any suspected devices for conflicts. If you find any, you can sometimes use Start| Programs|Accessories|System Tools|Microsoft System Information Utility to find free resources (usually addresses or IRQs) and manually force one of the devices to a new, nonconflicting resource. Figure 6.16 shows the Microsoft System Information utility running, showing IRQ resources allocated.

FIGURE 6.16.

Windows 98, unlike most previous releases of Windows, has a full-featured diagnostic toolset.

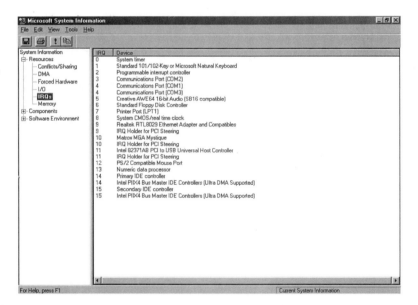

If you're unsure which component is causing problems, you can always disable a suspected component or components in a particular hardware profile. See Day 12, "Maintaining Your System," for information on how to do this.

A lesser-used, but extremely handy, utility within Windows 98 is MSCONFIG. This won't appear on a menu unless you take steps to put it there. To run MSCONFIG from a standard Windows 98 setup, choose Start|Run and then enter **msconfig** in the dialog box that appears. MSCONFIG will allow you to examine your initialization files, neatly categorized by function. To disable the loading or starting of any driver or program, just uncheck the box next to its entry; then restart Windows 98. You can also uncheck all the boxes not needed for basic Windows function and then add them back in one at a time. Figure 6.17 shows MSCONFIG displaying the SYSTEM.INI file for one Windows 98 computer.

FIGURE 6.17.

MSCONFIG *is a technically oriented, extremely powerful tool for diagnosing multimedia problems.*

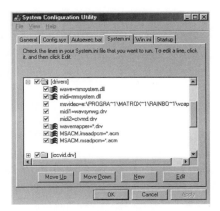

Although Windows 98 technically replaces files such as AUTOEXEC.BAT, CONFIG.SYS, WIN.INI, and SYSTEM.INI with the Registry, many third-party programs still use these files. Windows 98 is backwards compatible, using them in the same way as previous Windows versions. Disabling and enabling the drivers and programs within the initialization files is much easier in MSCONFIG than using an editor to remark out the lines, as you were forced to do with earlier Windows versions. MSCONFIG also leaves you with a visual record of what you've done.

One final note: Multimedia hardware and software, even the latest, aren't foolproof. There are products on the market, and there will be products coming onto the market, that you won't be able to run. This often is due to incompatible hardware installed in the same machine. In these cases, there's nothing to be done for it other than to try other hardware. Figure 6.18 shows a nonlinear video editing session on a computer. This particular computer, a standard setup, required three video capture boards and two editing programs until it found a combination that worked.

Summary

Multimedia was once the buzzword of the year. Now it's settled down to being such a common part of computing that there really aren't any computers sold today without some multimedia capacity.

6

FIGURE 6.18.

If at first you don't succeed, diagnose, fiddle, and then try other hardware or software.

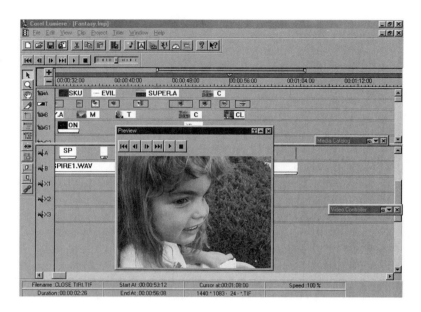

Windows 98 is as advanced a multimedia operating system as ever has been available for PCs. Arguably, it's the most capable operating system in wide distribution ever. It has built-in support for many graphics standards, from business to games to advance modeling. It supports various sound output and input devices, making it capable of being a full-featured music studio with the proper hardware, software, and most importantly, operator.

A Windows 98 computer can be an animation studio, a video editing device, a movie production studio, and a Web server and can serve many other functions.

Windows 98 is the foundation. The multimedia edifices you choose to build on it depend on your budget, your talent, and your inclinations. Such productions as movies with music, once the realm of only the most advanced and expensive workstations, are now possible using a modest PC with Windows 98 and a few hundred dollars in additional software.

Workshop

To wrap up the day, you can review terms from the chapter, see the answers to some commonly asked questions, and practice what you've learned. You can find the answers to the exercises in Appendix A, "Answers."

Terminology Review

ActiveX—A constantly emerging standard from Microsoft for distributed applications. This standard started with OLE and has moved through various iterations. Currently, Microsoft calls this family of standards DNA (Distributed Network Applications).

DirectX—A way for software to address Windows 98. Using DirectX, software programmers can get performance rivaling direct hardware addressing common in MS-DOS days—thus the name.

CD Plus—An enhanced standard that enables the encoding and playback of digital music and information at the same time. Using CD Plus, a music title can play back both the music track and textual information simultaneously.

MMX—Multimedia extensions for Intel and Intel clone processors. MMX inclusion in a processor permits the type of fast processing for matrix calculations previously requiring a separate DSP (Digital Signal Processor).

WDM—An integrated standard for driving hardware devices under Windows 98 and subsequent Microsoft operating systems.

WinToon—A special facility of Windows 98 that enables full-screen animation playback that matches, or closely matches, commercial cinema displays.

Q&A

Q When setting up Windows 98 over Windows 95, Setup disabled my proprietary sound card drivers and substituted those made by Microsoft. Is this normal?

A This is part of the grand plan. Whenever possible, Windows 98 will use the standard WDM drivers in place of the proprietary ones supplied by various vendors. If everything is working all right, you needn't change anything. If you want to replace the Microsoft drivers with proprietary ones, you can do so using the Update Driver option on the Driver tab. From the Control Panel, choose System|Device Manager|Properties|Driver tab for the device in question.

Q When using the Media Player to play `.avi` files from disk, the playback is jerky. How can I smooth it so that it looks like a real movie?

A The chief reason for jerky `.avi` playback (or any movie standard playback) is system speed. If large files play back poorly while small ones do all right, the culprit is usually the hard disk. There is little you can do to speed up a pokey system, other than replace hardware. However, in some cases, Windows 98 itself is slow due to having a lot of applications or services loaded. Before chucking your system, boot as cleanly as possible. Remove items from Startup, close any running services you can, and then try the playback again.

6

Q NetShow displays aren't smooth like normal television. What's up?

A NetShow's smoothness depends on system speed, Internet connection speed, and server speed. If any of these is slow, NetShow's display deteriorates. No matter what else is right, don't expect premium displays with 28.8 dial-up connections. Even the 56Kbps connections can be jerky.

Exercises

1. For this exercise, suppose that you're tired of seeing unlabeled CDs and songs when you use the music CD Player. Take your favorite CD and play it on the computer. While you are enjoying the music, type in the name of the artist, the CD's title, and the titles of the songs. When you're done, exit the CD Player, eject the CD, and then reinsert the CD to make sure the information was saved.

2. Install NetShow.

WEEK 1

DAY 7

Getting Help in Windows 98

by Michael Hart

No matter who you are, what your level of expertise is, what you're doing, or what software or hardware you're using, eventually you'll need help. It might be as simple as wanting to look up how to utilize a particular feature or as frustrating as an intermittent system error. Regardless, it's nice to know where to turn when you need assistance. In keeping with the mantra of making Windows easier to use, Microsoft has greatly enhanced the amount and type of help available to all users.

This chapter covers

- Windows Help
- Windows 98 getting started: online edition
- Technical help on the Web
- Using troubleshooters

- Using the System Configuration Utility
- Using Dr. Watson

In the dark ages of personal computing, there were demons who struck fear into the hearts of those unwary users unlucky enough to encounter them, known as GPFs (General Protection Faults) and UAEs (User Application Errors)—both technical sounding terms that just meant you had a problem. In our enlightened age, of course, these evil beasts are virtually unheard of. Right. The tooth fairy still visits, too.

Any system as complex as our current computer hardware and software is going to suffer the occasional problem, glitch, crash, whatever you want to call it. Sometimes we can determine the cause, oftentimes not. Even knowing the cause doesn't guarantee we'll be able to do anything to fix it—avoid it perhaps.

Help is one of those things that when you need it, you really need it. When you do need it, you're probably already going to be frustrated, so trying to figure out where and how to get help in your moment of crisis will just be doubly exasperating. Advance preparation will not alleviate the need for help but will certainly lower your frustration level.

Windows Help

Access to Windows Help is very convenient—it's located right on the Start menu. Click on Help to bring up the window shown in Figure 7.1. This is Windows Help. You'll find answers to all of your basic feature and usage questions here. Also included in the Help system is the online Windows 98 Getting Started book. As shown in Figure 7.1, there's a subject titled "Getting Started Book: Online Version" listed in the Help subjects. Displaying the subject and following the Click Here link will open another Help window containing the Getting Started book.

The Help system has changed from what you might be used to in Windows 3.*x* or Windows 95. The new look is a two-pane style window with subjects and topics listed in the left pane and the information shown in the right pane. Above the left pane you'll see three tabs: Contents, Index, and Search. Subjects are those broader categories shown with a book next to them. Opening a book (by clicking on it) displays the topics (shown with an icon that looks like a document with a question mark on it) in the subject. Clicking on a topic displays it in the right pane.

The Contents tab, displayed by default, lists all the subjects and topics of Help. Clicking on the Index tab displays a list of terms used throughout the Help file. So, if you wanted to find out how to hook up a digital camera to Windows but couldn't figure out the topic to look for under Contents, you could click the Index tab and then type in **cameras** or scroll through the term list. When you find the term you're looking for, click it; then click the Display button and the topic will be displayed in the right pane. If more than one topic contains the term, a small dialog box will appear listing the topics; select one. Then click the Display button in the dialog box.

FIGURE 7.1.

Windows 98 Help—the starting point for getting help.

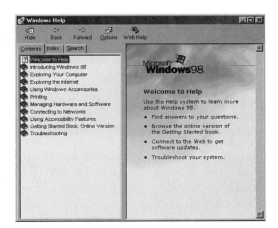

The Search tab works similarly. Type in the term (keyword) you want to find and then hit Enter or click the List Topics button, and a list of all the topics containing your keyword will be displayed in the left pane. When you select one and click Display, the topic will be displayed in the right pane. Many times a topic will have a link at the bottom of the page labeled Related Topics. Click this link to bring up a fly-out menu similar to what you see on the Start menu. Select one of the items on the fly-out to display the item.

Windows 98 Getting Started: Online Version

This Help file is just what its title would indicate: a basic introduction to using Windows 98. Beginning users will find more here than more experienced users, but there's still good information to be found.

Topics covered in the Getting Started Help include

- Windows 98 features
- Installing Windows 98
- Differences between Windows 3.*x*/95 and Windows 98
- Using and customizing your desktop
- Using a mouse
- Using the Internet

7

To open the online book by opening Windows Help, click on the Getting Started Book: Online Version subject, then click on the Microsoft Windows 98 Getting Started topic, and then click the Click Here link displayed in the right pane.

Technical Help on the Web

The Microsoft goal of integrating the Internet into Windows continues into the realm of getting technical assistance. Access to the vast technical support resources of Microsoft is available from Help in a number of ways.

On the menu bar in the Windows 98 Help window is an icon titled Web Help. Click the Web Help button (or make the menu selections Options | Web Help) to display a help topic with a Click Here link that will launch Internet Explorer, dial your ISP as required, and connect you to the Microsoft Windows 98 Web Update site.

The first thing you'll have to do when visiting the Windows Update or Web Help site is to register your copy of Windows 98. You'll fill in a couple of screens of information. You'll also be notified that an inventory of your system hardware has been taken. Don't worry; this is not an extensive examination of your programs and data files to determine what programs you have or any personal secrets. The system inventory, shown in Figure 7.2, is really only concerned with your hardware configuration: your processor, the amount of memory, display type, and so on. However, if you really have privacy concerns, you are given the option of not sending the inventory with your registration information.

FIGURE 7.2.

This is the listing of hardware configuration items collected during the registration process. You can choose not to send the inventory with your registration.

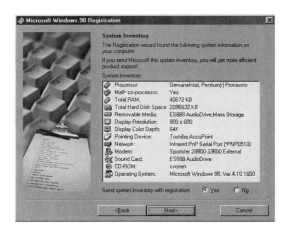

Note

Over time, the Windows 98 Web site will change in appearance, so don't be surprised if it appears slightly different than it does in screenshots in this chapter.

You will see how to use Windows Update to update system software on your computer on Day 10, "Managing Software." Click on Web Help to bring up the Support page on the Microsoft Web site, shown in Figure 7.3.

FIGURE 7.3.

The Web Help option in Windows Help brings you to this Microsoft Web page, where you can search for any Windows subject.

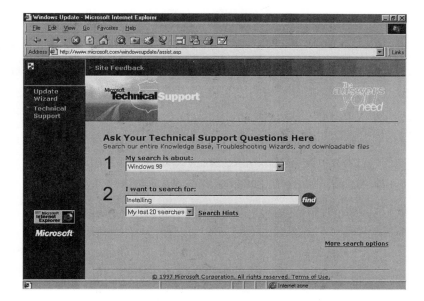

To use Web Help, select one of the categories listed under item 1 (as shown in Figure 7.3), such as Windows 98, as shown. Then type in a specific word or words in the I Want to Search For box. Click the Find button, and you'll get back a list of documents containing your search phrase, as shown in Figure 7.4.

7

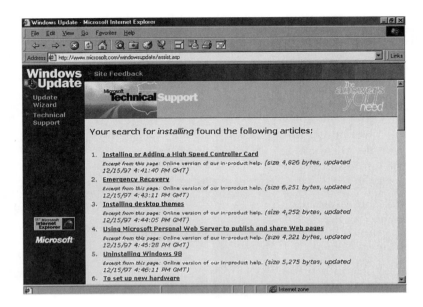

FIGURE 7.4.

A page full of results (also called hits*) from a search for the word* installing.

Using Troubleshooters

The last topic listed in the Windows Help file is Troubleshooting. This section contains information about using the many Windows troubleshooting procedures in the Help file and information on how to report Windows problems (covered in the following section). There are several troubleshooter wizards in the Help file that describe step-by-step troubleshooting procedures for LAN, modem, printing, startup, DriveSpace, memory, and other problems. These are procedures that have you perform some actions and then answer a question regarding the outcome of the action or what you saw. Based on your response, the next step of the troubleshooter is displayed.

Task 7.1. Using a Troubleshooter Procedure

Many common problems are addressed through the use of troubleshooters, available from the Help file. In this Task, you'll discover how to locate them and look at how they work:

1. Open the Help Desk by clicking Start | Help.

2. Open the Troubleshooting heading; then open the Windows 98 Troubleshooters heading. Notice the Troubleshooter topics available.

3. Click on one of the Troubleshooter topics, such as the DriveSpace Troubleshooter. In the right pane, read the description and then click the button to launch the troubleshooter. You might want to maximize the Troubleshooter window for ease of

▼   reading. All the troubleshooters follow a similar format. They present a question, and you pick an answer from a list of possible choices. Your answer determines what question is next asked of you. As you proceed from question to question, notice that each of the preceding questions, and your answer, is listed at the top of the page. Figure 7.5 shows a step from the Windows 98 Print Troubleshooter.

FIGURE 7.5.

This Print Troubleshooter is a typical troubleshooter. Answering questions as you go, the troubleshooters give you steps to take to figure out how to solve the problem you are having.

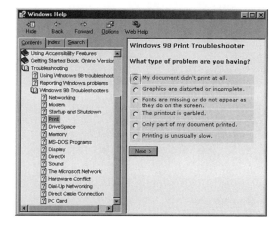

4. When you've gone as far through this troubleshooter as you care to on this practice run, simply exit Help.

You've now taken your first practice run through a troubleshooter. If you should
▲   encounter problems in the future, you'll know where to turn for assistance.

The System Configuration Utility

If you should encounter problems with system configuration or system startup, you'll probably wind up using the Startup and Shutdown Troubleshooter from Help. One of the tools used in this troubleshooter is the System Configuration Utility, `Msconfig.exe`. As shown in Figure 7.6, there are tabs for all the important system-related files: `Autoexec.bat`, `Config.sys`, `System.ini`, and `Win.ini`. There's also a Startup tab that lists all the tasks started automatically. If you have an idea about what particular device might be causing you problems, it's a relatively simple process to come to the troubleshooter, set your options to bypass the offending configuration settings, then reboot, and see if the problem(s) goes away.

7

FIGURE 7.6.

*The System
Configuration Utility is
used to selectively
enable or disable
various configuration
settings to assist in
troubleshooting system
and startup errors.*

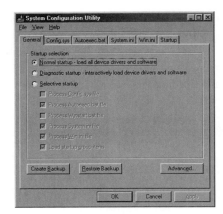

To start the System Configuration Utility, you'll have to either type **msconfig** in the Start
| Run box or launch the System Information Utility (Start | Programs | Accessories |
System Tools | System Information) and then select Tools | System Configuration Utility.
Feel free to start the System Configuration Utility and explore its dialogs and settings.
Just be sure to click Cancel when you've finished, so as to not accidentally change any-
thing that shouldn't be changed now!

Dr. Watson

Another available tool to assist in both capturing error-related data and getting it to the
support people or software vendors who can best analyze it is the Dr. Watson reporting
tool. The good doctor has been around for several years, and he's getting better, not
older. The current generation of Dr. Watson is a master detective and reporter rolled into
one. He'll take a snapshot of your system at the moment of failure, including all relevant
system files and process information; take your comments; save it all to a file; and usually save you the pain of having to reboot.

To load Dr. Watson, navigate to the Windows directory and launch the drwatson.exe file
there. You'll notice nothing happens; however, check down on the System Tray, and
you'll see doc down there with his stethoscope out.

You don't "run" Dr. Watson. When you find that you're having system or application
problems—an application starts crashing, or your system gets the blue fatal error
screen—load Dr. Watson; then try to cause the problem again. Alternatively, when you
start having problems, you might want to put him into your Startup group. That way, he's
standing by, waiting for the problem to reoccur. When it does, Dr. Watson will activate,
take a system snapshot, and allow you to enter comments as to what you were doing

when the error occurred. If the doctor doesn't automatically pop up, double-click on the icon in the System Tray to activate him. After you've entered your comments, click File | Save, enter a filename, and click Save. The default extension for Dr. Watson log files is `.wlg`. When you report problems to your software/hardware vendors, they might ask you to send them the Dr. Watson log file.

Task 7.2. Loading and Using Dr. Watson

Of course, you hope you'll never need the doctor's services, but if you do, it's nice to have visited with him before there's a problem. In this Task, you'll start him up and see what kind of information he will gather about your system:

1. Using Windows Explorer, start Dr. Watson by double-clicking on the `drwatson.exe` file located in the `C:\Windows` directory. Not much happened there, did it?

2. Verify that Dr. Watson started by checking to see if he's sitting in the System Tray.

3. Right-click on the doctor, and select Options. Click Open New Windows in Advanced View and then click OK.

4. Now double-click on the Dr. Watson icon in the System Tray. You'll see the Dr. Watson dialog appear, saying `Generating Snapshot...` and showing progress bars zipping across the dialog box.

5. Looking at the first tab, Diagnosis, you see confirmed that there is nothing obviously unusual (see Figure 7.7). Had this been an actual error, you would have seen a message here about the problem discovered. In an actual error situation, you'd want to enter as much information as you could about what you were doing before the error occurred—anything you could remember about the moments immediately preceding the error.

FIGURE 7.7.

Dr. Watson, here showing that nothing unusual was detected, will scrutinize your computer's current operating environment, looking for errors.

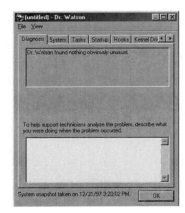

7

▼   6. Take a moment to look at the other tabs: System, Tasks, Startup, Hooks, Kernel
        Drivers, User Drivers, MS-DOS Drivers, and 16-bit Modules. Use the left/right
        arrow buttons to scroll the tabs. Do the tab names or the items listed on these tabs
        seem familiar? They should; you've seen them before—in the System Information
        Utility.

     7. Click File | Save. Type in a name for this Dr. Watson log and click Save.

     8. Click File | Save As. In the Save dialog, you can see the WLG file you just created
        listed in the file list. Click Cancel.

     9. Click File | Close to close this window and put Dr. Watson back on the System
▲   Tray, or File | Exit to quit Dr. Watson altogether.

There—you've just had your first house call by Dr. Watson. You might not need him for
a long time, but if you do, you'll know how to get him out.

Summary

These tools won't prevent you from having problems, but they can certainly be of assistance when you encounter trouble. Knowing how to use them properly, before you need
to utilize them during times of trouble, will go a long way toward getting you back to
doing what you want to be doing in the minimum amount of time.

Workshop

To wrap up the day, you can review terms from the chapter, see the answers to some
commonly asked questions, and practice what you've learned. You can find the answers
to the exercises in Appendix A, "Answers."

Terminology Review

bug—Any repeatable error in a program. Generally, something that doesn't do what it's
intended to do or interacts unfavorably with another program.

crash—Generally, a program crashes and is no longer usable until it is restarted.

snapshot—A recording of the current status of a machine's state.

troubleshoot—To systematically determine the cause of a problem.

Q&A

Q If I send a problem report to Microsoft, will a support engineer contact me with an answer?

A Probably not. Technical support from Microsoft is on a pay basis. You can pay by the incident or for a given period, such as a year. Problem reports submission will help Microsoft developers fix any bugs found before the next release of the related products.

Q I noticed that Dr. Watson doesn't normally run on my system. Should I put him into my Startup group?

A No. Dr. Watson doesn't need to be run unless you've been experiencing system problems. Then, load the program into your Startup group so it can take a system snapshot the next time you encounter an error.

Exercises

1. As a Windows user, you should frequently back up your important data files to ensure that you don't lose any work in the event of a hardware malfunction. Windows Help provides information about backing up your files; use the Help Search to find out how to back up your files.

2. Sometimes when you are troubleshooting a problem with your Windows system, it helps to know which programs are automatically started when you start up Windows. Display a list of all of the programs that are started automatically when Windows starts. (Note: The Startup folder in the Programs folder on the Start menu doesn't list all the Startup programs.)

7

WEEK 2

At a Glance: Getting the Most out of Windows 98 and Internet Explorer 4

WEEK 2

DAY 8

Customizing Windows 98

by Paul Cassel

Windows 98 offers a huge variety of options that enable you to change the way the graphical user interface (GUI) or desktop looks and behaves. You saw some customization options in the last chapter with the addition and removal of tool-bars from the taskbar as well as changing taskbar properties. This chapter adds to that information and extends itself to cover the entire desktop, not just the taskbar and Active Desktop.

This chapter covers

- Launching the Display applet
- Changing Display options
- Color resolution, display fonts, and color depth explained
- Choosing or making a custom desktop scheme
- Changing desktop system icons
- Configuring Windows 98 to look and act like Windows 3.1
- Adding, removing, and modifying your Start menu
- Making an Emergency Startup Disk (ESD)

- Adding, removing, and modifying your Windows 98 installation
- Accessibility options for those with special needs

Changing the Look and Feel of Windows 98

The look and feel of your Windows 98 computer greatly depend on the settings you apply to the desktop and the Start menu part of the taskbar. Easily the most customized feature of the desktop is its appearance. There isn't one single place to set all the desktop options that are available, but the single most feature-rich cyberplace is the properties of the desktop. To get to these properties, right-click the desktop anywhere away from the taskbar and any icons. Choose Properties from the context menu. Figure 8.1 shows the resulting screen of a representative computer. Keep in mind that your screen will vary from the one shown in Figure 8.1. The actual appearance of any computer depends on its hardware and installation options.

FIGURE 8.1.

The properties of a representative desktop in Windows 98.

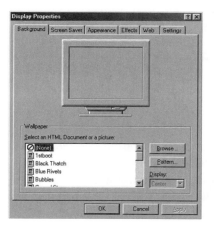

Examine the tabs and the title bar of the dialog box shown in Figure 8.1 or the one on your computer. Note that the properties for this dialog box all have something to do with display attributes. This is why the actual dialog box you see on any specific computer varies, depending on the options provided by the manufacturer of the display adapter. Just as automobile interiors vary from manufacturer to manufacturer and model to model, display features vary, depending on manufacturer and model. You can also reach this dialog box through the Display applet in the Control Panel. For information on the Control Panel, see the following section.

All display adapters have some standard tabs for their properties. All, for example, have a Settings tab where you set your resolution and color depth, an Appearance tab to set default Windows 98 colors, and an Effects tab to set the icons for system objects on your desktop. Effects also includes some animation and window display attributes, as you'll see in the screens for Task 8.1. System objects vary, depending on your setup, but always include such items as the Recycle Bin and My Computer.

Task 8.1. Changing the Icon for My Computer

▼ TASK

The following steps show you how to vary the icons for system objects on the desktop:

1. Right-click the desktop and choose Properties from the context menu. Click the Effects tab (see Figure 8.2).

FIGURE 8.2.

The Effects tab in Properties is where you set the icons for system objects located on the desktop.

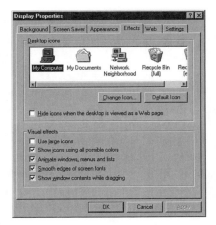

2. Click the My Computer icon in the dialog box to highlight it. Click the Change Icon button. The Change Icon dialog box appears, as shown in Figure 8.3.

FIGURE 8.3.

The Change Icon dialog box starts you on a hunt for a new icon.

The top text box shows which file you've opened to look for new icons. The box below this shows the icons embedded in the file. Icons are elements bound into files (usually files having the `.exe` or `.dll` extension) or can be standalone icon

▼

▼ files with the `.ico` extension. To choose an icon from the file displayed in the top text box (in this case, `explorer.exe`), scroll through the choices, highlight your choice, and click OK. Click Apply or OK on the Properties dialog box to apply your changes to the My Computer item.

3. If you want to use an icon from somewhere other than `explorer.exe`, click the Browse button and search for other files with icons. Unless you know exactly what you're looking for, your search might be somewhat haphazard. Figure 8.4 shows the icon available from the Metatools Painter program file, `Painter5.exe`.

FIGURE 8.4.

Many files have embedded icons, enabling you to have an interesting mix of desktop icons if you're willing to hunt for them.

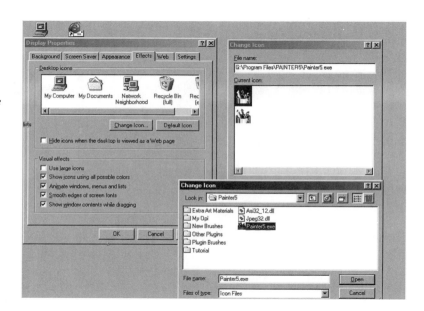

4. Choose the icon you want and click OK to close the dialog boxes. Figure 8.5 shows the result of applying the icon from `Painter5.exe` to My Computer.

To change the icon used in a shortcut, right-click the shortcut, choose the Properties entry on the context menu, and click the Change Icon button on the Shortcut tab. Your screen should resemble Figure 8.6. As in Task 8.1, you can browse for additional icons or use those embedded in the currently used file.

Changing Desktop Colors

You can change Windows 98's system colors (the active palette) for items such as menu bars, window backgrounds, and so forth through the Desktop Properties dialog box's Appearance tab, shown in Figure 8.7. Beware of bizarre combinations. They can be fun but also distracting.

8

FIGURE 8.5.

Windows 98 applies changes made to desktop items immediately after the OK or Apply button in the Properties dialog box is clicked.

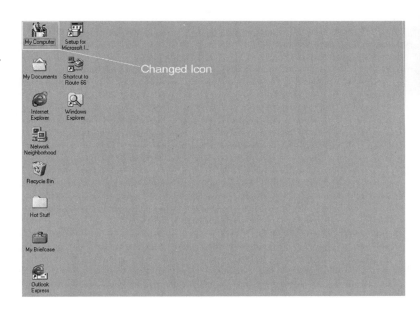

FIGURE 8.6.

This shortcut points to the RealPlayer add-in for Internet Explorer.

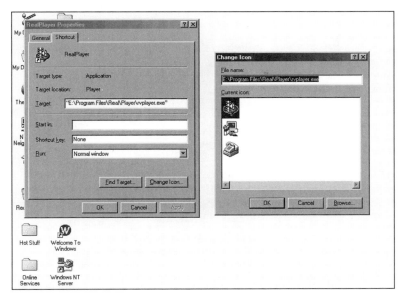

FIGURE 8.7.

The Appearance tab is where you change the system palette.

To make palette changes, either pull down the Item combo box or click the item you want to change in the large graphic display box at the top of the tab. Depending on the item selected, you have a choice of changing the foreground, background, and font or some combination of all three. Figure 8.8 shows the Appearance tab with standard settings from a normal Windows 98 setup.

FIGURE 8.8.

Windows 98 enables you to choose many appearance schemes— both wise and unwise.

Figure 8.8 shows an unusual set of choices for the Menu bar. This includes a dark background, a light foreground, and a decorative font. Figure 8.9 shows the results of those choices in Microsoft Word 97 and Corel Lumiere. Figure 8.9 also shows the taskbar Start menu.

FIGURE 8.9.

The results of your Appearance options can actually decrease the utility of your programs and system.

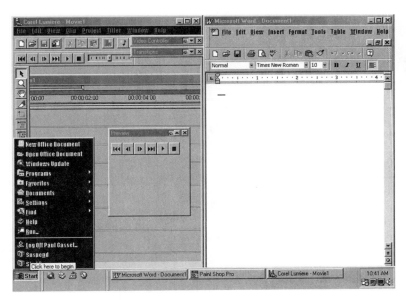

Changing colors for your system also changes colors for all those programs that obtain their color information from Windows 98. This is the vast majority of programs and their objects. If, after making some color changes, your programs start looking odd, the problem might be that the great color combinations for the desktop that you chose don't cut it for application programs.

As you can see from Figure 8.9, not all changes make sense. In this case, the readability of many Windows 98 objects has decreased dramatically. The Start menu is practically unreadable.

You can also pull down the Scheme combo box and choose from the supplied predefined schemes supplied with Windows 98. Although some supplied schemes are of questionable artistic merit, none of them dramatically decrease your computer's function.

BEWARE THE MONO ATTACK

Be careful of setting your background and foreground values to the same. This makes your text invisible. Unless you're a good Windows 98 navigator, it can also make changing them back to have some contrast quite difficult. Changing the background and foreground colors to the same value, such as white, is a favorite practical joke workers play on one another if and when they get access to another's machine.

You can also define your own scheme and then add it to the combo box list by clicking the Save As button in the Appearance tab. Figure 8.10 shows the Scheme combo box expanded.

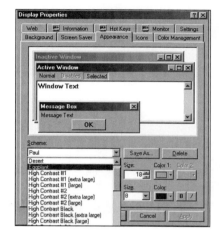

Choosing a scheme places a representation of that scheme in the Appearance preview box. Figure 8.11 shows how the Eggplant scheme alters your system colors. Of course, because this is a black-and-white figure, you can't see the exact color variance, but you can see the contrast. The Eggplant scheme will surely appeal to some but not all users. If you like the representation, click OK or Apply. If you don't, choose another, or you can cancel the entire operation by clicking the Cancel button.

FIGURE 8.11.

The quality of any color and font scheme varies, depending on the eye of the beholder.

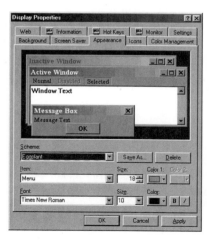

Resolution and Color Depth

The *resolution* of a desktop is how many *pixels*, or dots, a desktop contains in both the horizontal and vertical directions. The standard VGA resolution is 640×480, meaning there are 640 dots across the screen with 480 dots in the up-and-down direction.

The higher the resolution, the more dots your screen displays. It also means the smaller every displayed object must be because your monitor screen doesn't grow or shrink when you change resolutions. The higher the resolution, the more information displayed, but in the same physical area. There are more and more applets and even fairly large applications that don't work well in less than 800×600 resolution. For example, Microsoft Access 97 works indifferently at 640×480 and well in 800×600 but really shines in 1024×768. Its function increases with its capability to display more information at any given time.

Note
> Why these particular resolutions? The standard aspect ratio for PC screens is set at the same ratio as NTSC broadcast TV. That ratio is 4:3. Divide any standard resolution scheme, and you'll come up with the same 4:3 ratio. This might change when HDTV's 16:9 ratio becomes the new standard for television, but for now, the PC computer world is all 4:3.

Figure 8.12 shows a desktop in standard VGA resolution of 640×480. The standard VGA resolution shows large objects, but a desktop is limited in how many objects it can show.

FIGURE 8.12.

A desktop with 640×480 resolution.

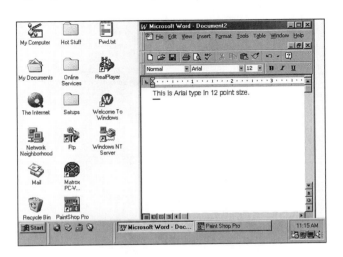

8

Figure 8.13 shows a higher resolution, 1152×864, available only with some display adapters. The 1152×864 resolution setting makes for many more objects on the desktop, but at the cost of making any item much smaller than with lower resolutions.

FIGURE 8.13.

*A desktop with
1152×864 resolution.*

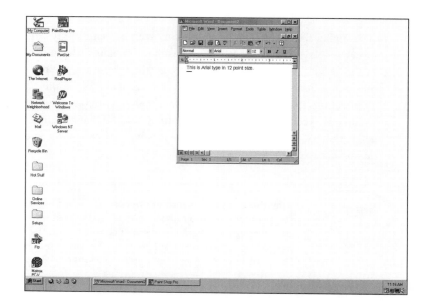

You control the display depth and resolution of your desktop on the Settings tab of the Properties dialog box, shown in Figure 8.14. *Color depth* is how many bits the computer is permitted to use to define a color—the more bits, the more color variety.

FIGURE 8.14.

The Settings tab.

The tab shown in Figure 8.14 is one customized by the driver of the particular display adapter used in the sample computer. The Settings tab for other display adapters varies, depending on their features. In particular, the PowerDesk button and the four buttons on the left of the tab are features particular to this company's adapters.

However, all adapters other than the most basic have a slider to change resolution. In Figure 8.14 this is the slider on the left, labeled Display Area. Slide the bar to the right to increase resolution. This adapter goes all the way up to 1920×1080 if your monitor can handle that size.

The *display depth* is how many bits an adapter uses for each point on your screen. The greater the number of bits, the greater number of colors your adapter can show at the same time. The color depth is powers of two, so a depth of 6 bits can show 2^6, or 64, colors simultaneously.

Note

The greatest number of colors available in display adapters is 16.7 million, or 2^{24}, yet many color adapters refer to 32-bit color, which also shows 16.7 million colors. What do these extra bits do?

The answer varies from system to system. In many cases, the extra bits act as modifiers of the alpha or transparency channel. However, there is no industry standard overall on what the extra memory can be used for.

Most modern computers have as their least colorful setting 8-bit depth for 256 colors at the same time. However, this is just the beginning. Even modestly priced displays sport more color depth than this, with many going to the limit of 16.7 million colors at 24- or 32-bit depths.

Note

Often color adapters refer to color depth using the words *high* or *true color* rather than a number. High color is 15- or 16-bit, displaying roughly 33,000 to 65,000 colors at the same time. True color shows the full 16.7 million colors simultaneously. Even the trained eye has a very difficult time distinguishing between high and true color schemes. However, certain high-level artistic programs are adversely affected by less than true color depth. If in doubt, crank the color depth up to the maximum you can. You pay a slight performance penalty (unnoticeable on most modern systems) and gain a beautiful display.

Remember that the more information on your screen, the more work it is for your adapter to refresh your view. Also, as you add resolution or color depth, you lose the capability to increase the other; display adapters are limited by their memory in what they can display. A display adapter with 2MB of memory can show true color, or 24-bit depth, in at most 800×600 resolution. The rough formula for determining how much memory a card needs at any resolution and color depth is as follows:

Vertical resolution×horizontal resolution×(bit depth/8) = Memory needed in bytes

To set your color depth, pull down the Color Palette combo box and choose from the offerings on the list. Figure 8.15 shows this combo box opened up for one particular display adapter.

FIGURE 8.15.

The Color Palette combo box sets the depth of color for your desktop.

Decorating Your Desktop

You can instruct Windows 98 to use different graphics as a background to your windows. You set this option on the Background tab of the Display Properties dialog box (see Figure 8.16).

Microsoft supplies quite a few selections for your desktop's background listing in the Wallpaper list box. As you select the entries in the list box, a representation of what your desktop will look like appears in the monitor graphic at the top of the tab.

The selections are bitmap graphics having the .bmp extension. The two wallpaper display options are center and tile. A centered bitmap appears only in the center of the desktop surrounded by the desktop color (if the bitmap is small enough). A tiled bitmap is repeated, like bathroom tiles, all across the desktop.

FIGURE 8.16.

The Background tab enables you to tile or center backgrounds from either the Microsoft-supplied selection or one of your own.

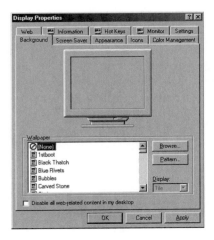

Figure 8.17 shows a tiled wallpaper selection. This particular bitmap is one supplied by Microsoft called Business.

FIGURE 8.17.

You have a wide variety of wallpapers to choose from, but how well you think they work out depends on aesthetic concerns.

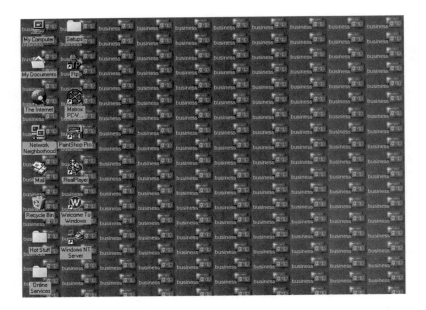

You can manufacture your own wallpaper by creating a bitmap graphic with any program that supports the file type. Figure 8.18 shows a bitmap created in Paint Brush Pro, saved to a bitmap format with the filename Windows Rules and then chosen as wallpaper.

FIGURE 8.18.

You can make up your own wallpaper using any program that creates a bitmap (.bmp) image.

If you make your own wallpaper images and want to find them in the Wallpaper list box by default, make sure that they're saved to the same folder as Windows 98 itself. Usually this is C:\Windows. You can also search for any bitmap by using the Browse button.

To set a pattern to appear outside your wallpaper, choose the Pattern button on the Background tab. This enables you to choose a pattern to use wherever your wallpaper ends. You also have an option to edit the pattern. Adding a busy pattern to a busy wallpaper can make a desktop virtually unusable. Figure 8.19 shows the Pattern dialog box, reached through the Background tab.

The Nostalgic Option

When Windows 95, the precursor to Windows 98, was in the early stages of development, Microsoft figured it had a clearly superior graphical user interface, compared to the then-existing Windows 3.1 and 3.11. Most users enthusiastically agreed; however, a few holdouts liked the added function of Windows 95 but pined for the Program Manager look of Windows 3.x.

Windows 98 carries forward the GUI of Windows 95 with added features such as the consistent appearance of all windows, the vastly improved taskbar, and the Active Desktop, but there are still those who prefer the old Program Manager look.

FIGURE 8.19.

The Pattern dialog box contains a simple editor to vary the supplied patterns.

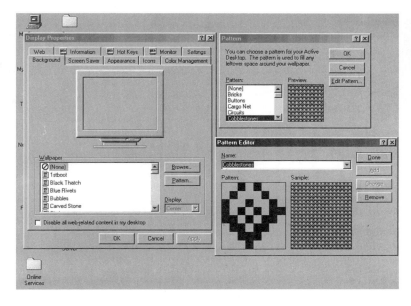

To satisfy the few old crusts who wanted Windows 95, but who didn't want to use the newer GUI, Microsoft offered the option of the old look over the new system. That tradition has been carried forward in Windows 98.

To see what the old Program Manager looks like in the new system, use Windows Explorer to locate a file called `Progman.exe` in the Windows 98 folder.

Run this program and your desktop is transformed to an interesting 1989 look, as you can see in Figure 8.20.

`Progman.exe` loads with the contents of your Start menu already set up. If this is the look you like, you can include `Progman.exe` in your Startup group. The next section discusses how to do this. You lose much Windows 98 function under `Progman.exe`, such as context menus and Active Desktop. However, you retain the stability and 32-bit application capability of the newer system. In other words, running `Progman.exe` as your GUI costs you quite a bit in features but nothing in architecture.

There are also some add-ons from third-party suppliers that add interesting variations to the Windows 98 GUI. Some of these are shareware available from the usual sources. Others are commercial programs available at common retail sources.

FIGURE 8.20.

Running Progman.exe *gives you a look similar to older versions of Windows.*

Taking Charge of the Start Menu

Most people are content to enable the setup and uninstall routines of applications to configure their Start menu's programs. However, with little effort anybody can learn how to change the contents and arrangement of Start to their personal preferences.

As with so much of Windows 98, this version of the Start menu is just a new view of something else. To open the Start menu for custom configuration, right-click the Start button and choose Open from the context menu.

Figure 8.21 shows the Start menu opened.

Your screen will very likely vary from the one shown in Figure 8.21. That system has Office 97 installed and is in Active Desktop configuration.

FIGURE 8.21.

The Start menu is one of three views of the same data.

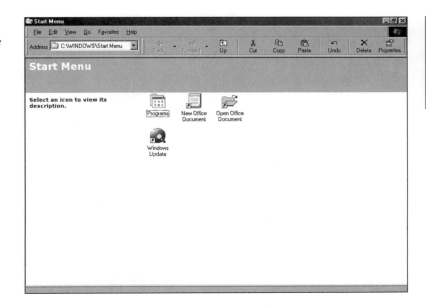

8

Task 8.2. Customizing the Start Menu

▲ TASK

This example rearranges the folders and files in the Start | Programs menu. You'll see these changes reflected on the Start | Programs menu after you complete the following steps:

1. Open the Start menu group by right-clicking the Start button and then choosing Open from the context menu. Your screen should resemble Figure 8.21, but will vary in the details.

2. Double-click (or single-click in Active Desktop view) on the Programs icon to open the Programs group. You see all the programs and program groups that you would if you clicked Start | Programs. Figure 8.22 shows the Programs group opened by double-clicking. Figure 8.23 shows the Start | Programs list. Note that the entries are identical.

3. As you add, edit, or change the contents of the Programs group shown in Figure 8.22, you affect the entries on the Start menu. To see the contents (drill down) of any folder in Programs, open it. You can place folders in folders just as you can in Explorer. In fact, you can use Explorer to manipulate the Start menu, as you'll see

▼

▼

in a little bit. Right now, locate the MS-DOS Prompt icon and drag it into any group. For example, you can place the icon in the Real (for RealPlayer) group.

FIGURE 8.22.

Double-clicking or opening the Programs group reveals its contents.

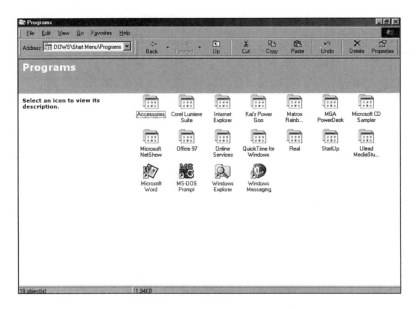

FIGURE 8.23.

The contents of the Programs group are reflected on the Start | Programs menu selections.

4. Click the Start menu. Choose Programs and then the group where you dropped the MS-DOS Prompt icon in step 3. You will see the new entry. Figure 8.24 shows the results if you dropped the MS-DOS Prompt icon in the Real group.

5. To return your MS-DOS Prompt icon to its previous place, open the Start | Programs group, open the Programs folder, and open the folder where you dropped the MS-DOS icon. Locate the icon, then right-click it, and choose Cut from the context menu. Close the folder by clicking the X icon in the upper-right corner.

▼

▼ This returns you to the Programs group. If you are in Active Desktop view, you can alternatively click the Back arrow to move up a level. In any view, you can choose the Up button on the toolbar. After you're back in Programs, whatever method you used to get there, right-click an empty area and then choose Paste from the context menu. Naturally, you can use your other cut-and-paste or drag-and-drop methods if you choose.

FIGURE 8.24.

You can drag and drop your way to the Start | Programs menu view you choose.

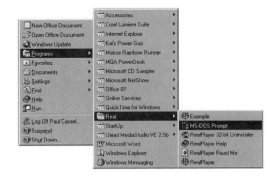

6. Close the Programs group if it's still open, and open Windows Explorer. Locate the Start Menu folder in the Windows folder and open it. Open the Programs folder, and you'll see an Explorer view of the same objects that you saw in Figures 8.22 and 8.23 (see Figure 8.25).

FIGURE 8.25.

Two views aren't enough. You also have an Explorer view of the objects on your Start | Programs menu.

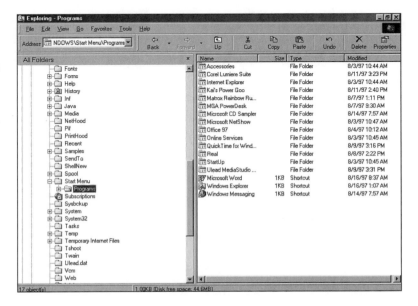

▼

▼   You can add, move, copy, delete, or rename any objects in the Explorer view and
     have those changes reflected in the Start menu, as you saw in the Open (icon)
     view.

7. If you right-click the Start button and choose Explore instead of Open, the view
   you get is the same as directly using Windows Explorer. The Find entry in the con-
   text menu for the Start button launches the same utility as the Tools | Find menu
▲ entry in Explorer but loads the \windows\start Menu folder on startup.

The Control Panel

The Control Panel appears as a program group containing applets for controlling the
function and appearance of your Windows 98 system. The panel is really a program
called Control.exe, located in your Windows 98 directory. If you search your Windows
98 folder for Control.exe and then start that program, you'll launch the Control Panel.

You can also start or open the Control Panel through the Start menu Settings entry or
access any of the applets (small configuration applications) in it from Windows Explorer.
Figure 8.26 shows the Control Panel entry in Explorer, whereas Figure 8.27 shows the
Control Panel opened.

FIGURE 8.26.

*You can launch any
applet in the Control
Panel through
Windows Explorer.*

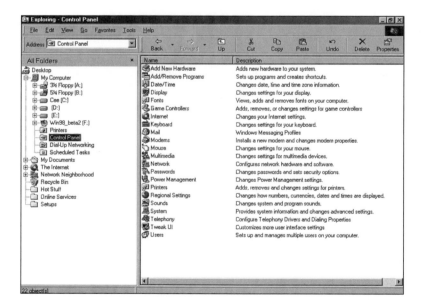

The Explorer view of the Control Panel is particularly useful because the right side of
the applet display holds a short description, almost like a ToolTip, of any entered applet.

Figure 8.26 is a good short reference for the applets installed in the sample computer. The opened Control Panel fails to have such tip help. However, the applets are fairly self-explanatory, based on their labels.

FIGURE 8.27.

To see the entire open Control Panel, choose Start | Settings | Control Panel.

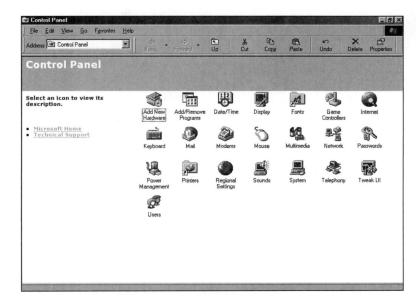

Each computer's Control Panel is a country unto itself. The entries vary, depending on the particular setup and often optional programs that might not even come from Microsoft. In many cases, you can effectively launch a Control Panel applet through other means or at least have the same effect on your machine.

Here are two examples. You can start the setup program for a new application by clicking the Add/Remove Programs applet or, in most cases, just by running the program `Setup.exe` or `Install.exe` from the distribution disk. In many cases, programs distributed on CD-ROMs start themselves upon being placed in the CD-ROM reader.

Similarly, most modern hardware is Plug and Play (PnP) enabled. When you add such hardware, Windows 98 detects it on the next startup and offers to install the needed drivers (interface programs) for the new gadget. The Add New Hardware applet is only for very old hardware that isn't PnP, or for those who like to beat PnP at its own game.

The Display applet starts the same program you can get by right-clicking on the desktop and then choosing Properties. In many displays, the same applet is available through a Display entry in the tray of the taskbar. As is the case with so many things in Windows 98, there are diverse approaches to the same end.

Changing Windows 98's Installation

The setup program for Windows 98 is a simplified version of previous Windows setup programs. This works for the vast majority of people, but for those who like to fiddle and tune their computers to get them just right, the one-size-fits-all approach isn't ideal.

Windows enables more flexibility in its setup after it's installed than during its initial setup. To vary your installed options, start the Add/Remove Programs applet in the Control Panel, either through the opened Control Panel (Start | Settings | Control Panel) or through a direct launch in Windows Explorer. Your screen should resemble Figure 8.28, although the actual entries in the installed programs in the list box vary, depending on what programs you have on your computer.

FIGURE 8.28.

The Add/Remove Programs applet enables you to modify applications or Windows 98 installation options.

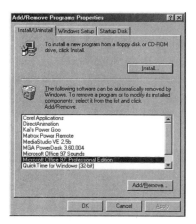

To add a program or application, click the Install button. Windows 98 searches for a setup program and offers its idea of what you want to do. You can accept this or directly instruct Windows 98 what to do. If you want to remove or modify the installation options of an existing application, highlight it (by a click) and then click the Add/Remove button (shown in the lower-right corner of Figure 8.28).

The Startup Disk tab gives you a chance to create an Emergency Startup Disk (also called an Emergency Boot Disk [EBD]) that will rescue you when your computer won't start normally. (For more information about creating an Emergency Startup Disk, see Day 2, "Installing Windows 98.") Usually, three occurrences cause this situation:

- Your computer has caught a virus that affects its boot process.
- Your hard (fixed) disk has developed a bad sector or sectors in an area that affects the boot process.

- Windows was damaged during an unexpected shutdown due to an event such as a power loss.

These occurrences are rare, but they do happen. An ESD enables you to start your computer and often fix the problem. Make sure you write-protect your ESD after making it. This protection keeps your ESD safe if you develop a virus. The middle tab shown in Figure 8.28 is one affecting Windows 98 itself. Click this tab and you'll see a screen similar to Figure 8.29, but the details will surely vary.

FIGURE 8.29.

The Windows Setup tab of the Add/Remove Programs Properties dialog box.

The optional components of Windows 98 are grouped according to classification in the list box shown in Figure 8.29. To see the details of any group, highlight the group by clicking on it; then click the Details button. You can also just double-click the group to open it. Figure 8.30 shows the Accessories detail.

To add or remove a component from any group, check or uncheck the check box next to its entry. To add or remove an entire group, check or uncheck its check box in the group screen shown in Figure 8.29. If you're adding a component or group, Windows 98 needs the distribution CD-ROM or access to the server where the distribution files reside.

Adding or removing parts of Windows 98 is as simple as clicking a check box. Note in Figures 8.26, 8.27, 8.29, and 8.30 that the Accessibility group isn't part of the sample computer's setup. Figure 8.31 shows the result of checking that group's check box and letting Windows run its setup program from a CD-ROM.

FIGURE 8.30.

The Accessories dialog box.

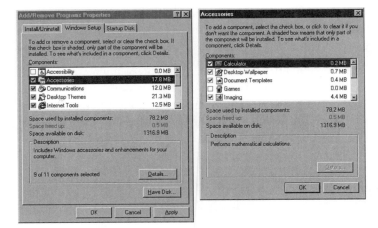

FIGURE 8.31.

Here you can see the Accessibility group addition reflected both in Windows Explorer and the Windows Setup tab.

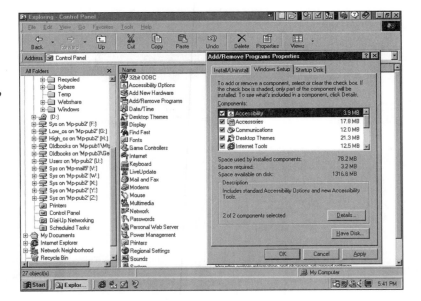

Accessibility Options

Windows 98 offers many standard options to make a desktop more usable. You can vary the font size and the screen resolution and even make the fonts dynamically resize themselves in those programs so enabled. For the latter, click the Custom button (refer to

Figure 8.14) and slide the ruler shown in Figure 8.32 to enlarge or decrease the font size within applications, somewhat independently of screen resolution. You can also directly enter a font scale in the combo box. This allows you to have, for example, your enabled applications show large fonts within themselves while Windows 98 itself uses a very high screen resolution.

FIGURE 8.32.

You can tell Windows 98 to enlarge the fonts used by enabled applications somewhat independently of its screen resolution.

You can also use the Sounds applet within Control Panel to add noise to system and application events. Adding sounds to events can be useful for those who have some visual impairment and can be amusing for all. Figure 8.33 shows the Sounds applet launched and browsing for a sound to attach to the Default sound Windows event. By scrolling through the Events list box shown in Figure 8.33, you can locate and assign sounds to many Windows occurrences. Some applications such as Microsoft Office 97 come with their own sounds and sound attachments.

FIGURE 8.33.

Aural annunciation of system and application events can be useful and amusing or both.

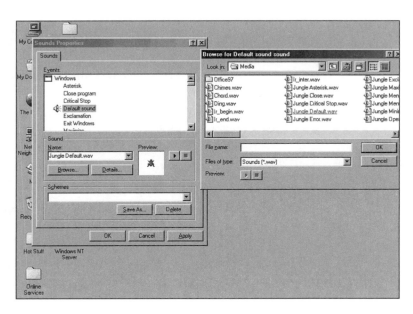

The real meat of Accessibility Windows 98 style comes from the Accessibility Properties dialog box in the Control Panel, however (see Figure 8.34). Like most dialog boxes, this one has various tabs, each with specific options.

FIGURE 8.34.

The Accessibility applet is a dialog box with tab options.

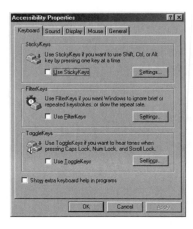

The following sections describe the tabs with a quick explanation of each entry on those tabs.

The Keyboard Tab

The following options are on the Keyboard tab of the Accessibility Properties dialog:

- Use StickyKeys—Enables the sequential rather than simultaneous use of the Ctrl, Alt, and Shift + other keys.
- Use FilterKeys—Enables the filtering or ignoring of quickly doubled keystrokes. Good for spastics or others with shaky hands.
- Use ToggleKeys—Makes a sound when the toggle keys such as Caps Lock, Num Lock, and Scroll Lock are hit.

The Sound Tab

Figure 8.35 shows the Sound tab; its options are described in the following list:

- Use SoundSentry—Flashes the screen to make a visual clue when a system makes a sound. This is good for those with sharp eyes but dull ears.
- Use ShowSounds—This is a closed-captioned TV, Windows 98-style. When an enabled application makes a sound, Windows can display text with the sound spelled out.

FIGURE 8.35.

The Sound tab extends the Sounds applet for those with special needs.

8

The Display Tab

The High Contrast option on the Display tab configures your machine for a high-contrast, high-visibility color scheme. You can choose a predetermined screen (from Microsoft or one you make) or just choose white on black or black on white. Figure 8.36 shows the results of applying a high-contrast scheme in Explorer. As you can see, this also enlarges the system font somewhat.

FIGURE 8.36.

When Windows 98 says high contrast, it means high contrast.

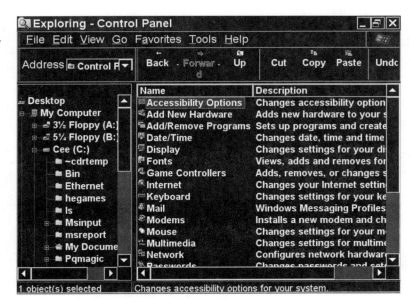

The Mouse Tab

The MouseKeys option is a holdover from Microsoft Natural Keyboard development. It enables the use of the arrow keys on the keyboard to move the mouse about. This is a handy option for those with problems gripping, such as arthritis sufferers. People who have trouble with mice sometimes find trackballs to be a good alternative.

The General Tab

The following options are on the General tab of the Accessibility Properties dialog:

- Automatic Reset—Turns off special access features after a certain period of computer idle time.
- Notification—Makes a sound when an access feature turns on or off or when activating an access feature.
- SerialKey devices—Adds support for devices attached through alternative input hardware such as serial ports.

System Sounds

Windows 98 enables user-defined sounds to be attached to various system events. Certain applications such as Exchange and Office also enable custom sounds to play on predetermined events.

To see the dialog box responsible for sound assignment, open the Sounds applet in the Control Panel. You must have audio hardware installed in your computer to use the Sounds applet. Figure 8.37 shows the Sounds Properties dialog box.

FIGURE 8.37.

The Sounds Properties dialog box is where you assign sounds to system and application events.

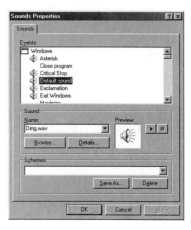

To assign a sound to an event, first locate that event by scrolling down the list box. The first section of the list box shown in Figure 8.37 has Windows 98 events. Further down you can see (if you have them installed) events applying to application programs such as Office.

After you've located the event you want to assign a sound to, highlight it by clicking on it with your mouse and then click the Browse button to locate a .wav file (Windows sound) to attach to that event. The Details button gives details about the highlighted sound, but not the event. You have to speculate on when Windows or its applications will trigger specific events. After a little experimentation, you'll learn the vaguely named events. Most events, such as Exit Windows, are self-evident as to their triggering points.

After you've located the .wav file you want to associate with an event, click the Play Sound button in the dialog box. Figure 8.38 shows browsing for a .wav file. The figure has the Play Sound button circled in white. The Play Sound button for sounds already associated in the Sounds Properties dialog box is also circled, but in black.

FIGURE 8.38.

The Browse for Sound dialog box has a Play Sound button to let you play the highlighted sound.

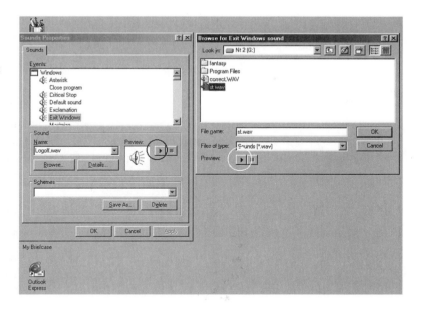

You can create your own sounds either using your microphone or from other sources such as video or audio tapes. Keep in mind that commercial audio sources are protected by copyrights. Those copyrights might not show up in the Details tab. Although this isn't a concern for most when it comes to private computers, it is something to keep in mind if you get it into your head to distribute what you think is a neat .wav file. This is doubly important if you are paid for this distribution.

To associate the sound file with the event, highlight the sound and click OK. To hear installed sounds, highlight the event in the dialog box shown in Figure 8.37 or with the Browse dialog box in Figure 8.38 and click its Play Sound button.

Figure 8.39 shows the Sound Recorder applet recording via microphone. You need a microphone attached to your sound interface to use the Sound Recorder. Look for the Sound Recorder applet in Start | Programs | Accessories | Entertainment. If you don't see it, you can install it from the distribution CD-ROM through Control Panel | Add/Remove Programs | Windows Setup.

FIGURE 8.39.

The Sound Recorder applet is Windows 98's answer to karaoke.

You can use predefined or your own Sound Schemes by pulling down the combo box at the bottom of the Sounds Properties dialog box. Microsoft supplies several sound schemes. If your combo box is empty, you don't have these installed but can obtain them by the usual route of Control Panel | Add/Remove Programs | Windows Setup.

Summary

You can change the look and feel of the Windows 98 GUI with many variations. The most obvious and often-used change is in Display. You can access the Display options through the context menu on the desktop or through the Control Panel. Some setups include a Tray icon for starting the Display applet as well.

Display enables you to change the colors, color depth, resolution, and font size of your desktop. You can do this either by making up a custom scheme or using one of the prepackaged schemes that come with Windows 98 or by modifying a prepackaged scheme.

You can also change the desktop icons through the Display applet, but icons for short-cuts, desktop or not, need to be changed on the Properties sheet for that shortcut.

You can change the programs on the Start | Programs menu by opening the program group, using Windows Explorer, or choosing Explore on the context menu of the Start button. Operations in the opened or explored Start menu are the same as under the Windows Explorer.

8

The Control Panel is where most configuration applets reside. The contents of any Control Panel depend on the Windows 98 options installed and, in some cases, the specific applications installed. The most used applets within the Control Panel are the Add/Remove Programs and Display. You can launch Display through the Control Panel, through the context menu of the desktop, or in some cases, through the Tray. Add/Remove Programs enables the addition of programs, their components, and Windows 98's optional extensions. It also enables the creation of an Emergency Startup Disk. Because bad happens, all computers should have a write-protected ESD on hand.

The most variant of Windows 98's options are available only through the Accessibility Options applet in the Control Panel. This applet enables configuration for those with special needs.

Workshop

To wrap up the day, you can review terms from the chapter, see the answers to some commonly asked questions, and practice what you've learned. You can find the answers to the exercises in Appendix A, "Answers."

Terminology Review

aspect ratio—The ratio of height to width.

color depth—How many bits Windows uses to display colors. The greater the bit depth, the more total colors in the palette, up to a theoretical total of almost 17 million (2^{24} = 16.7 million) colors at 24 bits. Some adapters refer to 24-bit depth as true color or 32-bit color. Actually, the extra 8 bits do other things (such as control of alpha) than define more colors.

palette—The array of colors Windows has to choose from for its display.

`Progman.exe`—An alternative shell or GUI that gives Windows 98 the look and feel of the Windows 3.x series.

resolution—The amount of dots, horizontally and vertically, in your monitor. IBM-style PCs use a 4:3 or $1^{1}/_{3}$:1 aspect ratio.

Sound Recorder—An applet for making your own sound files (`.wav`).

Q&A

Q **All the color schemes I try to make come out looking bizarre. How can I make a decent color scheme, given my limited (nonexistent, really) artistic ability?**

A Open the Desktop Properties dialog box. Choose the Appearance tab and pull down the Scheme combo box. Choose from one of Microsoft's predefined color schemes. Some are quite attractive. All are highly functional. Note that some don't work well at low color depths.

Q **How can I add sounds to my Microsoft Office program?**

A The easiest way is to run the sounds.exe program from the Office distribution CD-ROM. You also need to activate the sound feedback option in Office applications.

Q **Can I remove the My Computer icon from my desktop?**

A Yes, but to truly remove it, you must do a Registry hack that might have adverse consequences. A better solution to actual removal is to hide the icon (and other icons) by choosing Web view and setting the Hide Icons When Desktop Is Viewed as Web Page option in the Folder Options dialog box.

Q **Can I use TWEAKUI to modify my Windows 98?**

A This is an unsupported tool, so if it gets you in trouble, don't call Microsoft for help. However, many people are happily running late versions of TWEAKUI under Windows 98 and seeing few or no problems. Proceed if you want to, but at your own risk.

Exercises

1. Try out some of the Display settings by changing the Windows background to a nice, partially cloudy sky. (Hint: Windows comes with a cloudy bitmap.)

2. It's very important to maintain an up-to-date Windows startup disk so that you can easily recover from problems that can occur. Make an updated startup disk.

DAY 9

Managing Hardware

by Michael Hart

Sooner or later, you're going to change a piece of hardware on your computer. This might be something you want to do, such as adding a larger, or additional, hard drive, a tape backup, a new graphic card, or a faster modem. Or, it might be something you don't want to do—a hard drive crash or component failure could require it. In either case, you don't want to dive in blindly.

Yet, despite my cautionary warning, manipulating your own hardware isn't a task that must be reserved for the specialists. With a little care and preparation, you will be able to perform all but the most demanding hardware tasks required. This chapter covers several aspects of the hardware realm. You'll receive some background on hardware by learning about legacy devices, Plug and Play devices, hard drives, controllers, modems, and graphics cards and perform those tasks that you're most likely to have to do on your own. This chapter covers

- New generation hardware
- Plug and Play hardware

- Installing Plug and Play and non–Plug and Play devices
- Storage device controllers
- Installing a disk drive
- Parallel port peripheral installations
- TV devices
- Installing memory, common peripherals, and multiple monitors
- Control Panel hardware controls

Note Prices referenced in this chapter are current estimates at the time of publication. Actual prices of particular items might vary depending on your vendor.

Using a Professional Service to Upgrade Your Computer

Now, I recognize that for some of you the prospect of rounding up suitable tools, opening the case, and digging into the heart of your computer sounds about as much fun as watching paint dry; that's okay. Just about anywhere you're likely to go to buy new hardware for your PC will be more than happy to install your new toys for a nominal fee, usually $30–80, depending on the upgrade. If you don't have the time or desire to do it yourself, follow this handy-dandy checklist for upgrading:

1. BACK UP YOUR SYSTEM!!
2. If you skipped step 1, go directly to step 1. Anywhere you go to have your system upgraded, there will be a sign, sometimes with big letters, sometimes with fine print, saying that they are not responsible for your data.
3. With the PC power off, unplug all the cables from the machine.
4. Safely transport to your computer upgrade store of choice. I don't recommend strapping it onto the back of your motorcycle.
5. Purchase your upgrade.
6. Drop the upgrade hardware and computer at the computer service desk.
7. When you return to pick up your computer, ask to see it working. Make sure you check that the new stuff works. It's much more difficult to get them to fix something if you take the computer home first and then come back and say something isn't working.

8. When you get the computer home, reconnect everything and verify again that everything works.

See Day 12, "Maintaining Your System," for more information on backing up your system.

Note

Before making any changes to your system, you'll also want to be sure that you have an Emergency Startup Disk (also called an Emergency Boot Disk [EBD]), just in case you encounter any boot problems after making your changes. See Day 2, "Installing Windows 98," and Day 8, "Customizing Windows 98," for information on creating an EBD.

9

Regardless of whether you're going to enlist the help of a service center or the 14-year-old neighborhood whiz kid, you'll find helpful and interesting information in this chapter.

Preparing to Upgrade Your Computer on Your Own

If you're more of the do-it-yourself type, you'll need the following items:

- Small and medium Phillips screwdrivers
- Small and medium flat blade screwdrivers
- A pair of small needle-nose pliers
- An antistatic wristband or mat, if available

Let's talk about static for a second. Static electricity (yes, that stuff that makes your hair stand up and tickles your fingers when you reach for the doorknob in the winter) is death to the electronic components in your computer. Static electricity discharges, which seem just zzzzzt! little shocks, can actually be thousands of volts—more than enough to zap any component in your computer.

Using a static wrist strap or static mat, you can avoid wrecking your computer. A static wrist strap is just a stretchy bracelet with a metal button that touches your skin, connected to a length of wire with an alligator clip on the end. Put the bracelet on, with the metal button touching your skin, and clip the alligator clip onto the frame of your computer. This will ground out any static buildup. If you don't have a wrist strap or mat (either should run less than $20), just be sure to frequently touch the metal frame of your computer while working with boards.

An Overview of Hardware

Because you're going to have your hands right in the guts of it all, and you're going to be making purchasing decisions based on the equipment you have, you might as well know just what the heck all these things are. As you've no doubt learned, the computer industry loves TLAs (Three Letter Acronyms).

Let's start with the box itself, the computer. Way back, there was the original PC—big, heavy, built like a tank, 10 grand. Then there were the XT and the AT. Since the AT, there have been no real computer designations; now we identify our machines by their processors: 386, 486, Pentium, and so on. If you're running Windows 98 (and you are reading this book, right?), you're running at least a 486 computer.

Inside the computer is a bus, which all the adapter cards plug into. The buses—and there are many—all have names. The ISA (Industry Standard Architecture) bus comes in 8- and 16-bit flavors, but the 8-bit is never found in today's PCs. The 16-bit ISA bus, also called the AT bus, hangs on primarily because of the vast number of cards designed to work with it. The next bus to come along was the Micro Channel Architecture bus (MCA) by IBM, which found very little acceptance and faded relatively quickly.

The more successful counterpart to the MCA was the EISA bus (Extended Industry Standard Architecture). Although it was a high speed 32-bit bus, EISA could not meet the demands for bandwidth required by the emerging graphical applications. The VL bus, or VESA Local bus, developed by the Video Electronics Standards Association, was the next bus implemented for PCs. The VL-local bus was very popular for a couple of years (around '93–'94), until the PCI (Peripheral Component Interconnect) bus, designed by Intel, became widely available.

 Note

Bandwidth refers to how much data can be moved in a given time. As an analogy, a highway with a speed limit of 30 miles per hour can handle maybe 10,000 cars per hour. However, that same highway with a speed limit of 65 miles per hour can handle many more cars; it has a higher bandwidth.

ISA bus slots typically run on a clock speed of 8 to 16MHz, VL-bus slots at up to 33MHz, and PCI slots at 66MHz and higher. As you can guess, the higher the clock speed (and the wider the bus), the higher the bandwidth. Almost every computer will have several 16-bit ISA slots. If you have a 486 computer or a 60–120MHz Pentium computer, you'll probably have one or two of the VL bus slots. Newer Pentium computers will probably have just the ISA and PCI slots. Table 9.1 shows what bus types you're likely to have in a personal computer.

TABLE 9.1. COMPUTER TYPES AND LIKELY BUS TYPES.

Type	ISA (8 bit)	ISA (16 bit)	VLB	EISA	PCI
386	Yes	Yes	No	No	No
486	Yes	Yes	Occasionally	Occasionally	No
Early Pentium	Occasionally	Yes	Occasionally	Occasionally	Occasionally
Later Pentium	No	Yes	Occasionally	Occasionally	Yes
Pentium Pro	No	Yes	Occasionally	Occasionally	Yes
Pentium II	No	Yes	No	Occasionally	Yes

Disclaimer: This is a general configuration rule of thumb. Differing configurations are certainly possible.

When you're adding or replacing adapter cards in your PC, you'll need to be sure which bus you have. Many computers have a dual bus structure, for example an ISA bus and a PCI bus. If you have an option when adding cards, I always suggest going with a PCI card whenever possible, except for cards where the additional bus speed doesn't translate into processing speed. As an example, let's look at modems. The fastest modem available today is a 56K modem. Even if you could have that modem transferring data at full speed, its total bandwidth requirements would be well within the capability of the ISA 16-bit bus. Therefore, it wouldn't make a lot of sense to take up a high speed PCI bus slot with a device that will live quite happily in an ISA slot. This, by the way, is why you'll almost never see PCI bus internal modems. You'll definitely want to use PCI cards when choosing graphics cards, drive controllers (IDE or SCSI), or network cards.

The main circuit card inside the computer box is the *motherboard*. On the motherboard reside the central processing unit (CPU), support circuitry, cache memory, main memory, and in modern computers, built-in graphics, disk, or port controllers. The bus itself—that is, the circuitry that manages the bus and the connectors into which you plug the adapter cards—is also a part of the motherboard.

Also found on the motherboard is the BIOS (Basic Input/Output Services) chip. The BIOS stores very low level configuration information necessary for the computer to function. If Windows 98 provides the brains and personality of the computer, think of the BIOS as its DNA. When you make basic changes to the machine such as reconfiguring the memory or changing the ports that are built into the motherboard, the BIOS configuration needs to be changed so everything functions properly.

Connected to the adapters plugged into the motherboard are any disk, floppy, hard, and CD-ROM drives in your system. Hard drives and their controllers come in a number of flavors, which is discussed later in this chapter in the section "Storage Device Controllers."

The last remaining items you'll find inside the case are a power supply and some cables running to the front panel for the switches and lights on the control panel. There you have 15 years of computer history in just a few paragraphs.

An Overview of Plug and Play Hardware

Adding adapter cards to your computer was always a pain in the neck because you needed to know some very specific settings in order for everything to work. Adapter cards needed to have particular IRQ (Interrupt Request) settings, I/O addresses, port settings, memory addresses, or DMA settings before they'd function properly. Naturally, you couldn't just pick these settings out of the blue because you'd often conflict with some other device in the system. So, you'd have to go dig up the list of settings that you wrote down the *last* time you were in the box, assuming you wrote them down. If you didn't, you'd have to run a program to gather some information, and possibly pull out other cards to see what settings they already used. This whole situation became untenable because it was just too much work to add a card in.

Enter the Plug and Play specification. Plug and Play (PnP) is a spec that defines the way adapter cards, motherboards, BIOSes, and software should work together to configure themselves when installed. The idea is that no settings have to be made manually; the computer talks to the cards, they decide who is going to use what setting, and nirvana ensues. Things are never as rosy as the marketers would have you believe, but they're getting there. Many times these days, adding a card to your PC is really a case of Plug and Play—plug it in, reboot, and you're up and running.

The PnP specification actually defines several standards, such as a specification for the BIOS, the ISA devices, the SCSI and IDE devices, the LPT and COM ports, and device drivers.

Task 9.1. Checking If Your Computer Is Plug and Play

If your PC is less than two years old, you've almost definitely got a PnP machine. If your PC is older than that, follow these steps to determine whether or not your PC is PnP compliant:

1. Open the System applet under the Control Panel.
2. On the Device Manager tab, click View Devices By Type.

▼   3. Find System Devices in the list and expand the item. If you see Plug and Play
       BIOS listed, you're the proud owner of a PnP computer (see Figure 9.1).

FIGURE 9.1.

*The Plug and Play
BIOS line listed under
System Devices shows
that this computer is
PnP capable.*

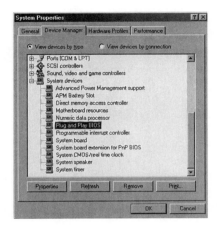

▲

Before You Begin

Before you begin any modifications or changes to your equipment, you'll want to take
some precautions. Despite the effectiveness of Plug and Play technology, sometimes
things happen that require you to back up and start over. If you don't know where you
were before you started, it's hard to return to that point.

There are two things you should definitely do before getting out the screwdriver and
opening the case. The first is to do a backup. Murphy always seems to be right around
the corner, just waiting for an opportunity to ruin your day. Back up. There's nothing
worse than trying to do something, realizing that it's not going to work, returning your
system back to where it was, and then finding out that you've lost all those files you
needed. Arrggh! Make a backup.

The second thing you should do is obtain a listing of what configuration settings are
already used in your computer; this will be a list of what IRQs are already used, what
cards are using what IO addresses and memory ranges, and so on. This is fairly simple to
do, and will not only help you if you need to put things back, but also helps you when
you install.

Task 9.2. Creating a System Summary

To create the configuration list, called a system summary, perform the following steps:

1. Open the System applet on the Control Panel.

2. Click the Device Manager tab.

3. Click the Print button near the bottom of the dialog box. You'll be given another dialog box with the option to print a system summary, a report on the selected device or class, or all devices and a system summary. Select All Devices, ensure that the proper printer is selected, and then click OK. Notice that you can also print to a file if you choose.

   Figure 9.2 shows an edited, condensed version of the system summary. The sections shown are the ones that will be of particular interest if you need to install a legacy card that requires you to set the IRQ, IO, and DMA settings manually.

FIGURE 9.2.

An edited sample of a system summary report showing IRQ, IO port, and DMA information.

```
System Resource Report    - Page: 1
****************** IRQ SUMMARY ******************
IRQ Usage Summary:
    00 - System timer
    01 - Standard 101/102-Key or Microsoft Natural Keyboard
    02 - Programmable interrupt controller
    03 - Communications Port (COM2)
    04 - Communications Port (COM1)
    05 - ALS100 Logical Device 0 Wave Audio Device
    06 - Standard Floppy Disk Controller
    07 - ECP Printer Port (LPT1)
    08 - System CMOS/real time clock
    09 - ALS100 Logical Device 3 External Midi (Mpu401) Device
    13 - Numeric data processor
    14 - Primary IDE controller (dual fifo)
    14 - Intel 82371SB PCI Bus Master IDE Controller
    15 - Intel 82371SB PCI Bus Master IDE Controller
    15 - Secondary IDE controller (dual fifo)
****************** IO PORT SUMMARY ******************
I/O Port Usage Summary:
    0000h-000Fh - Direct memory access controller
    0020h-0021h - Programmable interrupt controller
    0040h-0043h - System timer
...
****************** DMA USAGE SUMMARY ******************
DMA Channel Usage Summary:
    01 - ECP Printer Port (LPT1)
    02 - Standard Floppy Disk Controller
    03 - ALS100 Logical Device 0 Wave Audio Device
    04 - Direct memory access controller
    07 - ALS100 Logical Device 0 Wave Audio Device
****************** MEMORY SUMMARY ******************
640 KB Total Conventional Memory
48668 KB Total Extended Memory
****************** DISK DRIVE INFO ******************
A:  Floppy Drive, 3.5" 1.44M
        80 Cylinders   2 Heads
```

After you've created a system summary, store it away so that you'll have it for reference. Also, whenever you finish making changes to your computer's configuration, rerun the report and store away the new one.

Installing Plug and Play Devices

Installing Plug and Play devices is, when all goes well, an almost trivial process. Even when things don't go so well, it's still not too bad. Why might things not go so well?

With so many different motherboards, adapters, BIOSes, and individual configurations, it's bound to happen. If and when it does, don't panic. Just let the process proceed along as best it can; then try to ascertain the cause after it finishes the installation attempt.

In its simplest incarnation, PnP installation follows these steps:

1. Install the adapter card into the PC.
2. Turn the power on and reboot.
3. Insert the Windows CD-ROM or device driver disk if prompted.
4. Perhaps reboot a final time.

For an example, let's step through the installation of a PnP sound card, the Creative Labs AWE64 PnP. This installation is a representative illustration of most PnP adapter installations.

Task 9.3. Installing a Plug and Play Adapter Card

Before beginning, make sure that you read the section "Before You Begin," earlier in the chapter.

1. With the power off, open the computer case. You'll probably find it easier to remove all cables and lay the computer on its side on a table or desk.

2. Read the manufacturer's instructions. Make any jumper settings that might be required. Although there shouldn't be any jumper settings required to enable the card to work in the computer, there might be other jumper settings that control feature options on the card itself. On this card there were no other jumpers to set.

> **Note**
>
> Jumpers are not a new name for frogs or grasshoppers! *Jumpers* are used to make configuration settings on some circuit cards. Since the introduction of Plug and Play devices, there are fewer and fewer cards that require any jumper settings, but they are certainly still around. A jumper is sort of like a plug that you put onto or remove from a pair of metal pins sticking up from the card. When you place the jumper across two pins, a signal connection is made, telling the card what to do. Frequently, there will be a row of several pairs of metal pins (collectively called a header) in the same location on the board used for making configuration settings. There might also be other individual pairs of metal pins scattered across the card.

3. Locate an open bus slot of the right type. In the case of the AWE64, it's a 16-bit ISA slot. Plug the card in, seating it firmly in the connector.

▼   4. Tighten down the hold down screw. For this particular card installation, I also
         installed an audio cable between the card and the CD-ROM drive.

      5. Reattach all cables to the computer and turn the power on.

      6. During the boot process you might see references to the card being configured by
         the PnP BIOS. For this card, there are no messages. However, the BIOS does dis-
         play a summary of the PnP devices it finds, and the Creative SB AWE64 PnP is
         now listed.

      7. When Windows loads, enter your logon password, if you are normally asked to do
         so. You'll see dialog boxes indicating that Windows has found your new hardware
         and is installing the software for it. This is followed by several other similar dialog
         boxes that indicate the installation of the other devices on the newly installed
         board. On this sound board, there are three devices: the 16-bit audio device, a
         Wavetable device, and a joystick device. You'll be asked to insert your Windows
         CD-ROM.

      8. After Windows resumes loading, the installation is complete. Viewing the System |
         Device Manager tab now shows the devices listed under sound, video, and game
         controllers.

▲ That's about as easy as any installation gets! May all of yours be as smooth.

   You'll notice in Task 9.3 that Windows will ask for the Windows CD-ROM. That's
   because this particular card is one of the hundreds of peripheral adapter cards for which
   drivers are included on the Windows CD-ROM. If your card isn't one of those whose
   drivers are included, you'll be asked to supply a manufacturer's driver disk during step 7.

Installing Non–Plug and Play Devices

   This is the real world, so as you know, it's not all going to be as easy as the Plug and
   Play installation you just covered. When installing non–Plug and Play devices, also
   called legacy devices, things won't go quite as easily and will require a lot more intervention on your part.

   Don't be scared off, though, because it can be done; it just takes more work and some
   preparation. As you saw during the earlier discussion of PnP, the settings that many cards
   need to have configured in order to work are the IRQ, IO address, and DMA level. Some
   cards use all of these, some one or two. When installing these legacy devices, you'll be
   setting these configuration options via jumpers on the board. As you can surmise, reading the installation guide is a critical success factor for this task!

Having the system summary that you prepared in Task 9.1 will be immensely helpful now. For Task 9.4 in this section, you install a legacy network adapter. This card will be used to connect the computer to a network. Even though you haven't yet learned about networking, just think of it as a non-PnP device that needs to be configured and installed.

The particular device that I installed is a generic NE2000-compatible network adapter called a SimpleNet SN2000. This type of adapter is available by mail order or at retailers like CompUSA or Best Buy. If you look at a SimpleNet SN2000 card, you'll notice that there are no jumpers on it. Although this isn't a Plug and Play card, it's sort of a half step between legacy and PnP. On cards like this, a software utility supplied by the manufacturer is used to make the jumper settings. For my card, whatever documentation that might have originally arrived with it had long since been lost. So, I had no idea what the default settings of this card might be.

The general procedure in a case like this and with most legacy cards is to

1. Read the installation instructions.

2. Make reasonable assumptions about which IRQ, I/O, and DMA settings to use.

3. Set the jumpers.

4. Install the card in the computer.

5. Turn the power on and ensure that the card is recognized by the computer.

6. Install any software or drivers needed by the card.

As I said before, on my particular card the jumpers are set using a piece of utility software. So for my installation, I installed the card first and then made the jumper settings using the special software.

Task 9.4. Installing a Legacy Adapter Card

Before beginning the following steps, as always, make sure that you've completed the preparatory steps listed previously in the "Before You Begin" section.

1. Turn off the computer and open the case.

2. Locate an empty slot of the appropriate type. For the SimpleNet SN2000 card, you need a 16-bit ISA slot.

3. Remove the slot covering the case opening for this slot by removing the screw and slot cover.

4. Insert the card carefully into the slot. Press straight down on the card, carefully seating it into the connector. Use the hold down screw to secure the adapter card into the slot.

5. Power up the computer and enable it to boot to Windows. It's possible that you'll receive error messages during the boot process. Continue past them.

(If your card uses a utility program to make software jumper settings, continue here. If your card has actual jumpers, skip to step 9.)

6. Click Start | Shut Down, select Restart in MS-DOS Mode, and then click OK.

> **Tip**
>
> If you can't boot completely into Windows, you can boot directly to DOS. Press the Reset button on your computer to force a cold boot. Press F8 just after you see the memory count, and you'll be presented with the DOS boot menu. Select Command Prompt Only; then press Enter and you'll be booted up to a DOS prompt.

7. From the DOS prompt, run the utility program used to set the configuration parameters.

When running the utility for my NE2000-compatible network card, I saw that it would work on IRQs 3, 4, 5, 9, 10, 11, and 14. I also found out that my card will work on I/O ports 200h, 220h, 240h, 260h, 300h, 320h, 340h, and 360h. My card doesn't use a DMA channel, so I didn't have to worry about configuring that. Using the system summary (refer to Figure 9.2) and looking at the IRQ Usage Summary section, I saw that IRQ 10 was available. Because there were no devices listed as using that IRQ, it was free. Looking at the I/O Port Usage Summary section of the system summary, I saw that 340h wasn't listed, which meant that it too was free and available for use. These seemed like nice numbers, so I decided to set my card to use IRQ 10 and I/O port address 340h.

> **Note**
>
> There's no secret formula for choosing what settings to use. Just see what your card is able to use, find out what isn't currently used on your computer (from the system summary report), and there you are.

8. Having finished using the utility program, power off the computer. It's always a good idea to power down after making hardware changes like this because some cards only check their jumper settings on power up.

9. Turn the power on and boot to Windows again. This time you should have few, if any, error messages. If you do, you've probably got a resource conflict, and should review the configuration settings you chose earlier.

▼ 10. Because this isn't a PnP card, Windows won't detect it; therefore, you have to tell Windows that it's there. To do that, open the Add New Hardware applet in the Control Panel. Click Next twice to move past the Plug and Play detection. You'll then be asked if Windows should search for your new hardware. Most of the time, Windows will find it; if not, you'll be given the opportunity to pick it from a list. If you receive a message that your device was not detected, click the Back button until you return to the choice of selecting the device from a list rather than having it detected automatically.

11. When the detection is finished, a dialog box is displayed that says the detection has finished. Click the Details button just to ensure that the device that Windows found is what you're installing (see Figure 9.3). If not, click the Back button until you are given the choice to select your device.

FIGURE 9.3.

The Add New Hardware Wizard showing the details of the device about to be installed.

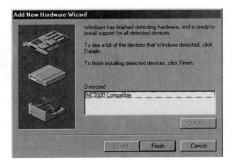

12. Click Finish. You might see another configuration screen like that shown in Figure 9.4. In this case, Windows is showing you the IRQ and I/O port settings. Looking at Figure 9.4, you see that the I/O port setting has # next to it, indicating that it is the current hardware setting. This is expected, as I set the I/O port to that address in step 7. Notice the asterisk (*) next to the IRQ field, which indicates a conflict with some other piece of hardware. By using the up or down buttons, I changed the setting to 10, which is what I configured in step 7. At 10, the asterisk goes away, indicating no more problems.

Note

It's possible that Windows won't recognize your device or won't be able to find a driver for it. If this is the case, you'll be prompted to select a driver. At that time, click the Have Disk button and insert the driver disk from the device's manufacturer.

▼

FIGURE 9.4.

*Properties box for a
legacy device showing
IRQ and I/O port set-
tings.*

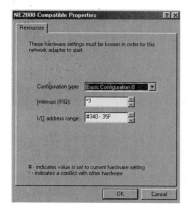

13. Click OK, and Windows suggests that you reboot to finish the setup.

After rebooting, verify the operation of the installed device. Because this installation is a
network adapter, I verified proper operation by accessing other computers on the net-

 work.

Storage Device Controllers

Hard drives are a crucial part of your computer system. Without today's large drives, you
would boot up by swapping 54 floppies in and out!

Note

(Turn on crotchety old man voice here.) "I remember, waaay back, why, computers didn't even have floppies. You had to use switches on the front panel
to enter a series of machine code instructions just to boot the computer. You
young whippersnappers don't know how good you've got it."

This was called *bootstrapping*. The computer looks for instructions to tell it
what to do. The first set of instructions normally tells it where to go to find
the next, more complete set of instructions, finally finding and loading the
operating system. Your computer still does it, except it automatically looks
for drives to bootstrap itself from.

However, you do have drives of all sorts—floppies, hard drives, little drives, big drives,
fast drives, slow drives. No matter what type of drive you have, you also have a drive
controller—a device that not only controls the operation of the drive itself, but also over-
sees the transfer of data to and from the drive.

Controllers are categorized by their type, and drives designed for a certain type of controller will only work with that type of controller. In the days of the original PC, XT, and AT computers, MFM and RLL drives and controllers were the standard. These have since become obsolete and have been replaced by an array of common controller types—IDE, EIDE, SCSI, and a number of SCSI variants (see Table 9.2).

TABLE 9.2. COMMON DRIVE CONTROLLER TYPES.

Type	Name	Throughput	Comments
MFM	Modified Frequency Modulation		Obsolete
RLL	Run Length Limited MFM		Obsolete
IDE	Intelligent (or Integrated) Drive Electronics	3.3MB/sec.	Very common
ATA	AT Attachment	3.3MB/sec.	Equivalent to IDE
EIDE	Enhanced IDE	11MB/sec.	
FAST ATA		11MB/sec.	PIO Mode 3
		13.3MB/sec.	DMA Mode 1
Fast ATA-3		16.6MB/sec.	PIO Mode 4
		16.6MB/sec.	DMA Mode 2
SCSI	Small Computer System Interface	5MB/sec.	8-bit transfers
SCSI Fast		10MB/sec.	8-bit transfers
SCSI Fast Wide		20MB/sec.	16-bit transfers
SCSI Ultra Wide		40MB/sec.	32-bit transfers

If your computer is a mass market, general category machine purchased in the past two to three years, you probably have one of the IDE controller types. If you have a workstation class computer, it's likely that you have a SCSI setup.

Tip

> If you're not sure and you want to know, right now, display the Properties for My Computer, or open the System applet in the Control Panel. On the Device Manager tab, expand the Disk Drives and Hard Disk Controllers lines, and your drive/controller type(s) is displayed.

Is one type better than another? That depends. No one controller type is the worst or best; they all do their jobs. Determining the best will depend on what your particular criteria might be. Is your first criteria cost or performance; drive capacity or selection? Let's spend just a moment to talk about the differences before returning to installation.

There are two main types of controllers on the market today—IDE, short for Integrated (or Intelligent) Drive Electronics, and SCSI, pronounced "scuzzy," short for Small Computer Systems Interface. IDE controllers typically have two channels, a primary and a secondary, each of which will support two drives, a master and a slave. The type of devices supported by IDE controllers are disk drives, CD-ROMs, and some tape devices.

SCSI controllers are a bit more versatile. A SCSI controller actually controls a SCSI bus. You might have up to eight devices on the bus, including the controller. Each device has its own address, or SCSI ID. Unlike IDE, these devices might be of a much wider variety. Besides disk drives, CD-ROMS, and tape drives, SCSI devices can also be scanners or video capture devices.

Both types have a number of improved variants also on the market. On the IDE side, there is the EIDE class. These generally have faster controller throughput and support faster data transfers with faster drives. You'll also hear the terms ATA and ATAPI used; these also refer to IDE. The EIDE equipment, also referred to as ATA-2 or Fast-ATA, supports drives with faster transfer rates, and also supports faster transfers to your computer memory, via PIO Mode 3 or 4, or DMA Mode 1 or 2 transfers.

Note

> *PIO* stands for Programmed Input Output, and is a transfer method where the CPU stops what it is doing and handles the transfer of data between the controller and memory. DMA stands for Direct Memory Access, and is a transfer method where the controller itself handles the data transfer to memory.

Note

> I'm not going to go too deep into all the details, as this book is about Windows 98, not PC industry equipment standards. Just the details on controllers and drives could fill a book. For those who must know more, there are many sources of information available, both in print and on the World Wide Web.

9

On the SCSI side of the market, there is Fast SCSI, Wide SCSI, Fast Wide SCSI, and so on. Each variant has some feature(s) that distinguishes it from the rest. In most cases, performance versus cost will be the deciding factor.

Your typical home market computer will have an IDE or EIDE drive and controller installed. In many cases, especially on the newer machines, the drive controller won't even be a separate controller board, but will be integrated right onto the motherboard. Some higher-end PCs will come with SCSI controllers and drives also.

Whether you're talking SCSI or IDE, you won't obtain optimum performance unless two considerations are also observed. The first is the bus type that the controller is to plug into, and the second is the drive being controlled. The bus type refers to the bus in your computer where you'll actually plug the adapter card in—ISA, VLB, or PCI. The different bus types were covered earlier in this chapter. The second consideration is the drive being controlled. If you buy a Fast ATA controller, hoping to use PIO Mode 4 transfers to achieve 16MB/sec. transfers, but the drive you're controlling is an older drive that only supports a 3MB/sec. transfer rate, guess what your maximum throughput will be?

So, you want to upgrade your drive/controller for enhanced performance; what do you do—EIDE or SCSI? I hate to say it, but the answer again begins, "It depends." In the first place, if you have a newer motherboard, it's very possible that you have an IDE or EIDE controller built in to your motherboard. To check, use the System applet in the Control Panel and look in the Devices list.

You'll have to trade off the cost versus the performance gains. One last thing that might sway you toward SCSI is to consider whether you'll ever want to add any other devices such as external drives, tape backups, or scanners. These devices are all available as SCSI devices, and their installation is exceedingly simple if you already have a SCSI controller installed.

Installing a Disk Drive

It's a classic chicken and egg scenario; which came first, larger drives, or hunger for more storage space? It seems like the larger the drives become, the more stuff you want to store on them, which means you need more space, which leads to larger drives, and, well, you get the picture.

Fortunately, adding a hard drive to your computer is very simple. No matter what type of computer you have, the basic procedure is this:

1. Mount your drive into the PC chassis.
2. Connect the power and data cables.
3. Boot Windows 98.

In 999 out of 1000 cases, Windows 98 will recognize your drive. Even that one in a thousand is easy to fix. Before you can use the drive, it has to be prepared. This means creating one or more partitions on the drive, and then formatting them. The procedure for installing and preparing a new drive will be practically identical, whatever type of drive you may be installing.

There might be one other problem getting your system to recognize the new hard disk. On older machines—most 486s and earlier Pentium systems—the BIOS might not be able to recognize and use all of a large hard disk. Early BIOSes were limited to using 528MB disks. Newer systems, or systems with upgraded BIOS chips, have no problems recognizing and using all the available capacity of today's large drives. Fear not though. The drive manufacturers include software in the form of a patch or driver that enables these older machines to use the newer, larger disk drives. Usually, the installation disks that come with the drives have a utility program that detects whether or not your machine needs to have the additional software loaded and advises you what to do.

The following example is the process used to add another hard drive, a slave, to an existing EIDE controller. In the example, the controller has two channels, each of which is capable of controlling two devices, four in all. One channel is considered the primary channel and the other the secondary. On each channel, one device is considered the master and the other the slave. In this example, the new drive will become the slave device on the primary channel of the controller.

Task 9.5. Adding a Hard Drive

Although the following isn't a difficult process, it might not be appropriate for the faint of heart! If you're unsure whether you *really* want to do this, I suggest you don't. Read through the steps and even open up your computer and visualize where the pieces are and how they hook together just to gain some additional familiarity with your computer.

1. Back up your system. This should always be your first step.
2. Read the manufacturer's instructions. Observe and follow any special notes included in the instructions.
3. Shut down the computer. Remove the power cord. Open the case. You might find it easier to lay the computer on its side. You might also find it easier, especially if

▼   your machine usually sits on the floor, to remove all cables from the PC and work
           on a table or desk.

    4. Using static protection if you have it, remove the drive from its static bag. Make
        any jumper settings that might be required. In this example, we're installing a slave
        drive, and because most drives ship with the settings for a primary, you have to
        move a jumper to indicate that this will be a slave.

    5. Mount the drive into a drive bay. If the drive is a 5 1/4-inch drive, you will only be
        able to mount it into a 5 1/4-inch bay. If it's a 3 1/2-inch drive, you will either
        mount it into a 3 1/2-inch bay or in a 5 1/4-inch bay with a mounting kit. Because
        hard disks don't need to be accessible from outside the case, you won't need to
        remove any faceplate covers from the case. You might want to do this temporarily
        though, to make it easier to place the drive into the bay.

9

Note

> Disk drives actually have two different sizes. When I talk about the size of a
> disk drive being 1.2GB or 500MB, I'm really talking about its *capacity*—how
> much data it will hold. The other size description of a disk drive is its form
> factor. The actual size of the spinning platter inside the drive itself will be
> either 3 1/2-inch or 5 1/4-inch in diameter, and in many notebook drives, it'll
> be as small as 2 1/2-inch inches. All 3 1/2-inch drives fit into a 3 1/2-inch drive
> bay, and all 5 1/4-inch drives fit into 5 1/4-inch drive bays.
>
> Disks might also be referred to by their height or thickness. You'll hear of
> full height, 1/2 height, and 1/3 height drives. The most common these days is
> the 1/2 height, which has a thickness of approximately 1 inch.

    6. The existing drive will have a 40-pin ribbon cable attaching it to the motherboard
        or drive controller. Follow the cable from the connector on the drive toward the
        controller and see if there's another unused connector on the cable. The connector
        could be between the drive and the controller, or after the drive. If there is no sec-
        ond connector, you'll have to replace this cable with a 40-pin IDE drive cable that
        has two drive connectors.

    7. After the drive is mounted, attach the 40-pin IDE cable to the drive connector,
        being careful to observe proper pin 1 orientation. The red stripe on the cable
        should be pointed to the pin 1 end of the connector on the disk drive.

    8. At this point a paradox arises. Inevitably, if you close up the case now, you'll need
        to open it back up to do something—reseat a cable, track down a loose screw, or
        whatever. If you don't close it up now, everything will test out okay, and you'll
        have to disconnect everything to close it up anyway. Your choice. I usually leave
▼   the cover off, test, and then close it up.

▼ 9. Power up. When the POST (Power On Self Test) memory count is complete, press whatever key combination takes you into the BIOS setup for your computer; often just pressing Delete during the boot will do it.

10. In the BIOS setup, tell the computer that the slave device on the primary IDE channel is now installed. Depending on the BIOS, you might have to tell the BIOS what the settings of the drive are—the sector, head, and cylinder count. Most newer BIOSes will have an Auto setting, where they'll automatically detect the drive parameters. For my motherboard, I set the primary channel, secondary device to AUTO Configure.

11. Save your BIOS settings; your computer will usually reboot. During the reboot, you'll probably see it detecting the IDE devices. You should see an indication that your new drive was detected.

12. If you encounter an error, you'll have to verify whatever changes or settings you've made. Verify also that your hardware connections are correct and secure. Unfortunately, there's no way to provide a detailed troubleshooting checklist here, as there are literally thousands of motherboard/drive/controller/BIOS combinations possible.

13. After Windows comes up, open the System Properties box. Click the plus next to Disk Drives, and your new drive should be listed there. Figure 9.5 shows the System Properties of my computer after my new drive was installed. Notice that I've clicked the View Devices by Connection option at the top of the Properties box. Figure 9.5 clearly shows two drives connected to my primary IDE controller.

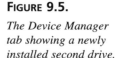
FIGURE 9.5.

The Device Manager tab showing a newly installed second drive.

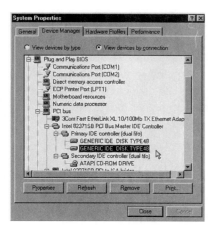

▼ Figure 9.6 shows the Settings tab of the Properties box for the second drive. Notice that the Current Drive Letter Assignment box, near the middle of the dialog, is

▼ blank. This indicates that Windows has not assigned a drive letter to the new drive
   and that you therefore cannot use it yet.

FIGURE 9.6.

*The Properties box for
the new drive.*

14. Click Start | Shutdown | Restart in MS-DOS Mode. When the DOS prompt comes
    up, type **FDISK**. You'll see a screen of information from the FDISK program asking
    if you want to enable large disk support. Answering Yes here will turn on FAT32
    support for the new disk. Even if you choose No, you can later convert this disk to
    FAT32 if you want. I answered No.

15. At the next menu, select 5—Change Current Fixed Disk Drive. You'll see a listing
    of the drives in your system; your C drive should be listed as Disk 1. Disk 2, the
    new one, won't have a drive letter next to it, and the Free column will display the
    same number as the Mbytes column. The Usage column will have a blank. Type **2**
    to select the new drive. Any settings you make from now on will pertain to the
    new drive.

16. Next, you have to create a primary DOS partition on the new drive. Select option
    1—Create Primary DOS Partition. FDISK will quickly verify the drive's surface
    integrity, and then ask if you want to use the maximum available size for a primary
    DOS partition; answer Y. After verifying the disk again, it will create the partition
    and so indicate. FDISK also indicates that drive letters have been changed or added.
    Press Esc to return to the previous menu.

17. To verify the new drive letters, select Change Current Fixed Disk Drive (option 5)
    again. This time in the drive list, you'll see both your C drive and the newly parti-
    tioned D drive. Press Esc twice to leave FDISK. The last FDISK message tells you
▼ that you must reboot for changes to take effect.

▼   18. Reboot your PC. When Windows 98 appears, open My Computer using Explorer and navigate to the new D: drive. Trying to open the drive will display a warning dialog box like that shown in Figure 9.7, indicating that there is a problem with the drive. The problem is that the drive hasn't been formatted for use yet.

FIGURE 9.7.

The warning dialog that comes up when you try to access a new drive that hasn't been formatted yet.

19. Right-click on the drive; then select Format from the context menu. On the Format dialog box, select Full Format and then OK. You'll see a message that all data will be lost. Click OK.

20. When Format finishes, roughly two seconds later, you'll see a summary like the one shown in Figure 9.8. You'll also be advised to run ScanDisk to verify the surface of the disk. A Help page will be opened with instructions and a link to start ScanDisk. Don't skip this step; if there are any problems with the drive, you want to know now, before you start loading it up with data.

FIGURE 9.8.

Summary information after formatting the new drive.

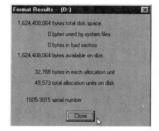

▲   That's it. Your new disk drive is ready for use. Don't forget to add your new D: drive into your Backup jobs. If you're not running regular backups, I'll let you slide, this time; be sure to pay extra attention on Day 12.

Just one last note about adding IDE drives. When you are running two IDE devices on the same channel, as master and slave, you might be lowering your overall performance to that of the slowest device. Some IDE controllers (more so the older ones) can't do separate timings for same-channel devices. In other words, they can't talk at high speed to the fast device and low speed to the slower device, so they talk at slow speed to both devices. If you have a hard disk and a CD-ROM on the same controller, you could be slowing the hard disk way down.

Also, with two devices on the same channel, only one device can be talking to the controller at a time; the other must wait patiently until the controller is free to talk to it.

Taking these two points into consideration, you might want to change the way your IDE devices are configured and use both controller channels. Your only cost will be some time and an additional IDE drive cable, perhaps $10. See Table 9.3 for a matrix of configuration options.

TABLE 9.3. IDE DRIVE AND CHANNEL CONFIGURATION ALTERNATIVES.

Configuration Number	If You Have Hard Disks	If You Have a CD-ROM	Comments
1 (Default)	1	1	Both the hard disk and the CD-ROM are connected to the primary channel of the controller, with the hard disk being the master device and the CD-ROM being the slave device. PC vendors will usually do this because it saves them work and the cost of an extra IDE cable.
2	1	1	Put each device on its own channel. Because the hard disk and the CD-ROM transfer data at different speeds, putting the hard disk on the primary controller channel (as the master device) and the CD-ROM on the secondary channel (as master on that channel) might improve your overall disk performance.
3	2	1	As with configuration 2, put both hard disks on the primary channel, with the slower CD-ROM on the secondary.

If you decide you want to reconfigure your IDE drives onto their own channels on the controller, perform the steps in Task 9.6.

Task 9.6. Reconfiguring IDE Devices onto Separate Controller Channels

As always, remember to back up before beginning.

1. Use the Device Manager tab of the System applet to verify that you have a dual channel IDE controller.

2. Decide which IDE devices will reside on the primary channel, and if more that one device, which device will be the master. Do the same for the secondary channel.

▼   3. Power down your system; disconnect cables as required. Open up your computer.

4. Identify your IDE controller, whether it's an adapter card or built in to the motherboard. Use the documentation to identify the primary and secondary channel connectors. The primary channel will already have a 40-pin ribbon cable connected to it.

5. If more than one device will be attached to either channel, verify that the IDE cables you have (you might need to purchase another cable for the secondary channel) enable the connection of two drives.

6. Using the manufacturer's documentation for your drives, set the Master/Slave jumper to Master for the devices that will be the master devices on each channel.

7. Set the Master/Slave jumpers to Slave for the slave devices on each channel.

8. If it's not already installed, install an IDE cable to the primary channel connector on the IDE controller. Plug the connectors on the other end of the cable into the data connectors on the master and slave devices. Order doesn't matter; either connector can connect to either drive.

9. Install the cable for the secondary channel in the same fashion.

10. Reconnect cables and power. Power up and reboot.

11. Verify proper configuration using the Device Manager tab of the System Properties box.

Adding a SCSI drive to your system will be roughly similar. The primary difference will be that, instead of setting a drive to be a master or slave and then determining which channel to connect the drive to, SCSI devices have an ID configured—an address. The SCSI device will have a SCSI ID setting on it, either via jumpers or a twist or click control, and you just set the ID of this device to an unused number on the SCSI bus. If you're not sure what IDs are in use, you can check the properties of the SCSI devices in System Properties. You must also use FDISK on SCSI disk drives and format them before
▲   using them with Windows.

Parallel Port Peripheral Installations

Over the past few years, the market for add-on peripherals that connect not to a specific controller board in the PC but connect instead to the parallel port has grown from nothing to a plethora of devices. Now you can obtain almost any kind of low-cost peripheral in a parallel port version.

These devices are typically low cost, serve specific functions, and are consumer oriented. I believe the popularity of these devices derives from the same problem that Plug and Play is intended to solve—the difficulty the average computer user encounters when installing boards into his computer. The parallel port devices are easy to configure, don't require opening the case, and can be removed in a flash.

Popular parallel port devices range from tape backup devices like the Iomega Ditto series or the Sony StorStation tape drive, to video capture gizmos like the Snappy, to page scanners like the PaperPort, to removable disk drives like the 100MB Iomega Zip drive or the Syquest EZ135. These devices all share common characteristics that make them attractive to consumers; they're cheap (less than $200), easy to attach to the computer, don't interfere with printing, and provide reasonable functionality.

The downside of parallel port devices probably won't be noticed by most consumers. Not, at least, until they attempt to attach that PaperPort and find their Zip drive already plugged there. Most parallel port devices support printer pass-through (for example, plugging your printer into your Zip drive, which is plugged into the parallel port), but whether other devices will work in tandem is a hit-or-miss proposition. The usual answer is no.

Hooking up a parallel port device is even simpler than the best of the PnP card installations. For this example, I hooked up an Iomega 100MB Zip drive to my computer.

Task 9.7. Hooking Up a Parallel Port Device

My standard disclaimer about backing up actually might not apply here. The risk factor when installing a parallel port device is pretty low because you're not even opening the case. However, backing up before making changes of any sort is a good habit.

1. Shut down your computer and turn the power off.

2. If you have a printer hooked up to the parallel port, which might be marked with a printer icon, Parallel, or LPT1 on the back of your computer, remove it.

3. Plug the computer end of the Zip drive cable into the parallel port. Finger tighten the hold down knobs.

4. Connect the other end of the Zip cable to the back of the Zip drive, observing the markings on the cable and the back of the drive.

5. Connect your printer cable to the printer port on the back of the Zip drive.

6. Insert the power connector into the proper receptacle on the side of the Zip. Plug the AC adapter into an AC outlet.

7. Turn on your computer. Log on when Windows starts, if required.

8. Insert your Zip installation floppy. Using Explorer, find and double-click Setup.exe on the installation disk, or click Start | Run and type **A:\Setup.exe**.

▼   9. Follow the directions from the setup program. You'll see it assign a drive letter to your Zip drive.

10. Finally, you'll be asked to remove the floppy so your computer can reboot. When it does, log back on.

11. Open Explorer or My Computer, and you'll see your new icon for the Zip, labeled Removable Disk.

Adding this particular parallel port device adds a SCSI Controller device to your system. To see it, open the System applet under the Control Panel. On the Device Manager tab, find SCSI Controllers and expand it. You'll see Iomega Parallel Port Zip Interface, listed as shown in Figure 9.9.

FIGURE 9.9.

Iomega Parallel Port Zip Interface is listed as a SCSI adapter.

▲

TV Devices

Isn't modern technology wonderful? With today's add-in peripheral cards, it's now possible to turn a $2,000 computer into a $200 television. But seriously, there are some fantastic video capabilities just $200–300 away from your computer. There are many add-in cards available today that enable you to view TV channels (either cable or broadcast) on your computer monitor, as well as enabling you to capture full motion video for later playback, capture stills from the video, and even hook up your camcorder or digital camera to capture video input from those devices.

Before you become overly enthused about the idea of getting rid of your VCR and using the computer to record your favorite TV shows, let's look at some numbers. The average hard disk in the average home computer is about a 1.2GB disk, with perhaps 50% free space, or 600MB. A DVD (digital versatile disc) can hold up to 4.7GB of data—enough for about 110 minutes of video. That works out to roughly 42MB per minute of video, which means your 600MB of free space will store maybe 14 minutes of *Star Trek*.

On the other hand, being able to keep a small video window running on your desktop (I like to watch CNN) while working, especially when running multiple monitors (covered later in this chapter) is pretty spiffy.

There are several television/video boards available currently, with more becoming available all the time. As of this writing, the only fully supported TV board under Windows 98 is the ATI All-In-Wonder card. However, by the time you read this, other vendors will have released Windows 98–compatible products also.

Note When using a TV tuner type card, it must usually be installed as the primary display adapter. Most video cards will not operate as secondary adapters.

Installing Memory

I won't spend much time on installing memory, even though it's one of the best upgrades you can get. Despite the requirements list on the side of the Windows box that says it runs in 16MB of memory, don't do it if you value your sanity. Memory is one case where more, much more, is always better.

If you're not happy with the performance of your computer and you have 16MB of memory or less, don't spend money upgrading to a faster CPU or a new motherboard or a better hard drive: Get more memory. Sixteen megabytes is the practical low-end limit for memory when running Windows. You'll see a phenomenal improvement moving from 8MB to 16MB; for about $25 you can't find a better deal anywhere. Moving from 16MB to 32MB will cost you about $50 and yield a similar performance increase. Unless you run several memory-intensive applications, you might see little apparent performance enhancement upgrading from 32MB to 64MB or more.

Tip My advice is to upgrade to 32MB if at all possible. Future versions of software will always require more, not less, memory.

When you go out to purchase a new machine and you're trying to decide what to buy, I recommend you take a slightly slower processor with more memory than a faster processor with less memory. You always pay a premium for the faster processor anyway, so save that money and spend it on memory instead.

It's almost impossible to tell you what kind of memory to get for your machine; once again, there are too many variables to say authoritatively. However, the following general rules apply. If your computer is a 486 or more than two years old, you probably need 30 pin SIMMs (single inline memory modules) and can install them singly or in pairs. If you have a Pentium class machine that's less than two years old, you probably need 72 pin SIMMs, which must be installed in pairs.

Newer motherboards might also have a 168 pin DIMM (dual inline memory module) slot. Even though they're named Dual, they actually look just like the SIMMs, but longer. These DIMM slots usually appear solo (although occasionally in pairs), along with the SIMM slots. The DIMM slot is designed to take a single, high capacity DIMM; typical DIMM capacities start at 16MB, with 32MB and 64MB common and 128MB readily available.

There are other options you might need to know before purchasing your memory expansion, such as the memory speed (generally 60ns or faster) and standard versus EDO memory, or with parity. As a rule of thumb, 72 pin SIMMs, 60ns, EDO should do, but again, I can't caution you enough to verify for your computer. If need be, take one of your SIMMs, along with the make and model of your computer, with you when you go to purchase your memory. The technical support people at the computer store should be able to assist you in obtaining the proper memory.

Most newer motherboards have four 72 pin SIMM slots; a few have six, and even fewer have eight. As mentioned previously, SIMMs must be installed in pairs. Because of this and the limited number of SIMM slots, it's entirely possible that you might have to replace memory that you already have, ending up with unused memory after your upgrade.

For example, say you have 8MB in your computer right now, and you want to upgrade to 16MB. Knowing what you know already, you can guess that your machine has two 4MB SIMMs in it. You should only have to purchase two more 4MB SIMMs to bring yourself up to the desired 16MB total. You open the case, only to discover that all four SIMM slots have SIMMs present. Hmmm, you think to yourself, I guess that means I have four 2MB SIMMs. If you take out two 2MB SIMMs and replace them with two 4MB SIMMs, you'll only have 12MB. To get to 16MB, you'd have to pull all four and replace them with either four 4MB SIMMs (not a good idea, as you'll run into the same problem again if you decide to upgrade to 32MB or higher), or two 8MB SIMMs, the recommended solution. In the end, you'll have paid for 16MB of memory and have 8MB of unusable (to you) SIMMs. All's not forsaken, though, because that unused memory has value; you might be able to sell it or trade it in. Don't just throw it away! (I'd rather you send it to me than throw it away!)

Task 9.8. Upgrading Your Memory

If you're not sure what kind of memory you need, take an existing SIMM out of your system and show it to the technician where you purchase your upgrade. Be sure to also tell him the make and model of your computer so that he can look it up in a cross-reference to verify.

1. Use a static strap or work mat if you have one.

2. Power down your computer. Unplug it.

3. Open the case and lay the computer on its side if necessary so the motherboard is at the bottom.

4. You might find it necessary to remove adapter cards or internal cables from their motherboard connectors to access the SIMMs. If you must do so, be sure to mark not only where each cable came from, but the orientation of pin 1—the red stripe at one edge of the cable.

5. SIMMs have a spring-loaded holding clip at each edge of the motherboard connector. A slight pressure on each clip, in the outward direction, will release the SIMM, and it will lay forward or back in the slot.

6. After the SIMM has moved, gently pull it free of the slot. Pull it straight up.

7. Before turning the SIMM, look at the bottom edge (that came out of the connector). You'll notice a notch cut out that goes to the left or right of center. Remember which way the notch is oriented.

8. If you're taking the SIMM to the computer store, place it into a static protective bag if you have one. Handle the SIMM only by the short edges, not the plated connector edge.

9. When installing SIMMs, note that the connector is keyed, so it only fits in one way. Hold the SIMM with the notch in the bottom edge oriented in the same direction as it was when you removed it in step 7. If you didn't remove any, try to orient the SIMMs the same based on the way the chips are mounted to the SIMM. If that doesn't work, try one way, then the other. Just be gentle; when it's right, it'll slip right in.

10. When installing the SIMM, slide it into the connector at about a 45 degree angle. Orient it end-to-end so it seats properly; then, lift gently, and when it is upright you should feel and hear the clips on each end click into place.

11. You'll need to install the SIMMs in sequence based on the way they tilt when installing into the socket. You might have to remove the ones still installed so you can tilt, install, and then lift it. Click! It's installed.

▼ 12. Repeat for any remaining SIMMs.

13. When finished, reinstall any adapter cards you might have had to remove. Reconnect any cables you might have had to disconnect to gain access to the memory.

14. Verify that everything is secure; then close up the case, reconnect the cables, plug it in, and power it up.

15. Watch the POST (Power On Self Test) and verify that the memory count is correct. On some older BIOSes you might have to enter the BIOS setup to configure the new memory amount. If the memory count is incorrect, turn off your machine, open it up, and verify that everything inside is correctly installed.

16. When Windows finishes booting and you've logged on, call up the System proper-ties. On the front tab you'll see an updated memory count in the lower-right corner,
▲ under the Computer section.

Installing Common Peripherals

I've already talked about installing Plug and Play and legacy devices. I won't rehash every possible type of adapter installation. What I do want to mention here are some generalities.

The common types of peripherals that you might install include internal modems, video graphics cards, network cards, and additional port controllers. A short word about each is in order.

Modems are generally 16-bit ISA devices. Newer ones will be PnP, so they'll automati-cally configure themselves to an unused COM port. Very seldom will Windows or any other software ever have trouble locating such a modem. The only problem you might run into is a case in which a modem configures itself onto a COM port that's already in use. This normally won't happen, but it could. The symptom will just be that the soft-ware can't find the modem; your computer could occasionally lock up, too. In a case like this, you'll have to find and disable the other COM port manually. Many times, the offending port will be a built-in (on the motherboard) COM port, and it can be disabled from the BIOS setup program.

If you're upgrading your video card or installing another one, go with a PCI card if at all possible. Good graphics demand bandwidth, the more the better, and PCI has the band-width. Also, if you want to run multiple monitors (see the next section) PCI graphics cards are required. Graphics cards tend to be have good drivers and good PnP support. Video drivers also are updated fairly frequently, so you'll want to keep an occasional eye on the manufacturers' Web sites.

Note

For those gamers out there or those wishing to move to 3D graphics applications, you might have seen some video cards that enable the addition of companion cards or daughterboards to enhance the video cards' performance and capabilities. My personal preference would be to just purchase a new video card rather than attempt to prolong the life of an older card.

9

Network cards are harder to generalize. If you're installing a home or small office LAN (see Day 20, "Windows 98 Networking"), the cheaper ISA cards (at least 16 bit, not 8 bit) are hard to pass up. For larger office environments, or when network throughput is important, splurge and get the PCI-based card when possible. It will have superior performance and probably be PnP also.

Lastly, you might find you need additional serial (COM) or parallel (LPT) ports. ISA bus cards that support additional ports, in almost any number and combination, are widely available. These cards will generally be 16-bit ISA; you might find one on a PCI card, but I doubt seriously that you'll need that bandwidth for those ports. Save your PCI slots for the bandwidth hungry cards like disk controllers, video controllers, and network cards.

Installing Multiple Monitors

One of the really nifty features of Windows 98 is its capability to support multiple graphics cards and multiple monitors. Can't afford that 21-inch monitor? No problem; just install two 15-inch or 17-inch monitors, for less money, and get more desktop area! The possibilities for a little bragging about how cool this little feature is are nearly endless. Just don't go mouthing off to any Macintosh fans though; they'll tell you that they've had the capability for multiple monitors for years now. Oh well, better late than never, eh?

But seriously, you might well ask why would you ever need two (or more) monitors. There are several uses that come to mind:

- Data monitoring, perhaps in financial applications, where you just don't have enough screen real estate to keep all the windows visible that you need to be able to see at one time
- Creating CAD-type drawings, where you might have a large drawing window on one monitor and three-axis drawings on another
- Almost any imaging application where a data window is needed alongside a large image window

- Desktop publishing
- Because you can, it's neat, and you want to

Windows 98 will support up to nine graphics cards and monitors. The toughest thing you're likely to encounter when installing multiple monitors is finding enough space on your desk to place them! The process is fairly simple, and there are only a few restrictions:

- All graphics adapters must be PCI or AGP adapters.
- If your motherboard has a built-in video adapter, the add-in card(s) will become the primary adapter, with the built-in adapter becoming a secondary adapter.
- The adapter in the lowest numbered PCI slot will be the primary adapter.

Beyond those restrictions, the use of multiple monitors is really wide open. You can run different resolutions on each display—for example, 1024×768 in 24-bit true color on your 17-inch monitor and 640×480 in 256-color mode on the 15-inch monitor. You can pull toolbars off the taskbar and dock them on any edge of any monitor, or float them. You can also orient the monitors left to right or top to bottom. A list of supported video chip sets is presented in Table 9.4. You can use any video adapter based on one of the listed chip sets as a secondary display adapter. Other chip sets will undoubtedly become supported as secondary adapters over time, so check the Microsoft Web site for a current list of supported video chip sets.

TABLE 9.4. SUPPORTED VIDEO ADAPTER CHIP SETS FOR USE AS SECONDARY DISPLAYS.

Manufacturer	Chip Set
ATI	Mach64 GX, Rage1 & 2 (VT and greater), 3D Rage Pro
S3	764V+(765), Trio 64V2, ViRGe, Aurora (S3M65)
Cirrus	5436, 7548, 5446
Trident	9658, 9680, 9682, 9385, 9382, 9385-1 PCI

Note

If you have a motherboard with built-in video, you must configure Windows 98 first, before adding any additional display adapters. After successfully setting up Windows, follow the procedure in Task 9.9.

Task 9.9. Installing Multiple Monitors

Enabling multiple-monitor support isn't difficult, but it does take some steps. For this Task, I assume that you're only adding in one additional monitor and graphics adapter:

1. Have your Windows 98 CD-ROM handy. You might need any driver disks that came with your video card(s) also.

2. Shut down Windows 98. Turn off your PC.

3. Install the secondary graphics card into a PCI slot, following the instructions in the previous section and any additional instructions given in the video card's manual.

4. Replace the PC cover. Connect the video cable for the secondary monitor.

5. Power up your PC.

6. Log on to Windows. After the logon, the Found New Hardware dialog pops up, telling you that Windows has found new hardware and is installing the software for it. You might be asked for the Windows CD-ROM or driver disks.

7. When Windows has finished installing the new hardware and continues loading, you'll be asked to reboot. Your secondary monitors won't work until you reboot.

8. When you reboot, you'll see a text message on the secondary monitor, indicating that Windows has successfully initialized the display adapter. If you don't see such a message, display the properties of the adapter. If it won't support multiple monitor use, you'll see a message so indicating, as shown in Figure 9.10.

FIGURE 9.10.

A message indicating that this adapter doesn't support multiple monitor mode.

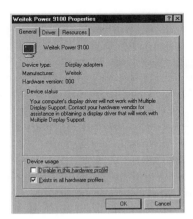

Tip

Bear in mind that it's only your secondary adapter that must provide this multiple-monitor support. If you install an unsupported adapter alongside an already-present supported adapter, Windows 98 will probably be smart enough to switch and make the existing card the secondary adapter.

▼ 9. After logging on, open the Display Properties box by right-clicking on the desktop and selecting Properties. Click the Settings tab; you'll notice right away that the tab is different (see Figure 9.11).

FIGURE 9.11.

The Settings tab now shows two monitors available for use.

10. In the middle of the dialog box, you'll see two monitors numbered 1 and 2. Each is a representation of the desktop area displayed on that monitor. Below that is the Display box, with your primary video adapter listed. Below that are the Colors settings and the Screen Area settings for the primary monitor. Click the image for monitor 2, and you'll see the dialog box shown in Figure 9.12. Click Yes in the dialog box to enable your second monitor.

FIGURE 9.12.

This dialog box asks if you'd like to enable the secondary monitor and describes what can be done with it.

The monitor numbered 2 becomes blue highlighted. Also, the video adapter for this monitor is now listed in the Monitor box; the Colors and Screen Area settings also reflect settings for the secondary monitor. Your secondary monitor has just come to life. Success!

11. To change the properties of the adapter and monitor, besides the screen size and color depth, click the Advanced button.

12 To rearrange the positioning of the monitors, drag the boxes on the Settings tab to
▼ the desired positions and then click Apply.

▼ That's it; you've configured multiple monitors. If you want to disable the second monitor, bring the Display Settings up again, select the second monitor either by clicking its icon or by choosing it from the Display drop-down list, and then uncheck Extend My
▲ Windows Desktop onto This Monitor.

Your monitors can be arranged in any position. Figure 9.11 shows the two monitors side by side, with the primary monitor on the left. You could arrange them in any position, top to bottom, diagonally, right to left; it's your choice. The mouse will transition from one desktop to the other, but only where the two desktops touch.

There are two ways to identify which monitor is the primary and what number the other monitors are. First, with the Display Properties box open to the Settings tab, click and hold on one of the desktop boxes. If you click number 1, the primary display will show a huge number 1 superimposed over the display.

The second way to identify the monitors is on the bottom of the desktop. There will be a listing such as Monitor1 800×600×16 (0,0,800,600). This indicates that this is the primary monitor; its settings are 800×600 pixels, with 16-bit color depth. The numbers in parentheses are the X,Y coordinates of the top-left corner of the monitor (0,0) and the bottom-right corner (800,600). With the monitors set up side by side (as shown earlier in Figure 9.11), the line at the bottom of Monitor 2 reads Monitor2 800×600×16 (800,0,1600,600). This also indicates the resolution and color depth of the second monitor and correctly lists the coordinates of the second monitor—starting at (800,0) top left to (1600,600) bottom right.

If you have a video card such as the ATI All-In-Wonder (or similar) discussed previously, you must realize that the video capabilities of that card will only be available on the monitor hooked to that card. In other words, with the All-In-Wonder installed as the primary video card, the WebTV for Windows window can only be displayed on the monitor connected to the All-In-Wonder card. Although you can drag the window to the second monitor, the TV signal will blank out.

Control Panel Hardware Controls

So far in this chapter, I've covered a great deal of the myriad types of hardware you might choose to add to your computer. In many cases I've discussed the software that goes along with it. What I haven't really discussed yet is the built-in control capability Windows has for many types of hardware.

Many of the hardware add-ins that you'll tack onto your system will come with their own special software applications. The PaperPort page scanner comes with scanning software; the Zip drive comes with Zip Tools, and so on. Let's take a little time to check out the applets on the Control Panel that enable us to control and manipulate your system's hardware.

The Add New Hardware Applet

First and foremost, and one that you've used in this chapter already, is the Add New Hardware applet. For some hardware, especially non-PnP devices, this is where you'll make your system aware of new hardware.

The Display Applet

The next hardware-related applet is Display. You've already visited this applet on Day 8 when you customized your desktop. The tab that really relates to hardware is the Settings tab (Monitors if you're running more than one graphics card and monitor). On the Settings/Monitors tab, you can control the size of your desktop in horizontal and vertical pixels. The amount of memory on your graphics card, combined with your selected desktop size, determines the color depth you'll be able to get.

Using the Adapter tab, you can get summary information about the video card and the drivers being used to drive it. Additionally, you have control, if the video card supports it, over the refresh rate used to drive the monitor. The refresh rate, if you don't already know, is the rate at which the video card repaints the image on the display. In general, the higher the refresh rate, the better. A refresh rate of less than 60Hz makes your screen look like a fluorescent light bulb; you can see the flicker in it.

Low refresh rates are very tiring to the eyes, because of the flicker effect; higher refresh rates are much easier on the eyes. To test this, pull up a full screen image on your monitor. Focus your eyes about 2–3 inches beyond the edge of the screen. If you can detect a flicker effect on the monitor, you've got a lower refresh rate. Refresh rates are a function of both the card and the monitor. Images displayed at a higher refresh rate on a good monitor appear rock solid.

Clicking the Change button on the Adapter tab launches the Upgrade Device Driver Wizard, which will search specified locations, such as floppy, CD-ROM, and even the Internet, for updated drivers.

The Monitors tab displays the currently configured monitor, along with three options. Properly identifying your monitor to Windows is important, so that any special features, such as Energy Star energy saving features, might be taken advantage of. The Change button on this tab also launches the Upgrade Device Driver Wizard.

The last tab, Performance, enables a degree of control over the hardware acceleration features of your card that Windows will attempt to use. If you find you're having intermittent troubles that you think might be caused by your video card, the Option setting on the Performance tab might alleviate it.

If you are using multiple monitors, the Settings tab enables you to control which monitors are used for display at any particular time.

The Game Controller Applet

Being a serious computer user, you'll never be interested in using a game controller, such as a flight yoke with pedals, a car simulator, or a 3-axis joystick, for anything even resembling a game. Your kids might, though, so it'll be your job to know how to configure the game controllers. Of course, you'll need to know how they function in an application, so be sure to thoroughly test out that F-16 flight simulator before turning it over; you want to ensure their satisfaction, after all.

The Game Controller applet has two tabs, General and Advanced. The General tab is where you add in your particular controller(s), choosing from a list of generic descriptions and brand and model names. After you've added your controller, selecting Properties brings up the Properties box, which also has two tabs: Settings and Test. On the Settings tab, you should use the Calibrate button to calibrate the controls on your game controller, at least the first time you use the controller. You'll want to recalibrate if you feel that the response of the controller isn't accurate after awhile. On the Test tab, an x,y display follows the controller as you move it around, and buttons light up in response to pressing buttons on the controller. If you have a rudder or pedals as part of your controller, be sure to click the check mark on the Settings tab also.

On the Advanced tab, you can assign particular controllers to controller IDs and change the Port Driver assigned to the controller, if required.

The Keyboard Applet

The Keyboard applet lets you change settings that affect your keyboard response. The first tab, Speed, has settings for Repeat Delay and Repeat Speed. Repeat Delay is the amount of time from when Windows detects that a key is held down until it begins repeating the character pressed. If you're heavy on the keyboard, like I am, you might want to set this to a longer delay, so you aren't as likely to inadvertently insert repeated characters. The Long setting delays repeating for about 2 seconds; the Short end of the scale sets the delay to about .5 seconds.

The Repeat Speed controls the rate at which repeated characters are inserted, after Windows has determined that you want to repeat the key being pressed. The Slow end of the range repeats characters at a rate of about one per second, and the Fast end repeats several characters per second.

Below the two slider settings just mentioned is a box where you can test out your settings. Click your cursor into the box and use any key to test out your settings.

Below the test box is a setting not really related to the keyboard itself—Cursor Blink Rate. This slider determines that rate at which a text cursor will blink, from very slowly to rather rapidly. Changing the setting causes the sample cursor displayed in the box to react appropriately.

Clicking the Language tab enables you to change both the language of the keyboard and the layout. In the United States, the default language will be installed as English (United States), and the keyboard layout will be determined by the keyboard detected by Windows, which will normally be a 101 key keyboard. If you don't like the standard 101 key layout, there are a number of alternative key layouts you can choose from by selecting the English (United States) line under the Languages box and then clicking Properties. You can actually choose any of the international keyboard layouts, but there are five specifically for the United States: the standard layout, Dvorak, International, and Dvorak LH and RH.

 Note

> The Dvorak keyboard is a keyboard layout where all the most commonly used keys are located on the home row, where your fingers normally rest. This layout is professed to give increased speed and accuracy, and less finger and wrist fatigue, by those who learn it. Dvorak keyboards have become increasingly popular in the past few years.

Changing your keyboard layout to another language is accomplished by clicking the Add button and then selecting the language and keyboard layout you desire. The two sections at the bottom of the Language tab enable you to set a hotkey for switching between keyboard languages and enable a language indicator on the taskbar in the System Tray.

The Modems Applet

Opening the Modems applet displays the Modems Properties box (see Figure 9.13). This properties box has two tabs, General and Diagnostics. On the General tab you'll find a list of all the installed modem devices on your system. Selecting a modem and clicking the Properties button displays the same Modem Properties box that you're able to access through many other routes.

FIGURE 9.13.

The Modems Properties dialog box's General tab.

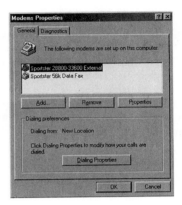

The bottom section of the General tab is the Dialing Preferences section. It lists the current Dialing From location and enables you, via the Dialing Properties button, to change the settings for this dialing location or to add new locations.

The Diagnostics tab is where the real value of the Modems applet becomes apparent. Click the More Info button. The More Info… dialog, shown in Figure 9.14, displays the results of Windows's query of the modem. The modem's answer, shown under the Response column, gives just about every conceivable bit of information you'd ever want to know about a modem, and then some. This will be one of your first stops whenever you have modem problems.

FIGURE 9.14.

The More Info… dialog box reveals everything Windows can discover about your modem.

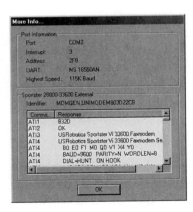

Looking at the screen shot in Figure 9.14, you can see that some of the modem responses scroll off the right edge of the screen. Unfortunately, the dialog box doesn't present a horizontal scrollbar by default. To obtain one, move your cursor over the divider bar between the Command and Response columns, and make the Command column a little narrower. That will pull the Response column to the left, making the right edge of the Response column visible. Now move the divider at the right side of the Response column to the right, and the scrollbar will appear.

The Mouse Applet

There are three devices that people use constantly when using a Windows PC: the monitor, the keyboard, and the mouse. The monitor is unequivocally the most used; second place is a tie between the keyboard and the mouse. Using the mouse properly can increase your proficiency and ease of use of Windows. It makes sense, therefore, that the mouse itself be adapted to your preferences as well. Enter the Mouse applet.

Opening the Mouse applet from the Control Panel displays a Properties box with three tabs: Buttons, Pointers, and Motion. Buttons and Pointers are the ones you will be most concerned with.

The Buttons tab enables you to configure the mouse to be either a left-handed or right-handed mouse. The determining factor is which button on the mouse is the primary button, the one that is clicked to select something. For a right-handed mouse, the left button (under the right index finger) is for Normal Select and Normal Drag, and the right button is for the Context menu and Special Drag. Configuring this as a left-handed mouse reverses the buttons, which makes the mouse easier for left-handed users to use.

The Microsoft mouse and its variations are very popular mice. However, its ergonomics clearly were designed for right-handed use. If you look for it, you will find a left-handed model available.

One of the things that really frustrates Windows users is the double-click. This is part of the reason for the Web-style action settings new to Windows 98; double-clicking isn't needed as much. A double-click is really nothing more than two clicks within a certain amount of time.

The Double-Click Speed section at the bottom of the Buttons tab enables you to set what constitutes a double-click. The time threshold between clicks is what you're configuring here. The range of click speed is almost two seconds apart at the Slow end of the scale and faster than I can click at the Fast end. Most intermediate-to-experienced Windows users will probably prefer the setting somewhere between the halfway point and three quarters. Test your settings by double-clicking the jack in the box at the right.

Clicking the Motion tab displays two more important settings, Pointer Speed and Pointer Trails. Pointer Speed adjusts the speed the cursor moves on the screen. Set it to the Slow end of the scale, and it takes a pretty fair amount of mouse motion to move the cursor from one side of the screen to the other. Set it to the Fast end, and the cursor moves across the screen with much less mouse motion.

Pointer Trails, despite its appearance, isn't something thought up by some '70s era programmers. Turning Pointer Trails on leaves a series of fading cursors behind the moving pointer. This serves to make the cursor much easier to find. This option is especially valuable for users who find it difficult to locate the moving cursor on the screen, and for laptop users using dual-scan screens. The dual-scan screens refresh somewhat slowly, and it's very easy to not be able to locate the cursor during movement.

The Pointers tab enables you to set a scheme for which pointers will be displayed under certain Windows circumstances. The settings on this tab are equivalent to choosing a desktop scheme, as covered on Day 8.

The Multimedia Applet

The Multimedia applet controls all the multimedia devices on your system. Multimedia is covered in more detail on Day 6, "Multimedia in Windows 98." The Multimedia Properties box displays five tabs: Audio, Video, MIDI, CD Music, and Advanced.

The Audio tab displays and enables the selection of the preferred playback and recording devices. A volume setting is also available for each. The Playback device also displays an option for putting a volume control on the taskbar (in the System Tray); this is a handy option to turn on, especially if you use your CD-ROM drive to play audio CDs. For the Recording device, you can also preset the preferred recording quality.

The Video tab enables choosing whether to show videos in a window at their original recorded size or scaling them to be displayed full screen. For best quality, show them at original size.

The MIDI tab is used for configuration of MIDI (Musical Instrument Digital Interface) devices. If you have more than one CD-ROM drive, use the CD-ROM Drive selection to set the headphone volume for each drive individually.

The Advanced tab can be thought of as the Device Manager for all multimedia devices. All the devices, both hardware and software, related to multimedia will be listed here.

Expanding a category, selecting a device, and clicking Properties will display the properties for the device, and depending on the device, might enable manipulation of some device settings.

The Network Applet

The Network applet is used to display the configured components used for networking your computer. Networks, and this applet, are covered in detail on Day 20. All the hardware, such as network adapter cards and modems, and software, such as protocols and services, configured on your system are listed in the Network Properties box.

The System Applet

The System applet is really the control panel for Windows and information central of your computer. The General tab displays high-level information about the version of Windows running on your machine, showing both the name and build number and, with the integration of Internet Explorer, the version of Internet Explorer installed.

Below the system information is the name and company of the user this copy of Windows is registered to, along with the product ID. The license key that you had to enter when installing Windows is displayed in the second and third section of the number. The Computer section displays information about your computer itself; the processor and whether it's MMX enabled.

The second tab, Device Manager, is one you're likely to visit many times. This tab displays all the devices, mostly hardware but some software, that comprise your computer. There are two ways to view this information, determined by the radio button choices at the top: View Devices by Type or View Devices by Connection. Both views display an expandable tree view, much like Explorer, of the devices in your computer.

Viewing by type displays a Computer icon at the top of the tree, with all the devices listed alphabetically below it, by type. Expanding any category displays the devices in that category, as shown in Figure 9.15, which shows the Disk Drives and Modem categories expanded. Under Disk Drives there are three drives shown: a hard disk, a floppy drive, and the Iomega 100MB Zip drive (which you installed earlier in this chapter). The Modem devices show five lines or devices: Parallel Cable on LPT1, Serial Cable on COM1 and COM2, Sportster 28800–33600 External, and Sportster 56k Data Fax. As you can guess, the first three aren't modems, so why are they showing up here? The reason is that direct cable connection, a type of networking that is covered on Day 20, is installed. Direct cable connection creates null modem devices on these ports, hence they show up here. If your system doesn't show these devices, it's okay.

FIGURE 9.15.

The Device Manager tab with View Devices by Type selected.

Clicking View Devices by Connection displays the same devices but in a very different order. View Devices by Connection shows each device listed under the device it is in turn connected to. Figure 9.16 shows a section of this view; notice how the disk drives are listed under their respective controller channels, which are listed under the controller device itself, which is in turn listed under the PCI bus. Following up the line (out of sight), the PCI bus connects to the Computer icon.

FIGURE 9.16.

The View Devices by Connection option shows devices hierarchically under their controllers.

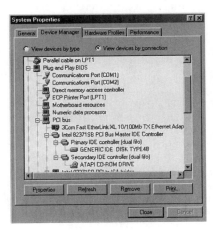

The next tab, Hardware Profiles, displays any profiles you might have configured. A hardware profile is a particular configuration for your computer, which might include some devices and exclude others. Profiles are used mainly by laptop users with docking stations or port replicators.

9

The final tab, Performance, displays information about your computer and the Windows configuration related to performance optimization and enables you to make configuration changes to those settings. The first line displays the amount of physical memory (RAM) actually installed in your computer. System resources show how much of the system memory is available for use. If this number becomes low, system performance will degrade.

The File System, Virtual Memory, and Disk Compression lines, shown in Figure 9.17, all display 32-bit. This indicates that 32-bit drivers are being used for each of these areas, which is what works best. If any of these indicate anything else, you've got some other drivers or programs controlling these areas and are likely not getting optimum performance. Near the middle of Figure 9.17, the message `Your system is configured for optimal performance` is displayed. If you are using anything other than 32-bit drivers for system functions, this area of the dialog box will be replaced with a list of the offending devices, and a Details button will be visible that provides additional information. See Figure 9.18 for a screen shot showing other messages.

FIGURE 9.17.

The Performance tab, configured optimally with 32-bit drivers installed for File System, Virtual Memory, and Disk Compression.

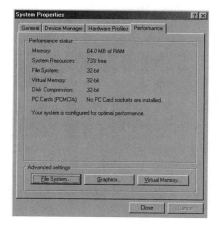

As described in the Help file, the MS-DOS compatibility mode file system is used when Windows detects that a real mode device driver has been loaded (usually from `Autoexec.bat` or `Config.sys`). For safety, Windows switches the disk drives to compatibility mode, which is generally slower than the 32-bit protected mode drivers normally employed. Unless you know that the real mode driver is needed for a specific device and reason, it should be removed from the configuration. Generally, Windows will be able to find and use a protected mode driver for better performance.

FIGURE 9.18.

The Performance tab showing real mode drivers installed for File System and Virtual Memory, reducing overall system performance.

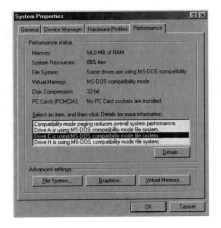

Under the Advanced Settings section there are three buttons: File System, Graphics, and Virtual Memory. You'll look at each in turn. The File System button brings up a File System Properties box, which itself has five tabs. The first tab, Hard Disk, contains two settings. The Typical role of this box enables you to select Desktop computer, Mobile or Docking System, or Network Server. The setting you select will be used to optimize disk performance for this computer's typical role. The Read-Ahead Optimization setting, which should always be set to Full, tells Windows to read ahead when fetching sequential blocks of data from the hard disk.

The Floppy Disk tab has a Search for New Floppy Drives Each Time Your Computer Starts check box. This will be primarily of interest to laptop users, who might or might not have a floppy attached when they start their machines. The CD-ROM tab settings should be set to Large in Supplemental Cache Size, and Quad-Speed or higher, unless your CD-ROM drive isn't at least a 4x drive. These settings help Windows optimize reading from a CD-ROM.

On the Removable Disk tab, the sole setting is Enable Write-Behind Caching on All Removable Disk Drives. The intent is that, because removables tend to be slower than normal hard disks, enabling this option will enable the program writing to the removable disk to continue on, and Windows will actually write the data out, in the background, as the drive can accept it. Although this is a great concept, it does open you up to potential data loss. What if your system crashes in the seconds between the time the program thought it wrote data out and when it actually got written? Or, what if the removable media was removed while data was queued up, waiting to be written out? Personally, I leave this unchecked.

The last tab, Troubleshooting, should only be used when attempting to resolve a system type problem. Even then, if you're not comfortable with what all the options mean, don't change them unless instructed to either by one of the Troubleshooters in the Help file, or on the advice of a support technician.

That concludes the File System properties. Clicking the Graphics button gives you the single option to slow down the graphics acceleration used on your graphics card. Leave this at Full unless you are having display-related problems.

The Virtual Memory button displays the settings that Windows uses to control the swap file. Unless you have specific knowledge and reason to do so, you should always leave this set at Let Windows Manage My Virtual Memory Settings.

The Telephony Applet

The Telephony applet is used as an access point to the dialing locations. Dialing locations are a set of rules that govern how your modem will dial a phone number: Should it prefix the number with a 9 to obtain an outside line? Should the area code always be used? Should long distance be dialed using a credit card number? These dialing locations can be accessed from the My Locations tab.

The Telephony Drivers tab is used to add or configure Telephony drivers. Telephony drivers support those modems or multipurpose telephone devices that provide such services as simultaneous voice and data, caller ID, distinctive ring, and so forth.

Summary

In this chapter you learned a lot about hardware. You learned some historical information, such as the lineage of computer buses. You learned about the Plug and Play standard—how it's used and why it's important. You also learned about installing legacy, or non-PnP, devices and about installing PnP cards. Storage controllers came next, and you learned about IDE and SCSI drive controllers and about the drives they control. You also learned how to install a controller and a disk drive.

Following those lessons, you learned how to install peripherals that attach to your computer's parallel port. Add-in devices that enable the viewing of television signals were also covered. You learned about installing memory, modems, and graphics cards. Windows 98's capability to support multiple monitors was covered, and you learned how to install and configure a multiple-monitor setup. Lastly, you learned about the Control Panel tools used to control all these devices.

Workshop

To wrap up the day, you can review terms from the chapter, see the answers to some commonly asked questions, and practice what you've learned. You can find the answers to the exercises in Appendix A, "Answers."

Terminology Review

backup—A copy of your system software stored on a removable media, such as a tape. To do a backup is the process of copying your software to such a medium.

BIOS—Basic input/output system. The BIOS chip resides on the motherboard and contains the basic low level configuration information and instructions to enable the PC to start up and operate.

COM port—See *serial port*.

controller—A device that manages the flow of data between the computer and a device under the control of the controller—such as a disk or tape drive.

DIMM—Dual inline memory module. A type of memory used in PCs. Usually 168 pins.

DMA—Direct Memory Access. Some peripheral devices are intelligent enough to bypass the CPU and put data directly into or get data directly from memory. These types of devices are configured to use a particular DMA channel.

EISA—Extended ISA. Higher performance ISA bus. Essentially obsolete today.

FDISK—A low-level program used to prepare a disk drive for use by the computer. FDISK prepares the partitions on a drive for use.

format—Once partitioned, a drive needs to be formatted before the operating system can access the disk.

graphics adapter—Also *video adapter* or *display adapter*. Circuitry, either on the motherboard or on an add-in card, used to control the computer display.

hard disk—A storage device for data. Consists of a rotating platter or platters of magnetic storage material, read/write heads for accessing the data, and control circuitry.

IDE—Integrated Drive Electronics. A popular standard hard disk type for personal computers.

IRQ—Interrupt request. A low-level hardware signal used to grab the attention of the CPU when a device needs service. Each device is enabled to use one IRQ when requesting service.

ISA—Industry Standard Architecture. Early and still popular 8- and 16-bit bus standard for add-in peripheral cards.

LPT port—See *parallel port*.

MCA—Micro Channel Architecture. Proprietary IBM bus architecture. Essentially obsolete today.

parallel port—An input/output port usually used for connecting a printer. Many low cost peripheral devices also connect using the parallel port.

partition—An area of a hard disk considered to be a logical drive. A single drive can be broken into multiple partitions, each appearing to the computer as a different disk drive.

PCI—Peripheral Component Interconnect. The current standard bus for personal computers. High speed.

PnP—Plug and Play. Devices that adhere to the PnP standard are self-configuring when installed into a PnP motherboard.

restore—To restore means to recover a file or files from your backup and return it to your system.

SCSI—Small computer systems interface. A versatile high-speed peripheral interface used for disks, scanners, and other high data throughput peripherals.

serial port—An input/output port usually used for connecting a modem or mouse.

SIMM—Single inline memory module. A type of memory used in PCs. Usually 30 or 72 pins per connector.

TLA—Three Letter Acronym.

VL-Bus—VESA local bus architecture. High-speed bus common in late model 486 and early Pentium computers. Still around today, but fading.

Q&A

Q Do I still need to use the driver disks that came with my peripheral?

A Usually not. Windows 98 ships with current drivers for hundreds of different peripheral devices. If you have a device that Windows doesn't have a driver for, it will prompt you for a manufacturer's driver disk.

Q **Why do I have to reboot so often when installing new devices or changing configurations?**

A Many configuration changes don't take effect until Windows is restarted. Additionally, some changes may not even be attempted until other changes have been made, possibly requiring multiple reboots.

Q **Can I use more than two monitors? If I do, can I use my TV tuner card as anything other than primary?**

A First, Windows 98 enables up to nine display adapters and monitors, provided you have enough bus slots! At this time, TV tuners are only supported as primary display adapters. Check with your card manufacturer to see if it has added or is planning to add support to its driver for use as a secondary display device.

Q **No matter what I do, I can't get my favorite five-year-old board to work under Windows 98. I've tried using the original driver disk, but Windows still won't recognize the board.**

A This can happen. In a case like this, the problem lies not with Windows but with the manufacturer for not providing updated drivers. Call the manufacturer or visit its Web site to see if it has or intends to provide updated drivers.

Exercises

1. Set your display adapter to display an 800×600 pixel desktop and a color depth of 16 bits (if your adapter will support these settings).

2. Describe two different ways to access the System Properties dialog box (the one that displays all the devices configured in your system).

3. Describe how and where you would find the following information:

   a) Your registered username

   b) Your Windows license number

   c) How much memory is installed in your computer

   d) Whether or not your PC has a Plug and Play BIOS

DAY 10

Managing Software

by Paul Cassel

Windows 98 would have little practical value if it weren't for the programs it hosts, or runs. The purpose of having a computer and an operating system such as Windows 98 is to be able to use the applications that increase your productivity or in many cases allow you to do things you couldn't otherwise do.

People vary quite a bit in how much they fiddle with their computers. Some people buy, or are given by their company, a machine with their applications and operating system already installed. In some cases they're prevented by company policy or their administration or both from altering their configuration.

Other people upgrade their applications or acquire new applications from time to time. These applications need to be installed or set up, whereas the older ones often need to be removed from the host computers. These same, more adventurous people also might tune their systems to make them leaner or tune them up for speed or to save disk space. It's for this latter group that this chapter exists. This chapter covers

- The basic structure of Windows 98
- How to install or set up programs
- How to uninstall programs
- What drivers are and how to update them
- Managing program group folders
- Updating programs
- Updating Windows 98
- Cleaning up unneeded files
- What the VCM is and how to launch it

The Structure of a System

Figure 10.1 shows a simplified schematic of how the software and hardware work together inside a modern personal computer running Windows 98.

FIGURE 10.1.

How the different elements of a modern computer interact.

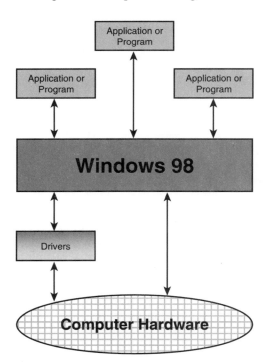

Here are the parts shown in Figure 10.1 and a small explanation for each one:

- Application or Program—The productivity tools for use with a computer. Examples are Lotus 1-2-3, Approach, Microsoft Access, Word, Excel, PowerPoint, Corel Lumiere, WordPerfect.

- Windows 98 (or another similar operating system)—This program, or set of programs, provides essential services identically to all applications or programs. For example, no native Windows 98 program contains file operation program code (such as open, save, delete, and copy). Instead, it requests these services from the operating system. That's why operations such as File|Open appear identical throughout various programs even from different vendors.

- Drivers—These are small programs that extend the operating system so that it can use the services of hardware that the maker of the operating system might not have even been aware of when it issued the operating system. The maker of an operating system, in this case Microsoft, will issue a standard set of hooks and tools to adopt hardware to its operating system. Microsoft calls its tool set the DDK (Driver Developer's Kit). If a manufacturer makes a new piece of hardware, such as a video adapter, it naturally needs that hardware to work with existing operating systems, or nobody will buy it. So the hardware manufacturer uses the DDK or the equivalent tools from other manufacturers to write drivers or adapter programs to extend operating systems to use its new hardware.

- Computer Hardware—Including firmware for the sake of simplicity in this chapter, this is the physical manifestation of a computer system. *Firmware* is a hybrid of hardware and software. It works like hardware in your computer but is programmable. An example of firmware is the BIOS on your mainboard. In most modern systems, the BIOS is upgradeable without chip replacement because it's firmware upgradeable by software programs.

Installing Applications or Programs

In the antiquity of MS-DOS days, installing programs was pretty simple. Each program was a world of one, itself. Installing such programs usually meant nothing more than copying the files to the user's intended installation folder (called directories and subdirectories back then).

However, those programs were pathetically limited compared to the programs native to such operating systems as Windows 98 and Windows NT. We demand much more from them, such as the capability to run all together and often interact without stepping on each other or fouling up the operating system.

10

For example, in the old days printing meant sending a job to a local printer attached to your computer. Today it might mean publishing to the Internet or an intranet, "printing" to a fax application, printing to a local printer, or printing to a printer attached to a network.

Similarly, programs once just ran until they ended either by plan or accident, and then the user could open another program. In some cases, programs could read each other's files.

Today, programs are busy talking to each other and sharing resources. Using Microsoft Office 97, for one example, you can create a Word document and include as part of that document an Access table and an Excel workbook.

All these extensions not only require many more operating system services but also require the operating system to "know" more about a program than just its location on disk.

Today it's just about impossible to manually install even fairly simple applications native to an operating system such as Windows 98. Programs need to not only install themselves in a folder as before but also add their information to the Registry and often install or update common support files.

To install such programs, specialized install or setup programs exist. In fact, some vendors specialize in making install programs for other vendors to use for their application programs. After installing a few Windows 98 applications, you'll notice the common threads that identify the few standardized setup routines.

Applications are, today, usually distributed on a CD-ROM, but some still cling to the older disk media. In either case, place the distribution media in the appropriate drive to start the installation procedure.

You can set off the installation program in four basic ways:

- The Control Panel
- Windows Explorer
- The Start | Run menu selections
- Directly, by command

The Control Panel

Open the Control Panel (see Day 8, "Customizing Windows 98," for information on how to do this) and click the Add/Remove Programs icon to run the Add/Remove Programs applet. After that launches, click the Install button on the Install/Uninstall tab (see Figure 10.2).

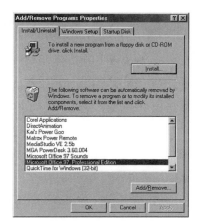

FIGURE 10.2.

*Adding programs
through the Control
Panel's Add/Remove
Programs applet.*

After you click the Install button on the tab shown in Figure 10.2, Windows 98 will hunt
through your removable media devices such as CD-ROM and disk drives, looking for a
program it thinks is an installation program. Usually those programs are called
`setup.exe` or `install.exe`.

Windows Explorer

Windows Explorer can directly start an installation program. You can browse for a setup
program just as you can any other program. After you've located it, double-click on it
(single-click if using the Active Desktop) or choose File | Open from the Windows
Explorer menu. Figure 10.3 shows Windows Explorer with a distribution CD-ROM as
drive F. The installation program visible in the right pane is called `install.exe`.

Opening or running the `install.exe` program launches the installation program. You can
see the first part of this program in Figure 10.4.

Start | Run

If you know the name of your installation program—check the documentation that
comes with the distribution media—you can directly launch the installation program by
making the menu selections Start | Run.

10

FIGURE 10.3.

Explorer set up with the Active Desktop and a Details view. Explorer has set the option to show all files including extensions for known file types.

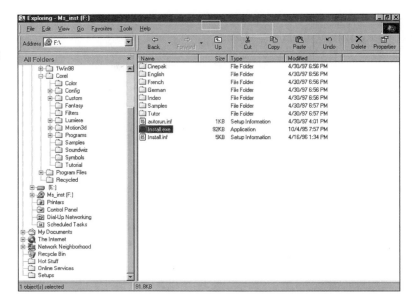

FIGURE 10.4.

Details of installation programs vary depending on the programs' requirements. This program supports several languages.

Click the Start button and choose Run from the menu. Figure 10.5 shows the resulting dialog box and the dialog box that appears when you click the Browse button in the Run dialog.

Start I Run remembers the past few programs it has launched. In the screen shown in Figure 10.5, the last program run is scanreg, the Registry scanner. If you pulled down the combo box showing scanreg, you'd see a list of other programs launched.

Note the Browse dialog box is set to drive F and the install program from Figure 10.3 is highlighted. Click once with the Active Desktop; otherwise, double-click or choose the Open button with install.exe highlighted to launch the program and start the install with the screen shown in Figure 10.4.

FIGURE 10.5.

Invoking a program directly. You can enter a program name or browse for it.

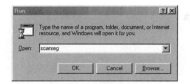

Alternatively, you could have entered

```
F:\install
```

or

```
F:\install.exe
```

in the dialog box shown on top in Figure 10.5 in the same area that you see scanreg.

Firing Up Programs Directly by Command

Although this is more trouble than it's likely worth, you can also start an MS-DOS session (or CLI for command-line interface) and launch a program from that. To fire up a CLI, choose Start | Programs | MS-DOS Prompt. This will result in a command line that looks similar to the old DOS command-line prompt.

Enter the program you want to launch; in this case it's

```
F:\install.exe
```

So you can either log on to the F: drive and then enter install, or you can enter the entire line

```
f:\install
```

from anywhere. This will start the installation program. Figure 10.6 shows the CLI and the launch of the program.

FIGURE 10.6.

For those who like to do it all themselves, Windows 98 has a command-line interface like MS-DOS.

The INF Install

A very few programs actually attach themselves to the operating system in a very intimate way. These programs occasionally use a slightly different approach to their installation and setup.

One such program is the famous TWEAK, or TWEAKUI, an optional part of the Windows 95 and Windows 98 family. TWEAKUI is part of some distribution CD-ROMs. If your CD-ROM or canned installation doesn't have it, you can get it from Microsoft at www.microsoft.com. Some of the elements of TWEAK work with Windows NT 4 also.

Rather than use a conventional setup.exe or install.exe program, TWEAK has all it needs for setup as part of an INF, or information file. Right-click on the INF file distributed with TWEAK, and choose the Install option from the context menu. Figure 10.7 shows the context menu for the INF file.

FIGURE 10.7.

The context menu for an INF file has an Install option. This system works for simple setups with few options.

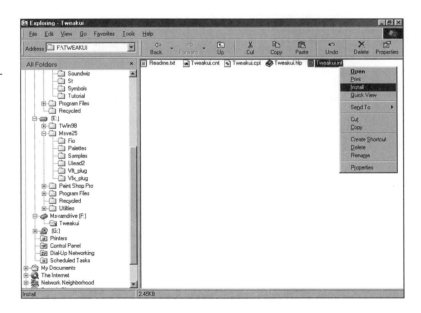

After you choose Install from the context menu, the setup routine proceeds without any choices to its conclusion. Figure 10.8 shows the INF setup running. There are no Next or Back buttons or choices of where to install the program, as you'll find in most conventional installation programs.

FIGURE 10.8.

After you start an INF install, it just runs along until it's done.

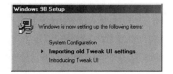

Reducing Program Group Size

Setup programs tend to dump all sorts of files into their created program groups. This can swell these groups to an unwieldy size. Many of these files, such as specific help or readme files, are of the type that you need to see once or refer to only rarely.

Naturally you can delete those files to reduce the size of program groups, but then you might later on regret not having them. Remember that Windows 98 gets rid of files in the Recycle bin from time to time. You shouldn't expect to be able to resurrect deleted files forever.

There are two ways to reduce program group size while preserving those elements you want to keep around in case you find you'll need them later:

- Create a subgroup within the main group and locate the elements there.
- Create a common high-level folder to store rarely used elements.

Remember that the Start menu system is just another view of a folder hierarchy. Refer to Day 8 for details on this hierarchy and its views. This chapter doesn't go into the same detail as Day 8 does on the Start menu topic but shows how to use the information in that chapter to reduce the size of your programs groups while preserving all the files installed by your application programs.

The steps to creating a new folder are worthy of review here, however. Here are ways to create folders in three different locations:

- To add a folder to the left pane hierarchy in Windows Explorer, click the item in the left pane under which you want the new folder to appear. Choose File | New | Folder from the menu. Change the name of the folder from New Folder to one of your choice.

- To add a folder to the desktop or an open folder, right-click anywhere away from an object (such as an icon) and choose New | Folder from the context menu. Change the name of the folder from New Folder to one of your choice.
- To add a folder to the right pane of Windows Explorer, right-click anywhere away from an object (such as an icon) and choose New | Folder from the context menu. Change the name of the folder from New Folder to one of your choice.

Creating Subgroup Folders

This example uses the Open or Large Icon view for altering a program group to one with a subgroup. If you prefer, you can do the same thing in another view such as Explorer.

First, take a look at Figure 10.9. This shows the Start menu with a program group open.

FIGURE 10.9.

The Start menu groups often contain extraneous items.

This group contains the following entries not needed in daily or even weekly use, so they're good candidates for the group size reduction scheme:

- Image Editor Tutorial
- ReadMe
- Ulead Products (a catalog)
- Uninstall
- What's New in 2.5
- Video Editor Tutorial

Task 10.1 shows how to reduce the group's size by creating a subgroup.

Task 10.1. Making a Subgroup

This example manually creates a subgroup and adds some programs and documents to it:

1. Open the Start menu by right-clicking on the Start menu and then choosing Open from the context menu. Open the Programs group by double-clicking it or single-clicking in Active Desktop. Open the target group. In the example, this is the Ulead MediaStudio VE 2.5b group. Figure 10.10 shows this group opened.

FIGURE 10.10.

Note that the Address shows the path to this program group.

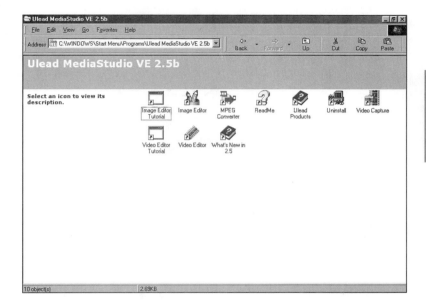

2. Right-click in the program group anywhere away from an icon. This will bring up a context menu with the New entry. Choose Folder from the fly-out menu, as shown in Figure 10.11.

3. Name the folder anything that suits you. For this example, I called the folder Rare Items. Drag the items from the group into the newly made folder. You don't have to open the new folder to add items to it. Just drag the existing items over it and then drop when you're over the new folder and Windows 98 highlights it. Figure 10.12 shows this operation.

4. If you want to make sure your items are really in the new folder, open it for a confirming sanity check. Close the group you're working in as well as the other groups of the Start menu. That's it.

▼

FIGURE 10.11.

The context menu for a program group works just like the context menu for any folder in Windows 98. Remember to click in an area without an icon to see the context menu shown here.

FIGURE 10.12.

You can open a folder to drop things into it or just bomb away, with it remaining closed, as shown here.

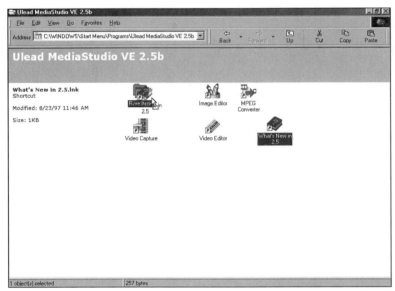

Figure 10.13 shows the results of trimming the original program group. Figure 10.14
▼ shows the new folder opened to reveal the removed items.

FIGURE 10.13.

The new group is much smaller and only includes often used programs.

FIGURE 10.14.

The rarely used programs now exist in a subgroup where they're available, but not in the way.

10

If you do much of this subgrouping, you can actually add complexity to your Start menu by making it deep. The next method avoids that.

Creating a Common Group

The procedure for creating a common group uses exactly the same technique as the one shown in Task 10.1, but instead of making a subgroup, it makes one high-level common group for rarely used items. You can combine the two techniques to create a common high-level group with subgroups of its own.

THE NAME GAME

Remember, you can't have files with the same name in the same folder. For example, the folder Microsoft Office can have only one file named readme. It can have more than one readme if they have different extensions, such as readme.doc and readme.txt. If you want to keep several files of exactly the same name in semicold storage, you'll have to make several subgroups to contain them.

To create a high-level group, open the Start menu and then the Programs group. Right-click on the desktop and then create a new folder, following the general outlines from Task 10.1. This example uses a folder named `Detritus`, as shown in Figure 10.15.

FIGURE 10.15.

You can create new folders to your heart's content. This one will hold rarely used pro-grams and shortcuts removed from their installation folders.

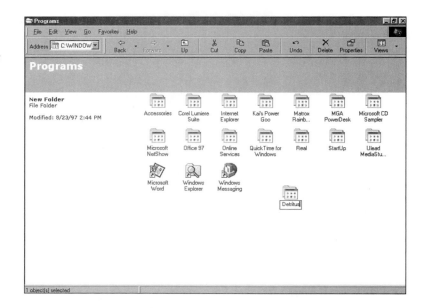

Now all that's needed is to open the folders with extraneous materials you want to include in the new folder and drag those items there. Make sure you drag them. Don't right-click, drag, and then put a shortcut in the new folder unless you want the entries in both folders.

You can also include whole existing folders or make new folders for sorting through the shortcuts and programs in the new group.

Figure 10.16 shows the `Detritus` folder with a collection of rarely used, but still valu-able, programs and shortcuts. It also includes the entire group created in Task 10.1.

The items were added to `Detritus` by opening up their groups, highlighting the items (using the Ctrl key to highlight noncontiguous items), and then choosing Cut from the Edit menu. Next, I opened the `Detritus` group and chose Paste from the Edit menu. That moved the items from their original location to `Detritus`.

FIGURE 10.16.

You can cut and paste your way to an interesting program lint collection from within the Start menu system.

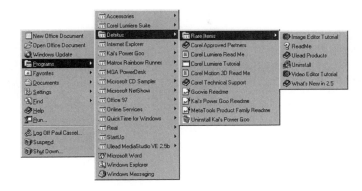

Uninstalling

10

The rather bizarre term *uninstall* has evolved into computer talk for *remove*. In other words, uninstalling a program means removing it from your computer.

Like installation, removal of software used to be an easy task when the Intel world ran under MS-DOS. Like installation, uninstallation has grown to be a real problem since Windows entered the scene. The reason is the same, albeit glanced in mirror vision, as installation.

Today, programs don't exist as solitary soldiers, glorious yet forlorn in their own folders. Instead, they're scattered hither and yon around your entire system and in some cases even your network. Although that presents problems, were that the limit of the difficulties, we'd be in our glory days.

Many programs share common files. Supposedly, when installing, the setup programs track the common file use and make sure that an older version of one of these common files doesn't overwrite the newer. Sounds simple, and in concept it is, but it doesn't work that way.

Simply put, there is no assured way to remove any install program perfectly. Depending on the effort a software vendor puts into it, an uninstall program can do a great to a terrible job of removing what its install counterpart set up.

There are two ways to uninstall any program lacking specialized software designed for program extraction. The first is to use the Add/Remove Programs applet from the Control Panel. Highlight the program you want to uninstall, and click the Add/Remove button. Figure 10.17 shows the dialog box with the Add/Remove button circled. Not all programs will appear in the Add/Remove Programs applet; to appear there, programs must be registered with Windows 98 in the approved Microsoft way. Any program that bears the Windows 98 or Windows 95 seal will have some sort of uninstall routine registered with Windows 98.

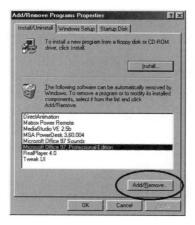

Uninstall varies among applications. When you click the Add/Remove button, what you launch depends on what the software vendor supplied. For example, if you click this button with Microsoft Office 97 highlighted, you go into a routine that will allow you to remove all of Office 97 or parts of it or even add some elements that might be missing from your Office setup.

Other programs don't allow this flexibility. Some will just allow you to either remove all of an application or drop the entire idea. This is because uninstall routines vary from vendor to vendor.

Figure 10.18 shows an uninstall program residing in a program group or folder. That brings us to the second way to uninstall a program: Locate its uninstall program and launch it either through the Windows Explorer or the Start|Run menu selections. Generally speaking, unless you're very secure in what you're doing, you'll be better off launching any uninstalls from the Control Panel rather than directly.

Picking Up the Pieces

Most uninstalls will miss a few pieces. The most obvious and, oddly, common miss is folders with program shortcuts. If an uninstall does miss these items, and you're sure they're now pointing to Nowheresville, open the Start menu, open Programs, and then delete them and the folder they rode in on.

Similarly, uninstalls often miss drivers, libraries (DLLs), and other bits and pieces. In some cases these files are necessary for the healthy functioning of other programs, or even Windows 98 itself. Don't willy-nilly delete these files unless you're quite secure in what you're doing.

FIGURE 10.18.

There is an uninstall program for every modern install. Here's one.

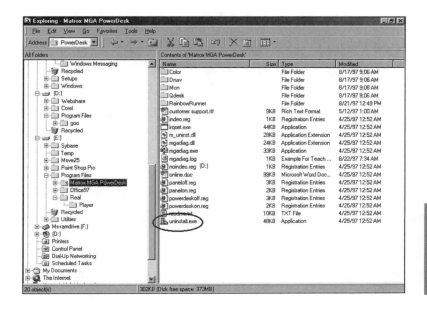

10

To be safe, don't delete the suspected files, but move them to a new place where Windows 98 and other programs can't find them. Any new folder will do as long as you don't have your path statement including it. If, after running a while, the system doesn't seem to miss the files, drop them into the trash. If you start getting messages like

```
Can't find blahblah.dll
```

you'll need to replace the missed file or files.

Drivers

Deep within the dark heart of the Uninstall morass lurk drivers. When you add a new piece of hardware, you'll almost always need to install new drivers for it. However nothing, including Windows 98 or the new driver set, will remove the old drivers that, upon removal of their hardware, do nothing but eat up disk space.

If you know which driver files are no longer needed, you can delete them, but this is tricky in the extreme. There's nothing that will make a Windows 98 setup fail faster than a lost driver. If you're lucky, you'll not have butchered your setup badly enough to prevent Windows 98 from starting. That's if you're lucky. If you're not, you will have to set up Windows 98 itself again.

The lucky ones will get an introduction to Safe mode. This is Windows 98 with utterly generic drivers and no optional hardware. You can go from Safe mode to the System applet in Control Panel to try to determine what's malfunctioning. If you find the felonious hardware, you can often rehabilitate it by reinstalling its drivers. Figure 10.23 (later in the chapter) shows a Windows 98 setup booted in Safe mode.

Figure 10.19 shows the System applet's Device Manager tab. This is where you can see what Windows 98 thinks is working and what doesn't seem to be. In this figure, there are slight problems apparent with both the parallel port and the IDE Controller, as you can see by the yellow bangs (exclamation points) next to their entries.

FIGURE 10.19.

The Device Manager is a good place to see what went wrong with your attempted uninstall for system devices.

For specific help with troubleshooting Windows 98 problems, see Day 12, "Maintaining Your System," and Appendix B, "Windows 98 Tips, Tricks, and Traps."

Updating Programs and Windows 98

Vendors constantly work on shipping products for three reasons:

- To fix bugs missed during the testing process
- To add features
- To improve performance

In the old days, the only way to update your software was to send off for or locally buy update disks. Today's online world gives you a virtual mall for downloading the latest drivers and program updates.

Microsoft and a few other vendors such as Symantec pioneered automated or semiauto-mated update services over the Internet. You visit a Web or FTP site, and the update soft-ware examines your system, compares that to the latest version, and brings your system into compliance if it's not.

The automated part places few if any demands on the user. Just click the Update Program icon and sit back. If you have a Dial-Up Connection (DUN) to the Internet, you might have to establish that first, but the locating and updating is automatic. The address for updating Windows 98 is `http://www.microsoft.com/windowsupdate`. You can start the Internet Explorer and enter that address or click on the Windows Update entry in Start to check for updates. Symantec's update service is called Live Update and is part of its programs' folder.

However, in many cases you'll have to do some manual work to update your configura-tion. In most cases this isn't any more difficult than finding your vendor's Web or FTP site, locating the files that you're interested in, downloading them, and installing them.

Figure 10.20 shows a Web page for a graphics vendor, Matrox. From this page it's only a matter of clicking on the product you have and then choosing whether to download the driver.

FIGURE 10.20.

Most vendors maintain Web sites for updates of their drivers or programs.

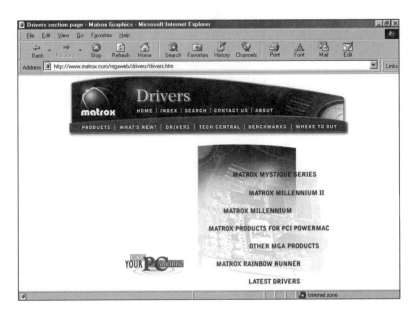

Most updates from Microsoft will update your system automatically. Other vendors tend to be less bold, requiring of you a two-step boogie. First, you download the files you need and then launch or open them to install the upgrade. The Matrox files, for example, arrive as executable (program) files. To run them, you first download them and then use Windows Explorer to explicitly run them.

Figure 10.21 shows the Windows 98 update page.

FIGURE 10.21.

Microsoft maintains a Web page dedicated to making sure your Windows 98 system is fully up-to-date and in tune.

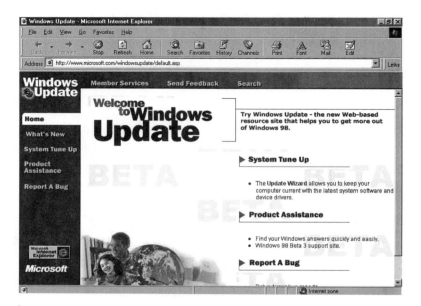

After it's downloaded, launching an update program usually means just running it from the folder you downloaded it into. Figure 10.22 shows the Matrox driver update program about to install a newer version of its drivers for Windows 98.

For the most part, the update programs run automatically with few if any user options. The vendors bank on painless updates for their software and hardware as a way to lure customers into buying their products again.

When Good Updates Go Bad

Sometimes updates don't help and can, in fact, hurt. This occurs when the new updates conflict with something existing on your computer. Although rare, such conflicts do occur. In many cases this will throw you into Safe mode. After you're there, your best bet is to undo what put you there, either by reinstalling the older drivers or uninstalling your program updates. Figure 10.23 shows a computer booted into Safe mode.

FIGURE 10.22.

Updating with new drivers after you've located and acquired the files is as simple as a few clicks.

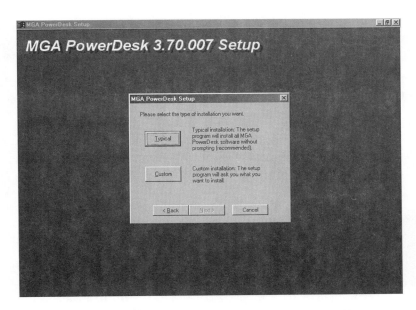

10

FIGURE 10.23.

Safe mode is the diagnostic mode of Windows 98 where you get to undo what forced you into it.

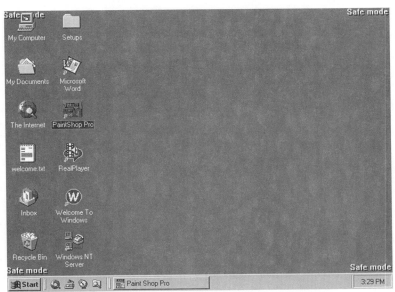

Notice that in Safe mode the screen resolution is at the lowest that Windows 98 is capable of—640×480—and only the standard VGA color set is available. Note also the tray in Figure 10.23. Safe mode launches no optional extensions to Windows at all. If booted normally, this system has four more applets running in the tray.

Windows has a Version Conflict Manager (VCM) that will allow you to restore versions of upgraded programs and utilities that use it. The working of the VCM is simple. It puts the old drivers in a folder called VCM, located underneath the Windows folder.

To run the VCM, choose Start | Run and then enter VCMUI in the dialog box. That will bring up a list of backed-up versions. To restore an older version of a driver, highlight it by clicking on it; then click on the Restore Selected Files button.

The only real problem with the VCM and any online updating that keeps the older files is disk space. Disk space under late versions of Windows is getting to be problematical, especially on the Windows host volume. Although the cost of disk space isn't the issue it once was, Windows 98 has a tendency to sneakily load up your disk with files you don't know you have. These files, such as old drivers and temporary Internet files, can be manually deleted if you know what you're doing. The Windows Maintenance Wizard will also remove some of these files.

Your best defense is to schedule the Maintenance Wizard to run weekly. Your computer will thank you and you'll experience better performance. You can find the Maintenance Wizard in Start | Programs | Accessories | System Tools | Maintenance. See more on the Maintenance Wizard in the section called "The Windows 98 Solution," later in this chapter.

Third-Party Uninstallers

The problems of removing old drivers and unwanted programs from Windows (all versions) have created a small industry of third-party uninstallers.

These programs often work similarly. Before installing a program, they inventory your system and Registry. After installing a program, update, or driver, if you aren't satisfied, you can ask the uninstaller to return your system to its previous state. The uninstaller has good and recent information to work with to restore your system.

Uninstallers also can march through your system locating files they think superfluous and then deleting them if you agree. What these uninstallers "think" depends on their built-in database of what can be removed from a Windows (or application) installation without adversely affecting function. For example, Windows 98, like previous Windows versions, insists on installing files for obsolete video adapters such as the EGA of circa 1984–1986. Few people, if any, use an EGA adapter for modern Windows machines, but the files remain.

You can manually thread through the \windows folder structure searching for such files and moving or removing them based on their names. Figure 10.24 shows the use of Tools | Find in Windows Explorer to hunt down an EGA file.

FIGURE 10.24.

A Windows 98 install includes many super-fluous files.

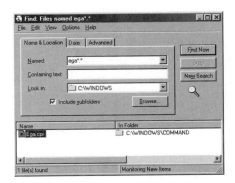

The problem with manually threading through the folders is that most people can't know what's important and what's not. For example, Windows 98 includes many information files for adding new hardware in the . . . \INF folder. Unless you will add a hardware piece associated with a particular INF file, the files are useless.

Take a look at Figure 10.25. This is a section of the . . . \INF folder. You can see a series of INF files for ISDN. At the right of the screen is one of those files opened with Quick View. If you will never use ISDN in any form, none of these files will ever have any use to you, yet they sit there eating up disk space.

If you're sure you'll never use a particular INF file, delete away. However, most of these files don't have particularly descriptive names, and you can end up in an inconvenient position if you do delete a file you later need.

The advantage of a commercial uninstaller is that it "knows" which files it can erase by asking you for instructions in plain language. For example, it might ask you if you'd ever use an ISDN connection. If you say No, it'll root out all those files related to ISDN.

Movin' On

One of the premiere headaches in Windows 98, as in previous Windows, is moving an application. Say you have WordPerfect Office on drive D, and you have run out of room. So you buy a new drive, install it as drive E, and now want your Office there. The only way Office allows you to do this is to uninstall from drive D and then install to drive E. You can do that with little or no danger of losing data, but you will lose a lot of time.

10

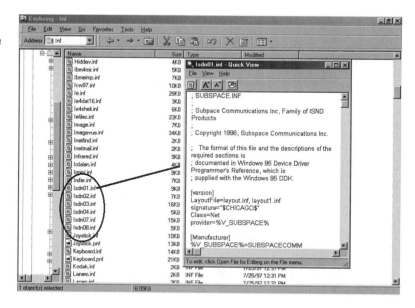

FIGURE 10.25.

You have many files on your disk that you'll never use.

The uninstallers come to your rescue by allowing you to move programs. The trick to a move isn't in moving the files. Windows Explorer can do that easily. The trick is getting all the INI and Registry entries to point to the new place. That's a specialty of uninstallers everywhere. One suite move and an uninstaller pays for itself.

Here are some third-party uninstallers and their Web sites:

Norton Uninstall Deluxe (http://www.symantec.com)

CleanSweep (http://arachnid.qdeck.com/qdeck/demosoft/CleanSwp)

Uninstaller (http://www.1stopsoft.com/uninstall.htm)

The Windows 98 Solution

Windows 98 does provide a cleanup solution of a lukewarm nature. The Maintenance Wizard will, as part of its options, delete certain files you define as useless. Figure 10.26 shows the dialog box where you can activate file cleanup. To get to this dialog box, choose Start | Programs | Accessories | System Tools | Maintenance Wizard.

Figure 10.27 is the dialog box you get if you click the Settings button shown in Figure 10.26. As you can see, this will allow the deletion of some files but isn't nearly as aggressive as third-party uninstallers are. However, it's better than nothing and more than any previous Windows version has had.

FIGURE 10.26.

Part of the Maintenance Wizard has an option to clean up (or delete) useless files.

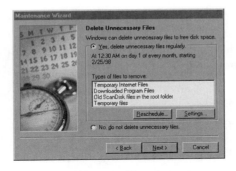

FIGURE 10.27.

The Settings button shown in Figure 10.26 allows a limited selection of files for cleaning up.

10

Starting, Saving, and Exiting Applications

After an application is installed on your computer, you should find it on the Programs menu in whatever group (folder, really) you specified. Some applications will also install themselves on the desktop or in the area of the Start menu above the Programs entry. The variety of installation options is vast, to say the least. However, well-behaved programs will give you the option of installing their launch points wherever you choose. Figure 10.28 shows the option dialog box for a well-designed program.

FIGURE 10.28.

A courteous setup program will allow the end user to specify how a program installs on a computer. This setup screen is from Nico Mak's WinZip version 6 for Windows 95/98.

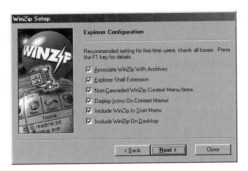

Note that the program in Figure 10.28 is more flexible than most programs. This screen shows that besides offering the end user installations on the Start menu and the desktop, this application (a graphic zip file manager) can associate itself with the Windows Explorer and be called from context menus there.

Some other applications will install to run invisibly in the background or visibly from the System Tray. Figure 10.29 shows a System Tray with several applications running. The two icons on the far right of the System Tray are applications that don't come standard in Windows 98 or from Microsoft.

FIGURE 10.29.

These applications have installed themselves both in the Programs menu and in the System Tray.

The two far right applications are PowerChute, a UPS (Uninterruptible Power Supply) manager, and the Hot Synch Manager for a 3Com Palm Pilot PDA (Personal Digital Assistant), respectively. Their visible presence in the System Tray is a reminder to the user that these services are running in the background.

You can launch most System Tray services by double-clicking on their icons. This will either launch the service or bring up a menu, depending on what's appropriate for the program. Double-clicking or right-clicking on the icon will allow you to shut down some services. Remember, you can prevent the launching of such services by removing them from the Start | Programs | Startup folder or by removing them from startup by using MSCONFIG. (See Day 7, "Getting Help in Windows 98," for more information on MSCONFIG.) Figure 10.30 shows the Startup tab of this utility. You can duplicate the screen shown in the figure by choosing Start | Run and entering MSCONFIG in the dialog box. Click on the Startup tab, and your screen will resemble Figure 10.30.

After you've located your application, you're ready to start it. If the program or its shortcut is on the Start menu (as is usual), click the Start button, choose Programs, and then locate the group (folder) where the shortcut lies. The Start menu will cascade out to drill down to locate the program icon or shortcut. Figure 10.31 shows the Start menu cascading.

FIGURE 10.30.

MSCONFIG *is the place to prevent services or programs from launching automatically.*

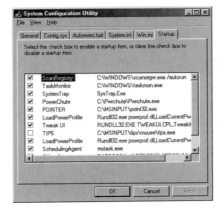

FIGURE 10.31.

The Start menu cascades to reveal its layers.

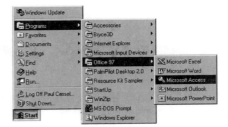

Your Start menu will surely look different in certain specifics from the one shown in Figure 10.31. The appearance of any Start menu depends on the install programs, their arrangement on the menu, and the desktop configuration. The Start menu in Figure 10.31 has been configured to show small icons. The group, Office 97, isn't a standard group created by Microsoft Office 97's Setup program. See Day 8 for details on how to change the look of your Start menu and other related items.

After you've highlighted an application or a shortcut, as shown in Figure 10.31, clicking the mouse will launch the associated application.

Some applications, such as Word or WordPerfect, will require you to specifically save your work. How you do so depends on the program. Most, if not all, programs that have user-savable type documents use the standard Windows menu choices File | Save and File | Save As. Most also have a key combination to enable you to save files without using menu commands. Other programs, such as Microsoft Access, automatically save data as you enter it. This action can be disguised by Access and other database programs if they're asked to do transaction processing, but the underlying dynamic save remains.

Exiting a program again depends on the program itself. Most programs use the standard Windows convention of a File | Exit menu command. Most also show the Minimize, Window, and Close buttons as well as the Control Menu buttons on their title bars. Windows 98 will also shut down most active programs and processes by use of the Alt+F4 key combination.

Finally, in the case of a runaway program, you can force a shutdown by pressing Ctrl+Alt+Delete to bring up the Task Manager (TaskMan). This will force a shutdown of the selected program or process, or you can use it to shut down Windows 98 itself. Use the Task Manager only as a last resort. Its forced shutdowns can cause data loss in open documents. Shutting down Windows 98 by way of the Task Manager can save your Windows 98 setup, but at the cost of maybe damaging installed programs that are open when you initiate the shutdown procedure.

Summary

As with any operating system, the purpose of running Windows 98 is to use the applications or programs it hosts. Managing those programs and their groups is fairly simple.

Managing the programs themselves boils down to installing them, configuring them, and, in some cases, uninstalling them. Managing their folders for quick access is a drag-and-drop procedure done by opening or exploring the Start menu.

You also need to manage the Windows 98 software itself. That amounts to mostly preventing excessive bloat, if possible, by deleting unneeded system files. Although it's possible to do this manually, it's time-consuming and can lead to system instability if you delete a file that was needed after all.

Third-party uninstallers and cleaners go further than the Windows 98 Maintenance Wizard in scrubbing your system clean of unneeded files. They also have the advantage of doing a better job of uninstalling unneeded application programs than most uninstall programs bundled with those applications.

The Version Conflict Manager is a Windows 98–supplied utility that catches installation of older drivers and allows the restoration of newer ones.

Workshop

To wrap up the day, you can review terms from the chapter, see the answers to some commonly asked questions, and practice what you've learned. You can find the answers to the exercises in Appendix A, "Answers."

Terminology Review

applications or *applications programs* or *programs*—These are the reason you use computers. These are the word processors, databases, games, modelers, and other software that you use to gain productivity or to amuse yourself.

CLI (command-line interface)—The MS-DOS prompt. There are three paths to a CLI in Windows 98. You can bypass the GUI of Windows 98 during boot (usually by using the EBD) or launch command.com either by choosing MS-DOS Prompt from the Start menu or by entering that string in the Run dialog box. Finally, you can shut down into MS-DOS mode. Windows 98 can support multiple MS-DOS sessions simultaneously.

driver—A nonaddressable program that allows your operating system (like Windows 98) to address specific hardware.

firmware—Embedded software not changeable by the user. In modern computers, most firmware are chips such as the Basic Input/Output System (BIOS).

program group—A folder subordinate to the Programs folder, which itself is subordinate to the Start menu folder. The term program group is left over from Windows versions prior to Windows 95.

uninstalling—Removal of a program and its specific support files from a computer or network.

VCM (Version Control Manager)—This is a utility you won't find on the Start menu after a standard setup. Using the VCM, you can restore older drivers saved by the update routine, usually after an automatic update through the Internet.

Q&A

Q Can I add programs to the System Tray?

A Technically yes, but it's not really a user-type task. You can drag and drop shortcuts or applications into the Quick Launch Toolbar. This will have an almost identical effect as having the application in the System Tray.

Q What use is `Win.ini` or `System.ini` in a Windows 98 installation? Doesn't the Registry functionally replace these files?

A Primarily, these files remain for backward compatibility with setup programs that aren't fully Windows 95– or Windows 98–compliant.

Q How can I get the VCM to kick into action during a driver update?

A You can manually copy drivers (if you know their names) into the `%windows%\vcm` folder prior to updating. For the most part, the update routine must be VCM-compliant for this utility to be useful. As Windows 98 grows more widespread in use, more update routines will use the VCM.

Q How safe are the third-party uninstallers?

A This is like asking how safe an automobile is. The answer is in how you use it. All third-party uninstallers will safeguard your vital files and back up before they delete files they consider superfluous. All will allow you to override their safeguards, too. Proceed carefully and keep backed up, especially when using one of these programs. You should be backed up anyway, but realistically, few people are. Data loss due to careless use on a non–backed up computer is the prime reason that some of these utilities have garnered a bad name.

Exercises

1. Use the Control Panel to determine whether or not you have the optional Windows Quick View utility installed.

2. Display a list of all the currently running programs. (Note: Please be careful!)

DAY 11

MS-DOS and MS-DOS Applications

by Paul Cassel

When Windows 95, the familial ancestor to Windows 98, arrived on the scene, Microsoft made a big fuss that it was a complete operating system utterly bereft of Microsoft's once leading, but now obsolete, operating system, MS-DOS. Critics of Microsoft soon chimed in with the observation, along with some technical information, that MS-DOS was, in fact, alive and well as the underpinnings of Windows 95.

The entire debate that then broke out, and still rages, is more structural than functional. The pure truth exists, as is often the case, on neither side of the argument. There was a version of MS-DOS underpinning Windows 95's boot process, but Windows 95, when actually running, made that fact irrelevant.

Similarly, there is a version of MS-DOS hanging around the periphery of Windows 98. It doesn't adversely affect how well Windows 98 works, however. From a user standpoint, the legacy of MS-DOS and some other debated architectural aspects of Windows 98 mean that the operating system has the flexibility to run often recalcitrant older 16-bit Windows and MS-DOS programs. Although not 100 percent compliant, it's a true winner for these purposes compared to the only real competition it has: Microsoft's own Windows NT. The beauty of Windows 98 is that it has this flexibility while exhibiting an amazing stability. This combination is the result of the amount of time Microsoft put into honing this operating system.

This chapter covers

- The three ways into the CLI or MS-DOS
- What the CLI is
- How to run commands from the CLI
- How to address MS-DOS program problems
- How to fool programs into thinking they're running under an obsolete version of MS-DOS
- Version adventures in SETVER

Ways into MS-DOS

There are three ways to access the MS-DOS subsystem:

- Press the Ctrl button during the Windows 98 boot process. Choose Command Prompt from the resulting menu.
- Choose Start | Programs | MS-DOS Prompt from the default Windows 98 menu.
- Use the menu choices Start | Shutdown, choosing Restart in MS-DOS Mode from the shutdown dialog box.

There is a further option for those who want to launch MS-DOS upon every startup and have the Windows 98 GUI callable from the command line. This technique is outlined in Task 11.1.

Caution

This advanced technique shows you how to modify one of Windows 98's configuration files to perform in a manner not approved by Microsoft. This modification will boot your computer into MS-DOS, requiring you to call the Windows 98 GUI manually or from a batch file. This task will substantially alter the way your computer boots. This is an advanced technique. **Use with great caution.**

Task 11.1. Editing `MSDOS.SYS`

1. Open Windows Explorer. Locate the file `MSDOS.SYS` in the root directory of your boot drive. If your options in Windows Explorer don't allow the display of hidden or system files, you must alter those options (View | Folder Options | View tab) to Show All Files. Figure 11.1 shows this dialog box.

FIGURE 11.1.

You need to be able to see all files before doing this task.

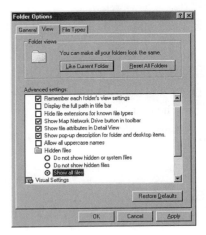

11

2. Right-click on the `MSDOS.SYS` file. Choose Properties from the context menu. Remove the read-only property by deselecting its check box. Figure 11.2 shows this operation.

FIGURE 11.2.

Before editing, you have to remove the read-only attribute from a file.

▼

▼   3. Close the Properties dialog box by clicking OK. Right-click again on the
        MSDOS.SYS file and choose Open With from the context menu. Locate Notepad or
        any other straight text editor from the resulting dialog box. You can see this opera-
        tion in Figure 11.3.

FIGURE 11.3.

*You need also to
choose an editor for
this text-only file.*

    4. The editor you choose will open with the file MSDOS.SYS loaded (see Figure 11.4).

FIGURE 11.4.

*After the file is loaded
into an editor with the
read-only attribute
cleared, you're free to
edit away.*

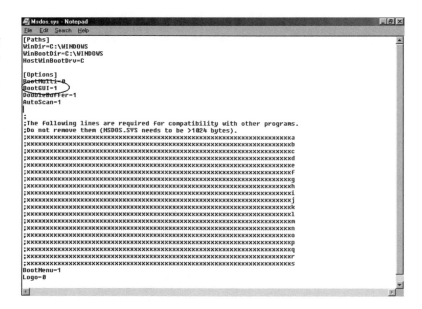

    5. There are several tweaks you can safely apply to this file, but be careful because
        you can tweak yourself into a lot of trouble by experimenting. A safer course
        would be to create a backup of the file on a bootable floppy before doing any
▼   experimenting.

▼ 6. For this demonstration, locate the line with BOOTGUI=1 on it (refer to Figure 11.4). Edit this, replacing the 1 with a 0. Save the file (File | Save) and exit Notepad (File | Exit).

That's it. The next time you launch Windows 98, you will end up at the old MS-DOS C:\ prompt. To launch the real Windows 98, type WIN at the command line. You can also add the line WIN to your AUTOEXEC.BAT file. That will have the same effect as leaving BOOTGUI=1 in MSDOS.SYS but will give you the flexibility of adding a command after the WIN that will, in effect, be an exit command for Windows 98. Use this latter facility with great caution. Because of some advanced power management built into Windows 98,
▲ such exit techniques won't work on all systems.

Things to Do While Alive in MS-DOS

After you've launched an MS-DOS session by booting with the technique shown in the Task 11.1, launching an MS-DOS session by choosing Start | Programs | MS-DOS Prompt, or exiting to MS-DOS mode, you'll be faced with the famous (or infamous) command-line interface (CLI).

The general way to use the CLI is to enter a command and then press the Enter key to tell MS-DOS that you're done with the command line. There are three general tasks that you can accomplish within the CLI:

- Run an MS-DOS program.
- Manually launch a native Windows program. This won't work unless you've booted into the Windows 98 GUI and are running MS-DOS on top of or within Windows 98.
- Run commands including batch files.

There is no advantage to launching a native Windows program from the CLI. People seem to enjoy doing it just to feel more in command of their computers. This feeling seems to hark back to the days when the only way to interact with a computer was to enter obscure commands, dozens (or even hundreds) of which a hopeful computer user needed to memorize before entering this new world.

Running Commands

Users who were brought up with the CLI as their only way to interact with computers got used to it and often tend to distrust the GUI most people prefer. Those people, analogous to those who kept a crank in their cars after the invention of electric starters, are the most common users of CLI. They will argue, if pressed, that the CLI (or DOS command line) is faster and more precise than the Windows GUI. This might be technically correct, but for the vast majority of users, the GUI is good enough and more.

11

Windows Help is annoyingly quiet about the CLI. It suggests typing the command followed by /? to get help on that command. That's fine as long as you already know the command you need help on. Microsoft seems reluctant to give any assistance to create future legions of MS-DOS users, it seems.

For an idea of what commands you can use, look in the [%windows%]\command (usually c:\windows\command) folder to see a list of the MS-DOS external commands. Ironically, those are the commands least used, but they will give you an idea of the variety of the CLI.

The most often used commands don't exist as discrete files but are inherent in MS-DOS itself. These are the *internal* commands. The commands in [%windows%]\command are the *external* ones. The three most often used commands are all internal. They are

- DIR—List a directory's or folder's contents.
- COPY—Copy a file or files from one location to another.
- DEL—Erase a file. Similar to moving it to the Recycle Bin, but unless you use a third-party uneraser, the deletion is permanent.

To see a list of a command's parameters, type the command name followed by /? at the CLI. To toggle full screen and windowed modes, press Alt | Enter. Figure 11.5 shows the results of getting help for the COPY command.

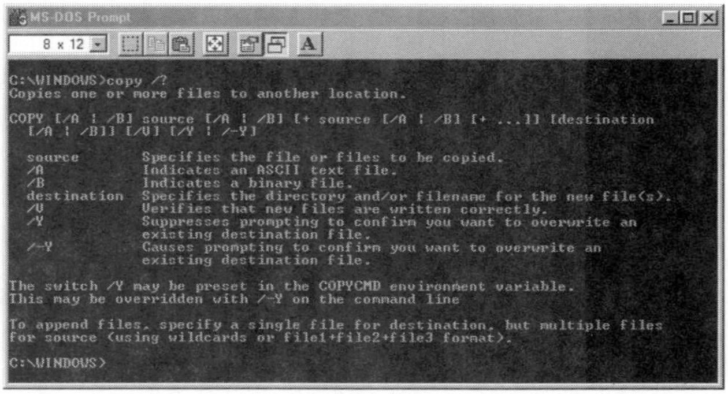

FIGURE 11.5.

After you've figured out what you need help on, that help is just a command away.

If you want to customize the MS-DOS prompt, click on the A icon in the toolbar. This will bring up a familiar tabbed dialog box, the MS-DOS Prompt Properties dialog box, allowing a blizzard of options for this facility. Figure 11.6 shows this tabbed dialog box.

As you'll see later in this chapter, the dialog box in Figure 11.6 comes into prominence when tweaking DOS programs.

FIGURE 11.6.

This dialog box is a vital part of making hard-to-run DOS programs operate under Windows 98.

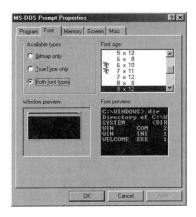

There isn't room here for even an elementary discussion of MS-DOS commands and their parameters. Whole books have been written on that topic. If it interests you, you can wade through the Help system or buy a full reference volume such as

Using DOS, ISBN 0-7897-0095-6, by Que Corporation

Peter Norton's Complete Guide to DOS 6.22, Sixth Edition, ISBN 0-672-30614-X, by Sams Publishing

If you want to try the do-it-yourself help method, here are some of the more useful commands to look up. More than 90 percent of MS-DOS commands issued are the following:

- DIR—Lists the files in the current folder (directory was the original name for a folder, hence the command's name). This command has many options you can see by entering DIR /? at the CLI.
- COPY—Copies a file or files (using wildcards) from one place to another.
- XCOPY—An advanced COPY command.
- DEL—Erases (deletes) a file or files.
- RD (or RmDIR)—Removes (erases) a folder (directory).
- MD (or MkDIR)—Creates a folder (directory).
- CD (or ChDIR)—Changes from one folder (directory) to another.

Running Programs from the CLI

To run native Windows programs from the command line, just type

```
[program name or shortcut]
```

where *program name* is the name of the program you want to launch. The program must be either in the currently active folder or on the path. You can also use the Start command to launch a program. For example, to start Microsoft Excel from the command line, enter the folder where the Excel executable file (`excel.exe`) or a shortcut to that file exists and enter

```
Start excel
```

or just

```
excel
```

or the name of the shortcut, if it's not the same as the program filename. There is no benefit to launching programs from the command line, other than that you can interactively feed them parameters. For example, if you want to launch Word (`winword.exe`) with the file `budget 99.doc` loaded, you can enter the command line

```
Start winword "budget 99.doc"
```

You can have the same effect by using the menu commands Start | Run and then filling in the line as you would from the CLI.

In the same way, you can launch an MS-DOS program from the command line. When you do so this way, Windows 98 will make a best guess as to the parameters the program needs. This works surprisingly often, but you need to be prepared for when it doesn't. That's what the following section is about.

Tuning MS-DOS Programs for Use in Windows 98

When you run an MS-DOS program under Windows 98, the operating system dynamically creates a PIF file. PIF stands for *program information file*. This text file tells Windows 98 which settings to use to run the MS-DOS program specified in the file.

During the transitive period when MS-DOS still ruled, but was yielding to the Windows onslaught, the limitations of MS-DOS and its native programs became apparent. For a short while a huge industry popped up, extending MS-DOS programs to stopgap these shortcomings. As soon as Windows and its native programs grew dominant, the need for those extenders died, but many programs, especially games, continue to use this jury-rigged technology.

Additionally, MS-DOS allowed programmer flexibility in how the program used the computer. Skilled programmers got more out of old Intel technology than many imagined they could, but in doing so they often broke certain programming rules that today make running such programs quite problematical under Windows 98. Again these unlawful but high-performance programs are usually games.

The reason for problems with games stems from the demands of the users. A word processor doesn't mind if a program takes a few extra tenths of a second to run a spell check on a word. The difference isn't noticeable. However, a gamer will not only notice, he won't buy a game that lags a few tenths of a second during critical action game play. These gamer demands led to superior MS-DOS games and to problems running them today. Windows 98 is a rules enforcer. To keep order between running programs, it has to handle all the tricks and traps those old time DOS programmers put into their programs.

For the most part, Windows 98 handles things well without any extra help from you. When MS-DOS programs fail under Windows 98, there are three things you can try:

- Tune the PIF using the Properties sheet in the program's context menu (right-click) to try to accommodate the program under Windows 98.
- Boot into MS-DOS mode and run the program there. In many cases, typing `exit` after the program exits restarts the Windows 98 GUI, but not always.
- Really give the entire thing up and use the Boot menu to select Command Prompt.

11

In some cases, you may want to use the second or third choice for those programs, like MS-DOS backup programs, with which you absolutely don't want any other processes or file accesses going on at the same time.

Keep in mind that when under MS-DOS from the CLI, the Boot menu, or in MS-DOS mode, you don't have long filenames active. That requires the Windows 98 GUI. Files created or backed up will be limited to the old MS-DOS 8.3 filename format or the long filename MS-DOS equivalent. Figure 11.7 shows a folder listing under Windows Explorer and the CLI to show the truncation of filenames under the CLI. Figure 11.7 has two lines drawn, linking the Windows Explorer file display with the CLI to give you a feel for how the names relate to each other.

The extension under MS-DOS for a shortcut is `.lnk`. The term *link* was the original term for a shortcut under Windows 95 (during early development). The file extension remains, although the name *link* yielded to *shortcut* a full year before the commercial release of Windows 95. The extension persists in Windows 98 for compatibility reasons.

FIGURE 11.7.

Simple truncation of long filenames uses the formula of the first six alphanumerics, a tilde, and then a number.

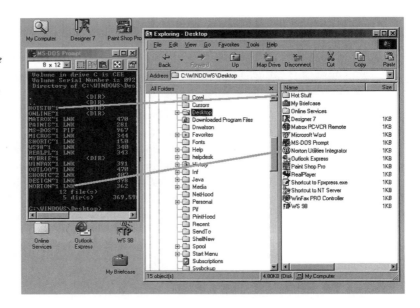

Problematic MS-DOS Programs

To customize the settings for MS-DOS programs that exhibit trouble running under Windows 98, locate the file, right-click on it, and then choose Properties from the context menu. Windows 98 is quite sly. It can tell if the program is an MS-DOS one. If so, it brings up a Properties dialog box appropriate to setting parameters for such programs. If you want to test the intelligence of Windows 98, right-click on a known MS-DOS and native Windows program to see the different dialog boxes.

Figure 11.8 shows the MS-DOS program dialog box.

FIGURE 11.8.

Six tabs and a very important Advanced button (on the Program tab) are the whole of the MS-DOS Properties box.

Of the six tabs, the last three contain the most important settings for adjusting the way Windows 98 runs an MS-DOS program. However, there is an Advanced button on the Program tab that hosts what can be the most important set of properties for one of these programs.

IT WILL RUN IF YOU MAKE IT

Using these adjustments, you can make any, or just about any, MS-DOS program run under Windows 98. As a last resort, it will run under MS-DOS mode. If you're desperate, you can boot directly into the DOS system underlying Windows 98. However, you don't need to try these latter two strategies until you've exhausted the options in the dialog box shown in Figure 11.8.

The problem you face is what adjustments to make. In most cases, you're on your own. You will be in high luck if you can locate the makers of the MS-DOS programs and they can suggest any remedies. Many of these programs were written by houses long gone. If they were around, they would have Windows programs out now, removing the need for the entire exercise. In many cases, these problem programs were written in-house, using a home brew–type tool such as Clipper. Much of the system work with such tools is beyond the control and knowledge of the programmer, so finding the maker of the home brew program usually won't help you at all.

Programmers using home brew tools such as Turbo Pascal or Clipper were quite good at what they did. The tools were excellent for their time. However, the ascension of Windows caused their time to pass, and the detritus of their techniques lives on in programs that behave badly when run under Windows—a situation the tool makers never envisioned.

Note

If you hit a badly behaving MS-DOS program under Windows 98, take the time to evaluate if it really makes sense to diddle it to run right. In almost every case, there is a Windows solution, either on the shelf or that you can easily make using modern Windows tools such as Visual Basic, Microsoft Access, Clarion, or Corel Paradox. In almost every case you'll end up with a better program than the one you're struggling to get to behave under Windows 98.

The secret to making MS-DOS programs run under Windows 98 is guessing. After doing this for awhile, you develop a "nose" for what stinks in these older programs, and you can address it. Until then, you need to start with a somewhat educated guess and go from there.

If you have the documentation for the older program, you might have a head start. Take a look at the Memory tab shown in Figure 11.9.

FIGURE **11.9.**

The Memory tab controls the various kinds of MS-DOS memory.

MS-DOS programs have various schemes to let them put data or even code in areas originally forbidden to them. Windows 98 is generally good about detecting what a program is asking for in any type of memory and then foxing the program into thinking it has received what it asked for. In some cases the program doesn't ask but assumes something is there. In those cases, Windows 98 itself can be foxed. If your program isn't running right and you know you need a specific amount of, say, EMS memory (the docs will tell you), you might try adjusting the EMS Memory box from Auto to the specific amount of EMS your program demands. Treat XMS and DPMI memory similarly. Some programs also demand a weird amount of environment. The Initial Environment box allows you to customize this.

In most cases, Windows 98 will handle the Conventional Memory setting, but if in doubt and you know exactly how much conventional memory (also called DOS memory or TPA) your program needs, you can try setting this away from Auto.

The Screen tab allows several adjustments of how the program interacts with the display—or how it thinks it's interacting. Windows 98 intercepts screen calls, making some programs think they're directly addressing the hardware as they did under real MS-DOS. Games not only often need special memory settings but also have troubles with the display under Windows 98. Mostly you'll want to run these programs in full screen; windowed makes for more problems. However, also try disabling—individually—Fast ROM and Dynamic Memory Allocation at the bottom of the dialog box shown in Figure 11.10.

FIGURE 11.10.

The Screen tab allows overriding of several display characteristics for Windows 98's MS-DOS emulation.

If the program you're running requires a nonstandard number of columns or lines, the Initial Size box will allow some adjustment there. Usually, the only programs requiring that are MS-DOS spreadsheet compilers, but oddities exist.

The Misc tab shown in Figure 11.11 has two important settings, although all might come in handy. Allow Screen Saver will permit you to suspend the screen saver when the program is active. Many programs fail to recover from a Windows-type screen saver, so this is where you can save the day in those cases. If you're having mouse troubles, try enabling the Mouse Exclusive Mode check box at the upper right on this tab.

FIGURE 11.11.

The Misc tab has several settings, two of which, screen saver and mouse exclusivity, can be real program savers.

When All Else Fails, You Can Still Succeed

The final place to explore the misbehavior of an MS-DOS program is the Advanced button on the Program tab. Figure 11.12 shows the resulting dialog box when you click the Advanced button.

FIGURE 11.12.

The Advanced button is the key to running many poorly behaved MS-DOS programs that respond to nothing else.

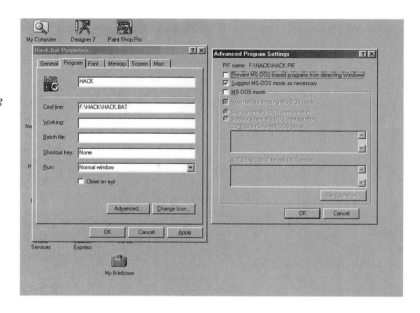

This fantastically flexible dialog box enables you to force just about any MS-DOS host setting. Some programs, for example, refuse to run under Windows. For those, you can make it impossible for them to detect Windows 98 by checking the top check box in the dialog box shown in Figure 11.12.

As said before, the key to running really strange programs can be MS-DOS mode. However, exiting to MS-DOS mode from Start I Shutdown will leave you with a generic MS-DOS session. Using the MS-DOS Mode check box in the Advanced tab, you can customize a CONFIG.SYS and AUTOEXEC.BAT specifically for your MS-DOS program. If your problem program demands certain entries in either or both of these MS-DOS initialization files, this is the place to set up a special host environment for it.

SETVER and the Wrong DOS Version

Many MS-DOS programs test for the version of DOS they're running under. This made sense when these programs were current because versions of MS-DOS differed as to the services they offered. Each subsequent version of MS-DOS was a superset of subsequent ones. However, all too often the programmers were shortsighted in how they checked for an MS-DOS version. Rather than check for a version or greater, they just checked for a version. Thus, a program that needed, say, MS-DOS version 3.3 might fail the version check if run under MS-DOS version 5, although the program would function just fine under that later version if it tried to run. The programmers usually put in a logic that would stop a program execution if the version check failed.

Microsoft solved that problem by creating a version faker program called SETVER. This allows the aliasing, or false reporting, of the MS-DOS version to specific programs. SETVER is itself an MS-DOS program run from CONFIG.SYS. Windows 98 has its own SETVER located in [%windows%]\command, which usually works out to be c:\windows\command.

You need SETVER if your pesky MS-DOS program says something like Wrong DOS Version when you try to run it. You need to find out what version it wants. This is part of the documentation for the program. If you can't find the docs and the error message doesn't include what version the program demands, try

- Version 2.0 or 2.1 for programs dated before 1985
- Version 3.0 (rare), 3.1, 3.2, or 3.3 for programs after 1985, but before 1989
- Version 4.0 (rare) or 5.0 for programs after 1989

Don't let yourself be limited to this list. There might be some program written in 1987 that demands 2.1, although such a program would be one for the Microsoft museum.

Remember, you must include SETVER in a CONFIG.SYS. A good place is the CONFIG.SYS for the MS-DOS Mode setting for the particular program. The general syntax for SETVER is

SETVER [path] Filename VersionNumber

So to report an MS-DOS version of 3.3 for a program called BUNKERS.EXE located in d:\warfare, you'd enter

SETVER d:\warfare\bunkers.exe 3.3

as a line in CONFIG.SYS. This will solve your version problems.

The Absolute End of the Road

Sometimes nothing works. In that case, you must run your MS-DOS programs utterly outside Windows 98's environment. The best way to do this is to create a boot floppy disk, add the needed commands to CONFIG.SYS and AUTOEXEC.BAT (don't forget SETVER), and then boot the computer using that disk. If your DOS program runs from a disk, you'll have no problems at all, although you'll have to ask yourself if a modern version of whatever you're trying to do exists. Using a modern 300+ MHz, 128MB machine to run a floppy-based program is strange indeed.

11

You can boot another version of MS-DOS (or PC-DOS or DR-DOS) from a floppy and run the problem program under that. However, if you plan on running from a hard disk, you need to understand that older versions of DOS can't recognize some of the newer Windows 98 disk storage schemes such as FAT32 or DriveSpace. You simply can't access a FAT32 partition from an older version of DOS.

If you're planning to run a troublesome MS-DOS application, it's a good idea to reserve at least one partition as FAT16 for compatibility. That will give you the boot floppy option.

Consider it a very rare program that can't be made to run under Windows 98 if you throw at it all the custom Properties and run it under MS-DOS mode with its own CONFIG.SYS and AUTOEXEC.BAT. As a final measure, don't forget SETVER.

You should never have to boot a Windows 98 computer into a previous version of MS-DOS (or another DOS) to run a particular program. But it's nice knowing you can if you are forced into that position.

Summary

MS-DOS, in a particular form, does exist within the Windows 98 environment. There are three roads into MS-DOS: You can boot there from the Boot menu, you can launch an MS-DOS session (which means to run the program, COMMAND.COM), or you can exit Windows 98 into MS-DOS mode using the Start | Shutdown menu commands.

Some veteran users coming to Windows 98 from MS-DOS prefer doing some operations from the command-line interface (CLI). You can do the same either because you enjoy doing things for yourself or because you want to experience what computing was like in pre-Windows days.

To use the CLI, you need to learn not only a plethora of commands but also their parameters. Microsoft likely doesn't want to remind users that MS-DOS still lives in one form under Windows 98, so it doesn't provide help on those commands in the usual Help system.

You can use an old MS-DOS reference or seek command-line help after you've learned the names of the commands. To use CLI help, type the command, followed by /?. Most of the old MS-DOS commands, and all of the important ones, remain in Windows 98's "DOS."

There are several strategies to pursue if you want to run an MS-DOS program under Windows 98 and it doesn't want to run. The chief tool is the Properties dialog box for the particular program. There you can set memory and screen settings if Windows 98 is guessing wrong. You can also disable the screen saver and give great priority to the mouse.

The big stick for running MS-DOS programs is MS-DOS mode and its custom settings under the Properties | Program | Advanced button. Here you can customize everything from environmental settings to the version of DOS that Windows 98 reports to your program. Use as an almost last resort. As an utter last resort, you can boot from a disk, including an older version of MS-DOS, but keep in mind that these older versions can't access the newer hard disk storage schemes used by Windows 98.

Workshop

To wrap up the day, you can review terms from the chapter, see the answers to some commonly asked questions, and practice what you've learned. You can find the answers to the exercises in Appendix A, "Answers."

Terminology Review

Boot menu—An option menu for booting Windows 98 into various modes such as Command Line and Safe mode.

CLI—The command-line interface, where you can enter keyboard commands followed by options or parameters and hit Enter to execute the command.

`Command.com`—A program that launches an MS-DOS session within Windows 98.

EMS—An obsolete "windowed" memory specification still required by some old MS-DOS programs.

MS-DOS—The original Microsoft operating system. Available in many versions over the years; each newer version has enhanced capabilities. For the most part, MS-DOS only accepted command-line commands until Microsoft released first Windows and then `DOSSHELL`. Other vendors, such as IBM, offered graphical user interfaces that ran on top of MS-DOS.

MS-DOS mode—Running almost identically to the original MS-DOS by exiting Windows 98 (leaving only a stub behind). MS-DOS mode is a Shutdown option in Windows 98.

`start`—The command to launch a Windows 98 program from the CLI.

Q&A

Q Can I boot various configurations of MS-DOS using Windows 98?

A You can fox programs by changing their Property sheets (right-click | Properties) into thinking they're running under almost anything. If that fails, you can create floppy boot disks and try that to create distinct profiles for distinct boot sessions. You can even boot old versions of MS-DOS such as the venerable 3.3, but keep in mind that you won't be able to see any FAT32 volumes from such a boot.

Q What is a wildcard in MS-DOS?

A A wildcard is a character to substitute for many other characters. For example, the asterisk (*) means "accept any characters after this," so the command

```
DIR *.doc
```

means to list all files having the .doc extension. The ? means to take any character in this place, so

```
DIR mine.?oc
```

means to take any character following the dot. This command will list the files

```
mine.1oc
mine.doc
mine.roc
```

and so forth.

Q Why do some MS-DOS programs require older versions of MS-DOS?

A Poor programming, plain and simple. Still, if you use such programs, you have to accommodate the errors of their programmers.

Q What types of programs seem to cause the most troubles under Windows 98?

A MS-DOS action games such as fly-bys as well as custom programs for insurance companies. The latter is a real mystery.

Exercises

1. One of the most useful features of the DIR command is that it can be used to create a text file listing of a directory. Use DIR to create a listing of the files in your Windows directory, sorted by file size.

2. The DIR command is extremely powerful. You can use it to get a listing of all the files in a directory and its subdirectories. Use it to make a listing of all the files in your Windows directory and below.

DAY 12

Maintaining Your System

by Michael Hart

In the past days you've learned a lot about running Windows 98 on your system: how to install it, configure it, use it. Now you need to learn some things about how to keep it running smoothly.

Like any finely tuned machine, your Windows 98 computer requires some periodic attention to maintain its top operating condition. For some things, you can configure Windows to automatically run maintenance programs on a regular basis. Other maintenance needs require manual intervention. In any event, the toolbox of utilities and wizards built into Windows 98 will assist you in keeping your computer doing what it does best—computing.

In this chapter, you'll learn about the tools you need to keep Windows 98 running smoothly on your computer. You'll learn how to configure them, how to run them, and, just as importantly, why you should run them. More specifically, this chapter covers

- Windows Update
- The System Information Utility

- The System File Checker
- Automatic ScanDisk
- The Drive Converter (FAT32)
- Disk compression
- The Maintenance Wizard
- Using the Task Scheduler
- The Backup program
- Using System Recovery

The Maintenance Tools: An Overview

The many system maintenance tools are listed in Table 12.1. These tools assist you in just about everything you'll need to do to keep your system in tip-top shape, from backing up on a regular basis to recovering an accidentally deleted system file, from optimizing your hard disk to getting onto the Microsoft Web site to search for additional technical assistance.

TABLE 12.1. WINDOWS 98 SYSTEM MAINTENANCE UTILITIES.

Name	Description
Windows Update	Automatically checks for updates to device drivers and system files from the Microsoft Web site. Allows user intervention or automatic operation; includes an uninstall option.
System Information	Displays more than you could ever want to know about what's loaded and configured in your system.
System File Checker	Verifies that all the system files are the proper version, size, date, and so on and reports problems; allows restoration of affected files.
Maintenance Wizard	Automatically runs programs to keep your hard drive running smoothly.
Scheduled Tasks	Allows scheduling of tasks at predetermined times or recurring intervals.
Disk Defragmenter	Rearranges programs on your hard drive to speed up your frequently used programs.
Dr. Watson	Gathers complete system information after a program crash.
Backup	Improved program for backing up your programs and data files.
Disk Cleanup	Automatically cleans unneeded files off your hard disk to free up additional storage space.
Automatic ScanDisk	When Windows isn't properly shut down, ScanDisk will automatically run when your PC is rebooted. ScanDisk can also be run at any time to verify disk integrity.

Windows Update

If you've been a Windows user for a while, you know that keeping up on which updates, patches, or new drivers are available for your system is a never-ending, tedious task. Windows Update helps to alleviate some of this headache. Conveniently located right at the top of the Start menu, it means you are only a click away from system updates.

Windows Update connects you to the Windows Update site. There, your system will look for any available software updates that are applicable to your particular system configuration. If any are found, you can view information about each, download any or all, and presto, they're installed. Figure 12.1 shows the welcoming screen of the Update site. Clicking Product Updates takes you to another page offering options for downloading add-on products for Internet Explorer 4.0. The Active Setup dialog box will appear; click No for now. Scroll down to the bottom of the page to the Device Drivers and System Files banner and click the link to check for new updates. This takes you to the actual Update Wizard page; click Update to get to the screen shown in Figure 12.2.

FIGURE 12.1.

The Welcome to Windows Update site allows you to search for and install or remove any available system updates.

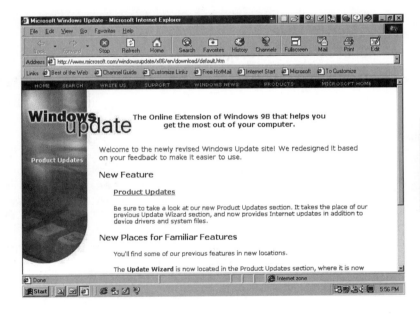

12

If you should find that you are having problems with a new update, you can also choose to remove an update from your system, restoring it to the condition it was in previously.

When you first connect to the Update site, you'll be presented with some VeriSign certificate dialogs asking if you want to install and run several components of the Windows Update system. You should answer yes to these dialogs; otherwise, you won't be able to complete the update process.

FIGURE 12.2.

The Update Wizard displays any updates that apply to your particular hardware and software configuration.

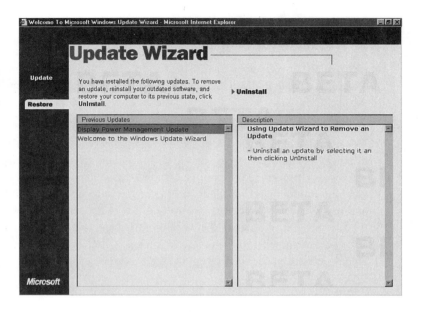

Task 12.1 walks you through the process.

Task 12.1. Checking for Available System Updates

In this Task, you'll connect to the Update site, specify which updates you want, then download and install them.

 Note

> If you have not yet established a connection to the Internet, probably via a service provider, the next two tasks won't work. You may want to just read these now and try them after you have an Internet account set up. For assistance in getting connected to the Internet, see Day 21, "Mobile Computing with Windows 98."

1. Click Start | Windows Update. If your connection to the Internet is a dial-up, you should see the Internet Connection Manager make the connection to your Internet service provider.

2. If necessary, click to accept any certificates presented by the site. If this is the first time you've been to the Update site, you'll also have to accept the download of components to allow the update process to complete.

▼   3. After any preliminary downloads have completed, click on the Update button. You'll see the notices, under Available Updates, that your system is being checked for configuration. As relevant patches are found, they'll be listed.

   4. Click on one of the updates listed for you. The right side of the table will display information about the update, including a description, the date of the update, its size, and the approximate time required to download the patch. With one of the updates selected, click the Install button. At the next dialog, confirm that you actually want to install the update.

   5. A download progress indicator will appear. While one update is downloading, you will not be able to start the download of another. When the download has completed, the selected update will no longer be listed as an available update.

▲   6. If you've downloaded a patch that requires rebooting your machine, you'll see a dialog asking if you want to reboot your PC now. I usually answer No and then reboot as soon as possible.

Congratulations! You've just downloaded and installed a system patch from the Update site. This procedure is one you'll use periodically to keep abreast of available updates and retrieve and install those that will help you.

Unfortunately, not every system or driver update will be good for your system. Occasionally, you'll find that "new and improved" is actually worse. If this happens to you with an update you got from the Windows Update site, you can simply have Windows Update remove the patch. Task 12.2 shows you how.

Task 12.2. Removing an Installed System Update

▼ TASK

The reverse of the System Update you did previously, this procedure shows you how to remove an already installed patch or driver:

   1. Launch the Windows Update by clicking Start | Windows Update.

   2. After you've arrived at the Update site, click the Remove button to bring up the Uninstall page.

   3. Windows Update will automatically scan your system, looking for previously installed updates. These updates will be listed under the Previous Updates column.

   4. Select the update you want to remove; then click the Uninstall button. Exactly what you see will depend on the individual update being removed. In general, you'll see the file-copying progress dialog, and possibly the question asking if you'd like to reboot now. If you're asked to reboot, as before, I suggest saying No until you're ready. If the update can be removed without rebooting, it will be

▼   removed from the Previous Updates column immediately. If the update requires a

12

reboot, it will still be listed in the Previous Update column, but in a different font. After you've rebooted, it'll be removed from the list.

You've now come full circle—both installing and removing updates to your system via the Windows Update. Remember that when you hear of new drivers or Windows updates, you should use Windows Update to visit the Update site and see what's useful to you.

The System Information Utility

Whether you're a curious person, you're trying to troubleshoot a problem, or you're just poking around, there are times you'll want or need to know just exactly what's happening with your system—what DLLs are loaded, what tasks are running in the background, what driver is currently being used. If that's the situation you find yourself in, then the Microsoft System Information Utility is for you.

If you've used the old MSD (Microsoft Diagnostics) program that's been around for some time, you'll immediately understand that the System Information Utility is MSD on steroids. Everything you could possibly want to know about your system (and a lot of things you don't care to know) is reported in the System Information Utility (SysInfo).

Start up the System Information Utility from the System Tools group. On the opening screen, shown in Figure 12.3, are the menu bar with the File, Edit, View, Tools, and Help menus, the toolbar, and below the toolbar, a two-pane window with a hierarchical tree of information types on the left and a display area on the right. This chapter doesn't cover every menu choice and option, but it does touch on the important ones.

FIGURE 12.3.

The Microsoft System Information Utility displays more information than you ever wanted to know about your system.

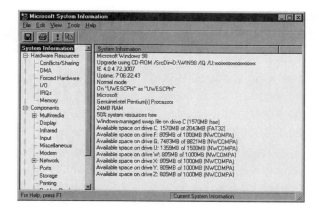

The System Information Utility can store all the information it gathers about your system and write it out to a file (an MSInfo file, with an .nfo extension), or read in a previously stored MSInfo file. The MSInfo files are fairly large, several hundred kilobytes, and may take a minute or two to generate. They are binary files, so you can't view them using a word processor or text editor. However, by using the Export function under the File menu, this information can also be written out to a text file, which could then be opened in any word processor.

You can also use SysInfo to view a previously saved NFO file by clicking File I Open and selecting the file you want to view. When you open an NFO file for viewing, the first line of the tree in the left pane will change to say File: xxxx.nfo. To see current system information again, select File I Close.

Tip

It might be a good idea to take a "snapshot" of your system, using File I Save, before making any significant changes like installing new hardware or software. Then, take another snapshot after the installation or other modifications are completed. That way, you have a complete before and after picture of what's under the hood, in the event you need to do some troubleshooting or undo the changes you've made.

The Edit menu contains a Copy command and a Select All command, both of which can be used to copy information from the right pane (the display pane) onto the Clipboard. The Tools menu contains menu shortcuts to several other system tools—Update Wizard Uninstall, Signature Verification Tool, Windows Report Tool, System File Checker, Registry Checker, Automatic Skip Driver Agent, Dr. Watson, System Configuration Editor, ScanDisk, and Version Conflict Manager—all covered separately.

The list of all the categories of information the System Information Utility will gather is shown in Figure 12.3, earlier in the chapter. Much of the information shown in this utility is only of interest to software or hardware technical support people, so each type is not covered in detail here. I do point out which types contain information that might be useful to you.

Does it feel like your system is running a little sluggishly today? Take a look at the Running Tasks category in the Software Environment branch to see a list of all programs currently running. You may be surprised to see so many programs listed. Even though you may not have started any programs, Windows has, and usually a lot of them. You may be able to determine where some of them got started by looking at the Startup Programs category. This will also tell you where those programs were started from— your startup group or from a Registry setting.

12

Task 12.3. Running the System Information Utility

This example shows you how to use the System Information Utility to save a snapshot of your system and check out some detailed information about your computer:

1. Start the System Information Utility from the System Tools group. Maximize the window for ease of viewing.

2. Expand all the branches of the information tree by clicking all the + signs.

3. Click on the Input heading under Components. A lengthy listing of information should appear on the right side.

4. At the top of the right half of the window, click the Basic Information radio button. You should see information listed similar (but not identical) to what's shown in Figure 12.4. You will also probably have listed at least a mouse and a keyboard.

FIGURE 12.4.

Basic Information for input devices listed in System Information.

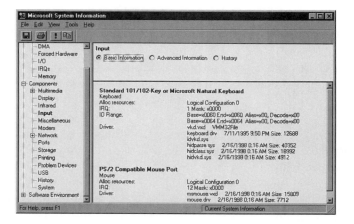

5. Select File I Save. In the dialog box, enter a name for this NFO file, such as MyPC. Click Save.

6. Now select File I Open; then click on the NFO file you created in step 5. Notice that the left pane now displays the name of the NFO file at the top of the information tree.

7. Close the System Information Utility.

Now that you've had a chance to view very detailed information about your system in a compact detailed form, via the System Information Utility, you'll be more comfortable when adding or changing hardware or software configurations.

The System File Checker

One of the common problems PC users encounter is accidental, or at least unintentional, changing of system files—perhaps as a result of cleaning up the hard drive too enthusiastically or an accidental click and delete. Even more likely is the scenario that after the installation of a new piece of software, some program that previously worked, doesn't! Not only can this be very frustrating, but it's also darned hard to track down.

In response to this problem, Microsoft has created the System File Checker (SFC) utility. Elegantly simple, this little utility can save you hours of frustrating troubleshooting. It has the capability to track changes not only to system files but also to any set of files that you specify. It's important to remember, though, that the SFC only tracks and alerts you to changes to system files; it doesn't prevent them. SFC does its job thoroughly, telling you which files have been changed and providing an easy means of restoring the proper version of the file.

The heart of the System File Checker is the DEFAULT.SFC file, a list of all the filenames, sizes, dates, locations, and version numbers of the files to be tracked. DEFAULT.SFC—the list of all the files for the Windows installation—lives in the C:\Windows directory. When the System File Checker is started, DEFAULT.SFC is automatically loaded.

Start the System File Checker from the Tools menu of the System Information Utility; it can also be started by double-clicking on the SFC.EXE file located in C:\Windows\System. The SFC window appears, as shown in Figure 12.5. Operation of the SFC is very simple. In the middle of the dialog box is the What Would You Like to Do? section, with the choices Scan Files for Errors and Extract One File from Installation Disk. You will probably choose Scan Files for Errors 90% of the time. Choosing this option sends SFC off, madly checking all the files listed in DEFAULT.SFC against what's currently installed on your hard disk.

12

FIGURE 12.5.

The System File Checker main window.

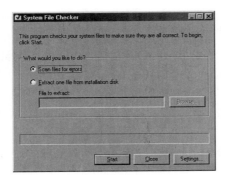

If any file is found whose size, date, or version doesn't agree with what it should be (as defined in DEFAULT.SFC), you are given these options:

- Update Verification Information
- Restore File
- Ignore
- Update Verification Information for All Changed Files

If you want to keep the flagged file as the proper version, select Update Verification Information. This will update DEFAULT.SFC with the new file information for the flagged file. This means that the next time SFC is run, this file won't be flagged as having been changed.

The second option, Restore File, is used if you do not want to keep the flagged file but want to restore the original file back to its rightful place. When you select Restore File, you'll be asked where to restore the file from (usually this would be the Windows 98 CD-ROM) and where to save the file, which will already be filled in with the correct location. You'll be asked if you want to keep the file being replaced, and if so, where. Don't worry, SFC will suggest a place to store the replaced file.

Selecting Ignore essentially tells SFC to skip over the flagged file but not to update the verification information either. The next time SFC is run, you'll receive notification about this file again. You might want to select Ignore when running SFC just after installing software. You'll get a list of changed files listed in the SFC log. After testing the results of your software installation, you can run SFC later to either update the verification information or restore the original files.

The last option, Update Verification Information for All Changed Files, tells SFC to continue through the rest of the file check operation but not to alert you to changed files. Instead, SFC will update the verification information for each changed file it encounters, as if you had personally approved it. Each file whose information is being updated will be logged in the SFC log, however.

After SFC finishes running, you'll be notified via dialog box and given the option to display a synopsis of SFC's actions, as shown in Figure 12.6 (later in the chapter). SFC keeps a very detailed log of its activities also, which may be viewed directly by opening the SFCLOG.TXT file in the C:\Windows directory, or by clicking the Settings button on the SFC main window and then clicking the View Log button.

You can configure SFC for what actions it should take when restoring a file. The default action is to prompt you for a decision as to whether or not SFC should back up the existing file before restoring the original file. You may set this to automatically back up changed files or not to back them up at all. You may also use the Change button to change the default directory where SFC will store those changed files.

How does SFC know which files to track—which files are "its own"? SFC has a list of folders, subfolders, and file types that it tracks. The folders and subfolders are listed in Table 12.2, and the file types in Table 12.3. This list, as mentioned before, is contained in the DEFAULT.SFC file.

TABLE 12.2. FOLDER AND SUBFOLDER SETTINGS FOR DEFAULT.SFC.

Folder	Subfolders
C:\Program Files	No
C:\Program Files\Accessories	Yes
C:\Program Files\Common Files	Yes
C:\Windows	No
C:\Windows\Command	No
C:\Windows\Downloaded Program Files	No
C:\Windows\Fonts	No
C:\Windows\System	Yes
C:\Windows\System32	Yes

TABLE 12.3. FILE TYPE SPECIFICATIONS DEFINED FOR DEFAULT.SFC.

File Spec.	Description
*.386	Device drivers
*.com	Executable commands
*.dll	Dynamic link libraries
*.drv	Device drivers
*.exe	Executable files
*.ocx	ActiveX controls
*.scr	Screen savers and script files
*.sys	System files
*.vxd	Virtual device drivers

12

So, what do the Folder and File Type sections define for us? Here's how they work together. For each folder listed, SFC looks for every file contained in that folder that matches one of the file type specifications listed. When it finds a matching file, SFC then checks DEFAULT.SFC to see if the filename is listed there. If it is, SFC then checks to see if the size, data, and version (if determinable) of the found file match what is listed in the DEFAULT.SFC. If anything doesn't match, SFC presents the File Changed dialog, asking you for instructions on what to do.

Additionally, if SFC finds a file that is not listed in the DEFAULT.SFC list, the file is added so that it can be verified the next time SFC is run. You are not asked if you want to add the file to the verification data; SFC automatically adds any file that matches the folder and file type criteria. If SFC determines that a file listed in DEFAULT.SFC is missing, either moved or deleted, you are presented with a File Deleted dialog, similar to the File Changed dialog.

Task 12.4. Creating a Baseline System File Check

◀TASK

This example shows you how to do two important things: first, to learn how to run SFC for a routine file scan, and second, to update DEFAULT.SFC so that it'll properly detect any file changes from here on in:

1. Start the System File Checker. Click Settings.

2. Verify that Prompt for Backup and Append to Existing Log are selected. Click both Check for Changed Files and Check for Deleted Files so that they both have check marks. Click OK.

> **Caution**
>
> If Check for Changed Files and Check for Deleted Files are not checked, you won't be prompted for an action when SFC encounters a changed file or deleted file—it will always just update the DEFAULT.SFC list. You want to know if files have changed or been deleted, so be sure to check these settings.

3. Select Scan Files for Errors and then click Start.

4. If the File Changed dialog appears, click on the Update Verification Information for All Changed Files option. This tells SFC not to bother you again, that all the changed files it encounters are okay, and to make them the new "OK list."

> **Note**
>
> If the File Deleted dialog appears, click Cancel and do Task 12.6; then redo this Task. If the File Changed dialog doesn't appear, proceed to the next step.

▼ 5. When SFC has finished, click the Details button and view the results, as shown in Figure 12.6.

FIGURE **12.6.**

FIGURE **12.6.**

Details from a System File Checker file scan showing the deleted or changed files count.

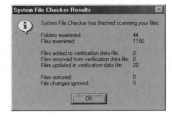

 Tip

The results can also be viewed in the SFC log. Using Windows Explorer, open the file C:\Windows\SFCLOG.TXT with either Notepad or WordPad. Notice the level of detail presented. Close the log file.

You'll also be able to view the log by clicking the Settings button and then clicking View Log.

▲ 6. Close the System File Checker.

You've just created your baseline file verification list. From now on, SFC will let you know whenever any files that are on your system are changed, the moment it happens.

So, how will SFC help maintain the integrity of your system files? Using Task 12.5 every time you install software on your computer will help. (Don't do this now, only when installing software.)

Task 12.5. Safely Installing Software

Using SFC before and after installing and testing new software can go a long way toward catching potential problems before they become real headaches.

1. Create a baseline system file check, as described in Task 12.4.

2. Install the software according to the manufacturer's installation instructions.

3. Verify that the new software operates correctly.

4. Run SFC, selecting Ignore whenever a File Changed or File Deleted message appears. Your SFC log now contains a full list of all system files that were added, changed, or deleted by the new software just installed.

▼ 5. Verify that your other major applications continue to function correctly.

▼

6. If you encounter problems with your other previously installed applications, use the file listings in the SFC log to narrow down the potential causes. Use SFC to restore changed files.

7. Test the new software and your other applications.

8. In some cases, you may not be able to both restore your existing applications to working condition and run the new software. Contact your software vendors, detail the problem you've encountered, and offer them your SFC log as supporting evidence.

▲

This task should serve you well as a general installation guideline and may save you much frustration if a newly installed program kills another program.

The last task you need to learn to do with SFC is to actually use it to restore a file that's been deleted.

Task 12.6. Using SFC to Detect and Restore a Deleted File

It's not considered good form to delete Windows files willy-nilly, but since we know what we're doing, this little controlled demonstration will be okay. This task shows you how to delete a file that SFC is tracking and then use it to restore a copy of the file to its proper location.

1. Have your Windows 98 CD-ROM or other installation media at hand.

2. Using Windows Explorer, delete the file C:\Windows\Command\extract.exe.

3. Start SFC from the System Tools folder.

4. Click the Start button to start the file check.

5. In a minute or two, you'll see the File Deleted dialog shown in Figure 12.7. Notice that it's saying that extract.exe, which you just deleted, is missing. The default option selected is to restore the file from the installation disks. Click OK.

6. The Restore File dialog shown in Figure 12.8 appears. You see that the destination for the file is already entered in the Save File In box. You just need to tell it where to restore the file from.

7. Put your CD-ROM into the drive. Click the Browse button and navigate to the CD-ROM drive and the Win98 folder; then click OK.

8. The file is immediately restored, and SFC continues with the file check. When it has finished, click the Details button to view the summary, which should indicate one file restored. Click OK and then OK again.

9. Click the Settings button; then click View Log. Go to the bottom of the file, where the latest information was written, and you'll see listed that extract.exe was restored to C:\Windows\Command.

▼

FIGURE 12.7.

SFC File Deleted dialog, showing the discovery of the missing extract.exe.

FIGURE 12.8.

The SFC Restore File dialog, in which you tell SFC where to recover the deleted file and where it should be placed.

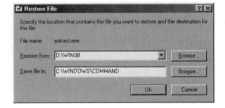

▲ 10. Close the log. Close SFC.

That's about as easy a system fix as they come.

12

SFC also allows you to create your own SFC files. You can specify which folders and file types to track. This could be useful when you want to be able to track when specific files have changed. To create your own SFC file, use the Settings button; then go to the Advanced tab. Specify which folders and files on the Search Criteria tab.

The System File Checker is very good at its primary function: alerting you to changes in system files and restoring them to originals if desired. Using the customization features available, you'll undoubtedly be able to find your own useful applications for SFC.

Automatic ScanDisk

Occasionally, Windows will not be properly shut down—an application might lock up or crash the machine, or your toddler might nose up against the reset button (it happens!). When your PC reboots, your system will want to run an Automatic ScanDisk on your disk(s) before going into Windows. It will launch the MS-DOS version of ScanDisk, which will scan the drives, fixing any errors it finds before loading Windows.

The Drive Converter (FAT32)

The Drive Converter program converts the file structure of your disk drive from the older FAT system to the newer FAT32 system—all of which may mean nothing to you, unless you read on.

Back in the old days—that is, up until 1995 or so—disk drives for PCs were generally in the 250MB to 1GB (1000MB) range. In the ancient days, the people who wrote the code that allowed programs to manipulate disk drives were pretty visionary, so they built flexibility into the disk drivers to allow the drivers to operate on disk drives of up to 2GB capacity. In today's world, disk drives of 2GB and more are increasingly common. Because of this, a new disk driver system had to be developed.

When a disk drive is formatted, a file system is installed on the drive. The file system determines how files are stored. For PCs, the file system has almost universally been the File Allocation Table (FAT) file system—a 16-bit FAT. The FAT itself is a special area where the operating system keeps track of what files are stored where. The FAT is a list of each storage unit on the disk. The 16-bit FAT can keep track of only so many storage units. However, the physical disk drive stores data in small pieces called sectors. Because there are many more sectors on the drive than the file allocation table can keep track of, each storage unit, called a cluster, encompasses many sectors. The exact number of sectors per cluster varies depending on the physical size of the disk. For disk drives in the 2GB range, a single cluster could be as large as 32KB (32,768 bytes, or 32 kilobytes). For smaller drives, a cluster could be as small as 2KB. The cluster is the smallest unit that can be tracked or allocated in the file allocation table, so every single file stored on a 2GB drive will require at least one cluster, or 32KB of space—even if the file has only a single character in it. As you can see, this is a terrible waste of space. The same single character file stored on a small drive would use only 2KB of disk space.

To get around this limitation, the FAT32 file system was developed. Still using the file allocation table, but with twice as many addressing bits, the FAT32 file system can be used on drives up to 2TB (that's terabytes, or 2,000GB, or 2,000,000MB) in size. More importantly, on the drives you and I are more likely to have, those in the 2GB–4GB range, cluster sizes are kept smaller, reducing the amount of wasted space on our drives. The FAT32 file system is not necessarily more efficient than the FAT16 file system in terms of speed, but it is certainly more efficient in terms of utilization of the drive space. The maximum drive size for a FAT32 drive is 2TB—or two million megabytes!

A picture is worth a thousand words, so take a look at Figures 12.9 and 12.10. To illustrate why a FAT32 drive is more efficient at storing files, I created a text file with a single character in it on both a FAT16 drive and a FAT32 drive. Figure 12.9 shows the properties of the one-byte text file when stored on a FAT16 drive. Notice the Size line; it shows that the file is one byte but that 16,384 bytes are used. Because the FAT16 drive uses 16KB clusters, this one-byte file takes up 16,000 bytes of disk space! Next, I converted the drive to FAT32 and displayed the properties of the text file again, as shown in Figure 12.10. Look now at the Size line in Figure 12.10 and you'll see that the one-byte file now takes up only 4,096 bytes of disk space, or only 25% as much room as it did on the FAT16 drive. Although there is still lost space, you can see that the FAT32-formatted drive is making better use of the available disk space.

FIGURE 12.9.

Properties of a single byte file stored on a FAT16-formatted drive. Notice that this one-byte file requires 16KB of storage space.

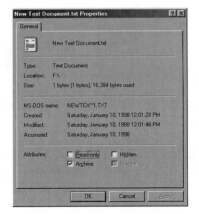

12

Windows 98 includes the Drive Converter, which converts your hard disk from FAT16 to FAT32. In general, there should be no problems doing so. What you will want to do is take inventory of what third-party disk utilities you may be using and see if the manufacturer has a patch or update to allow the utility to function with a FAT32 drive. Most packages should already have updates available; be sure to verify that the programs you rely on are FAT32-capable before converting.

Converting your drive from FAT16 to FAT32 is a one-way process. There is no conversion utility in Windows that will convert a FAT32 drive back to FAT16. So, as with all system configuration changes, be sure you back up your data before converting your drives.

Figure 12.10.

The same single-byte file stored on a FAT32-formatted drive requires only 4KB of disk space.

Note

Windows doesn't convert from FAT32 back to FAT16, but there are third-party utilities available that will do this conversion. Look for them in the Utility section of your favorite computer software store.

There are some issues that you need to know about before converting your drive(s) to FAT32. See Table 12.4 below for a list of known issues with FAT32 drives.

TABLE 12.4. KNOWN COMPATIBILITY ISSUES TO BE AWARE OF WHEN CONVERTING DRIVES TO FAT32.

Issue	*Description*
Dual booting	If you dual boot your computer between Windows 98 and another operating system, your boot drive should not be converted because other operating systems cannot access FAT32 drives.
Virus programs	Some virus programs cannot access FAT32 drives. Contact your virus program vendor for update information.
Free space reporting	Some older applications will not be able to report free space greater than 2GB. There should be no operational problems when running these programs.
Windows 98 uninstall	After you convert your boot drive (usually your C: drive) to FAT32, you'll no longer be able to uninstall Windows 98.
Compressed drives	DriveSpace3, used to create compressed disks, cannot be used on FAT32 drives. If you want to use drive compression, do not convert it to FAT32.

Disk Compression

Converting your drive(s) to the FAT32 file system is one way to wring extra storage space out of your hardware. Another way is to utilize the optional disk compression facility of Windows. Called DriveSpace3, this compression scheme has been around since Windows 95 and was available in two versions: the standard DriveSpace, which was included in Windows 95, and DriveSpace3, which was in the optional Plus! pack.

DriveSpace compression creates a new compressed drive that is actually resident on your existing drive. The new drive will appear in Windows Explorer, and all your existing programs will be able to access the new drive, just like any other drive. When you create a compressed drive, you have two options: You can either compress an entire drive to get maximum storage space, or you can use just a portion of an existing drive as a new compressed drive.

Because your compressed drive employs software compression, you'd be correct in guessing that there might be a performance penalty exacted against a compressed drive. Certainly if you are running on a 486 class machine, or a lower-speed Pentium (under 100MHz), you might notice a slight slowdown. However, on today's modern, 150MHz+ machines, the slowdown will not be noticeable.

Another question that might arise would be that of the safety of your data. I have used disk compression software for more than three years without a single incident of data loss related to disk compression. I would not, and do not, hesitate to recommend it as a viable option to anyone.

When creating a compressed drive, you have the options of compressing an existing drive, thereby giving it additional free space, or of creating a new drive by using some of the free space on an existing drive. Figure 12.11 illustrates both methods. The top half of the dialog shows that by compressing the entire drive, an additional 1200MB of free space would be gained; this drive is a 1.2GB one with 100MB free. The second half of the dialog shows that an additional 238MB drive could be created from the free space on drive D. The rest of drive D would not be compressed.

These numbers, however, are not completely accurate. First of all, compression figures are always estimates. Different file types compress differently. Also, DriveSpace3 can handle only an uncompressed drive of 1GB or less; the maximum compressed size is 2GB. Referring back to Figure 12.11, recall that the top half of the dialog box indicated that 1200MB of free space would be gained by compressing the entire drive. Figure 12.12 shows the Compress a Drive dialog from DriveSpace3. Notice both the text at the top of the dialog regarding the 1GB limit and the breakout displayed on the right half of the dialog.

12

FIGURE 12.11.

The Compression tab of an uncompressed drive's Properties box shows the two ways this drive can be compressed and provides a button to launch each.

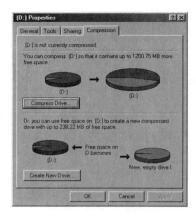

FIGURE 12.12.

The Compress a Drive dialog shows the before and after effects of compressing a drive using DriveSpace3.

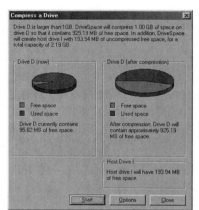

The after-compression configuration shows that drive D will contain 925MB of free space and that Host Drive I will contain 194MB of free space.

What is this host drive? DriveSpace works by creating a hidden Compressed Volume File (CVF) on an existing drive. The CVF becomes the new compressed drive. The DriveSpace3 software compresses and decompresses all the files that are read from and written to this new compressed disk. The physical disk where the CVF is located is called the host drive. When you compress an entire disk, the compressed disk is given the drive letter of the original disk, and its host drive (the actual physical disk) is given a new drive letter.

On the Properties dialog for a compressed drive, you'll find a check box labeled Hide Host Drive. This setting effectively makes the host drive invisible to the rest of Windows. If you have a drive under 1GB that you've compressed, this is a convenient option because you don't have the extra drive showing up. However, if your host drive is larger than 1GB, as is the drive shown in Figure 12.12, hiding the host drive will also make the free space on it unavailable to you.

Note

> The following tasks should not be done just to experiment. Use these as reference if/when you decide to employ compression on your hard disk(s). When compressing a hard disk, the entire process could take several hours.

Task 12.7. Compressing an Existing Drive

Don't actually do this now. Use this Task as a reference when you decide to compress a drive.

If DriveSpace3 is not in your System Tools folder, you'll have to install it from your Windows distribution media. See Day 2, "Installing Windows 98," for directions on installing optional Windows components.

1. Start DriveSpace3 in one of the following ways: by clicking Start | Programs | Accessories | System Tools | DriveSpace or by right-clicking the drive to be compressed in Windows Explorer and then clicking the Compression tab.

2. If you started DriveSpace3 from the System Tools folder, select the drive to be compressed in the list; then click Drive | Compress. If you are looking at the Compression tab of the drive Properties dialog, click the Compress Drive button.

3. In either case, you'll now be viewing the Compress a Drive dialog box, shown earlier in Figure 12.12. Clicking the Options button allows you to change the drive letter that will be assigned to the new host drive. You're also given the chance to change the amount of uncompressed free space that will be left on the host, as well as hide the host drive. Click OK.

Note

> While setting up compression, you'll be asked if you would like to update your Emergency Boot Disk, which you absolutely should do. If you don't, and you experience system problems, it's possible you won't be able to access your drives because your boot floppy won't have the necessary DriveSpace drivers.

4. Click the Start button. You'll see a progress box with an indicator and messages relating to the progress of the task. When it's finally finished, you'll see a dialog like the one in Figure 12.13. Next, you'll be warned to restart your system before using your compressed drives, which you should do.

12

FIGURE 12.13.

After completing the compression, you're shown the actual before and after capacity figures for the drive.

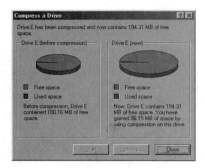

5. After your reboot has completed, check the Properties of your new compressed drive by right-clicking on it in Windows Explorer. The first thing you should notice is that the amount of free space is greatly increased.

6. Click on the Compression tab, and you'll see that this tab has changed. Whereas previously it displayed your options to compress this drive, it now displays statistics about the compression ratios of the files on the drive.

7. Click the Advanced button. This dialog box will show you more details about the compressed drive, including telling you where the compressed drive actually is (including its actual filename—usually DRVSPACE.000 on the host drive). You can also hide the host drive and launch DriveSpace from the button. Click OK.

8. The last button on the dialog is the Run Agent button, which launches the Compression Agent task. This task is covered in more detail in the next section, "The Maintenance Wizard." Click OK and you're done.

The Maintenance Wizard

Our computers are a lot more like us than perhaps we realize. I know that I start out with great intentions—I organize my files, I put all the documents related to a particular project in one folder, I alphabetize my project folders, clean up my desk, and throw out junk papers. Sooner or later, my desk starts getting cluttered again, my project files are no longer alphabetized, paper scraps start accumulating, and I have to schedule another cleanup. Does this sound like your desk? How about your computer?

The Maintenance Wizard is a handy little utility that can help optimize your computer by scheduling some of the housekeeping tasks that we all mean to do but sometimes don't get around to. Table 12.5 lists the things the Maintenance Wizard will do.

TABLE 12.5. MAINTENANCE WIZARD TASKS.

Optimization Area	Description
Optimize Compressed Drive	Schedules periodic recompression of compressed disks.
Speed Up Programs	Defragments the hard disk by moving files around so that all the pieces of the files are in a contiguous group. Also rearranges the physical location of program files so that your programs start more quickly.
Scan Hard Disk for Errors	Schedules periodic disk surface scans to detect and fix errors.
Delete Unnecessary Files	Schedules a task to remove certain unneeded "waste" files to free up disk space.

When the Maintenance Wizard is launched, it walks you through a series of dialog boxes where you can configure the various tasks the wizard can launch. The following paragraphs walk through the process of running the wizard, discussing those settings that are common across all the tasks you can configure, and then visit each maintenance area in more detail.

You'll notice that these tasks are all getting scheduled. You'd conclude that later, some other program will run these tasks, and you'd be correct. The Task Scheduler program keeps a list of what programs should be run when and executes them at their appointed times, if possible. The Task Scheduler is covered in more detail later in this chapter.

Each task has a Yes, <Do Something> Regularly option. Selecting the option enables the Reschedule button and a Settings button. The scheduling options are extremely flexible, ranging from as simple as Run This Program Once at 2:00 a.m., August 13 to as complex as Run Every 2nd Tuesday of the Month, the 15th of the Month, and the Last Friday of the Month. The scheduling options are covered in more detail later in the chapter in the section "The Task Scheduler."

12

The last dialog box you'll see when running the Maintenance Wizard is the one pictured in Figure 12.14, which is a summary page of what you've just configured. It will show each task, if and when it's been scheduled to run, and what the schedule is. More than one person has scheduled tasks for execution, only to find out they weren't completed because he or she turned the machine off or because the machine put itself into energy-saving standby mode.

Note

In the interest of conserving energy, you probably don't want to leave your machine on all the time. But picking a single night to leave your PC on and scheduling all your maintenance tasks for the same night of the week seem a reasonable compromise.

FIGURE 12.14.

The Maintenance Wizard summary showing task schedules for the Optimize Compressed Drive, Speed Up Programs, Scan Hard Disk for Errors, and the Delete Unnecessary Files tool.

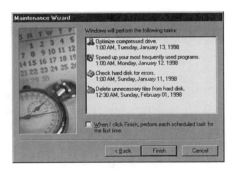

So, you've completed the Maintenance Wizard. Now what? Nothing happened, did it? If you look in the taskbar, you'll see a new icon (it might have been there before now), the Task Scheduler icon. Double-click the icon to open the Scheduled Tasks window, shown in Figure 12.15. The Maintenance Wizard created the last three tasks listed in the window, each starting with Maintenance. I've adjusted the columns so that the task names and dates are more visible. Rest assured, if your computer is on when those tasks come due, they will be run.

FIGURE 12.15.

The Task Scheduler showing the maintenance tasks scheduled by the Maintenance Wizard.

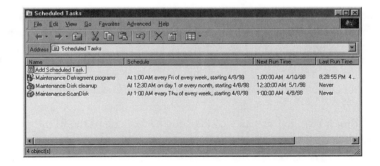

Task 12.8. Running the Maintenance Wizard

For right now, consider this a practice run. You'll actually run the Maintenance Wizard, but you'll then delete the scheduled tasks. This is because you'll need to decide, after reading the rest of this section, which tasks you actually want executed. When you're ready, you'll perform this task again, minus step 14.

1. Start the Maintenance Wizard from the System Tools group. Click Next.

▼   2. You're given the option of selecting the Express method, which automatically configures the maintenance tasks with the most common configuration settings, or the Custom method, which lets you select your own schedule and settings. Click Custom and then Next.

3. Now you're asked to select a schedule: Nights, Days, Evenings, or a custom schedule. This setting determines when Windows will initially schedule each task. You'll still be able to individually set a schedule for each task. Click Nights and then Next.

> **Note**   If you don't have a compressed drive, go to step 6. If you do have a compressed drive, go to step 4.

4. At the Optimize Compressed Drive dialog box, click Yes, Optimize My Compressed Drive Regularly.

5. As you see, Windows has set the default schedule for this task to be 01:00 a.m. every Tuesday (your day of the week may vary). Clicking the Settings button brings up the Compression Agent settings, discussed earlier in this chapter. Click OK and then Next.

6. You're now at the Speed Up Programs dialog. You see that the default schedule is to run this task at 01:00 a.m. every Monday (again, your day of the week may be different). Click Settings and verify that All Hard Drives is selected and that the Rearrange program files option is selected. Click OK.

7. Click Next and you're now at the Scan Hard Disk for Errors task. It is also scheduled to run every week, but on Sundays, at 01:00 a.m.

8. Click Settings and verify that the Thorough Testing is selected, along with Automatically Fix Errors. Click OK and then Next.

9. You're now at the Delete Unnecessary Files task. The scheduled time should show 12:30 a.m. on day 1 of every month.

10. Click Settings. Look at which types are selected by default, but don't change these until you've learned more about this task.

11. Click on each file type in turn, and notice that the Description changes and describes what each file type is. Be sure not to add or remove any of the default selections.

12. Click OK and Next. You're shown a summary of what you've just scheduled. Click Finish, and your Maintenance tasks will be automatically added to the Task
▼   Scheduler.

12

▼   13. Open the Task Scheduler window by double-clicking on the Scheduler icon on the System Tray or by opening the Scheduler from the System Tools group.

Note

> You can delete the newly scheduled tasks as in the next step if you like. You just created them here for familiarization. At any time, you can rerun the Maintenance Wizard and re-create the tasks.

▲   14. Select each task that starts with Maintenance and then press the Delete key. Click OK when asked to confirm deletion of the item. Close the Scheduler.

That's it for the Maintenance Wizard. You probably won't need to run the Maintenance Wizard more than once. If you do want to redo these task schedules, you can do it either from the Task Scheduler or by deleting those scheduled tasks and rerunning the Maintenance Wizard.

The following sections discuss each of the maintenance tasks in detail, in the order they were encountered when running the Wizard.

Optimize Compressed Drive

If you're running a drive that's been compressed with DriveSpace3, you'll want to be sure that you get maximum available space on your compressed drive. To that end, the Optimize Compressed Drive task schedules the Compression Agent for regular execution.

If you remember back to when you created your compressed drive, you made some configuration choices that determined how your files were compressed. You were able to select both the type of compression (HiPack, Standard, or no compression) and when to use compression (only when drive is X% full or not at all). Using the Compression Agent actually introduces yet another level of compression, UltraPack, and gives a large degree of flexibility in determining how and when files should be compressed.

Task 12.9. Configuring the Compression Agent

If you're running a compressed drive, this task will assist you in learning how to configure the Compression Agent for optimum drive utilization:

1. Start the Compression Agent from the System Tools folder. The main Compression Agent window opens. This window will display statistics relating to the compression task as the program runs.

▼   2. Click the Settings button.

▼ 3. You have two questions to answer: Which files do you want to UltraPack, and Do you want to HiPack the rest of your files? Click UltraPack Only Files Not Used Within the Last 30 Days, and Yes (good performance, good compression). These should be the default settings.

4. Explore the settings behind the Exceptions and Advanced buttons. Click OK when ready to proceed.

5. Click the Overview button to read the related Help topic. Close the Help topic when you've finished reading.

▲ 6. Click Start. When the Agent has finished, review the statistics to verify the space recovered and then click Exit.

Use this procedure to configure the Compression Agent when you're ready to set up a schedule to run it periodically.

The Help file on compression states that UltraPack compression takes the longest to read and write but typically compresses files to approximately one-third of their uncompressed size. HiPack compresses files to about one-half of normal but has different access characteristics. HiPack files don't write very quickly but read very quickly. This makes HiPack a good compression choice for certain kinds of files—those that are read but seldom, if ever, written. This could include DLL files, Help files, even executable (.exe or .com) files. You could use the Exceptions button in the Compression Agent settings to specify that these files are always HiPacked.

One more consideration regarding the compression used is the processor in your computer system. Microsoft says that UltraPack can be rather slow on 486 class or earlier machines and that you'll want at least a Pentium class computer. Let me put my own spin on this. If you're using a 486 or older computer, you have two options: Don't run Windows 98 with a compressed drive, because you're not likely to be content with the performance, or run—don't walk—to the nearest computer store and upgrade to a Pentium class or better machine.

Additionally, consider these facts. If you're running on a machine with enough power to do the compression—that is, a Pentium class machine—it's a newer machine (let's say less than two years old) and probably has at least a 1GB disk on it. So, ask yourself if you really need to run a compressed drive. I'm not saying there's anything wrong with doing so (I do because I always seem to be short of drive space); just don't run compression simply because it's there.

12

Speed Up Programs

The Speed Up Programs task rearranges where your programs' files are stored on the disk, moving them so that each file is not only contiguous but so that they are all close to each other, thereby speeding up access. You should know that this task is actually two: defragmenting and optimizing.

As you use your computer, reading and writing files and making modifications to existing files, the files slowly become fragmented. This means that they are not stored in a contiguous group of clusters, but perhaps in multiple groups of clusters scattered across the hard disk wherever there was room available. The reason for this is fairly simple to understand. Say that from within Microsoft Excel you create a spreadsheet. You work on it for awhile and then quit, intending to come back to it later. For the sake of argument, say the computer writes the entire file into contiguous clusters on the disk. Over the next few days, you create some other files, which get written behind the spreadsheet. Now you have files both ahead of and behind your spreadsheet. Finally, you come back to Excel and finish the rest of the spreadsheet, which is now substantially larger than it was before. Since the file is larger, it can't all be stored in the same clusters where it was stored before, can it? So, the computer writes as much of the changed file back to its original location as will fit and then has to locate some free space elsewhere on the disk to store the rest of the file. You might be lucky enough that there are some clusters nearby that will hold the rest of the file. It could also turn out that it has to write the rest of the file into several different groups of clusters spread all across the surface of the disk. This is called fragmentation.

In and of itself, fragmentation is neither good nor bad—other than just seeming messy. However, a fragmented file does cause performance issues because the read/write head(s) of the disk drive must seek back and forth to find the different clusters storing the file; since this is a physical movement, it takes time. When lots of files are badly fragmented, you can hear your disk drive seeking back and forth, and the system will be slower.

Defragmentation is a process that will look at each file, determine if it's fragmented, and attempt to move files around so that all the clusters of each file are now together. This reduces or possibly eliminates the need to move the read/write heads to get the entire file read, thereby greatly decreasing the time needed to access the file.

File fragmentation increases as time goes by. Fragmentation also affects data files more than program files because your data files are the ones that are created and then modified again and again, leading to fragmentation. Program files typically aren't modified after they're on the hard disk. However, they might have been installed on a disk that was already fragmented, which means that each program file that needs to be opened to launch an application (or Windows itself)—and most Windows applications require many files to be opened when launched—might have been fragmented to begin with. The result is that every time that application is started, you'll be waiting for those disk drive read/write heads to jump all over the surface of the disk, finding the next clusters of the files—all just wasted time.

Carrying the discussion of defragmentation just one step further, let's suppose that the defragmenter just finished running and that every file on the machine is now stored in contiguous clusters. Not a single fragmented file in the bunch, which means that you should get the absolute fastest access time to each file. Can you increase the performance any more than that? Yes! Sure, each file is defragmented. But, when you launch an application like Excel, are all the Excel program files located physically close to each other? Not likely. Chances are that they're spread all over the disk. The heads might have to seek to the beginning of the disk to get the first file needed, then to the middle for the next, the beginning for the next, and so on—again, wasting time. Clearly, even if each of the files is defragmented, you could see even more speed improvement if all of a single application's files were close together. Enter the Speed Up Programs task.

The first part of Speed Up Programs is defragmentation. The second part is the optimization. If you remember the Settings dialog from Speed Up Programs, the first thing you do is select the hard disk you want to optimize, if you have more than one. If you only have one, C:, it'll already be selected. You then select via the check box whether or not you want to rearrange your programs on the hard disk.

How does Windows know which applications you use? Every time you launch an application, it gets logged. By watching which programs you run and which files those programs load, Windows can then calculate how to arrange files on your drive so that the most frequently used files are close together and therefore quick to load.

Scan Hard Disk for Errors

The ScanDisk utility program does comprehensive testing of the surface of your disk drive(s), verifying that the directory structures are valid, checking that every file entry is valid, and reading every sector of the disk, checking that it can get a good read of the data stored and then writing the data back to the same sector to verify correct writeability.

There are a number of different errors you might develop on your disks. There's the bad sector, the cross-linked file, and the lost file fragment.

The bad sector error is what you have when a sector on the disk surface just won't reliably read or write anymore. Disk drives have areas set aside for emergency use; this can be thought of as the system area. When a cluster on the drive is determined to be bad, it must be taken out of service. Drives and/or controllers do this by marking the affected

12

cluster as bad, and logically relocating it to some of the spare clusters in the system area. In this way, repeated data errors from reading the same bad clusters are avoided. More importantly, your system doesn't write a piece of some important file there, only to be unable to retrieve it later.

The cross-linked file is a sector (cluster actually) that just isn't sure which file it really belongs to. Remember, files are stored on the drive in clusters. Each cluster should contain data from only one file. Sometimes, the file directory entry in the file allocation table will record two or more files as claiming that a particular cluster belongs to that file. Clearly, this cannot be. One cluster, any cluster, can belong to only one file. If a cross-linked cluster is encountered, you can safely assume that *at most* one of the files claiming to own that cluster is correct; it's possible that the cluster really doesn't belong to any of the claiming files.

The last error is a lost file fragment. This is a cluster that appears to belong to a file, but there's no file entry in the file allocation table claiming this cluster; it's lost.

Task 12.10. Configuring the ScanDisk Utility

This Task shows you, by doing, exactly what ScanDisk can do for you. By setting the various options available, you can keep your disk drives running smoothly.

1. Start ScanDisk from the System Tools folder.

2. The window at the top displays all the local drives (no network drives will be shown) on your system. Select C:. Also put a check mark in front of the Automatically Fix Errors option.

3. Click Thorough under Type of test. Go ahead and click the Options button, and verify that the System and Data Areas option is checked and that both of the Do Not options are unchecked. Click OK.

4. Click the Advanced button. Make the following settings: Under Display Summary, select Always; under Log File, select Append to Log; under Cross-Linked Files, select Delete; under Lost File Fragments, Free; under Check Files For, Invalid filenames. Also check Check Host Drive First. If you run MS-DOS mode programs (that is, from the C:\ prompt), you should probably check Report MS-DOS Mode Name Length Errors, also. For this task, I selected Always Display Summary. In the real world, you'll probably want to select Only If Errors Found.

5. Click OK; then at the main ScanDisk window, click Start. Depending on the size of your drive, this could take a while.

6. When ScanDisk finishes, you'll see a summary box like the one shown in Figure 12.16.

On a Pentium 150 with 48MB of memory, running ScanDisk on a 1GB drive (either FAT16 or FAT32) took about 17 minutes.

FIGURE 12.16.

When complete, ScanDisk will display a summary dialog that lists disk statistics and error information.

As you can see, ScanDisk is a powerful ally to have. If you use the Task Scheduler to run ScanDisk when you're not using your machine, you should very rarely, short of an actual hardware failure, encounter a disk error.

The Do Not Repair Bad Sectors in Hidden and System Files option on the Options page is worth noting. This option is really intended for those who might be using some of the older programs that were install locked. Some programs would install hidden system files in specific locations on your hard disk during installation as a means of determining that yours was a valid copy of the program. The scheme worked by not allowing the program to run if this hidden file was not in the specific location the program expected to find it. If this hidden file were to have a disk error in it and ScanDisk moved the file, the program would cease to function. If you don't have any of this type of program, leave this box unchecked.

12

The Log File option allows you to not log, add to an existing log file, or create a new log every time ScanDisk runs. The log file, ScanDisk.log, is created in the C:\ directory. It's a text file, so it can be opened with any text editor or word processor.

Selecting the Delete option under Cross-Linked Files instructs ScanDisk to delete all files claiming the cross-linked cluster. Is this potentially a bad thing? Sure. However, it's just as likely that if you choose Make Copies or Ignore, you'll encounter errors anyway. If you select Make Copies, ScanDisk will make a copy of the cross-linked cluster and rewrite the cross-linked files so that they all have their own copy of the cross-linked cluster. Remember, though, that only one of those cross-linked files can be correct, and it's possible that none of them are. The last option, Ignore, does just that—leaves cross-linked files and clusters alone.

Your options under Lost File Fragments are Free or Convert to Files. There might be useful data in the cluster, but probably not. If you select Free, ScanDisk will mark the cluster as available so that it can be used to store other data. Selecting Convert to Files will direct ScanDisk to gather up any lost clusters that seem to belong together and create files called FileXXX.CHK in the root directory of the drive. The first converted file will be File000.CHK, the next File001.CHK, and so on. You might be able to recover data from these files; usually there's nothing of value in them.

The Check Files For section let's you instruct ScanDisk to look for Invalid Filenames (which you might be unable to open in other programs), Invalid Dates and Times (which might cause programs that check file dates, like Backup, to miss files), or Duplicate Names. (There should never be duplicate filenames in a folder.)

The Check Host Drive First setting is only applicable if you have compressed a drive using a compression tool, such as DoubleSpace or DriveSpace. This option will cause the physical, uncompressed drive to be checked first, followed by a check of the compressed drive. If you have a compressed drive, you'll want to select this option. The last option, Report MS-DOS Mode Name Length Errors, is a directive to ScanDisk to report into its log any files it finds whose name under MS-DOS, which doesn't support long filenames like Windows does, would not be valid. Under MS-DOS, filenames must be of the format *xxxxxxx.yyy* (commonly called the 8.3 filename), and total length, including directories, must be fewer than 66 characters.

Delete Unnecessary Files

The last of the tasks that the Maintenance Wizard will configure is the Delete Unnecessary Files job. This task is the one that will run through your computer, deleting leftover, unnecessary files. Table 12.6 lists the files that will be deleted. Select each type you want to have automatically deleted. Unless you know that you have files of these types that you want to save, there's really no reason not to let these all be deleted.

When you make your selections, several of the file type selections will have a View Files button that allows you to see which files would be removed.

TABLE 12.6. FILE TYPES, LOCATIONS, AND DESCRIPTIONS FOR THE DELETE FILES TASK.

Files to Be Removed	Description
Temporary Internet files	These are Web pages that have been downloaded to your computer.
Temporary setup files	Many setup or installation programs create temporary files that are generally deleted when the setup program exits. Sometimes these files don't get deleted, but should be.
Downloaded program files	These are ActiveX controls and Java applets that were downloaded from some of the Web sites that you've visited. Keeping them will speed up your browsing the next time you visit the same site.
Recycle Bin	The Recycle Bin is where all the files you delete go to. They sit in the bin until you empty it or until it grows to a certain size.
Old ScanDisk files in the root folder	If ScanDisk is configured to save lost fragments as files, they get stored in the root of the drive. Usually these files are of no value.
Temporary files	Many programs will write temporary files into the TEMP folder. If these files are a week old, they're considered safe to delete.
Windows Setup temporary files	These are files that might have been left over from an unsuccessful setup of Windows.
Delete Windows 98 uninstall information	During Windows 98 installation, you were given the option of saving your previous Operating System information so that you could uninstall Windows 98. The option takes up a lot of space. If you don't want to be able to uninstall Windows, select this.

12

The Task Scheduler

The Task Scheduler is a very flexible program scheduling utility. As you've already discovered, Windows itself makes use of the Task Scheduler by scheduling the jobs configured during the Maintenance Wizard. Open the Task Scheduler by double-clicking its icon in the taskbar System Tray, or from the System Tools folder (Start | Programs | Accessories | System Tools | Scheduled Tasks). The Task Scheduler window was shown earlier in Figure 12.15.

The Task Scheduler window displays any scheduled tasks. There will always be at least one entry listed there: Add Scheduled Task. On the Advanced menu on the menu bar, you'll find the menu choices Start/Stop Using Task Scheduler, Continue/Pause Task Scheduler, Notify Me of Missed Tasks, and View Log. The Scheduler can be running or not; if it is currently running, the first Advanced menu will read Stop Task Scheduler, and vice versa. If the Scheduler is not running, you'll not see the icon in the System Tray area of the taskbar. Even though the Scheduler might be running, you could pause or continue it using the Pause/Continue Task Scheduler option. When the Scheduler is paused, the icon in the System Tray will change to show a white *X* in a red circle on top of the icon. Also, the pop-up ToolTip will indicate the current status of the Scheduler.

Task 12.11. Creating a Scheduled Task

There are many, many options available to you when creating a scheduled task. During this Task, take the time to explore and investigate the many options on the dialog tabs. Many of them are discussed after the Task.

1. Open the Task Scheduler. Verify that the Task Scheduler is active by looking under the Advanced menu. If the first option is Start Using Task Scheduler, select that option to start the scheduler. If the first option is Stop Using the Task Scheduler, it's already running.

2. Double-click on Add Scheduled Task, and the Scheduled Task Wizard appears. Click Next.

3. If the application you want to schedule is shown in the list, select it. If it's not there, you can use the Browse button to find it. For now, scroll the list and click on ScanDisk; then click Next.

4. Enter a name for this task if you want. The default will be the name of the application. You might want to enter a name like Tuesday Disk Verify. Click Weekly under Schedule to Run; then click Next.

5. On the next dialog, change the time to 01:00 a.m., run weekly on Tuesdays, starting next Tuesday. Click Next. The check box labeled Open Advanced Properties for This Task When I Click Finish will display the properties dialog for the scheduled task to allow you to make even more configuration settings. For now, don't check it.

6. Click Finish, and you're done. Listed in the Task Scheduler window will be your newly scheduled task, awaiting the proper time to be executed.

Don't delete the scheduled ScanDisk task; you'll use it for the next Task. You just used the wizard to add a scheduled task. For most of the programs you'll want to run on a regular basis, the wizard will meet your needs. As you'll see in the next Task, there are many more scheduling options available.

Double-clicking on any of the scheduled tasks listed in the window (except Add Scheduled Task), or right-clicking and selecting Properties, will call up the Task Properties dialog box. There are three tabs available: Task, Schedule, and Settings. At the bottom of the dialog is a check box for enabling or disabling this task. The Task tab describes what program is to be run and whether it's enabled, allows you to enter comments about the scheduled job, and, if the program supports it, allows you to directly set options in the program via a Settings button.

The Schedule tab contains all the scheduling information for this task. Using the Advanced button, you could also set a range of dates for this task to run (for example, between July 1 and September 1) and even set it to repeat every 15 minutes for 2 hours. Sitting at the bottom of the Schedule tab is the Show Multiple Schedules option. Why would you want to be able to set up multiple schedules for a task? As an example, say you want a program to run every Tuesday, the 13th of the month, and the last Sunday in October. You could set up three scheduled tasks in the Task Scheduler, each running the same program but with different schedules, or you could enable multiple schedules for a single task entry.

The Settings tab allows you to specify whether the task should be terminated if you start using the PC or whether it should even start if the PC is running on battery power.

Task 12.12. Modifying the Schedule of a Scheduled Task

In this task, you'll investigate more fully the many scheduling options available to you. You'll also create a scheduled task with multiple schedules enabled.

1. Open the Task Scheduler. Double-click on the ScanDisk task you created in Task 12.11.

2. Click on the Schedule tab. In the Schedule task box, select each option (Daily, Weekly, Monthly, Once, At System Startup, At Logon, and When Idle) in turn, and observe the different choices available depending on the schedule selected. Notice, too, that as you make a selection, the schedule is described in plain English at the top of the dialog box.

3. After you've explored the Schedule options, set this ScanDisk task to run Once, about three months from now, during the middle of the night. Finally, place a check mark next to the Show Multiple Schedules option at the bottom of the dialog.

4. Notice the change at the top of the dialog. The Run Once schedule you entered previously is showing in the box as schedule 1, and clicking the drop-down arrow confirms that there are no other schedules enabled.

5. Click the New button. Listed now in the drop-down box is schedule 2, a Daily schedule.

▲ TASK

12

▼ 6. Click the New button again. Schedule 3 is now listed. Select schedule 2, and change it to be a Weekly on Thursday task.

7. Click OK. Go back to the Task Scheduler window and observe the listing for the ScanDisk task you just created. If it hasn't changed, press F5 or click View | Refresh. Your ScanDisk task should now show Multiple schedule times under the Schedule column.

▲ 8. Delete your newly created task.

You've not only created a scheduled task but have also enabled multiple schedules for it and looked at the multitude of configuration options the Task Scheduler offers. Whenever you need to schedule a program to be run at a later time, you'll be able to quite easily.

> When you schedule a task to run on Day 29, 30, or 31 of the month, the task will run only in months that have those day numbers. There is no Last Day of the Month setting.

Backup

Despite our best efforts, sometimes things go south on us. Disk drives fail, laptops get dropped, applications crash, files are corrupted. It happens. We deal with it.

When it happens to your critical project plan, the one you've been working on for three weeks, what do you do? The answer, of course, is simple: Get out your backup and restore the file. Sure, you might have lost a little bit of work, whatever you've done since your last backup, but hey, that's better than losing everything, isn't it? What's that you say, you don't have a backup? Ouch. So sorry; back to square one for you.

Backup and restore programs have been around for a long time; probably since the first time a programmer spent hours working on a program, only to have to rewrite it because the computer crashed. No one likes doing backups—they've always been tedious, they take time, and you almost never need them. The operative word of course is *almost*. When you do need them, you're awfully happy you've been making them.

So, what is backup, and the restore that goes with it? Often referred to as making back-ups, or backing up, it is the process of transferring data from your fast, expensive storage devices, your hard disk(s), to slower, cheaper storage devices, such as tape drives or CD-Rs (recordable CDs). Restoring, or doing a restore, is the reverse process: locating the files you want recovered on the backup media and copying them back to your disk drive.

There are two ways that your data gets written out to a backup device: as an image or file by file. An image backup is one in which, literally, a snapshot of your disk is written out to a tape device. In other words, if your disk has 10,000 sectors, they are read from the disk in order, 1 through 10,000, and written out to the tape in that order. The disadvantage of doing an image backup is that there's no way to recover an individual file; the only way to use the image backup is to restore the entire backup image—in other words, completely restore the entire disk. If you only wanted to recover a file or two, this type of backup is clearly not ideal. It's for this very reason that image backups are seldom used anymore. In fact, I don't know of any image backup programs for Windows.

The other type of backup, by far the most common and certainly the most flexible, is the file backup. In a file backup, files are read from the disk and written out to the tape, as files. A catalog or directory is also written to the tape, listing every file stored in the backup. With backups created in this fashion, you can select a single file for restoration from the tape. The backup program included with Windows 98, called Backup, is the file backup type.

In deciding how often to do backups, the prime question is always: How important is your data? How long would it take you to re-create it? If you manipulate lots of data files—whether they're documents, spreadsheets, or databases—you'll probably want to back up more frequently, perhaps as often as every day. If your data files don't see as much activity, a weekly or even monthly backup schedule might be appropriate. For purposes of discussion, a daily backup schedule is assumed here.

In general, you have two types of files on your system: program files and data files. Data files are the ones that contain data: again, documents or spreadsheets that you create. Program files are all the files that are part of a program, whether that program is Windows itself, Lotus Notes, Microsoft Excel, or that great golf game. Program files don't change regularly, in fact, almost never. For that matter, most of your data files won't change every day either. For these reasons, you can see that backing up all files on your disk every day is really not necessary because most of them are the same today as they were yesterday. What you need to develop is a backup scheme. There are two types of backup schemes: incremental and differential.

Incremental Backups

First and foremost, all backup schemes start with a full backup—every single file on your disk is backed up. This becomes the baseline backup. Label this full backup Monday. When Tuesday rolls around, you need to decide what files have changed since your Monday backup. Do you remember every file that you've used since Monday? You might not remember, but your system does (sort of). As you might already know, for each file, Windows keeps track of things like its size, creation date, last modification date, and its attributes—such as whether it is read-only, or a system or hidden file. Another attribute that each file has is the archive bit. When you created your Monday backup, the backup program cleared the archive bit on every file it backed up. Every time you modify a file, Windows will set the archive bit.

So you can see that when you run the Tuesday backup, you just tell Backup to back up all the files that have the archive bit set. This is called an incremental backup. As your backup program is backing up those modified files to the tape, it is also clearing the archive bit. When Wednesday's job runs, once again only those files with the archive bit set will be backed up.

This pattern of incremental backups continues through Monday. On Monday, you'll want to do a full backup again. Why not just continue with another incremental? Assume that the worst has happened and on Friday you accidentally deleted a full directory of data files, the C:\Data directory. How do you recover those files? First, you might not know exactly which files were in that directory, right? Let's look at the catalog of files that were backed up on Thursday for that directory. The catalog lists two files. What does that mean? That means that between Wednesday and Thursday, those two files were modified. You still don't know what other files might have been in the directory. Now, look at the Wednesday backup catalog. Wednesday's catalog shows no files for the C:\Data directory. Tuesday's catalog shows five files, including one that was also backed up on Thursday. Do you yet know the entire contents of the directory? Nope. Looking at Monday's backup (the full backup) shows us the full file listing for the directory.

How would you restore the directory? In this case, you'd have to restore the entire directory from Monday and then restore the directory from Tuesday's backup, then from Thursday's backup. Remember that Monday's backup contained all the files from the directory, as they were on Monday. Restoring Tuesday's tape brought back the files modified between Monday and Tuesday. Restoring Thursday's tape brought back any files modified between Tuesday and Thursday. Couldn't you have just restored Monday's and Thursday's tapes and have been done with it? No, because Thursday's tape only contained changes since Wednesday. Remember that five files were modified between Monday and Tuesday. If you restored only Monday and Thursday, you'd be missing Tuesday's changes.

As you can tell, this gets a little cumbersome, which is why you should periodically, like every week, do a full backup. This updates your baseline backup.

Differential Backups

The other common backup scheme is the differential backup. The differential also begins with a full backup on Monday. On Tuesday, all files changed since Monday are backed up, same as the incremental backup. The difference here is that the archive bit is not cleared. On Wednesday's backup, all files with the archive bit set are backed up—which now includes all files changed since Monday. Ditto for Thursday and Friday. Each day's backup will contain all the files changed since Monday. Because of this, each day's backup will take longer because each day's backup will include not only files changed since yesterday but also all the files that were backed up yesterday. On Monday, you again run a full backup.

Restoring from a differential is a bit easier than from an incremental because at most only two tapes are required: the last full backup and the last differential.

Regardless of whether you use incremental backups or differential backups, consider this question: Should I overwrite last Monday's backup tape with this Monday's backup? Generally, no, although again, your data needs will determine what's best for you. Another example will illustrate what I mean. You have a full backup from last Monday and daily backups (incremental or differential) from every day in between. On Thursday, you deleted a file. On Monday you erase last Monday's backup and do another full backup. On Tuesday you realize that you really didn't want to delete that file that you deleted last Thursday. Can you recover that file? No, it's gone forever because the last copy of the file was on last Monday's backup, which has since been erased. For this reason, you should consider using multiple backup sets. I use five backup sets, on the rotation shown in Table 12.7.

TABLE 12.7. BACKUP SET ROTATION SCHEDULE.

Backup Set	When Used
1	First Monday of the month
2	Second Monday
3	Third Monday
4	Fourth Monday
5	Fifth Monday (if there is one)

12

Using this rotation, I can recover a file from as long ago as a month. If you need data retention longer than a month, you could easily extend the schedule to include a monthly backup, perhaps done on the first Monday of the month. Then, every month, you'd use a new tape for your monthly full backup. Commercial sites use a rotation like this for data retention of a year or more. For most users, a one-month retention will be more than enough.

The last thing I want to talk about before jumping into the Backup program is the concept of backup jobs. I mentioned doing full backups every Monday, then daily backups the remaining days of the week. The settings for these backups are repetitive. It's time-consuming to have to configure a backup every day. For that reason, Backup makes it possible to save settings for a particular backup as a backup job. That way, when you want to run the daily differential, you just specify the daily backup job with its stored settings.

When you start the Backup program, you're brought to a simple menu, which can be disabled. The main window is shown in Figure 12.17. As you see, there are two main tabs, one each for Backup and Restore. For either, you select a job name to run (if the one you want already exists; otherwise, create a new one). Select the files you want backed up or restored; then launch the task. Let's configure a backup job right now.

Note

Because everyone might not have a backup device handy, please note this departure from the normal procedure. The next three Tasks describe the steps necessary to create a full backup job, create a differential backup job, and do a restore. Even if you do have a backup device available, these Tasks could take several hours. Refer to these Tasks when you are ready to perform them. For right now, as you're learning about backing up and restoring, skip ahead to Tasks 12.16 and 12.17. In these two Tasks, you'll back up just a few files onto a floppy disk and then restore them.

Task 12.13. Configuring Backup to Do a Full Backup on the C: Drive

This backup job can serve as the weekly full backup for your backup schedule:

1. Open Backup from the System Tools group. The first dialog is the "easy menu" shown in Figure 12.17. Click Close.

2. In the main window, you'll see that this new job is an Untitled job. The center portion of the window, What to Back Up, is where you'll select files for backing up. Click the All Selected Files radio button.

3. The two-pane view works just like the Windows Explorer: objects and folders on the left, contents of the folders on the right. Click in the empty box just to the left of the icon for the C: drive. This sets a check mark into the box.

   To verify that everything on the C: drive is actually selected, expand the folder tree for C: by clicking the + next to the drive icon. Notice that every folder now displayed also has a check mark next to it. If you continue navigating to the file level, you'll see that every file has a check mark also.

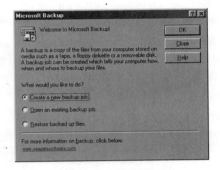

FIGURE 12.17.

Backup program "easy menu" makes it easy to get started backing up or restoring.

4. Set your Where to Back Up options in the bottom section of the window. Your backup device should already be displayed; select it from the list if it's not.

5. Set your How to Back Up options by clicking the Options button. For this job, leave them at their default settings, but take a minute to peruse the settings available on the six tabs, shown in Figure 12.18.

FIGURE 12.18.

The Backup Job Options tabs give you nearly complete control over how your files get backed up.

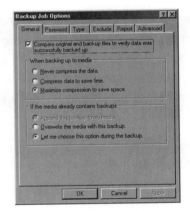

12

6. Click the Start button. You'll be asked to give this backup job a name. Call it Monday Full Backup – C. Click Save. You'll see Backup counting the files and total number of bytes that will be backed up.

7. If you haven't already, you'll be asked to insert a media into the backup device. After doing so, you'll see the backup progress dialog. If this is the first time you've used this tape, you'll be asked to enter a unique name for this media; enter **Monday Full Backup**. What you enter becomes the name of this tape.

▼ 8. If this tape already contains a backup set, you'll be asked if you want to append the current backup job to the tape, overwrite what's on the tape, use another tape or cancel. For your full backups, you'll usually select Overwrite.

9. The backup will proceed to completion, updating the progress window as it goes. After the files have all been written to the tape, the tape will rewind, and the verify pass will commence. After the verify has finished, remove the tape and store it
▲   away.

Congratulations! You've just backed up your drive. To complete your backup process, you'll need to create a job for the daily backups (differential backups are the default) and learn how to do a restore.

Task 12.14. Creating a Daily Differential Backup Job

This backup job will complete your backup schedule:

1. From the Backup main window, click the New Backup Job tool, or select Job|New.

2. In the What to Back Up section, select New and Changed Files. Click the box next to the C: drive icon.

3. In the Where to Back Up section, ensure that your backup device is selected.

4. In the How to Back Up section, Click Options and then click the Type tab. Verify that Differential backup is selected.

5. Click OK in the Options dialog and then Start on the main window.

▲ 6. Save the job as Daily Differential. The backup will finish as before.

That's all there is to it.

Depending on the size of your backup media, you might be able to get more than one day's differential backup on a tape—possibly the whole week's worth.

Tip

You might want to use the Task Scheduler to create an automatic backup schedule; unfortunately, you can't. In order to do that, the Task Scheduler would need to be able to pass parameters to the Backup program to tell it what backup job to perform. The version of Backup included with Windows won't do this. You can, however, upgrade to the full Seagate Backup program by contacting Seagate Software.

The last thing you'll have to learn to make your knowledge of backing up and restoring complete is how to restore. You have the means to restore a single file, multiple files, an entire directory, or even an entire disk drive from your backups. It's not likely that you'll often, if ever, restore an entire drive—that usually only happens after a catastrophic event like a drive failure or sometimes a case of extreme user fiddling. The next Task you'll perform will be to restore a single file from a backup set.

Task 12.15. Restoring from a Backup Set

This process will be nearly the same whether you use it to restore a file, a directory, or an entire drive:

1. Start Backup. Click the Restore tab.

2. Make sure that your backup device is selected in the Restore From box. Insert the Monday Full Backup tape you made earlier and then click Refresh. The tape catalog will be read from the tape.

3. You'll be presented with a list of all the backup sets on the tape. Click next to the one you want to use. Backup will then load the file list from that backup.

4. In the What to Restore section, navigate through the folders to the C:\Windows directory. Click on the folder. In the right side of the window, scroll the list until you find the file SYSTEM.INI. Place a check mark next to it.

5. In the Where to Restore box, select Alternate Location. When you do, another field will open up below the Where to Restore box. Click the Folder button next to the new field. Navigate to C:\Windows\Temp; then click OK.

6. Under the How to Restore section, click the Options button. Read the choices on the General tab. For this task, leave it as it's currently set. Click OK.

7. Click the Start button. Backup will tell you which tape to insert. Do so and then click OK.

8. When Backup has finished, open Windows Explorer, navigate to the C:\Windows\Temp directory, and verify that the SYSTEM.INI file was restored there.

You now know most of what there is to know about Backup, certainly enough to allow you to safely back up and restore files as needed. The only thing left to do is DO IT! Knowing how to back up files won't help you if you don't actually back them up. Get in the practice of backing up your files on a regular basis. Someday, you'll be glad you did.

Now, for practice, let's do a quick backup to floppy and a restore from floppy. This will get you comfortable with the Backup program.

▼ TASK

12

Task 12.16. Backing Up to Floppy

As mentioned, this Task is a practice run for familiarization purposes. What you'll do here is, however, absolutely applicable to the real backups you'll do to protect the data on your system:

1. Put a blank floppy in your floppy drive.

2. Start the Backup program.

3. Click Create a New Backup Job and then OK.

4. On the What to Back Up dialog, click Back Up Selected Files, Folders, and Drives and then click Next.

5. The next dialog shows a view that looks a lot like Windows Explorer—drives and folders on the left side, files on the right. You're only doing a practice backup here, so click on the drive icon for the C: drive. Don't place a check mark in the box next to the C: drive; just click on the icon for the drive.

6. In the right window, click on the column heading Type. You might have to use the horizontal scrollbar to make the Type heading visible. Clicking the heading will sort the files by type.

7. Place a check mark next to the following files (all four of these should exist; don't be alarmed if they don't): Setuplog.txt, Detlog.txt, Bootlog.txt, and Netlog.txt. If you don't have any of these, select three or four other small files.

8. When you've checked those files, look at the check box next to the C: drive icon on the left side. See the gray check mark? That indicates that some files are selected. If all the files were selected, the check mark would be black. Click Next.

9. Ensure that All Selected Files is clicked and then click Next again.

10. You are now at the Where to Back Up dialog. If you have a backup device installed, it will be showing in the top box; change it to File. If you don't have a backup device, it'll already say File.

11. The next line should say C:\MyBackup.qic. This setting is the filename that you will be backing up to. Change this to read A:\MyBackup.qic (or B:\MyBackup.qic, if you have a B: drive). Optionally, you can click on the Browse button (the one with the folder on it) and graphically select the floppy drive. Click Next.

12. On the How to Back Up dialog, you can select to do a compare after the backup is created and to compress the data being backed up. For now, check only the Compress option. Click Next.

13. Give the backup job a name: My First Backup. Notice that a summary of the options being used for this backup job is listed on the dialog.

▼ 14. Click Start. Probably too fast to see, a summary box listing the file count and byte count to be backed up flashes on the screen.

15. The Backup Progress dialog box will display, giving information about what is being done. When it's complete, you'll get a Backup Completed dialog. Click OK.

16. Click the Report button to view a text report of what was done. Notice that the names of the files backed up are not listed. When you've finished viewing the report, click File | Exit.

17. Click OK at the Backup progress dialog. You're now at the main Backup window, as shown in Figure 12.19. Click the Options button.

FIGURE 12.19.

The Backup main program window gives you control over everything Backup will do.

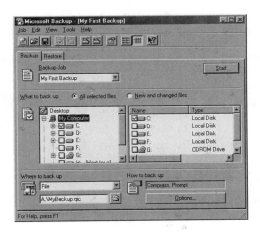

18. Take a minute to explore the configuration options available. Go to the Report tab. Click List All Files That Were Backed Up. This will include all filenames in the backup report the next time you run this job.

19. Click the Advanced tab. The sole option here is Back up Windows Registry. Click this on.

20. Click OK. Now click Job | Save. This backup job, with all its configuration options, ▲ is now saved, ready to be reused some day. Leave Backup open.

There, that wasn't so scary, was it? You've now done a backup of selected files. Your experience here will carry over when you begin doing backups of all your files.

12

Task 12.17. Restoring Files from a Floppy Backup

This Task will complete your practice usage of the Backup program by guiding you through a restore of files previously backed up:

1. Ensure that the floppy you backed up to in the previous task is in the floppy drive.

2. In the Backup program main window, click on the Restore tab. You might get a message asking you if you'd like to refresh the current view; click Yes.

3. You'll see it scan the floppy and then display a dialog box with My First Backup selected with a check mark. Click OK.

4. Backup now reads the backup set catalog to see what files are in it. Clicking on the C: drive icon in the left side of the window will display a list of the files you backed up on the right side of the Backup window.

5. Put a check mark next to the C: drive to restore all the files, or select one or two of the files by checking them individually.

6. Near the bottom of the window, under Where to Restore, select Alternate Location and then, using the Browse button, select C:\My Documents. Click OK.

7. Click the Options button. On the General tab, notice that the default is to not replace the file if it exists on your computer; this is the recommended setting. Click on the Advanced tab. For this task, we do not want to restore the Windows Registry, so uncheck the option. Click OK.

8. Click Start. Backup will tell you what media is required. In this case, it's the one in the floppy drive, so click OK.

9. The Restore will complete quickly, displaying the Operation Completed dialog box. Click OK and then click OK again.

10. You're done with Backup, so select Job | Exit. You've made changes to the My First Backup job, so you'll be asked if you want to save those changes; click Yes.

11. Using Windows Explorer, view the folder C:\My Documents and verify that the files were restored to that folder.

Done! You now have the knowledge and experience to successfully back up and restore files from your backup sets. Never again will you suffer from file loss.

Using System Recovery

In the unpleasant event that something goes terribly wrong with your system, you'll be extremely pleased to know that you can use a utility called System Recovery (or SysRec for short) to get everything back to normal. The only catch with System Recovery is that you must have used Backup to create a full system backup. Now, if that's not a reason to do a backup, what is?

If you should need to use SysRec, follow the procedure in Task 12.18.

Task 12.18. Using System Recovery

Don't do this task just for fun. If you're lucky, you'll never have to do it at all, but if you do, you'll know what to do. You'll need to have your Windows 98 CD-ROM, your Emergency Startup Disk, and your full backup handy.

1. Boot your PC from your Emergency Startup Disk.

2. After the boot finishes, insert your Windows CD-ROM. At the command prompt, type **x:** (use the drive letter for your CD-ROM instead of *x*) and press Enter.

3. Next type **CD \SysRec** and press Enter.

4. Now type **PCRESTORE** and press Enter.

5. You'll see the Windows Setup program start. Unlike normally, though, the dialog boxes will all be filled out for you. (It is possible you might have to manually select configuration information for legacy devices.) The normal Setup process will run through to completion.

6. At the Windows Logon, you'll see the username entered as System Recovery. Just hit Enter to log on; after logging on, you'll see the System Recovery Wizard. You'll be asked to have your backup media available. If your backup device(s) weren't installed automatically, you'll have to install the drivers needed.

7. Follow the directions given by the wizard, and your system will be restored from the backup.

▲

12

Note

Experienced users might find it just as easy to reinstall Windows and then restore from a backup manually. Fine. For less experienced users, the step-by-step direction given by the System Recovery Wizard can be very comforting.

Summary

Today you learned about keeping your system healthy and running well. You discovered how to get detailed information about your system using the System Information Utility. You learned how to determine and fix the problem of deleted or changed Windows system files by using the System File Checker. You used Windows Update to determine what system or driver updates are available that pertain to your system and to install or remove them.

Using the Maintenance Wizard, you discovered and configured various programs to assist in maintaining your system. First, you learned about the FAT32 conversion program, which converts your drive to the more efficient FAT32 file system. For those running compressed drives, you learned about the Compression Agent, which recompresses your files space savings or decompresses your files to give increased performance, based on your needs. Performance optimization was achieved by configuring the Defragmentation program, which both defragments files and intelligently rearranges program files to increase performance. You discovered the ScanDisk program, used to regularly test the integrity of your hard drive. The last Maintenance task you configured was the Clean Up Manager, which will remove clutter from your disk(s).

Following the Maintenance Wizard, you learned about using the Task Scheduler to automatically execute programs on a schedule. Finally, you learned about the all important task of backing up and restoring your files by using the Backup program.

Workshop

To wrap up the day, you can review terms from the chapter, see the answers to some commonly asked questions, and practice what you've learned. You can find the answers to the exercises in Appendix A, "Answers."

Terminology Review

back up—To store copies of files in another place to be used in case of emergency, such as accidental file deletion or hardware failure.

cluster—A number of hard disk sectors grouped together into an allocation unit. When additional storage is requested, another cluster is allocated for file storage.

defragmentation—The process of moving file segments around so that all the pieces of a file are contiguous, decreasing the amount of time required to access the file.

differential—As related to a backup, the backing up of all files that have changed since the last time a full backup was done.

driver—A small piece of software, usually related to a particular piece of hardware, that is used to control the device's functionality.

FAT (File Allocation Table)—A type of file system used in personal computers.

incremental—As related to a backup, the backing up of all files that have changed since the last time a backup was done.

log file—A file, usually text, where the actions and results of a process or program are written.

patch—A small update to an existing program or driver, typically done without replacing the entire program or driver.

restore—To recover files from previously created backup copies.

sector—A physical measure of the smallest storage unit available on a hard disk.

Q&A

Q If I want to minimize the time I spend doing backups, should I use the incremental or differential backup system?

A The general rule of thumb is that differential backups are slower to create but faster to restore from, whereas incrementals are faster to create and slower to restore from. The reason should be obvious: Today's incremental is a backup of any files that have changed since the last backup, which was probably yesterday's incremental backup. Today's differential backup is a backup of all files that have changed since the last full backup. If I have a disk crash tomorrow, using the incremental backups to restore would mean recovering from several tapes. However, with differential backups I could restore by using a single backup tape.

Q Can't I use the Task Scheduler to schedule an automatic backup with the Microsoft Backup program?

A No. MS Backup, as included in Windows 98, doesn't understand command-line parameters (the passing of parameters to the program), so it can't be used except interactively.

Q When I run the Maintenance Wizard, I don't see the Optimize Compressed Drive dialog.

A If you don't have at least one compressed drive, you won't see this wizard.

Q I have loaded the Compression software from my Windows CD-ROM, but I don't have a Compression tab when I display the properties for my C: drive. Why can't I compress this drive using DriveSpace3?

A Remember that a FAT32 drive cannot be compressed. If you do not have a Compression Properties tab, either the compression software has not been installed or you are viewing the properties for a FAT32 disk drive.

12

Exercises

1. Create a scheduled task to run ScanDisk regularly.

2. Describe the Compression Agent settings that would give maximum performance of a compressed drive. Describe the settings that would provide maximum storage space on a compressed drive.

3. Describe the procedure to create a compressed drive on your system using 25MB of free space on an existing hard disk.

DAY 13

Multiple Users and Windows 98

by Michael Hart

Many of us spend a lot of time on our computers (and many spouses might say too much!). As with that cubicle at work or the desk in the corner, we like to customize our working area. The Windows 98 desktop is chock-full of customizing options—not just its appearance such as background, colors, fonts, and so on, but the programs used, the contents of the My Documents folder, and the program folders. Sharing a PC opens personal workspace to changes by others.

Whether at work or at home, sharing a PC with several people is very common. At work, environments such as a shop floor or warehouse don't easily accommodate the one person/one PC concept, nor can it always be justified. Similarly, at home a PC is often shared between husband and wife, parents and children, or sisters and brothers. In any scenario, we all like to set up our own working space the way we want it and don't want it disturbed.

The examples in this chapter are based on the scenario of a home computer with multiple family members sharing access. In this chapter, you'll learn how to

- Configure Windows 98 to allow multiple user profiles or accounts
- Utilize multiple logons
- Control which settings each user is allowed to customize
- Configure the Microsoft Family Logon as the Primary Windows Logon
- Log on and log off of Windows 98
- Add, change, and delete user accounts
- Change your Windows password

A Word on Security

A bit of perspective is in order before proceeding. Remember what kind of computer you're running on here. This is not a multiuser system designed to allow 142 people to access a database or whatever. This is a personal computer, with emphasis on the personal.

Configuring your PC to allow multiple user logons makes it possible for individual users to define what their desktops look like, where they keep their documents, and some other preferences about how they like to use Windows 98. That's all! There is no security provided or enforced. If you create a document on the PC that you share and save it into your My Documents folder, you might log off that PC thinking that no one else can look at it. Not true! I come along later and log in to the PC as myself, which is perfectly okay, because we share this PC. While I'm fiddling about in Windows Explorer, I happen to find your document. Can I open it up and read it? Absolutely, no questions asked.

Not only can a "registered" user of the PC read it, but anyone who can physically walk up to the keyboard can also. (For more information about the logon prompt, see Day 20, "Windows 98 Networking.") Whether you see the Microsoft Networking prompt, the Windows Logon prompt, or the Family Logon, anyone who just hits Esc or clicks Cancel will also be allowed into the PC. Can they then get access to your file(s)? You bet.

The moral of this story is to be aware of the level of security you need for your files. If no security is needed, store them in your My Documents folder or anywhere else on the hard disk. If you need to protect your files from prying eyes, you have a few options. First, you can store your sensitive files onto floppies or other removable media and lock them up somewhere. Very secure, but less than convenient. Option two is to store them onto a file server, provided you are connected to a network. With the right access controls on your file server account, your files should be very secure. This is also generally convenient. A last option is to install a secure operating system onto those machines where you need user security and need the files local rather than on a file server. Windows NT Workstation is a good choice.

Configuring Multiple User Accounts

Very little work is actually required to configure user logons to Windows, although there are a number of options available for configuration.

The first thing to decide is whether all the users of this machine will see the same environment or whether they will each be allowed to configure their own desktops. For this chapter's scenario, a home system, assume that each user will get his or her own desktop to fuss with. This is the "major" control option, and is set on the User Profiles tab of the Passwords Control Panel applet (see Figure 13.1). Clicking All Users of This Computer Use the Same Preferences and Desktop Settings does just what it sounds like it does: Every user shares the same settings. Any customization by one user appears for every user. The Users Can Customize option is what you're interested in now.

FIGURE 13.1.

The Passwords applet has the main on/off switch for allowing users to customize their own desktops.

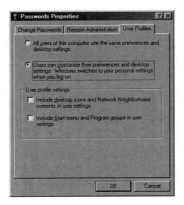

After you've decided to allow individualized desktops, you have two other options available—Include Desktop and Network Neighborhood Contents, and Include Start Menu and Program Groups. Both of these settings can be overridden by the settings in the Users applet of the Control Panel.

The real control over how much customization each user can control is in the Users applet. From the Users applet you add new users, change their default settings, and delete users. Additionally, you can add, change, or remove a user's password (if you know the original). The areas of customization are

- The Desktop folder and Documents menu
- The Start menu

13

- The Favorites folder
- Downloaded Web pages
- The My Documents folder

Here's the way these settings interact for the user accounts. There is a default group of settings—those settings that you get if you log on to Windows with no username or hit Esc at the logon prompt. You can think of these settings as the default or system settings.

The Desktop folder holds all the icons that appear on a user's desktop. The Documents folder, which holds a list of recently opened documents, shows up on the Start menu under Documents. The Start Menu setting obviously controls what shows up on the user's Start menu: the folders and items. The Favorites folder is a list of links to favorite items—Web sites, or files or folders on your local hard disk or on a network server. The Downloaded Web Pages setting controls the usage of the Temporary Internet Files folder and the Cookies folder. The Temporary Internet Files folder is also referred to as the cache for Internet Explorer and holds pages recently visited using Internet Explorer. The Cookies folder is where Web sites store cookies: small files that contain user information such as the password for the Web site or information the user might have entered into a form at the site. The My Documents folder controls the contents of the My Documents folder that is on the user's desktop.

Checking any of these options allows the user to have a personal copy of the item selected. Leaving it unchecked means that the user will use the system copy of the item. For example, if user Diana has her own copy of the Start menu, when she installs a new application, the application's folder and icons will show up on her Start menu, but not on anyone else's. Other users can add the icon and run the program, but they won't automatically see the new program folder on their Start menu.

Conversely, if a user who shares the system Start menu (in other words, who does not have a private Start menu) adds an application to the Start menu, all users who use the system default Start menu will see the new Start menu items; users who have a private Start menu won't see the new items.

The same concept holds true for each of the other options. The user either gets a private copy to personalize or shares the system copy. Now, there is one thing you have to be aware of. Do you remember that the major control setting for the personalization options was on the User Profiles tab of the Password applet? Refer back to Figure 13.1 to see a screen shot of the tab. Any user can change this setting! So you see that, once again, Windows doesn't really provide security and control in this regard. Although it might not be likely that users will be poking around in the Passwords applet, it could happen.

Fear not, though. If a user should turn off the Users Can Customize option, turning it back on will restore all the customizations that the users previously had; they won't be lost. Turning on the Customize setting will restore all user settings after a reboot of the PC.

Similarly, users also have access to the Users applet. Any user could get in and change the settings for any other user. However, here, too, should a customization option get reset (accidentally or otherwise), the user won't lose anything. When the option is turned on, the customization will be returned. However, anything that might have been in the system settings will have been added to the user's settings.

The following series of screen shots illustrate the customization settings—in this case, the Start menu. In Figures 13.2 through 13.5, as you look at the differences in the Start menu that result from changing the settings in the Users Control Panel applet, watch the Log Off option to see which user's Start menu is currently shown. Figure 13.2 shows the Start menu for Jaimie, showing the contents of her Programs folder. Notice that user Jaimie has, on her Start menu, a folder called Jaimie's Games.

FIGURE 13.2.

Notice the folder called Jaimie's Games. She does not show a Useful Utilities folder on her Start menu.

On the default Start menu there is a folder called Useful Utilities, as shown in Figure 13.3. To get the default (or System) Start menu, you'd hit Esc at the logon prompt.

Somehow, the Start menu customization setting for Jaimie's account gets turned off. When Jaimie next logs on, she sees the default Start menu, including the Useful Utilities folder (see Figure 13.4). You know Jaimie's logged in because her name shows on the Log Off option.

13

FIGURE 13.3.

The System default Start menu Programs folder includes a folder called Useful Utilities.

FIGURE 13.4.

Jaimie's Start | Programs folder after her Start menu customization was turned off. She now sees the System Start menu contents.

After the Start menu option for her account is turned back on, and she logs off and on, she now sees both the Useful Utilities folder and her Jaimie's Games folder, as you can see in Figure 13.5.

How does this happen? Jaimie previously had a customized Start menu with the Jaimie's Games folder on it. When her Start menu customization was turned back on, Windows copied the system settings, as they are right now, into her account. Because the Useful Utilities folder was in the system settings, it was copied into Jaimie's settings. The Jaimie's Games folder already existed, and was left.

So how does Windows do all this? Actually it's pretty simple, and even somewhat obvious, if you know where to look. Figure 13.6 shows Explorer displaying the contents of the Windows\Start Menu\Programs folder. Everything in the Start Menu folder is displayed—you guessed it—on the Start menu; Windows\Start Menu is the default Start menu discussed earlier.

FIGURE 13.5.

*Jaimie's Start |
Programs folder after
the customization
option is turned
back on.*

FIGURE 13.6.

*Explorer view showing
the folders that make
up the system default
Start menu contents.*

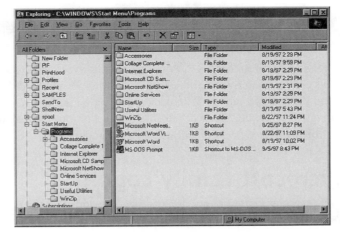

Look at the left pane of the screen shot, just about six folders above Start Menu, and
you'll see one labeled Profiles. Figure 13.7 shows the Profiles folder expanded. As you
can see, there is a folder shown for each of the customization options that can be set in the
user's Control Panel. You can see that the items listed on Jaimie's Start | Programs menu,
shown in Figure 13.5, match the folders in the Explorer view shown in Figure 13.7.

13

> **Tip**
>
> The easiest way to modify the contents of your Start menu is to click Start |
> Settings | Taskbar & Start Menu, click the Start Menu Programs tab, and then
> click the Advanced button. This will bring up an Explorer window displaying
> your Start menu contents. From this you can easily add folders, shortcuts, or
> icons to your Start menu.

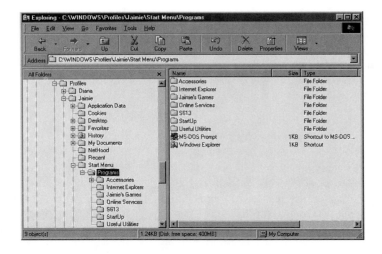

When a user logs on to Windows, Windows checks to see if the user is registered. If not, Windows creates an account for the user on the spot, using the default settings, as discussed earlier in this chapter. If the person logging on is a registered user, Windows uses the settings stored under his or her Profile folder. For those items not stored under the user's Profile folder, Windows will use the system default.

The Microsoft Family Logon

After all your configurations are done and you've added all the user accounts you need, there's one last step that will make logging on a little bit easier for your users.

If you have a network installed, you chose either the Client for Microsoft Networks or the Windows Logon as the Primary Network Logon. If you don't have a network, you might not even have to enter a username and password to get into Windows. Either way, you will be getting a logon prompt now—some method is required for your users to identify themselves to Windows.

The Client for Microsoft Networks logon prompt is shown in Figure 13.8. Except for the wording, the Windows Logon prompt looks the same. The username box will appear with the name of the last user who logged on already entered. A password needs to be typed into the password box. This all works well. The only problem comes when someone can't remember his username (usually those of us with more gray hairs!). Was that username Michael or mhart?

FIGURE 13.8.

The Client for Microsoft Networks logon prompt. The Windows Logon looks essentially the same.

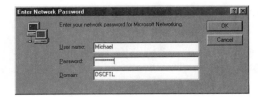

What happens if someone incorrectly types in his or her username? If Windows doesn't recognize the username, it assumes that this is a new user and creates a new user account on the spot. The user is prompted to enter a password for the new account (twice to ensure accuracy) and is then logged on. If this is really not a new user but one that spelled his username wrong, he will not see his old desktop, which of course sort of defeats the whole purpose, doesn't it?

Setting the Primary Network Logon to the Microsoft Family Logon, as shown in Figure 13.9, helps alleviate the problem. As you can see, the Family Logon lists all the known usernames in a scrolling list box. The user then simply selects the right username from the list, types in the password, and clicks OK.

FIGURE 13.9.

The Microsoft Family Logon showing a list of usernames.

Configuring the Family Logon for use is simplicity itself.

Task 13.1. Configuring the Microsoft Family Logon

The Family Logon will enable your users to log on with even less effort. This Task shows you how:

1. Open the Control Panel and then open the Network applet. Alternatively, if you have the Network Neighborhood icon on your desktop, right-click it and then select Properties.

2. On the Configuration tab, click the Add button. Select Client and then click Add again.

▼   3. Under the Manufacturers list, select Microsoft. Under the Network Clients list, select Microsoft Family Logon. Click OK.

4. You might be asked to provide a path for some files. As you've done previously, you might have to insert your Windows 98 CD-ROM.

5. When the installation is complete, you'll be back at the Network dialog box. The Family Logon client will now appear in the Installed Components list at the top of the dialog.

6. Under Primary Network Logon, select the Family client. Take a look at Figure 13.10, which shows the Family client listed in the installed components list, the Family Logon as the Primary Network client, and a description of the Family client in the Description area.

FIGURE 13.10.

The Network properties box showing the Family Logon installed and selected as the Primary Network Logon.

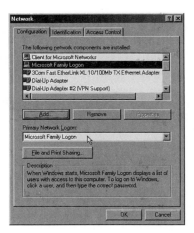

7. Click OK. You'll be presented with a dialog box asking if you want to reboot now. Click Yes.

8. After your PC has rebooted, you'll set the Family Logon prompt asking you to
▲   select a username and enter a password.

A simpler installation you couldn't ask for; now that you've done it, you'll be comfortable should you ever need to do it again (or undo it).

Controlling What Other Users Can Access

As already mentioned, Windows 98 does not provide any access control over local storage devices—your hard disks, floppies, removable drives, or tapes. The bottom line is this: If there's something on your computer, any user of your computer can access it. Many programs, such as Excel, allow you to password-protect individual files; those file protections still apply. If you don't know the password, you can't get into the file. Other programs, such as Lotus Notes, allow you to encrypt locally stored files (databases in Notes); these also are protected from prying eyes unless they have the correct password.

Repeating our earlier mantra, if it needs to be secured, you must secure it. On a Windows 98 PC, that means password-protecting or encrypting it (if the program supports it), or moving it elsewhere.

Setting Up Multiple User Accounts

Getting your user accounts set up on your Windows 98 PC is very easy. If you enter a username and password when you start your PC, you've already configured the first user account—your own. For each user account, you'll be able to set the options such as Desktop, Start Menu, Favorites, and so on.

Task 13.2. Creating User Accounts

▼ TASK

Even if you don't think you'll need multiple user accounts, go ahead and create one or two, just for practice; you can delete them later.

1. Open the Control Panel. Double-click the Users applet.

2. You'll either have one or no users listed, depending on whether you enter a username and password when starting Windows. Click the New User button and then Next.

3. Enter a username for the new user account. Usernames can be up to 128 characters long; however, you probably don't want to use anywhere near that many characters, as you wouldn't be able to see the complete name in the logon box. Click Next.

4. Enter a password for the new user, if desired. If you do enter a password, you'll have to also enter it in the Confirm Password box. Click Next.

5. The Personalized Items Settings box, shown in Figure 13.11, is displayed. Here is where you'll determine which elements of their desktop users will be able to customize. The five options listed—Desktop Folder and Documents Menu, Start Menu, Favorites Folder, Downloaded Web Pages, and My Documents Folder—can

▼ be individually selected.

13

▼

FIGURE 13.11.

The Personalized Items Settings options enable you to control which aspects of the Windows interface a user is allowed to customize.

▲

6. The final option on the dialog is Create Copies of the Current Items and Their Content or Create New Items to Save Disk Space. Choosing Create Copies will give the new user a complete copy of the current checked items—the Desktop Folder and the Start Menu, for example. Choosing Create New will give the new user the items selected, but without any content. Click Next and then Finish. You'll see progress boxes as Windows creates the new user account and copies the specified items and content, if specified.

Your new account has just been created, and the user can now log on to your computer and customize his or her own workspace, within the range of settings you've provided.

Duplicating Accounts

Another way to create a new user account is to select an existing user account in the Users applet and then click Make a Copy. The new user will be created with the same settings as the selected existing user.

If you'll have a number of people sharing a machine, all of whom will have a "standard" user profile, you might want to create a user account to be used as a model first. Create a dummy account, perhaps called Standard User Profile. Make the settings appropriate to your requirements. When you're ready to create the real user accounts, select Standard User Profile from the Users list and then click Make a Copy for each new user.

Removing an Account

When the time comes to remove a user from the system, you should use the Users applet. You could remove the user's files from under the Windows\Profiles folder, but for a safe, complete removal, use the Users applet.

When you remove a user account, which deletes all the user's settings, including the individual's My Documents folder, any files stored there are gone, deleted, banished from the earth. Be sure before deleting a user!

 Yes, it's true you might be able to restore a user account and a user's files from the Recycle bin, as long as the Recycle Bin hasn't been emptied yet.

Switching Between User Accounts

Having different people using your computer is not the only reason you might want to set up multiple user accounts. You might find that you have different needs at different times, and might be able to use user accounts to assist you.

As an example, suppose you do both graphics design work and document writing. When you do your graphics work, you prefer to have your monitor resolution set to 1024×768, at 24-bit color depth. You also prefer to have a neutral colored desktop background. When you sit down to write, you prefer to have your monitor set to 800×600, 256 colors, so the text is easier to read. When you're writing, you like to have your desktop set Active, so your stock ticker and headline news ActiveX controls get updated while you're working.

Normally, you'd have to reset your monitor adapter settings and desktop controls when changing between tasks. If, however, you created two different user accounts, Writing and Graphics, you could just log on as one or the other, and all your preferred settings would be restored for you.

To use this technique, you'd create user accounts as before, in Task 13.2. Give descriptive usernames to each account so their purpose and usage are easy to distinguish. Log on as each account in turn, and configure each account for its task. When you are ready to switch to one of your special-purpose accounts, you just log off your current username and then log on as the new name.

13

To log off from the current user account, click Start | Log off (username). You'll be asked to confirm logging off; just click OK, and the screen will reset and you'll be presented with the Logon dialog box.

Editing a Password

Passwords are one of those things we love to hate. You know they're necessary for security, but don't you hate having to remember lots of different passwords? Passwords work best when they're hard to guess, which usually means hard to remember, especially if you haven't used it in a while. In a business environment, you should change your password periodically: on the interval specified in your company's computer security policy, if there is one—at least every three months otherwise.

As far as Windows 98 passwords go, you've already seen that the passwords don't actually protect against much. It's still not a bad idea to change your password occasionally. Frequently, a user will forget a password. You can remedy this also, although in a different fashion.

Task 13.3. Changing a Windows Password

This Task shows you how to change your own Windows password and the password for another user account on your PC. It will only work if you know the original password to the account.

1. To change your own Windows password, open the Passwords applet in the Control Panel. Click on the Change Windows Password button. To change the Windows password for another user account, open the User applet, click on the username, and then click the Set Password button.

2. Enter the original password to the account and then type the new password in both the New Password and Confirm New Password boxes. Click OK. Notice that you don't see the passwords as you type.

3. If you mistype any of the three passwords, you'll be alerted to your error. When you've done it correctly, Windows will tell you that the password has been changed.

If you don't remember (or the user doesn't remember) the password, you must use a different procedure. If the original password isn't known, your only option is to clear the entire password list for the account. Each user account has its own password list. The password list is an encrypted file with the name (*username*).pwl, and is stored in the C:\Windows folder. So, the user Michael would have a password list called michael.pwl. Deleting the file will clear Michael's password but have no other effect on the account. Or will it?

There are many passwords stored in the PWL file. You know how Windows remembers passwords for you, such as your Internet dial-up password and the password for connecting to your dial-up server at work? Those passwords are stored in your password list. So, if you delete that PWL file, you'll have to reenter your passwords the next time they're required.

Summary

Today you've seen how to set up your computer to allow multiple users to share it, yet allow each to have their own customization settings, if desired. You learned about the different customization settings available, and how to turn them on and off. You learned about where each user's settings are stored. You also learned about the Microsoft Family Logon client and how to turn it on. Very importantly, you learned about the security aspects of Windows—what they will and won't provide for you and your users in terms of security and access control. Lastly, you learned about adding, changing, and deleting user accounts and passwords.

Workshop

To wrap up the day, you can review terms from the chapter, see the answers to some commonly asked questions, and practice what you've learned. You can find the answers to the exercises in Appendix A, "Answers."

Terminology Review

Microsoft Family Logon—The logon dialog box that lists all the users registered on a particular computer; includes a field to enter a password.

Password list—A list kept by Windows for each user that contains a name and password for a particular point of access. For example, a user might need a username and password (completely unrelated to his or her Windows username and password) to access a particular Web site. Windows will store each username/password pair used by a user in that user's password list, the .pwl file.

Profiles folder—The folder where Windows stores each user's individual Start menu, Desktop, Favorites, downloaded Web pages, and My Documents folder and account settings.

security—Keeping computers, files, and folders protected and only allowing authorized users to have access.

username—A name that identifies the current user to Windows.

user profile—Those settings that control how Windows looks for a particular user.

13

Windows Logon—The logon dialog box that enables a user to enter a username and password before gaining access to Windows.

Q&A

Q My computer has multiple user accounts configured, but I don't see a list of usernames when I start Windows.

A Make sure that you have configured the Microsoft Family Logon as the Primary Windows Logon. You'll find this configuration setting in the Network Control Panel Applet.

Q Every day I have to change my desktop to be the way I want it. Windows doesn't seem to remember my personalized settings.

A Be sure that your computer is set up to allow each user to maintain his or her own personal settings. Go to the Control Panel, open Passwords, and on the User Profiles tab, verify that the Users Can Customize Their Preferences and Desktop Settings choice is selected.

Q If I want to tell someone to get a file out of my My Documents folder when I'm not logged on, where do I tell them to look?

A Go to the folder `Windows\Profiles\`*(your username)*`\My Documents`. All of the files you've stored in your My Documents folder will be stored there.

Q One of the other users of the computer deleted my password list file (PWL file) and I don't remember what some of the stored usernames and passwords were. How do I get those back?

A I hope someone is doing a regular backup of your hard disk. That's your best bet. You could try looking in the Recycle Bin to see if your PWL file might still be there. If it's not, sorry. There's no other way to get it back.

Exercises

1. The people who share the computer with you don't want to have to type their usernames in; they'd rather pick them from a list. What would you do to accommodate them? How would you set it up?

2. Create an account for a new user that will allow users to customize their own Start menu settings, wallpaper, and Favorites lists, without interfering with anyone else's settings.

3. When setting up a computer for members of your family to share, you realize that everyone will need to use the same programs. What settings would you make or change so that whenever a new program is installed, everyone sees it on the Start menu?

4. You, your spouse, and your two kids all share the same computer, but you each have different programs listed on your Start menu. Your daughter installs a nifty game that your spouse would also like to run, but it's not listed on your spouse's Start menu. You know that installing the game a second time would just be a waste of disk space. What would you do to put the icon for the game onto your spouse's Start menu?

13

DAY **14**

The Internet and Internet Explorer 4

by Paul Cassel

Microsoft got Internet religion late, but that hasn't prevented it from catching on with great fervor at the company. In fact, by many measures, Microsoft is now the premier software company when it comes to Internet. Some will no doubt contest that assertion—with good reason, as this isn't an easily quantifiable measure. However, by anybody's ruler, Microsoft ranks as a strong influence when it comes to the Internet and online communications in general.

Windows 95 came out before Microsoft got the "Internet Everywhere" syndrome, but even so, it showed significant connectivity improvements over its predecessor, Windows 3.11. During Windows 95's gestation, Microsoft had hopes of becoming a huge online service provider itself. This led to the introduction of The Microsoft Network, or MSN, concurrently with 95. At that time the strong online presences were large services such as America Online (AOL),

CompuServe (then CIS), and Prodigy. The Internet was a playground for academic or defense types with few ordinary users having any interest in it.

MSN was neither a runaway success nor a failure. The surprising growth in interest in the Internet concurrent with the development of the World Wide Web (WWW or Web) and away from online services such as Prodigy, CompuServe, and America Online hit it hard. Soon Microsoft modified its corporate ambitions away from being a standalone service provider to becoming the Internet company.

It changed MSN's slant away from a full-service provider to an extended service provider with strong Internet connectivity. In the same way, other online services wanting to survive in the Internet era also added strong Internet connectivity to their online mix.

By the time Windows 98 showed up, the world had changed: Internet was the dog and the large online services were the tails. Not only did Microsoft change Windows to become fully integrated with the Internet, but it also changed all its products likewise. Office 97, introduced a year before Windows 98, became as comfortable handling Web-type documents and addresses (URLs) as it did filenames and its native file formats.

That Windows 98 grew into an operating system fully integrated with the Internet came as no surprise to anybody. Microsoft has done its best to make your local computer (workstation), your LAN, and any remote connections, such as the Internet, work as a seamless unit—or at least as much as possible.

Not all of this chapter applies to any particular circumstance. There are many ways to connect to the Internet, there are many service providers, and there are many services online. The following sections will broadly cover most people's situations, but in some instances, the details won't apply to your particular one. For example, if you connect to the Internet through a proxy server and firewall, this chapter won't describe in detail how to set up your workstation or what the firewall permits. That information is better left to your network administrator as it becomes more an issue of company policy than Windows 98. This chapter sticks to the Windows 98 side of things, for the most part. This chapter covers

- Connecting to the Internet
- Setting up Dial-Up Networking (DUN) for modem connections
- Using Dial-Up Networking
- Internet Explorer
- Searching the Web
- Your Web history

- Finding and saving Favorite Places
- Configuring and customizing Internet Explorer

Connecting to the Internet

Speaking in the broadest sense, you need only a few things to get online:

- A way to physically connect—This can be a gateway connecting your LAN to the Internet or a modem along with Dial-Up Networking (DUN). Day 9, "Managing Hardware," discusses installing and configuring modems, and Day 21, "Mobile Computing with Windows 98," discusses Dial-Up Networking.
- The right protocol—In the case of the Internet, this is TCP/IP. Most online services and bulletin boards use terminal emulation, so you won't need any additional protocols. Windows 98 comes with TCP/IP, but it isn't installed by default. Terminal emulation is the capability of a personal computer to "fool" a mainframe or host computer into thinking it's a terminal rather than an independent computing unit. In most cases, personal computers use software to create the emulation.
- Client software—Windows 98 comes with a wide selection of clients. Client software is the side of a host/client session the user interacts with. For example, if you connect to a network server that has central files or a mail system, your computer becomes the client. When connecting to the Internet, your machine becomes a client to the many interconnected servers that make up the Internet.

That's about it. While few in number, there is a wealth of complexity in the choices and configurations within those three items.

The Physical Connection

If you're connected to the outside world through your local area network, or LAN, you can skip this section because the work is already done for you.

Most people working at home or in small offices don't have the luxury of a LAN to outside connection. Many don't use a LAN at all. These people can establish an Internet connection by using Dial-Up Networking (DUN) to create an ad hoc network of which they are one node, or workstation.

Although you need a modem or a device analogous to a modem for DUN, you don't need DUN to use a modem. For example, you can use a modem along with service provider client software to establish a connection to the service provider or even the Internet without DUN. Long before there was any general interest in large service providers or the Internet, there were many small dial-up host computer systems called

14

bulletin boards. You accessed these systems using terminal emulation software with a built-in dialer. Here is a list of online services and their dial-up needs:

- Large multiservice providers such as MSN, CompuServe, or America Online—The client side software has a TCP/IP protocol for connection to the Internet. You can also connect to these services through the Internet, which would require DUN or an alternative physical connection.

- Bulletin board systems—Terminal emulation software such as HyperTerminal (part of Windows 98) or ProComm Plus from Quarterdeck software. Bulletin boards themselves don't require a TCP/IP protocol or DUN to be installed. They might require a TCP/IP layer if they in turn act as passthroughs to the Internet.

- Independent service providers—These are Internet gateways available by subscription to dial-up customers from the general public. They require both DUN and TCP/IP unless they provide an alternative way to physically connect. If so, that only covers DUN and they'll still require TCP/IP to be part of your Windows 98 setup.

The bottom line is that for Internet connectivity, you need either the proprietary client/dialer software from a large service provider like AOL or another way to connect. This is usually DUN.

If you need DUN, you must first check to see if it's installed on your machine. By default, Windows 98 Setup places DUN under Start | Programs | Accessories | Communications. Figure 14.1 shows the Start menu with DUN highlighted and the group opened on the desktop. You can also reach the DUN folder from My Computer or Windows Explorer.

The computer shown in Figure 14.1 has only one DUN connection configured. This is labeled NT Server and it's a remote connection (Remote Access Server, or RAS) for a company LAN. If you don't have DUN as part of your Windows 98 setup, run the Add/Remove Programs applet from Control Panel, click the Windows Setup tab, and locate the Communications option. Click the Details button and then check the box next to Dial-Up Networking. Figure 14.2 shows this operation.

Setup might ask for your distribution CD-ROM or the location of your Windows 98 setup files. After a bit of grinding around, Setup will add Dial-Up Networking to your Accessories group.

FIGURE 14.1.

The Dial-Up Networking group or folder has an icon to launch the DUN wizard and any existing DUN connections.

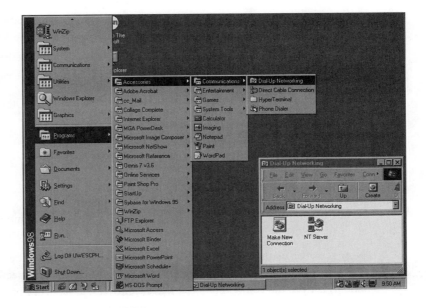

FIGURE 14.2.

You can add DUN using the Communications option from the Windows Setup tab of the Add/Remove Programs applet.

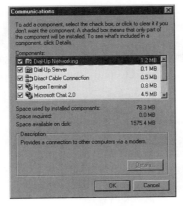

Setting Up Dial-Up Networking

How you set up DUN depends on what you'll be using it for. This chapter primarily covers Internet-specific DUN.

The most common reason people use DUN is to connect to their independent service providers (ISPs) for direct Internet connections, so this example shows how to set up a typical DUN to ISP connection. If you'll be using a large service provider such as AOL, its software should contain an equivalent to DUN.

14

To configure a DUN connection, choose Start | Programs | Accessories | Dial-Up Networking to open a group containing the Make New Connection Wizard shown in Figure 14.3. When you launch this applet, the screen shown in Figure 14.3 appears.

FIGURE 14.3.

To configure a new dial-up connection, launch the Make New Connection applet from the Dial-Up Networking group.

The first screen of the wizard gives you an opportunity to name your dial-up connection as well as specify the device the connection is to use. If your connection (usually a modem) isn't in the combo box, you need to install that device. For instructions on installing hardware, see Day 9.

This example uses the default 28.8 modem shown in Figure 14.3 and names the connection Route 66, the name of a large ISP for Internet services. Click the Next button to open a telephone number dialog box as shown in Figure 14.4. If you don't live in the United States of America, you'll also need to pull down the combo box in Figure 14.4 and make an appropriate choice.

FIGURE 14.4.

Here is the dialog box where you can specify a telephone number for each dial-up connection.

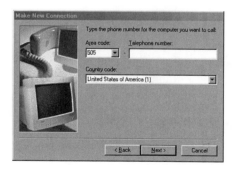

Enter a telephone number for your DUN. If you have an ISP, you should also have a numbers sheet with this information as part of your sign-up papers. Click Next and you're finished with the basic setup of a DUN. Figure 14.5 shows the success dialog box you'll see when you're done creating a DUN.

FIGURE 14.5.

Creating a new DUN takes only two steps. When finished, you'll be rewarded with this success dialog box.

Now that you've created a DUN, you must configure it for your particular server connection. Return to the Dial-Up Networking group. Locate the DUN you just created—in this case it's Route 66—and right-click on it. Choose Properties from the context menu. The resulting dialog is shown in Figure 14.6.

FIGURE 14.6.

Unlike creating a DUN, configuring one is somewhat complex.

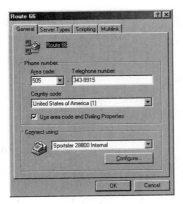

Here's what you can do at each tab:

- General—Edit the items you entered (such as telephone number) during the creation of the DUN. The Configure button opens the modem's (or similar device's) Properties for editing.
- Server Types—Tell Windows 98 what protocols it must use to connect to the server generally or, in this case, the ISP. For Internet connections, this is usually PPP and TCP/IP. Further alternatives are NetBEUI for connection to Windows- or Windows NT-only networks and IPX/SPX for connection to the older NetWare-type networks. If you're in doubt, contact your ISP's tech support people for what to enter on this tab.

14

- Scripting—Enter whether to use a log on script and if so, which one.
- Multilink—Enter whether to use more than one device for this connection. For example, some systems use one conduit for downloading from the Internet and another for the uplink side. In other cases, you can use two conventional modems along with two telephone lines to speed up an otherwise conventional Internet connection.

As the General tab has the correct information, the only configuring this DUN needs is on the second tab, Server Types. Figure 14.7 shows this tab as the Make New Connection Wizard left it.

FIGURE 14.7.

The Make New Connection Wizard left these selections behind.

As this is to be an Internet-only connection, the only protocol needed is PPP over TCP/IP. The vast majority of ISPs will accept this setup so for this example, and probably yours, uncheck the NetBEUI and IPX/SFX Compatible check boxes. If they are checked, Windows 98 can try to establish all three protocols. If your ISP is only TCP/IP (most are), this will lead to long logon delays and mysterious error messages.

The next step is to configure the TCP/IP protocol to match the requirements of your ISP. Click the TCP/IP Settings button. This brings up yet another dialog box, shown in Figure 14.8.

Usually, your ISP requires you to enter an IP for its DNS. Some ISPs will have you enter an IP for your station. You should find these addresses as part of your setup papers from your ISP. A TCP/IP address (or IP number) has four groups of up to three numbers each, separated by dots, in this form:

###.###.##[#].#[##]

FIGURE 14.8.

The last of the dialog boxes is for customizing your TCP/IP settings.

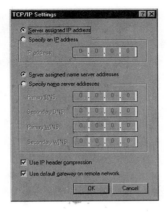

In most cases, the ISP will assign you a personal IP upon your connection to its server. For those setups (the most common), you need to choose the top option button in the TCP/IP Settings dialog, Server Assigned IP Address, and leave the boxes for specifying an address blank.

Examples of legitimate IPs are 198.45.123.3 or 201.123.23.111.

Enter the IP supplied by your ISP in the place indicated unless you're sure you don't need to do so. The second section of the TCP/IP settings dialog box concerns itself with connections to corporate type LANs, for the most part. If you're making such a connection, consult your network administrator for what you need in such settings. Specifically, this DUN will connect a Windows 98 computer to a Sun running SunOS (UNIX), hosting Apache Internet server software. If your ISP uses different host equipment, what you need to put in this dialog box can vary significantly.

That's it. Click OK to exit all the dialog boxes. You're finished setting up your new DUN.

How to Use Dial-Up Networking

There are two fundamental ways to use DUN connections. The first is to open or launch the connection (or a shortcut) directly. The other is to let your clients, such as Outlook Express (OE), launch the connection. When configuring OE, you will be asked what, if any, connection it's to use. You can specify a DUN. You can alter this option using the OE menu choices, Tools | Options | Dial-Up. In any case, the procedure is identical, although the screens will vary slightly.

This example uses the connection made in the preceding section by directly launching the DUN from the Dial-Up Networking group. This group is part of your Windows Explorer. Figure 14.9 shows the group opened from Windows Explorer.

14

FIGURE 14.9.

You can use any of your dial-up connections from Windows Explorer.

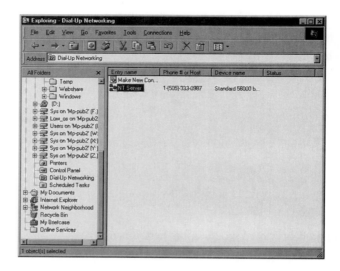

Launch DUN and the dialog shown in Figure 14.10 will appear.

FIGURE 14.10.

Enter your dial-up username and password in this dialog.

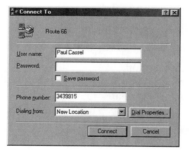

The dialog box shown in Figure 14.10 has some important features. First, the username in the box might not be (and usually isn't) your real name. Most usernames have no spaces. They can be handles, like

```
Flash
XeXiz
WingCommander
```

or variants of a real name like

```
Pcassel
TheTirilee
Paulc
cas2!73
```

Remember that the username and password can change depending on what you're logging on to. Your sign-on package from your service provider should provide you with an initial logon name and password. You'll probably want to change your password to one of your own choosing after your initial logon.

The Save Password check box will only be enabled if you log on to Windows 98 with a password. This prevents people from starting your machine and using your DUN to access your service provider. That is, if a Windows 98 machine without a startup password could save DUN passwords, anybody could not only start the machine, but also use DUN. This is a safety check. If you check this box, Windows 98 will remember your password from one DUN session to another. If you're concerned about security even slightly, leave this box unchecked, even though it means you'll have to manually enter your password at each session.

You've probably heard it before, but here it is again: Most hackers break into systems by guessing passwords rather than great feats of legerdemain in computer science. Here are some sample passwords that are commonly used:

- `8220` (house number)
- `031792` (daughter's birthday and most important holiday)
- `janie` (sister's name)

These kinds of passwords have a security rating of "bad." Anybody knowing a few facts about a user can guess things like telephone number, birthdays, relative names, and other easy-to-remember items. Fair passwords look like these:

- `$sammy$` (starts and ends with symbols)
- `saMMy` (mixed case, all alpha)

And here's a good password:

- `idKd#$&#!BBB` (mixture of cases and alphas with symbols)

The problem with good and even fair passwords is that they're so hard to remember that users tend to become locked out of their systems or prefer to use the Save Password check box to prevent such occurrences. There's nothing to be done for it. Good passwords require some work, whereas bad ones are easy to break. Only you can decide how secure you want to make your system, and choose a password accordingly.

The password will appear as all asterisks to prevent the common practice of shoulder surfing to acquire another's password. Shoulder surfing has two techniques. The first is to read a screen, which the asterisks prevent. The second is to watch a person's fingers as they type. There's nothing Windows 98 can do about the latter. That's up to you.

14

Figure 14.11 shows a DUN Connect To dialog box properly filled out.

FIGURE 14.11.

A Connect To dialog box shows asterisks in place of characters.

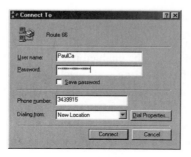

Click on Connect and let Windows 98 do the rest. If you've entered the connection information properly, you should log on automatically. If you fail to get a connection and are sure all your entries are right, check with your ISP or administrator, as you might have bad information. Also, remember that some usernames and passwords are case sensitive. Some systems see `tirilee` and `Tirilee` as the same, some don't. If in doubt, check with your ISP.

Internet Explorer

The Internet is a network with many aspects, including email, newsgroups (Usenet), file transfers (FTP), and many search engines such as Yahoo! or Gopher (to name two of vastly different types). Lately, the Internet has been used for communications previously the realm of noncomputer networks, including video and telephone.

Today's modern browsers, such as Internet Explorer, enable you to access most if not all of the Internet's assets. As providers increase the types of Internet assets, browser makers such as Netscape and Microsoft will surely expand the capacities of their products.

For many people, the World Wide Web is synonymous with the Internet. This is likely due to two things. Most of what people find interesting on the Internet is part of the Web and the new browsers themselves handle activities that have traditionally been part of other client packages.

So today, many people never have to leave their browsers to use the Internet. In fact, many people get good use of the Internet never realizing that the system can do more than support their browsing.

Windows 98 is a giant leap forward compared to any previous operating system when it comes to integrating the Internet (or intranets or extranets) into the desktop. Using the Internet with Windows 98 is seamless, especially if you have an Internet-aware productivity suite such as Microsoft Office 97 or WordPerfect Office 8.

Explorer's the Thing

From a user point of view, Windows 98 provides two browsers: Windows Explorer, optimized for use on local machines, local area networks, and non-Web type documents; and Internet Explorer, optimized for use with Web documents, wherever they're located.

To start Internet Explorer, choose the desktop icon Internet Explorer or choose Start | Programs | Internet Explorer | Internet Explorer. You can also find an icon for Internet Explorer in the Quick Launch toolbar.

Internet Explorer starts up with a default page loaded. This might be the Microsoft home page, a blank page, or any other page that you've chosen or that has been chosen by your network administrator for your workstation. If you're not connected to the Internet, you might get an error message saying the page isn't available. Click OK and then connect using whatever method you've chosen.

Note

This section uses the Internet for examples of using Internet Explorer. The information, with minor address and connection changes, also applies to intranets and extranets. The specific changes for addresses and connections are different for various individual network setups. For specifics on using your company's intranet or extranet, see your network administrator.

Figure 14.12 shows Internet Explorer with the Microsoft home page loaded.

FIGURE 14.12.

When you start up Internet Explorer, you might find yourself transported to the Microsoft site on the Internet.

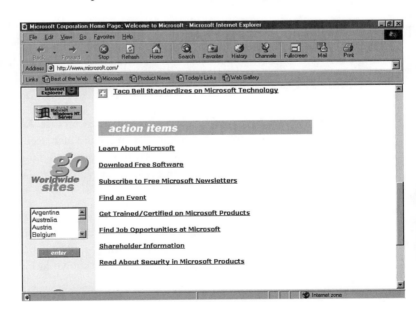

14

Most people prefer to navigate around Internet Explorer using the toolbar buttons. Starting with the first row in Figure 14.12 and moving down, these buttons are as follows:

Button	*Function*
Back	Moves back one page or to the last page shown.
Forward	Moves forward to the page accessed before you clicked the Back button.
Stop	Halts online operations immediately.
Refresh	Repaints the current page.
Home	Returns to the home page.
Search (toggle)	Opens the Search panel and initiates the search engine chosen by the user or by the search engine support software.
Favorites	Opens the Favorites folder.
History (toggle)	Opens the History panel to the left of the main panel.
Channels (toggle)	Opens the Channels panel.
Fullscreen	Alters the Internet Explorer display to full screen.
Mail	Launches Outlook Express or your selected mail client. If your client is Outlook Express, this gives you access to newsgroups also.
Print	Prints the current page.
Address	Shows the current URL for the displayed page. Pull down to see a short history of your Internet travels.
Links bar	Connects to hard-wired sites to see what's new on those pages. Microsoft maintains these sites in hopes that you'll find them of sufficient interest to visit them often.

The toolbars shown in Figure 14.12 are stacked on each other. As they are the usual toolbars found in Windows 98, you can move them around and stack them horizontally as well as vertically. As with all Windows 98 toolbars, you can drag them around by clicking near the bar on the left and dragging. Similarly, you can resize them by clicking and dragging on the bar.

The underlined phrases and words shown in Figure 14.12 are hyperlinks. When you click on these, you jump to another page containing (if the link is maintained correctly) detailed information underlying the link. For example, if you click on the link Subscribe to Free Microsoft Newsletters, you jump to the page shown in Figure 14.13.

FIGURE 14.13.

Internet Explorer uses hyperlinks for quick navigation.

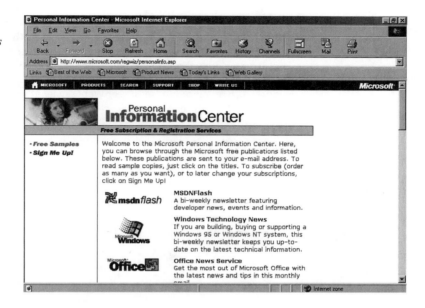

In this way you can jump from site to site or pages within a site.

Searching

The Internet is a huge agglomeration of information. Sifting through that information for what's interesting to you is the key to using the Internet in a practical way. You can just wander around in cyberspace or use other people's recommendations for what are interesting places to go, but the ability to search changes the Internet from an amusement to a useful tool.

Internet Explorer has a Search button on its toolbar. You can use that button to launch a search engine or, if you already know the address of the search engine you like to use, directly enter it by pressing Ctrl+O and then entering the address. This works with any address you know.

Task 14.1. An Internet Search

This example searches the Web for references to Mercedes-Benz automobiles:

1. Click the Search button on the toolbar. This brings up a search panel to the left of the original panel, now moved to the right.

2. Enter **Mercedes-Benz** in the space provided.

3. Press Enter or click Search.

TASK

14

Internet Explorer uses many different search engines. This search randomly chose the Excite search engine, which was the search engine of the day. If you try searching without specifying an engine, you only have a small chance of hitting Excite. You might hit any one of many other search engines, such as Yahoo!, AltaVista, or WebCrawler. If you want to use Excite (or any other specific engine), you can go to its site directly. Excite is located at www.excite.com.

The search engine returns any *hits,* or successful search results. Figure 14.14 shows the return from this search on Mercedes-Benz. The underlined hits in the left column are all hyperlinks. Click on them to bring up the linked sites.

FIGURE 14.14.

Searches return hyper-links, allowing fast navigation to the found sites.

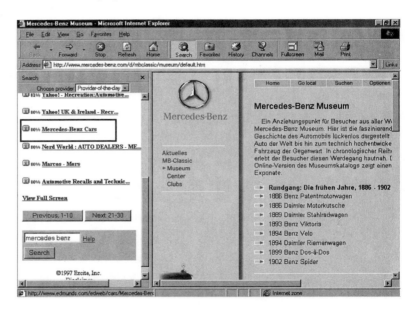

If you run your mouse over the links, Internet Explorer will bring up a ToolTip-like balloon expanding on the site information.

Clicking on the hyperlink highlighted in Figure 14.14 brings up the site shown in Figure 14.15. You can resize either column or close the search column by clicking on the X in the upper-right corner of the column.

FIGURE 14.15.

A couple of clicks bring you to this site.

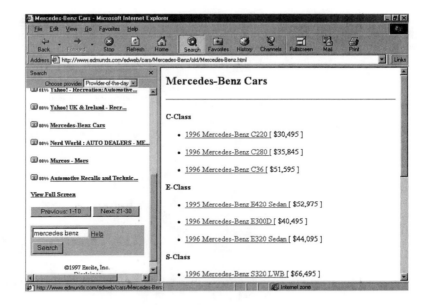

Favorites

When you've found sites you like and want to return to, you can save them like any other file. You can also create folders for grouping your favorite sites.

To save a site as a favorite, click on the Favorites menu. Click Add to Favorites, and Internet Explorer will open the dialog box shown in Figure 14.16.

FIGURE 14.16.

The Favorites menu allows creation of folders for grouping your favorite sites. Here, the Create In button is activated to show the folder structure for this copy of Internet Explorer.

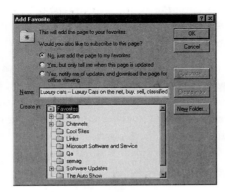

14

As you can see from Figure 14.16, you can store this page (and choose several updating options) in the main menu, or by clicking the Create In button (grayed out in Figure 14.16), you can store it in one of the existing folders or in a new folder you can make on-the-fly.

After you've stored a site or folder in Favorites, you can return there by opening the Favorites menu and the folder and then clicking on the entry. Figure 14.17 shows a new folder, The Auto Show, made from the screen shown in Figure 14.16. The site entered in Figure 14.16 is also shown.

FIGURE 14.17.

After you've entered a site in Favorites, you can return there easily.

Subscriptions

Designating a site as a subscription makes it a special type of favorite to Internet Explorer. This tells Internet Explorer that you want to update the site from time to time, either automatically or manually.

There are two Yes options on the Add Favorite dialog box. For a partial subscription, mark the first: Yes, But Only Tell Me When This Page Is Updated. Internet Explorer will notify you when changes are made to the page. For a full subscription, mark the second Yes option. Internet Explorer will not only notify you of changes to the page, but also download the page for offline viewing. You can manually update any subscribed to page by choosing Favorites | Update Subscriptions. You must be online to update or you'll get an error message in the Status column of the update folder view.

All subscriptions are located in the Subscriptions folder subordinate to the main Windows 98 folder. Choose Favorites | Manage Subscriptions in Internet Explorer to open a view of this folder optimized for use in Subscriptions.

History

Internet Explorer maintains a history of your Web wanderings in its history folder. The depth of your maintained history depends on your disk capacity, to some extent. This history makes it easy to return to a site you've visited recently, but neglected to place into your Favorites folder.

History is just a set of links grouped by the day or week you visited them. Figure 14.18 shows a History panel opened with a few sites shown.

FIGURE 14.18.

The History button is a toggle. Click to open it; click again to close it.

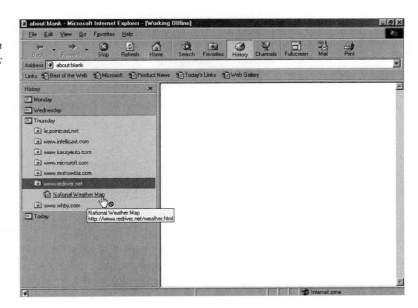

Each day and week in History is a folder under the History folder you can see within your Windows 98 folder. To open a day's history, click on it. Figure 14.18 shows one day open and a site within that day selected. The operation of the History panel is the same as using folders in other areas of Internet Explorer or Windows Explorer. Each day (or week) is a folder and a site within that day that has multiple pages is a folder containing those pages.

Internet Explorer Options

Internet Explorer is quite configurable in theory, but in fact, the default settings will work best for most people. Open the Configuration dialog box by choosing View | Internet Options from the menu. This opens the complex tabbed dialog box shown in Figure 14.19.

14

FIGURE 14.19.

Internet Options is the dialog box to configure Internet Explorer and its auxiliary programs.

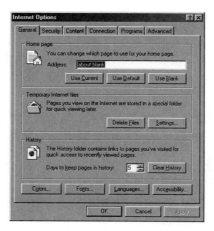

Following is a list of the tabs and a discussion of the most often used settings on each tab. This list isn't feature complete, as it glosses over the rarely used or obvious options on each tab:

- General—Use this tab to set the initial page, which in this case is a blank page. You can set this page to a URL such as www.microsoft.com or a page on your local computer or LAN such as \\Tirilee\Pages\opening.html. This tab also allows you to specify the location and size of your temporary Internet files. Keep in mind that a person browsing your computer can determine which sites you've visited by examining these files. Delete them for that secure feeling. You can also use this tab to set special accessibility features for the handicapped, the colors and fonts used in Internet Explorer, and the default language for the browser. You can also instruct Internet Explorer how long to keep its History and whether to purge the History files for your enhanced security or privacy or both.

- Security—This sets your zone for Internet Explorer's scope and how it should handle security issues for any given zone. Figure 14.20 shows the Security tab. The Internet is an utterly open and anonymous society. As such, it suffers from its criminal element. To some extent, if you can see a site, that site can, in theory, see you, too. Although Internet Explorer is as secure as any browser, any lock set can be picked. How high you set your security levels depends on your situation. You might be forced, due to the nature of your computer's records (mental health medical records, for example), to consider even the most remote possibility of access. In that case, you should consider not using an Internet connection at all. If your concerns are less pressing, you can set the scope of Internet Explorer in the Zone combo box and set the Security Level for that zone using the option buttons below it. If you connect through a gateway on a LAN, consult with your network administrator about the features and limitations of your firewall.

FIGURE 14.20.

The Security tab allows you to range Internet Explorer from wide open to locked down quite tightly.

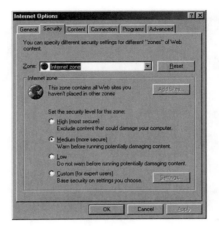

- Content—This is the personal identification and filtering tab for Internet Explorer (see Figure 14.21). The Enable and Settings buttons at the top of the dialog box enable you to set the ratings of the pages Internet Explorer will display based on language, violence, nudity, and sex. You will need to set a password to activate this feature. The reason for the password is to prevent unauthorized removal of these filers. Although this is usually thought of as a device for children, many adults prefer not to have to wade through the swamps of degradation, desolation, and debauchery so common to modern society and so set some filters for themselves. Figure 14.22 presents a chart describing the various levels of filters you can set. The Certificates section of the Content dialog allows the creation and setting of properties that will positively identify you and others you communicate with. This section is identical to the certificate discussed on Day 16, "Outlook Express for Mail and News." Similarly, the personal information is the same as using Outlook Express's Address Book, but the form you fill out refers to yourself.

- Connection—Usually this works fine by default. Don't change these settings unless you've been told to by your network administrator or know what you're about because these are advanced topics. Errors made here can prevent you from connecting until they're set correctly again. If you've had a change in ISP, you might choose to run the Connection Wizard from this tab to set up the new connection. To run the Connection Wizard, click the Connect button. Figure 14.23 shows this tab.

14

FIGURE 14.21.

The Content tab not only sets the dissolution level of Internet Explorer's allowed views, but also contains identification information.

FIGURE 14.22.

Here are the levels and their meanings for enabling content filtering in Internet Explorer.

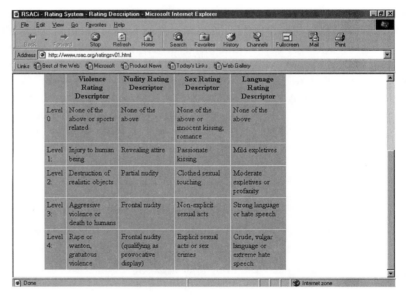

	Violence Rating Descriptor	Nudity Rating Descriptor	Sex Rating Descriptor	Language Rating Descriptor
Level 0	None of the above or sports related	None of the above	None of the above or innocent kissing, romance	None of the above
Level 1:	Injury to human being	Revealing attire	Passionate kissing	Mild expletives
Level 2:	Destruction of realistic objects	Partial nudity	Clothed sexual touching	Moderate expletives or profanity
Level 3:	Aggressive violence or death to humans	Frontal nudity	Non-explicit sexual acts	Strong language or hate speech
Level 4:	Rape or wanton, gratuitous violence	Frontal nudity (qualifying as provocative display)	Explicit sexual acts or sex crimes	Crude, vulgar language or extreme hate speech

- Programs—Here's where you tell Internet Explorer which programs to use for services it might need while you're browsing the Web. By default, Internet Explorer will use Outlook Express for mail and news and NetMeeting for Internet conspiracies. If you choose alternate clients like Pegasus for mail or Agent for news, this tab is where to tell Internet Explorer about them. You can also change your Calendar and Contact list program at the bottom of this tab. Figure 14.24 shows the Programs tab.

FIGURE 14.23.

The Connection tab allows you to switch from connecting through your LAN to a modem or back if you have the equipment to do so.

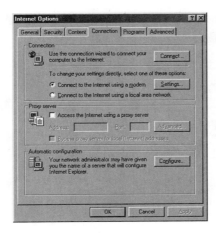

FIGURE 14.24.

Use the Programs tab to tell Internet Explorer which auxiliary programs to use.

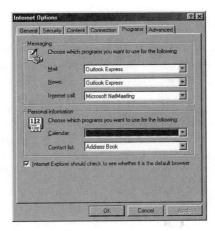

- Advanced—This tab contains a list box with dozens of check boxes allowing you to configure Internet Explorer in a variety of details from the way it scrolls (jumpy or smooth) to whether it should auto-complete URL addresses when you start entering them. Figure 14.25 shows the Advanced tab. Note that the check boxes in this tab will affect not only Internet Explorer online, but also how your desktop works when in Web view. Contrary to its name, the Advanced tab doesn't contain settings any more advanced than the other tabs. In fact, the settings here are quite safe to experiment with, as Internet Explorer has a Restore Defaults button that will get you out of any possible trouble you configure yourself into. The Advanced tab is the place to make Internet Explorer and the Active Desktop work just the way you want them to. Feel free to experiment to your heart's content. Just remember the Restore Defaults button in the lower-right corner of the tab. This is your escape hatch.

14

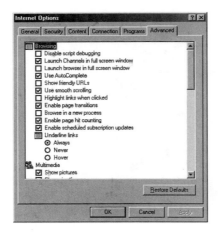

FIGURE 14.25.

The Advanced tab doesn't contain any options to be afraid of—just the contrary. Feel free to experiment with these settings to make Internet Explorer work just the way you want it to work.

Commercial Services

Bulletin boards (BBSs), not the Internet, were the start of the online experience for the personal computer industry. Although the Internet in one form or another has been around for more than 20 years, most personal computer users only heard of it, much less used it, within the past 3 or 4 years.

A bulletin board is a computer set up as a Dial-Up Server for exchange of messages, file uploading and downloading, and even chat. Most bulletin board systems were run by hobbyists, some charging a nominal fee for their efforts. Before long, large commercial services saw the potential for professionally run BBSs with true national, and even international, scope. These services started up and prospered during the 1980s and into the 1990s, but now are feeling extreme pressure from the Internet. Each offers Internet access, but for many users, the value added by the large commercial BBS itself isn't worth bothering with the service.

Still, for many, services such as CompuServe, America Online, The Microsoft Network, and Prodigy make a good deal of sense. They are all rather economical compared to their fees in the heady days of the 80s when they or their ilk were the only games in town. They offer easy-to-use interfaces, and they have sections private to their subscribers. For example, many software companies offer free (aside from connect time) support on CompuServe.

Each of these services sports individual characteristics. CompuServe is the most serious of the big services offering the largest selection of online support of all of them. AOL started out as a Macintosh-friendly service and remains very graphic-oriented today. AOL also tends to be a lighter service than CompuServe (although both are owned by

AOL), although many companies are now moving to offering CompuServe-style support at AOL. Prodigy strives to be a G-rated service suitable for the entire family. It largely succeeds, although from time to time it gets embroiled in controversies as it strives to keep its cyberspace clean. MSN originally was designed to be an improved version when compared to any competing service, but the Internet craze struck just as it was starting out. Microsoft has changed the slant of MSN to be partly a huge BBS and partly an Internet service provider.

Windows 98 comes with startup (or setup) programs for the larger online services. By default, Windows 98's setup installs shortcuts to these programs on the desktop in a folder called Online Services. You can access this folder through the menu choices Start | Programs | Online Services. If you have an account with any of these services and want to use that account, you can install the client software into Windows 98 if it's not already there or use one of the startup programs provided. You'll need your sign-on information to configure these programs.

Figure 14.26 shows the start of one of these setups—the one for CompuServe. Clicking Yes at this message box will install the CompuServe client software and start the automatic configuration process for this service.

FIGURE 14.26.

The Online Service folder's shortcuts will install online client software and then launch into a configuration routine.

14

The screen in Figure 14.26 uses a Web page as a background and has the desktop configured to hide desktop icons when in Web view. You can set this and many other options within the Folder Options dialog box.

Summary

If you're not online, you're missing a great deal. Windows 95 introduced The Microsoft Network, but that quickly got swamped by the rush to the Internet. Now many people skip online services such as MSN and connect directly to the Internet.

The three basic requirements for connecting are

- A service provider.
- A physical way to connect to the network. This can be wireless, such as with satellite linkups.
- Client software.

If you connect through your company's LAN, the first two items are essentially taken care of by your network administration. If not, you'll need to make some sort of business arrangement either with an independent service provider or a large online service such as MSN and then add a modem to your system.

Windows 98 comes with a great selection of client software. The first program is Outlook Express, which handles your email and newsgroup accounts and correspondence. Internet Explorer is a highly configurable browser useful for browsing your LAN, WAN, or the Internet. Both Internet Explorer and Outlook Express can handle links to URLs or other similar addresses furnished using the Universal Naming Convention (UNC) for filenames, and both are fully multimedia-enabled.

Both Internet Explorer and Outlook Express work in a fashion similar to Windows Explorer. Outlook Express uses the left pane folders, right pane files metaphor but with folders, headers, and messages rather then just folders and files. Internet Explorer also uses the left pane, but it's a toggle showing Channels, History, or a Search engine.

Internet Explorer is even more configurable than Outlook Express. The View | Internet Options menu choice will bring up a huge array of choices from cosmetic to security. The Advanced tab within this dialog box has some of the more interesting options. Using the options on this tab is actually safer than using other options as the tab has a button to reset defaults in case things really go awry.

Workshop

To wrap up the day, you can review terms from the chapter, see the answers to some commonly asked questions, and practice what you've learned. You can find the answers to the exercises in Appendix A, "Answers."

Terminology Review

DUN (Dial-Up Networking)—A way to make a client computer part of a network using POTS.

Favorites—Sites you retain the address to for quick return.

Internet Explorer—The Web browser optimized for use in Microsoft products.

POTS (Plain Old Telephone Service)—The standard analog packet network used by telephone systems such as US West and AT&T.

Quick Launch toolbar—An optionally shown area of the taskbar where user-selected shortcuts and applications reside for fast launching without using the Start menu. By default, this area is shown and includes Internet Explorer and Outlook Express.

subscriptions—A special type of favorite in Internet Explorer. Subscriptions are sites that can be manually or automatically updated for offline reading.

terminal emulation—Making a compatible connection with a host computer. This commonly is accomplished using specialized software.

Q&A

Q I can't find my Subscriptions when using the `DIR` command at the `Windows\Subscriptions` folder. Are they lost?

A Use your Windows Explorer to view this folder. You'll see your Subscriptions safe and sound. The nature of the folder makes the files "invisible" at the command line because they aren't real files in the sense that the command line (shell) understands files.

Q If I have my Subscriptions set to manual update, can I change that to automatic?

A Yes and yes to the other way around. Open Favorites | Manage Subscriptions in Internet Explorer. Right-click on the subscription you want to alter. Choose Properties from the context menu. The automatic/manual options are on the Receiving tab. This is also the place to Unsubscribe to a site.

14

Q Can I see the Internet through AOL or MSN?

A Yes. This is a flexible but often slightly more expensive option that gives you access to the Internet in addition to the provider's proprietary content. Depending on your provider, you might not have full Internet access. Check with the provider to be sure.

Q How can I prevent Internet Explorer from accessing "salty" material on the Web? I want my kids to use this, too.

A You can try enabling content screening by choosing View | Internet Options | Content from Internet Explorer. A cagey child can bypass any security by munging and then reinstalling Windows 98. Nothing replaces supervision.

Q Can I edit Web files in Internet Explorer?

A If you have the rights to, you can. Load the page and then choose View | Source from the Internet Explorer menu. This will load Notepad (or your designated application) with the page opened. Make your changes and then choose File | Save from Notepad. If you have change (edit or save) rights, you will see your edits the next time you load the page.

Exercises

1. Frequently, you'll find that a search on the Web returns lots of hits that don't necessarily make sense to you. Consequently, it can be useful to use a subject index. Yahoo! is one of the most popular subject indices. Use Yahoo! to find online tutorials for the Internet.

2. Change your home page to MSNBC so that you get a news update each time you log in.

WEEK 3

At a Glance: Extending Windows 98

15

16

17

18

19

20

21

DAY **15**

Internet Explorer Channels and the Active Desktop

by Paul Cassel

A channel is a Web site that can push, or download, information from itself to your computer. A channel site can function like a TV channel, which is where it got its name; it can also function just like any other Web site.

You can "tune in" to a channel-enabled site and let the site manage the content you'll see. Channel sites allow subscriptions, which are elements you can specify you're interested in. This gives the channel site information about what you'd like to see narrowcast to your computer and what you'd not like to see.

For example, a general news site like MSNBC has a broad scope of information it can push out to your computer. Most people would only like to see a small part of this information set. Subscriptions enable you to tell sites like MSNBC what you'd prefer not to have pushed to your computer.

In this chapter, you'll learn

- What a channel is
- What the Active Desktop means
- How to set up a channel
- How to subscribe to an Internet Explorer channel
- How to include active elements on your desktop
- About the TV tuner that comes with Windows 98

Internet Explorer Channels in Action

Figure 15.1 shows the Channels panel opened to the MSNBC site. To start using the site to its full capacity, you must download some enabling software. The link to do this is the Add Active Channel link.

FIGURE 15.1.

Channel sites are active. This requires you to download some software to your workstation.

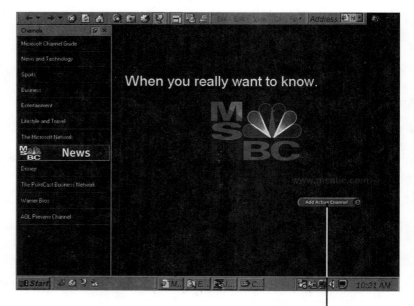

The Add Active Channel link

After you've downloaded the software to your computer, you can subscribe to the entire site or any parts of it. To get more channel sites into your Channels panel, choose the Channel Guide in the Channels panel or in the menu selections Go | Channel Guide. This takes you to a Microsoft-maintained site containing up-to-the-minute additions to channel-equipped sites. Figure 15.2 shows a partial selection from Lifestyle & Travel.

FIGURE 15.2.

Microsoft maintains a central directory of channel-enabled Web sites. This is the direct route to adding new sites to your Internet Explorer.

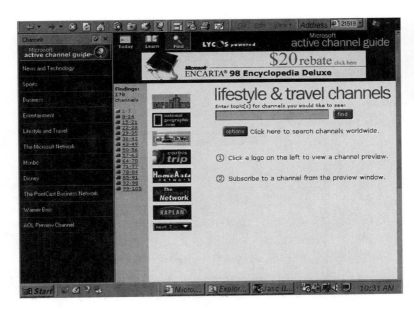

Using Internet Explorer Channels

Windows 98 installs by default with the channel bar open. If you have a custom install or have closed the channel bar, you will need to open it before trying this technology. You will also need a connection of some sort to a channel server. This is commonly the Internet, but it also can be a local area network (LAN) or other private network. In the case of a private network, the channel content will be whatever is appropriate to that network (such as company news) rather than the public or semipublic offerings on the Internet.

Seeing the Channel Bar

If you don't see a channel bar on your desktop, right-click on the desktop, choose Properties from the context menu, and choose Active Desktop if it's not currently checked. Again, right-click on the desktop and choose Active Desktop | Customize my Desktop. Click the Web tab. Your dialog box should resemble Figure 15.3.

Check the Internet Explorer Channel Bar check box. Click OK to close the dialog box shown in Figure 15.3. This will put the channel bar on your desktop. You can also see channels by choosing Start | Favorites | Channels.

FIGURE 15.3.

The channel bar display check box is under Web properties for your computer's display.

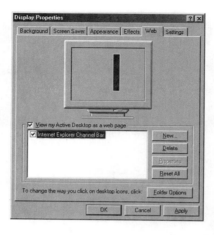

Task 15.1. Using a Channel

This example visits the MSN site and establishes a channel subscription to Carpoint, a Microsoft service:

1. Make sure that your desktop is configured to be active and the channel bar is visible. If it's not, read the preceding section, "Seeing the Channel Bar," for instructions on how to make it so.

2. If you're not online to the Internet, initiate such a session now. Click the MSN option on the channel bar.

3. Depending on your situation, Windows 98 might respond with a request to insert a CD or to connect via the Internet. Choose the connection option. Windows 98 will also offer first-time connectors a chance to look at a help-like file about channels. Feel free to read that and then return to continue this Task.

4. After you're connected to MSN, your screen should resemble Figure 15.4. This is the place where you can start subscribing to active content.

5. The content of all channels changes constantly. Your MSN might differ from the display shown here, but the gist of it will be the same. To subscribe to, say, Carpoint (circled in Figure 15.4), click on it. If you want to subscribe to something else, click on that option.

FIGURE 15.4.

The initial MSN screen offering channels to which you can subscribe.

6. Click on the Add Active Channel button at the bottom of the circle of choices. After a brief download period, MSN and Windows 98 will ask how you want to subscribe, as shown in Figure 15.5.

FIGURE 15.5.

You have three options for any subscribed channel. You can also click the Customize button to modify the default choices.

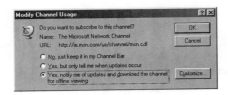

7. Internet Explorer will then go to a page containing many MSN-hosted sites. Your screen should resemble Figure 15.6.

8. Locate and click on CarPoint. This brings up the CarPoint home page site, shown in Figure 15.7.

▼

FIGURE 15.6.

Microsoft hosts a switchboard form with many hosted services and sites for active content.

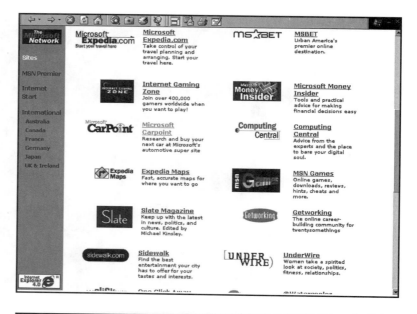

FIGURE 15.7.

The payoff is the site itself.

▲

Making a Site Part of Your Desktop

You can also make the site part of your desktop. This is most often done with sites or services that have continually updated information, such as weather or stock prices, but you're free to use whatever page you want.

You can also include subscribed sites on your desktop. If not subscribed to, Windows 98 will automatically subscribe you when you put them on the desktop.

Here are the steps to make any Web site part of your desktop:

1. Right-click on the desktop, choose Active Desktop, and make sure View as Web Page is active. Choose Customize My Desktop. This will open up the Web tab of the Display Properties dialog box (refer to Figure 15.3, earlier in the chapter).

2. Choose the New button. If this is your first time, Windows 98 will give you a hint message box with a check box to not show the message again. Click No. Add by direct entry or browse for a page you want to include on your desktop. This is usually a URL. For this example, I use the URL www.mrshowbiz.com.

3. Click OK to exit the browse or direct entry for the URL. The address www.mrshowbiz.com is added to the Active Desktop, as you can see in Figure 15.8.

FIGURE 15.8.

You can add as many sites to your Active Desktop as you want. Too many active at once can lead to a very cluttered screen, however.

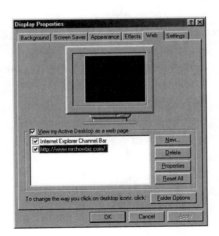

Size the displayed Active Desktop component to suit you. After finishing, your desktop should look something like the one shown in Figure 15.9.

If you don't see your active component on your desktop, make sure you're configured to view your desktop as a Web page.

FIGURE 15.9.

After adding a site to your desktop, you're plugged into the world of the Internet or any other world available to you.

The TV on Your Computer

Windows 98 also hosts the capability to receive true television broadcasts and place them on your desktop. You can also use the broadcasts for any other reason, including clipping and saving for later editing if you have the necessary software, such as Corel Lumiere or Adobe Premiere.

We're now in a transition period when it comes to delivering content from the Internet to most locations. The older dial-up modems running at roughly 50,000 baud or less will be supplanted by newer technology capable of speeds many times in excess of that. These speeds will allow user enjoyment of full motion TV-like broadcasts and other similarly dense transmitted material. The current technology in common use can't pull or push the material fast enough for such multimedia material to be delivered in a way satisfactory to most consumers.

Although such technology currently exists, it doesn't at a reasonable cost for most users. The new connection technologies should allow connection speeds at reasonable consumer-oriented prices. Whether this technology will be cable modems, ADSL, HDSL, fiber, satellite, or some alternative not yet even available experimentally is unknown at this time.

To receive television broadcasts, you need a TV tuner card. These are becoming more common all the time. Some video cards include a tuner "side" for just this purpose.

You'll also need to subscribe to this special service. If you just want to use your TV tuner card to place local broadcasts on your computer, the hardware itself should come with the necessary software. The WebTV for Windows that's part of Windows 98 allows you to subscribe to special 'casts in a way similar to the way large satellite dish users can see many 'casts not available to typical TV watchers. What's available depends on your subscription service.

If you have such a card and want to use Windows 98's TV tuner, you'll need to install it by choosing Control Panel I Add/Remove Programs I Windows Setup, and then scrolling down to the WebTV for Windows check box (last on the list). Figure 15.10 shows this option. You will also need your distribution CD-ROM or another distribution media.

FIGURE 15.10.

WebTV for Windows isn't part of the usual Windows 98 setup.

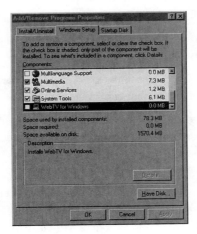

After WebTV is set up on your machine, start WebTV for Windows, go to Channel 1 (another type of channel than Internet Explorer channels), choose Go To, and then go to the section you want to configure. The WebTV for Windows configuration screen will also scan around to see if new channels have become available.

Summary

Windows 98 is entertainment enabled. Using either Internet Explorer or WebTV for Windows or both, you can subscribe to various online or 'cast content. You'll need a tuner card to use WebTV for Windows.

After you've subscribed to something using Internet Explorer, you can place that on your Active Desktop if you've configured it to act like a Web page. Most people use this ability to add items like weather maps or stock tickers to their desktops. If you use a dial-up connection to the Internet, you'll likely want to have the Active Desktop show a reasonably decent looking display offline as well as online.

Workshop

To wrap up the day, you can review terms from the chapter, see the answers to some commonly asked questions, and practice what you've learned. You can find the answers to the exercises in Appendix A, "Answers."

Terminology Review

Active Desktop—The configuration of Windows 98's desktop that allows viewing of Web content and a Web-like view of your local resources.

channel—A way for a server to push or for you to selectively pull down live content and updates from a network, usually the Internet.

channel bar—A bar, like the taskbar, with links to channel providers. Windows 98 comes with several links on its predefined channel bar.

WebTV for Windows—A TV add-on to Windows 98 to manage paid-for TV subscription services. You need a TV tuner card to use this service.

Q&A

Q I'm on a dial-up connection only. Will this cause a problem with my active subscriptions?

A No. They will update when you're back online. Windows 98 has been designed with dial-ups in mind.

Q I bought a tuner card, but it doesn't seem to work at all. What could be the problem?

A Some tuner cards require that specific video or add-on cards also be inside your computer. Read the requirements carefully.

Q I can't see my subscribed-to content on the desktop. Any ideas why?

A You must have your desktop configured to display Web-like. Right-click on the desktop, choose Active Desktop | Customize my Desktop, and make sure you have this option set.

Exercises

1. The MSNBC Web site has terrific news content covering a wide variety of topics. Add the MSNBC site to your desktop so that you can get updated headlines automatically. (Hint: The MSNBC site is `www.msnbc.com`.)

2. Windows Explorer is your gateway to almost anything on your Windows system. Use the Windows Explorer bar to view your current channel listing; then use it to view a helpful search guide.

15

WEEK 3

DAY 16

Outlook Express for Mail and News

by Paul Cassel

Outlook Express (OE), a subset of the Outlook program found in Microsoft Office 97 and subsequent Office products, is the common client distributed with Windows 98. OE allows full email and newsgroup services.

This introduction to Outlook Express is complex because it covers a lot of territory in a short space. Don't be discouraged. Using Outlook Express, or any email or newsgroup client, is simple after you've been through it a time or two. After skimming this introduction, move to the part where you gain hands-on experience with Outlook Express. The doing is simpler than the explaining, as you'll see. In this chapter, you'll learn

- How to configure Outlook Express
- Several specific Internet jargon terms
- How to compose an email

- How to send an email
- The nature of newsgroups such as the Usenet
- How to participate in newsgroup discussions
- How to filter out a twit
- How to add a signature to your messages

Setting Up Outlook Express

Your username and passwords for Outlook Express's services might, and usually do, vary from your Dial-Up Networking (DUN) logon name. For example, if you want to use OE for picking up and sending your mail using an Internet service provider (ISP), you'll need to use the username and password for your Post Office Protocol (POP) and Simple Main Transport Protocol (SMTP) (mail in and mail out) accounts. This is usually your interactive password and username. You'll also need to tell Outlook Express the IP or domain name for any newsgroups you want to use. Your ISP should provide you with the IP for the Usenet. This might appear on your sign-up sheet as the IP for the Network News Transport Protocol (NNTP) server. (NNTP is the protocol for newsgroups such as the Usenet.)

Some news servers are private. They require a username and logon for their particular server. The Usenet, or User Network, of newsgroups is public, as are many other newsgroups that exist apart from the Usenet. Microsoft, for example, has many newsgroups, some of which are private for subscription-only use. Many corporations today maintain a private newsgroup for company discussions, too.

You'll need to enter your password and username for your mail account, as well as any private newsgroups you wish to join—the procedure is the same as for making a Dial-Up Networking connection, or for that matter, logging on to Windows 98 at startup. Enter your username where indicated, keeping in mind the case-sensitive nature of some servers, and enter the password where indicated (getting asterisks instead of a literal representation of your password), and then you're done. The purpose of the asterisks is to thwart shoulder surfers who steal passwords by spying on your screen.

Adding Services to Outlook Express

Launch Outlook Express by clicking on the Mail | Outlook Express icon on your Desktop. If Setup didn't drop an OE shortcut on your Desktop, explore the Start menu under Programs | Internet Explorer for an Outlook Express entry.

After it is launched, Outlook Express is similar to the Windows Explorer. Containers are on the left side of the display, and details, or contents, are on the right. When you start OE, you'll have several entries on the left side. As you add services and folders, you'll add to the left. As you use OE to retrieve and send messages, you'll see them appear in the right pane. Figure 16.1 shows Outlook Express with a few additional services.

16

FIGURE 16.1.

After a bit of use, most people add services and folders to their Outlook Express installation.

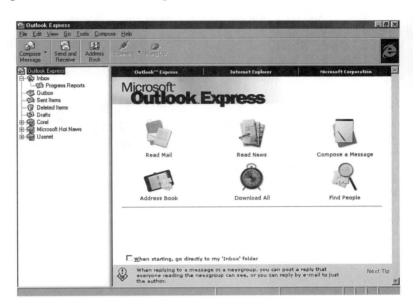

You have several navigation options when you are at the screen shown in Figure 16.1. If you're logged on to your server, you can go directly to pick up or send mail or to your registered newsgroups. If you're not logged on and choose the Read Mail, Read News, or Download All entry, OE will ask you for connection information. If you're using Dial-Up Networking, you'll have to direct OE to the DUN connection you want to use for this service.

Alternatively, to use the large icons in the right pane shown in Figure 16.1, you can click on the entries in the left pane, called the Resource pane. This will show you the contents of the folders in the left pane, just as the same operation in Windows Explorer allows you to explore the contents of folders. Here are the standard entries in Outlook Express:

- Inbox—Where your email messages land.
- Outbox—Where your outbound, but not sent, messages await disposition.
- Sent Items—Where your messages (email and newsgroup) land after successful transmission.

- Deleted Items—Similar to the Recycle Bin. Where items reside after you've deleted them. You can set an option to permanently erase the contents of this folder
upon exit from OE.

- Drafts—A residence for items in process.

In addition, the OE in Figure 16.1 has three newsgroups added and a folder under the
Inbox, called Progress Reports. You can add a new folder for storing outbound or incoming items the same way you add a folder in Windows Explorer. Right-click where you
want the new folder; then choose New Folder from the context menu. Figure 16.2 shows
this process for creating a new folder in the Drafts folder.

FIGURE 16.2.

*Outlook Express works
identically to the
Windows Explorer
wherever a design par-
allel is possible. Learn
one and you've
learned the other.*

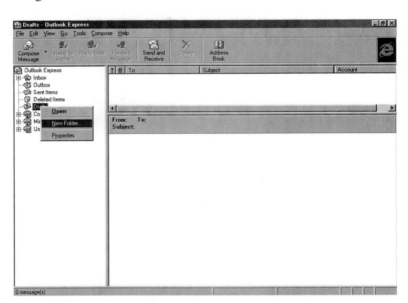

After adding a new folder, the Draft entry gets a plus sign when collapsed, just like in
Windows Explorer. Figure 16.3 shows the results of adding a new folder to the Resource
pane of Outlook Express.

Clicking on a Resource pane folder with entries will bring up a display of the entries and
the contents for the highlighted entries in the two right panes. Figure 16.4 shows the
Outbox with one entry. The top-right pane shows the title of this entry, and the bottom-
right pane shows its contents.

FIGURE 16.3.

You can create folder hierarchies within Outlook Express just as you can within Windows Explorer.

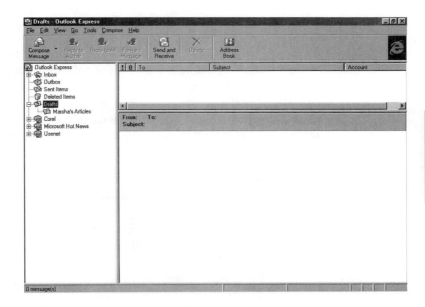

16

FIGURE 16.4.

Outlook Express uses three panes by default. Each pane provides a more detailed look at OE's contents.

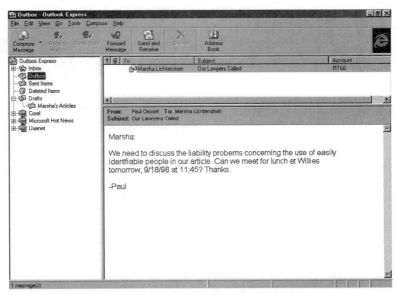

As with Windows Explorer, you can resize the panes and the columns within the panes by mouse dragging. You can also sort the contents of the top-right pane by clicking on the column heads or by making the menu choices View | Sort By.

Sending and Receiving Mail

After you've entered all your usernames and passwords, emailing using Outlook Express is simplicity itself. Assuming you're connected, you only need to click on the Send and Receive button in the toolbar or choose Tool | Send and Receive from the menu. If you're not connected, OE will offer to connect, using whatever connections you've defined for your email and newsgroup services. (For an example of using DUN, see Day 14, "The Internet and Internet Explorer 4." The example uses a predefined DUN connecting to an ISP called RT66.)

After you click on Send and Receive, OE will post your Outbox messages and then locate your incoming mail and download it to your Inbox. Figure 16.5 shows this process in action.

FIGURE 16.5.

Send and Receive is the right button for moving the emails.

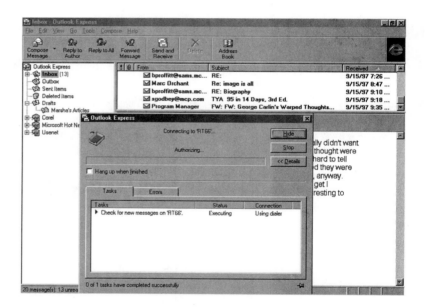

To read any received mail, highlight (if necessary) the Inbox folder in the Resource pane, find the mail in the top-right pane (called the Contents pane), click on it, and after a small interval, OE will display it in the bottom pane, the Preview pane. You can double-click it for immediate opening. Clicking on the Delete button will immediately move the mail from the Inbox to the Deleted Items folder. Figure 16.6 shows the Inbox with an email retrieved in Figure 16.5 displayed in the Preview pane.

Figure 16.6.

You can open mail or choose to display it in the Preview pane.

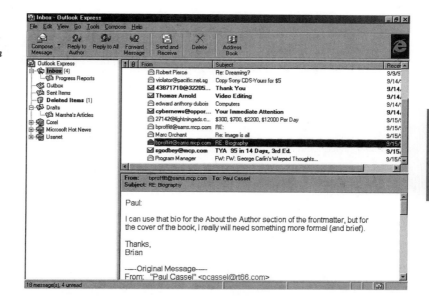

After reading your mail (if you choose to), you can click the Delete button to remove it to the Deleted Items folder, or you can drag it from the Contents pane to any folder, including ones you make, in the Resource pane. You can also reply to any email.

Replying to Mail

To reply to an email message, click the Reply to Author button in the toolbar. This button appears both in the main Outlook toolbar and the smaller toolbar visible when you have a message open. When you choose to reply to a message this way, Outlook will include the sender's message in your message.

This quoting of a sender's message is a standard for email and for newsgroup messages. It keeps all correspondents on track about what they're talking about because it might be several days or even weeks between receiving and responding to emails.

If you're sure your correspondents have kept track of the conversation, feel free to delete the quotation of previous messages. If all correspondents keep quoting each other, even short replies can end up as rather huge, unwieldy messages.

After several exchanges, the quoting of previous messages can get massive and irrelevant. Make sure that you cut out old parts of your exchanged messages, or you risk overwhelming your correspondents (and they you) with ancient drivel.

Composing a New Email Message

To create a new email message—that is, one that's not a reply to a message you received—click on the Compose Message button on the toolbar. By pulling down the Compose Message combo box, you can choose to have various Stationery formats for your messages. Unless you're sure your correspondents will be using Outlook or another email client capable of deciphering Stationery or other fancy formatting, play it safe and omit any such features from your mail. When in doubt, leave it out.

After you click on the Compose Message button (or choose the menu selections Compose | New Message), Outlook will respond with a form for creating an email. Figure 16.7 shows this form.

FIGURE 16.7.

The email form in Outlook Express contains fields for the address, copies, and subject, as well as a message area.

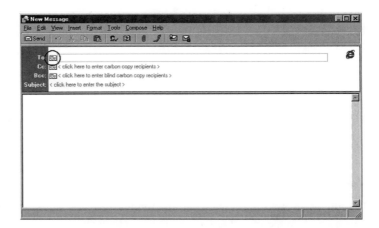

You can manually fill in the To field with your correspondent's email address or click the little Rolodex-like icon between the To label and the text box. This icon is circled in Figure 16.7. The To field is where you put the recipient's (or recipients', separated with semicolons or commas) email address. The Cc field is for open "carbon copies" of your email and the Bcc field is for blind "carbon copies" of your message. All fields can contain more than one email address, separated by semicolons or commas.

Clicking the icon will bring up your Address Book. The Address Book in Outlook Express functions just like a real-world address book or Rolodex. It has a listing of people, their contact information, and other relevant information. Figure 16.8 shows the Address Book opened, ready for copying recipients to the various To fields of an email message. (The Address Book is discussed in more detail later in this chapter in the section "The Address Book.")

FIGURE 16.8.

The Address Book allows you to add as many addressees as you choose to your email messages.

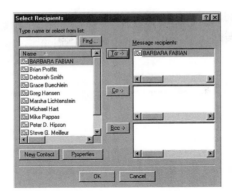

To add an addressee to the To, Cc, or Bcc field of your email message, highlight that entry or entries and click the appropriate arrow button. Figure 16.8 shows one entry added to the To field of the new message.

> **Tip**
>
> The list box in the Select Recipients dialog box accepts Ctrl+click and Shift+click to select multiple noncontiguous and contiguous selections, respectively.
>
> That is, to select several noncontiguous entries as recipients, click on one and then Ctrl+click on the others. If you want to select a series of contiguous entries, highlight (click on) the first one and then Shift+click on the last one in the group.

After you're done adding recipients to your message, add a subject if you choose, and then you're ready to write your message in the message body area. After doing so, your new message will look something like Figure 16.9.

After working on your message, you have four options:

- Discard it by closing and failing to save.
- Send the message immediately by clicking on the toolbar Send icon or choosing File | Send. If you're offline, Outlook Express will offer to establish a connection with your email server.
- Send the message later by choosing File | Send Later (Alt+S). The message will go out the next time you Send and Receive mail.
- File the message in the Drafts folder by choosing Save from the File menu.

FIGURE 16.9.

*A message finished
and ready for sending.*

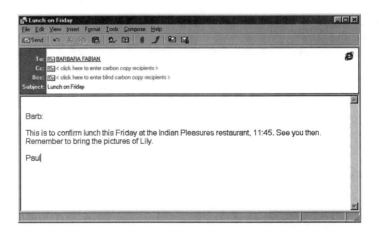

Remember, you can cut, copy, drag, and do any other standard Explorer-type operations on messages stored in Outlook Express. For example, if you're not sure you want to place a message in the Send (Outbox) queue, you can Alt+S it to Drafts. If you later decide to send it after all, you can drag it from Drafts to Outbox, where it will go out the next time you click the Send and Receive button.

Similarly, if you have a message in the Outbox and you wish to delay or avoid sending it, you can

- Open the Outbox and delete it.
- Open the Outbox and drag it to the Drafts, which will take it out of the Send queue.
- Open the Outbox and drag it to a folder of your own making. This too will move it from the Send queue.

Make sure when dragging from the Outbox that you move the email to a new folder rather than copy it there. Moving a file will remove it from the Send queue; copying it won't.

Sending Queued Messages

If you've been working offline and have queued up one or more messages and wish to send them, click the Send and Receive button in the main Outlook Express toolbar. If you're offline, Outlook Express will bring up a connection dialog to your email server. If you're online, Outlook Express will send all your messages in the Outbox and pick up any messages awaiting you on your server and deposit them in your Inbox.

This sounds simple, and it is. After a few runs through the reply or compose, send and receive routines, you'll find you can do these email chores without any thought at all.

The Address Book

In the section immediately preceding this one, you saw how to use the Address Book to add recipients to your new email messages. The Address Book can do more than just help you with your To: fields, however.

From the main Outlook Express view, click the Address Book button in the toolbar. OE responds with the screen shown in Figure 16.10, but naturally your entries will vary, or you might have a blank screen if you haven't added any addresses yet.

16

FIGURE 16.10.

The Address Book's opening screen is the entryway to all of the electronic features of the book.

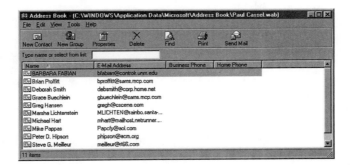

The toolbar really tells it all. The buttons are the gateways to all of the Address Book's functions. Here's a list of the buttons and their functions:

- New Contact—Add a single contact to the Address Book.
- New Group—Add the equivalent of an Address Book folder, that is, a place for adding many entries that can be treated as a single entry. A group is to an Address Book entry as a folder is to a file.
- Properties—Bring up detail information about any listing in the Address Book.
- Delete—Remove an Address Book entry.
- Find—Locate an Address Book entry. Similar in function to the Windows Explorer Find | Files or Folders entry.
- Print—Print an entry from the Address Book.
- Send Mail—Compose a new message to the highlighted recipient.

Clicking the New Contact button will bring up a complex dialog box for entering information. Clicking Properties will bring up the same dialog box for a highlighted entry. The Properties button is very much like an Edit button.

Figure 16.11 shows the New Contact dialog box. Note the title bar for this dialog box contains the word Properties.

FIGURE 16.11.

The New Contact dialog box is tabbed in the usual Windows 98 manner.

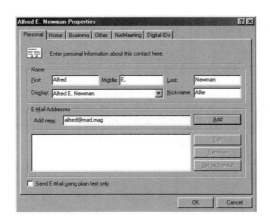

The tabs are mostly self-explanatory. You can add more than one email address to any entry by successively clicking the Add button and adding new addresses.

The only tab that's a bit confusing is the last one, Digital IDs. These are ways to authenticate correspondents in email. You need to receive a file with a digital ID, or certificate, to add it to a person's Address Book entry. After you have these files (usually with the .pub extension), click the Digital IDs tab, click the Import button, and then locate the file with the ID.

Clicking on Add New Group brings up the dialog box shown in Figure 16.12. Figure 16.12 shows a name given to the group and three existing entries from the Address Book added.

FIGURE 16.12.

You can create new groups with both new and existing Address Book entries. Such groups are treated as one entry.

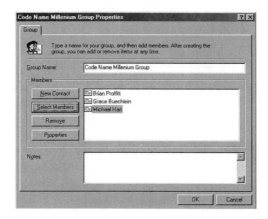

After you've created a group name and added your correspondents, click OK. Outlook Express will add the group to your recipients list box. Now if you want to send mail to this group, just add that group entry to the To: line of a new email. Figure 16.13 shows the group added to the recipients list box.

FIGURE 16.13.

A group is an easy way to manage mailing lists.

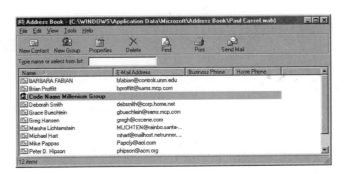

16

There are a few other noteworthy yet not too obvious facilities within the Address Book:

- Tools | Accounts: Allows the addition, deletion, and sorting of online directories of people. These directories are similar to the white pages of a telephone book, but they cover the entire world. Outlook Express comes with the more popular directories already included.

- Tools | Internet Call: Initiates a NetMeeting session. Depending on your hardware, this can include group whiteboarding, group video conferencing, a group telephone or email session, and more.

- File Import and File Export: This is the facility to import new Address Book data from common sources and to export existing data to several common file formats. For example, you can easily export your Address Book information to a comma-delimited file and then import it into a Microsoft Access table or tables.

Express Address Book Entries

An express way to add a correspondent's email address and name to your Address Book is to open the incoming mail and then right-click on the address. Select Add To Address Book from the context menu, as shown in Figure 16.14.

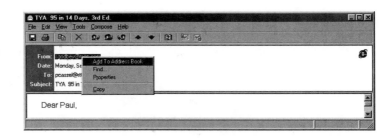

FIGURE 16.14.

An open email message has a shortcut to add entries to your Address Book.

Newsgroups

If you're unfamiliar with the concept of newsgroups on the Internet or extranet or intranet, in the case of private newsgroups, remember that this is one of those topics easier shown than discussed. Consider skipping right down to the section "Getting to the Newsgroups" to see what this is about and then, if you choose, return here for an introductory discussion of the topic.

An Introduction to Newsgroups

A newsgroup is an online place for private or public exchange of messages. The largest newsgroup is the Usenet, or User Network. This is a worldwide cooperative of more than 20,000 newsgroups, and it's growing each day. Each newsgroup exists to exchange information about a particular topic. Anybody can start a newsgroup and many do, so there are many spurious newsgroups. These are often started to make some sort of statement. For example, there is a newsgroup that has a title implying a dislike of Barney, the purple dinosaur puppet on television. This newsgroup doesn't exchange any information. It was likely started either as a joke or as a statement by someone who didn't like the TV show. The freedom of the Internet has as a side effect silliness of this sort.

However, among the real and active newsgroups, there are some to suit anybody's interest. Of the thousands of newsgroups, here are some of the more active categories:

- Serious political issues such as socialism, Whitewater (the scandal), political parties, individual liberty, and black nationalism.
- Hobbies such as collecting, boxing, shooting sports, archery, cars, planes, trains, and motorcycles.
- Any form of eroticism you can imagine and probably a few that will surprise you. Approach this with caution. The Internet is an international gathering with no regard for personal or regional behavioral norms.
- Recreation in the form of joke exchanges, social groups of all natures (and some not so natural), and so on.

- Support for any condition you can have, from divorce to acrophobia and maybe even hydrophobia.
- If it's a computer, it's here. Anything from Vic 20s to Windows NT, with UNIX on the way, exists on the Usenet. This is a terrific support place, second only to buying Sams books.

That's the Usenet. There are also non-Usenet servers, usually addressing a class of topics. For example, both Microsoft and Corel have servers dedicated to user-to-user (or peer) support of their products. In some cases the professional support staff monitors and contributes to these newsgroups.

16

The Usenet also has newsgroups dedicated to discussion of these vendors' products, but the vendors have no control over the messaging in the Usenet, whereas they do in their private groups. Often, discussions on controversial topics on the Usenet resemble a riot. It seems you can't have a discussion on certain topics without starting a fight. The topics range from political, moral, historical, and sporting issues to which operating systems are better—basically, anything people can have an opinion about and can argue.

There are two types of newsgroups: moderated and unmoderated. Moderated newsgroups run all the exchanges through one or more sysops (*system operators*, an obsolete term) or group moderators, who edit and censor to reduce or eliminate threads such as the ones in the preceding list or anything offensive or off topic. Unmoderated groups are free for posting any thoughts you or others have. The fires often burn brightly in the Usenet.

Many people intentionally (or not?) leave their manners behind when they enter newsgroups. Here is the domain of the racial or ethnic insult, the flame (a public attack on a person having made a post), and any other cowardly verbal insult perpetrated by the sleazy meek, made bold by anonymity.

The excesses of the Usenet have spawned a proposal to start a new version of the Usenet, Usenet II, a moderated-only forum for civil exchange. Many newsgroups, such as `alt.auto.mercedes`, by the nature of their populace, remain reasonable in tone and informative in nature. Others, such as the public religion newsgroups, usually don't.

Getting to the Newsgroups

If you have no interest in technical folderol, skip right to Task 16.1 for an example of how to set up a newsgroup in Outlook Express.

You can set up Outlook Express to monitor as many newsgroup servers and newsgroups as you wish. You'll need some information from your network administrator or ISP to access the Usenet. This information appears as an address such as `newsie.isp.com` or an IP number such as `111.111.1.11`.

If you have a numbers/sign-on sheet from your ISP, look for an entry for NNTP server information. This is often the same as your SMTP information. NNTP is the news protocol for the Internet. SMTP is the mail protocol. Your client software, in this case Outlook Express, "knows" whether to access news or mail by differing the port number on the server it's attaching to.

JARGON MADNESS!

The Internet is full of jargon and abbreviations that, when explained, are still murky. For example, SMTP stands for Simple Mail Transport Protocol. NNTP is Network News Transport Protocol. You don't need to know any of this to enjoy mail or newsgroups. The only reason to know these oddities exist is to be able to match up numbers on your sign-on sheet and Outlook Express. After you're up and running, you'll never refer to them again.

For those who like the tech stuff, the port number for SMTP is 25; for FTP, it's 20 and 21; for NNTP, it's 119; and POP3 uses 110. This information won't be on the test.

Task 16.1. Your First Newsgroup

This example shows you how to configure Outlook Express to access the Microsoft news server:

1. Launch Outlook Express by clicking on its Desktop icon or choosing it from the Start | Internet Explorer menu. Your Windows 98 might have Outlook Express located in a different Start menu location. Your screen should resemble Figure 16.15, although the Resource pane usually won't be so populated.

2. Choose the menu selections Tools | Accounts. Click Add and then News from the fly-out menu. This starts a wizard that will request the following information:

   - The Display name you want to use in the newsgroup. Use your real name or choose an alias (handle) such as "Xena, Warrior Princess." When messages appear from you, the others will see this name. When done, click Next.

   - Your email address. Use your real address or, if you desire anonymity, a false one. Outlook Express will accommodate you either way. When done, click Next.

   - The NNTP server address. Enter `msnews.microsoft.com` for the Microsoft news server. Here's where you'd add the NNTP IP or URL for your ISP server to connect to the Usenet. Similarly, you'd add other NNTPs for any other servers you wish to log on to. Some NNTP servers are secured, requiring a logon name and password. If your server requires this, check the check box at the lower-left corner and add the proper logon information when prompted. Microsoft's news server isn't secured, so you don't need to check this box. Your screen should resemble Figure 16.16. When done, click Next.

FIGURE 16.15.

Outlook Express waiting to be configured for using the Microsoft news server.

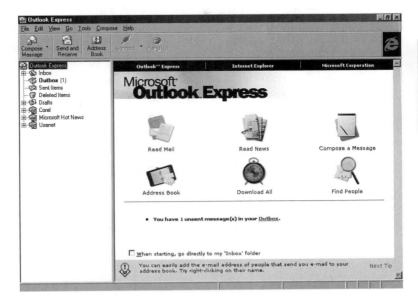

16

FIGURE 16.16.

Add as many newsgroup servers as you choose by entering their IP or URL to the NNTP text box in the Internet Connection Wizard.

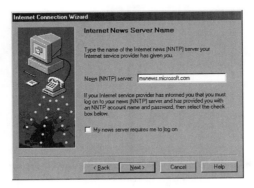

- Now enter a Friendly Name for the news server. This is the name you'll see in the Resource pane of Outlook Express. In this example, I call it Microsoft's Server. Use that or choose one of your liking. When done, click Next.

- Enter the method you'll be using to connect to this server. In most cases, this will be by phone line or manually. If you connect through a gateway on your

▼   LAN, check the middle box. If you connect through a modem, the top box
     will connect you automatically when you open Outlook Express. The bottom
     box won't. Click Next. Click Finish and you're finished.

3. After you're done with the wizard, click Close to close the Accounts dialog box.
   Outlook Express will offer to download the newsgroups from your newly entered
   server. Accept the offer. If you're not currently online, Outlook Express will hunt
   about and locate your Dial-Up Networking connection to log you on to your ISP
   and do the download from the server. This download can take several minutes,
▲ even with a fast connection.

The Newsgroups

If you did Task 16.1 or otherwise configured a news server and downloaded the newsgroups and you're logged on to the Microsoft News Server msnews.microsoft.com, your
screen should resemble Figure 16.17.

FIGURE 16.17.

*Outlook Express will
automatically down-
load the newsgroups
from any server it logs
on to.*

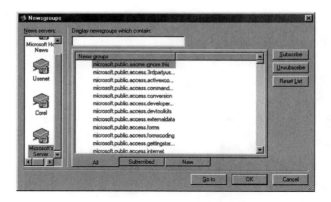

A subscribed group is one that will appear below the news server's Friendly Name in the
Resource pane of Outlook Express. You can see the messages from any newsgroup by
clicking the Newsgroups button on the toolbar when logged on to a server. Subscribing
to a newsgroup is handy if you want to easily access certain groups each time you log on
to this server. You can subscribe to any newsgroup by clicking on it and then clicking the
Subscribe button shown in Figure 16.17. You can also double-click on a newsgroup to
subscribe.

To narrow down the list of groups, enter a key word in the text box at the top of the dialog box. For example, to only see groups concerned with Microsoft Word, enter **word** in
this text box, as shown in Figure 16.18.

FIGURE 16.18.

A keyword will narrow down your newsgroup selection.

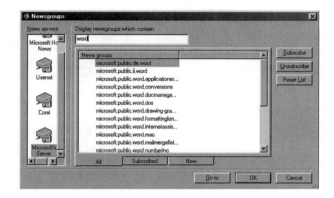

Choose any groups that interest you and click the Subscribe button. You can choose multiple groups by the Ctrl+click or Shift+click method. When you're done, click OK. Figure 16.19 shows a series of Word-related newsgroups subscribed to and the Resource pane entry for this news server expanded.

FIGURE 16.19.

Subscribed newsgroups appear under the server's Friendly Name in the Resource pane of Outlook Express.

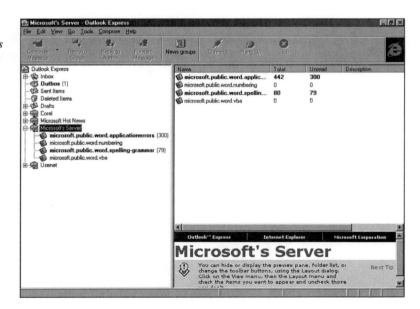

Now you can see the three-pane Outlook Express layout in action with newsgroups as you did earlier with mail. To see the message headers or subjects for any group, click that group in the Resource pane. If a header interests you, click on it in the Contents pane. That will display the message in the Preview pane. Figure 16.20 shows the message headers for the Spelling-Grammar group and a message from that group displayed.

FIGURE 16.20.

Outlook Express uses a drill-down approach to news. Here you see the Resource pane showing the group, the Contents pane the message header, and the Preview pane the message body.

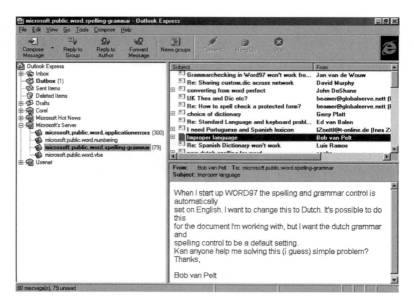

To reply to a message, click the Reply to Group button in the toolbar if you want your reply seen in the group. If you choose Reply to Author, your response will be emailed privately to the person who posted the message. Figure 16.21 shows a reply to the group being composed.

FIGURE 16.21.

You can reply to the group publicly or directly to the author if you prefer a private exchange.

After filling in your response, click Send and Outlook Express will post or mail your message. You can also file (by dragging) any message to any folder in the Resource pane or forward the message by clicking on the Forward button on the toolbar.

The little plus signs you see to the left of the headers indicate that this header has responses already posted. To expand the tree, click on the plus sign. For example, the header shown in Figure 16.22 has seen many responses, including responses to responses.

FIGURE 16.22.

The plus sign next to a header indicates a collapsed branch. A minus sign indicates an expanded branch.

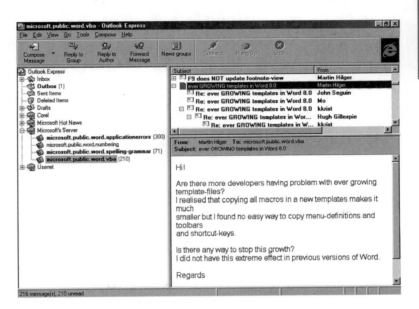

16

> **Note**
>
> A *thread* is newsgroup speak for a conversation. For example, say you post a comment such as "I think the Jets will win the next Superbowl" with the subject "Next Winners." Others might reply to your post, and others reply to those replies. The entire conversation is a thread.

Note the Re: addition to the header for responses. Outlook Express will automatically add the Re: part to any message without an Re: to indicate to all that you're responding to a message. You can keep this addition or change the subject line entirely for a new header posting.

Composing a New Newsgroup Message

To make a new newsgroup message, locate the server and the newsgroup you wish to post into; then highlight that group. Click the Compose Message button. That will bring up a form almost identical to the mail form you saw earlier but tailored for newsgroups. The newsgroup you've highlighted will be automatically entered in the Newsgroups (recipient) line. You can add more newsgroups to your recipients by clicking the newspaper-like icon to the left of the Newsgroups text box. Figure 16.23 shows a new message composed and the Pick Newsgroups dialog box open.

FIGURE 16.23.

To add newsgroups to your message, highlight the group or groups and click the Add button. Similarly, you can remove added groups using the Remove button.

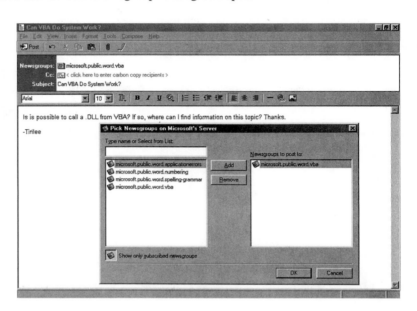

If you're online, you can send your messages immediately by clicking the Send button. If you're working offline, you can click the Send button or press Alt+S or choose the File | Send Later menu option to store your messages in your Outbox. The next time you're online and click the Send and Receive button, Outlook Express will log on and post all your email and newsgroups messages.

Spam, Sigs, and Twits

One of the chief annoyances of getting online is the so-called spam mail you'll likely start receiving. *Spam mail* is unsolicited commercial messages, often touting shady schemes of questionable ethics or marginal legality.

Many spammers, or senders of spam mail, garner email addresses from the Usenet or other public newsgroups. For example, if you spend time in a newsgroup dedicated to dogs, you might start receiving unsolicited dog-oriented solicitations. However, most spammers just garner all the email addresses they can and spread as wide an umbrella as they can.

Some people enter a false return address with a sig line with their proper mail address. This works but also acts as a slight block to legitimate people trying to contact you, so you might want to try another tactic, such as the kill filter technique discussed in the "Twits and Kills" section, later in this chapter.

As you wander through cyberspace, you'll meet unsavory people. These types either have abusive personalities or enjoy making others squirm for reasons of their own. These people are called *twits*.

Sigs

Sig is short for *signature*, a tag line that Outlook Express will attach to your emails or newsgroup postings. To enter a sig for yourself, choose Tools | Stationery in Outlook Express. Select the Mail or News tab and click the Signature button. Figure 16.24 shows the resulting dialog box and the Mail tab.

FIGURE 16.24.

The Signature dialog box has a place to add a signature for email and newsgroups.

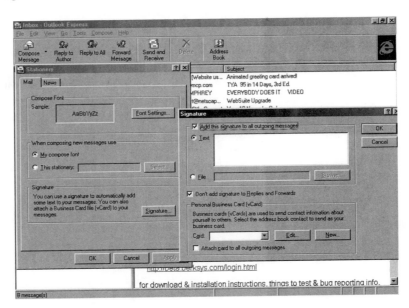

Enter any text in the box and Outlook Express will enter that text whenever you reply to a newsgroup message or compose a new message. You can have different sigs for newsgroups and mail. This dialog box will also allow you to set default Stationery for your news messages or emails. Stationery is like a background wallpaper for your messages.

Only those who have readers equipped to decipher Stationery will be able to see your artwork, so use it with caution unless you're sure your correspondents are using a fully enabled mail or newsgroup client like Outlook Express.

If you choose to eliminate spam by using a false email address in newsgroups, edit the newsgroup account (Tools | Accounts) to a fake address, such as `pcasselnospam@msn.com`, and also add a sig to your newsgroup messages saying something like this:

```
Remove the 'nospam' from my address to send me messages.
```

This will prevent automatic newsgroup scanners from acquiring your real email address. It will also prevent people from being able to automatically respond to your newsgroup posting by private email. It won't prevent people from automatically responding to your newsgroup postings in the newsgroup, however.

If you don't want any email from your wanderings in the newsgroups, enter a false email address and don't correct it in your sig.

Most people use sigs for personal or humorous touches to their newsgroup postings or emails.

Twits and Kills

You can also filter out messages from those you don't want to hear from or from known spam originators. Most people call these tools *kill filters* or *twit filters*, but Outlook Express has chosen to use the Inbox Assistant nomenclature for this facility. The menu choices Tools | Inbox Assistant will bring up the first screen of a complex dialog box for creating email and newsgroup rules. Figure 16.25 shows this dialog box.

FIGURE 16.25.

The Inbox Assistant is a sophisticated rules-based filtering system.

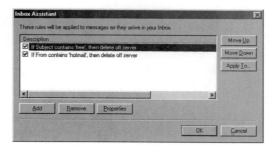

Say you want to not receive any messages from a person whose email address is `smutty@hotstuff.net`.

From the screen shown in Figure 16.25, choose Add. Fill in the From field with the person's email address, as shown in Figure 16.26.

FIGURE 16.26.

The Inbox Assistant will remove messages according to the criteria entered in this dialog box. This is a twit filter.

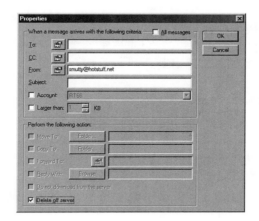

16

You must fill in two parts for the Inbox Assistant to know what you want. First, fill in the criterion or criteria for the messages you want to filter. Second, fill in the action you want the Assistant to take. In the case of the filter set in Figure 16.26, the user told the Assistant to apply the filter to anybody with the email address `smutty@hotstuff.net` and to delete those messages from the server without downloading them at all. You can also automatically move such messages to folders or forward them or any other action you see in the Assistant's dialog box.

If you want to remove all messages from a particular domain such as the `hotstuff.net`, enter **hotstuff.net** or just **hotstuff** in the From line of the dialog box shown in Figure 16.26. Keep in mind that `hotstuff` will not only filter out messages sent from `hotstuff.net`, but `hotstuff.com` and `hotstuff.edu` as well, so use with caution. Under no circumstances enter something like **com**, unless you're sure you don't want to receive any email from commercial (`.com`) domains. Figure 16.27 shows an Inbox Assistant dialog box with a fairly typical filter set. This person has chosen not to receive messages from the domains `juno.com` and `hotmail` and has filtered out any messages that contain the subject words `sex`, `adult`, `money`, and `free`.

Although these rules won't stop all objectionable spam mails, they'll keep out a good deal of them.

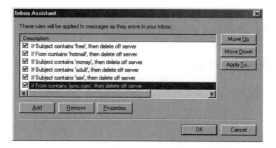

FIGURE 16.27.

One set of filters set for the Inbox Assistant. These will keep out some but not all objectionable material. Naturally, what this user finds objectionable isn't universal.

Summary

Outlook Express (OE) comes standard with Windows 98. It's a variant of the Outlook program that comes with Microsoft Office products.

Using OE, you can participate in the soon-to-be universal world of Internet email as well as local email, if your LAN has such a service.

You can also participate in the multitopic discussion group called the Usenet or any other private newsgroup you can subscribe to. It's getting to be quite common for companies, especially computer companies, to create public non-Usenet newsgroups dedicated to their company's policies or products.

In this chapter you learned how to configure Outlook Express, how to compose and send an email, the nature of newsgroups and how to participate in newsgroup discussions, how to filter out a twit, and how to add a sig to your messages.

Workshop

To wrap up the day, you can review terms from the chapter, see the answers to some commonly asked questions, and practice what you've learned. You can find the answers to the exercises in Appendix A, "Answers."

Terminology Review

Address Book—A part of OE that stores contact information about your correspondents.

flame—Rude, provocative reply to an email or newsgroup posting.

newsgroup—A discussion group.

NNTP (Network News Transport Protocol)—The protocol for newsgroups such as the Usenet.

OE (Outlook Express)—A subset of the Outlook program found in Microsoft Office 97 and subsequent Office products.

POP (Post Office Protocol)—The most common protocol for picking up email (receiving) from the Internet.

SMTP (Simple Main Transport Protocol)—The most common protocol for sending email on the Internet.

16

twit—Someone you don't want to get email from or see newsgroup postings from.

Q&A

Q I can't see all the newsgroups. Why?

A Some ISPs filter which newsgroups are available to their subscribers in hopes of keeping a modicum of decency in their service. The downside is that in judging what is decent, an ISP might not agree with your ideas. Before suspecting any OE malfunction, check with your ISP to see if the problem is at his end. If in doubt, open up Tools | Newsgroups and press the Reset List button to download the newsgroups again.

Q How can I add the neat > figure to quoted parts of my messages?

A In OE, choose Tools | Options | Send. Click the Settings button for Plain text and check the appropriate check box. You can choose the > character or any other (such as the :).

Q Can I create a folder beneath a folder of my making?

A Yes. The Resource pane is similar to the Resource pane of Windows Explorer. You can nest folders in both.

Q How can I reply privately (by email) to a Usenet posting?

A Choose the Reply to Author button rather than the Reply to Group. Your reply will arrive by email rather than find its way onto the newsgroup.

Q What is the meaning of the various categories in the Usenet?

A They're a voluntary system to give people an idea of what type of newsgroup is represented. `alt.` is for the alternative category, `rec.` for recreation, `comp.` for computer topics, `de.` for German (Deutsch), and so forth.

Q How can I start my own newsgroup on the Usenet?

A The exact steps vary, depending on which category you want and if you want it to be moderated or not. For information; look at the URL `http://cs1.presby.edu/~jtbell/usenet/newgroup/`.

Exercises

1. Use Microsoft Outlook Express to create a birthday email using the standard birth-day stationery.

2. When you've received a lot of email, it can be very difficult to find individual messages. Keep yourself organized by creating a new folder called Work-Related.

WEEK 3

DAY 17

NetMeeting

by Paul Cassel

NetMeeting is a network conferencing and application-sharing utility for use in any TCP/IP network including the Internet. Using NetMeeting, you can connect with others using voice, video, chat (keyboard entry), whiteboard, or various other media. The ways you can use NetMeeting are as varied as your needs and your hardware or software.

This chapter gives a quick overview of NetMeeting and some of the tools you can use with it. It is not a comprehensive survey of this versatile application—there isn't room for that in this book. However, it provides all the basics you need to be able to intuit the details. This chapter covers

- Internet conferencing
- Intranet conferencing
- Using NetMeeting

NetMeeting has a decent local help system. Because Microsoft is hoping NetMeeting will be a premiere product for the company, there is extensive discussion of NetMeeting at the Microsoft Web site, www.microsoft.com.

You can also access the Web site to download upgraded versions of NetMeeting, along with its tools and accessories. NetMeeting is a dynamic program constantly being updated by Microsoft and third parties in cooperation with Microsoft. Be sure to check with the Web site often for new developments.

What Is NetMeeting?

NetMeeting is a type of real-time groupware. People from various locations can hook up together to share information or even applications. These locations can be along the same LAN, WAN, or anywhere the Internet reaches.

You don't need Windows 98 to use NetMeeting. Prior to Windows 98's release, Microsoft released several versions for use under other operating systems. However, one of the stated goals of Windows 98 is Internet connectivity, so NetMeeting is not only bundled with this new operating system, it also integrates quite easily with it.

Starting NetMeeting

NetMeeting is part of the usual setup of Windows 98 but not a necessary part of the operating system. Usually you'll see it on the Programs menu. If you don't see it, select Start | Settings | Control Panel, click Add/Remove Programs, and click the Windows Setup tab to see if it's installed. NetMeeting appears as a detail of the Communications choices, as you can see in Figure 17.1.

FIGURE 17.1.

NetMeeting is a detail in Windows setup.

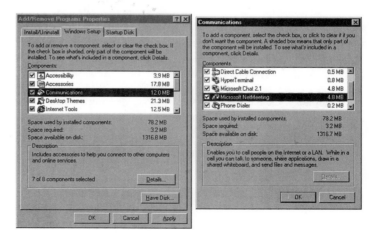

The Initial Startup Wizard

After you have NetMeeting installed, you must configure it for your particular system. This, for the most part, means tuning the audio so you can use it with a normal voice. To start NetMeeting, choose Start | Programs | Microsoft NetMeeting. You will be greeted by the dialog box shown in Figure 17.2. This dialog box appears automatically only the first time that you run NetMeeting. If you won't be using any audio, you can cancel this wizard.

FIGURE 17.2.

NetMeeting needs to be manually tuned for each computer before use.

Click Next to move to the speaker tuning section, as shown in Figure 17.3.

FIGURE 17.3.

The Test button generates a sound, and the slider adjusts the speaker volume.

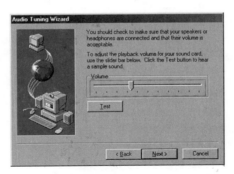

Click the Test button to generate a sound. Your correspondents will be at that volume when they talk. Consider privacy here. Some speakers have headphone jacks. If yours do and you plan to use headphones for audio, test this too. Click Next to move on to the microphone section of the Audio Tuning Wizard. You can see this section in Figure 17.4.

FIGURE 17.4.

The microphone tuning dialog box has a level bar allowing for the visual setting of gain.

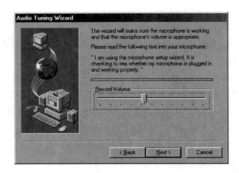

Read the suggested text or something of your own choosing. Make sure you're oriented toward the microphone in the same manner you'll be when online with NetMeeting. Set the volume slider so the volume is enough to show at least halfway up the graphic, but not so much that you run into the red LED-like display at the right end of the graph bar.

Click Next to finish the Audio Tuning Wizard and then click Finish to exit. Your audio settings are now ready.

Options

Before moving on, you should check the Options for NetMeeting, although for the most part the defaults will work fine. Knowing what's there before starting NetMeeting will give you an idea of what you can do to troubleshoot things if something misbehaves during your sessions. To see the Options dialog box, choose the menu selections Tools | Options. Figure 17.5 shows the resulting tabbed dialog box.

FIGURE 17.5.

The Options for NetMeeting aren't too terribly technical. They exist within the familiar tabbed dialog box.

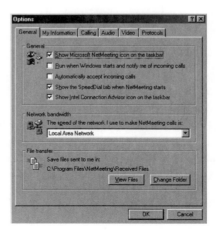

The tabs in the Options dialog and the important settings within each tab are as follows:

- General—Here is where you set options on startup, bandwidth, and file locations as well as indicate whether the application is to answer calls automatically. You can see this tab in Figure 17.5. Be sure to tune your bandwidth to match your actual connection scheme. Also, if you've found your %windows% volume (the logical drive, such as C: where Windows 98 exists) is running short on space, move the location of the sent files to a different volume. You can do this for Internet Explorer as well.

- My Information—This is your personal information for use in NetMeeting sessions. It establishes your identity on a server. Alter this to conform to your preferences for privacy if you'll be going online in any public venue. You can see how I set this tab in Figure 17.6. The option buttons at the bottom of this tab are somewhat optimistic. You can try to categorize your use, but you can't control what others will do online. If you care what your family will encounter online, supervision is the key, no matter which option button you check.

FIGURE 17.6.

The My Information tab is the place to enter data for your virtual online visage.

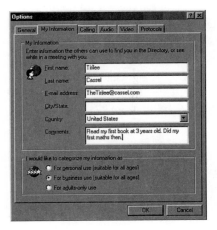

- Calling—In this tab, you can select options for placing calls, indicate whether or not your contact information is to be listed in directories, and choose which, if any, directory you log on to when NetMeeting opens. A directory is a server (online computer) with a public ULS (user locator service) allowing you to find others who are online with NetMeeting. SpeedDials are shortcut entries to other online users. Figure 17.7 shows the Calling tab.

FIGURE 17.7.

The Calling tab shows information about SpeedDials and directories (ULS computers).

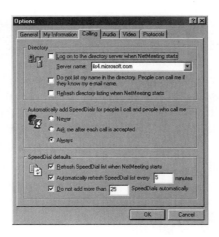

- Audio—This tab sets the options for the audio part of NetMeeting. Naturally you need an audio card to use the features of NetMeeting related to voice. These settings were made for you if you ran the wizard upon the first NetMeeting startup. You can manually change these settings if the results of the wizard aren't satisfactory. Figure 17.8 shows the Audio tab. There is an Advanced button and dialog box (also shown in Figure 17.8) where you can manually set the compression scheme (codec) NetMeeting uses if you're dissatisfied with NetMeeting's performance. There's also a button that triggers the Audio Tuning Wizard. Keep in mind that you can run the wizard from the Tools menu also.

FIGURE 17.8.

The Audio and Advanced dialog boxes enable you to manually override the audio settings created by the Audio Tuning Wizard.

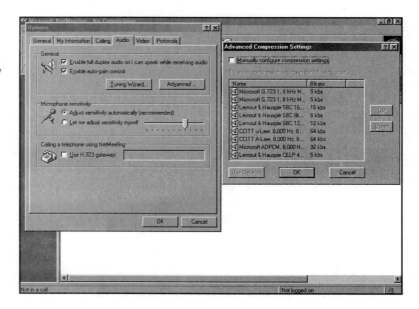

- Video—This is the tab that controls the defaults for video. You need a video camera and a capture card (or other interface setup) to broadcast (or narrow cast) video. However, you don't need any special equipment to receive video. The computer shown in Figure 17.9 is equipped with a video camera and an interface card (Rainbow Runner), so it has the tab fully filled out. The video camera pull-down list will have more entries if you have more than one device. Although the bottom section of the tab refers to a video camera, it really shows information about the capture card installed in the computer.

FIGURE 17.9.

The Video tab is relevant to computers with and without local video input capacity.

17

- Protocols—Here, you can choose a protocol for communicating using NetMeeting. The Null Modem choice allows connection with another computer via a direct cable and null modem. You can buy null modems for under ten dollars at most computer stores. Using NetMeeting with a direct cable is similar to using an intercom. You can also set the Properties for the Null Modem, such as which COM port to use and the characteristics of that port. Figure 17.10 shows the Protocols tab, the Null Modem Properties, and the Properties dialog for the port. The TCP/IP protocol is effective not only over the Internet but also locally.

Using NetMeeting

How you use NetMeeting greatly depends upon what you wish to do. You can connect to just about anybody online who is also using NetMeeting and willing to answer your call. Your correspondents might be any of the following:

- People within your company on your LAN.
- Fellow employees at far-flung locations connected through the Internet, a WAN, an Extranet, or a Virtual Private Network (VPN).

FIGURE 17.10.

The Protocols tab tells NetMeeting which protocol to use by default.

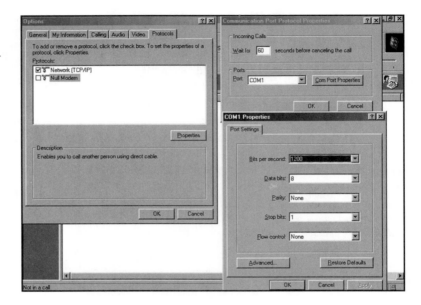

- Your customers.
- Your vendors.
- Continuing education sources. Virtual classrooms are becoming common in some fields, such as Continuing Legal Education (CLE).
- Strangers, listed and active on various directories, who will answer your calls. This works similarly to meeting in Newsgroups or in chat rooms.
- Your company through Dial-Up Networking (DUN) while telecommuting.

Task 17.1 uses DUN to connect to a stranger listed on a standard service.

Task 17.1. Using NetMeeting

This example uses the "public" aspects of NetMeeting to reach out to a stranger and initiate an exchange. Before following along, you must have a connection to the Internet established. Either a LAN gateway or DUN will do. You also need to have installed NetMeeting in Windows 98 if it wasn't installed during Setup (it usually is). Finally, if you want to use audio or transmit video, you need to install the appropriate hardware and in the case of audio, set your speaker and microphone levels. (See "The Initial Startup Wizard" earlier in this chapter for details on this wizard.)

1. Start NetMeeting by choosing Start | Programs | Microsoft NetMeeting from the menu (if your setup is left at defaults). Your screen should resemble Figure 17.11.

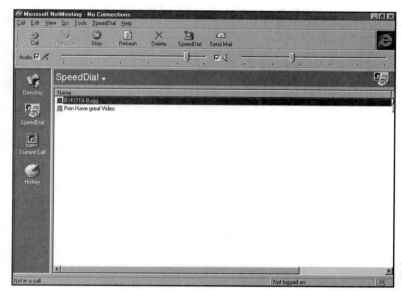

FIGURE 17.11.

The NetMeeting start-up screen has earlier connections listed as SpeedDials.

17

2. If you're on DUN, NetMeeting should initiate the dial-up sequence to connect to the Internet. Figure 17.11 shows the standard NetMeeting startup screen after a few SpeedDial entries have been made. Double-clicking any of these entries will cause NetMeeting to attempt to connect to the respective correspondent. (For more information on DUN, see Day 14, "The Internet and Internet Explorer 4," and Day 21, "Mobile Computing with Windows 98.")

3. Click the Directory icon at the left side of the screen. Choose a server and a category from the pull-down boxes (combo boxes) circled in Figure 17.12. Your screen should fill with active correspondents from this server. Figure 17.12 shows the Business category at the `ils4.microsoft.com` server.

4. To try to "call" any entry, right-click on the entry and choose Call from the Context menu (see Figure 17.13).

5. The server will try to locate the person you've chosen to call. If successful, it will "ring" the person. If the person answers, you're online with your correspondent. Figure 17.14 shows a connection made with the correspondent transmitting video while the local machine doesn't. Note the picture of the person who received the call at the lower right while the local person's video contains the Microsoft NetMeeting logo.

▼

FIGURE 17.12.

Directories have thousands of correspondents, some of whom desire encounters with strangers.

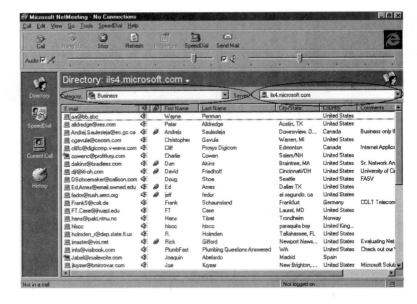

FIGURE 17.13.

Place a call by right-clicking on any entry.

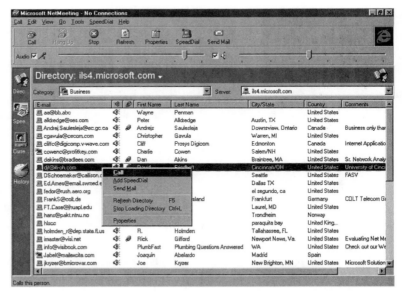

▼

▼
FIGURE 17.14.

You can have simplex or duplex multimedia using NetMeeting. Simplex is one-way, and duplex is two-way exchange.

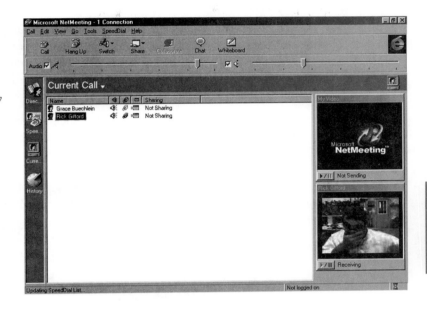

▲

That's it. Depending upon your hardware, you and your callers or callees (correspondents) can now converse using the following or any additions to NetMeeting issued by Microsoft or cooperative vendors:

- Audio
- Video
- Chat in NetMeeting
- Microsoft Chat (formerly Comic Chat)
- Whiteboard

NetMeeting's Applets

Pause for a minute to examine your screen or, if you're not online in NetMeeting, refer to Figure 17.12. Each entry contains a wealth of information about potential correspondents. The entries come from the My Information tab in Options along with connection details. The first column is the email address for everyone on the server. The second and third columns tell whether the person online is equipped with audio or video, respectively. The remaining columns, all the way out to the Comments column barely visible in the figure, are from My Information.

The Whiteboard

The Whiteboard tool is part of NetMeeting. It's a multiuser, multipage illustration and drawing program. When one user makes an entry on his Whiteboard, all users can see that entry. Others in the conference can add annotations to the common whiteboard. In other words, the changes on any Whiteboard tool are replicated or reflected in all whiteboards of that session.

Figure 17.15 shows a Whiteboard session online. Note the title bar contains the text Whiteboard - in Use by 1 Other(s). This indicates that one remote person is using the Whiteboard.

FIGURE 17.15.

The Whiteboard tool is invaluable for illustrating ideas or brainstorming with one or more persons.

The Whiteboard works just like a whiteboard or chalkboard in a meeting except that everybody participating in the meeting can add to what's displayed. Whiteboard tools, shown on the left side in Figure 17.15, are similar to those used in the Windows Paint program. To use a particular tool, click on it. To see what any tool does, let your mouse cursor hover over it to bring up the ToolTip.

Figure 17.15 shows the users trying to enter text ("Hi" and "Hi Back") using the mouse rather than the Text tool. As you can see, the results aren't too satisfactory. Using the correct tool for the job is important in whiteboarding, as in anything.

You bring up the Whiteboard by clicking on the menu choices Tools | Whiteboard or by pressing Ctrl+W while in NetMeeting. Once any person on a conference starts a whiteboard, all people have potential access to it.

Shared Applications

All participants in a NetMeeting conference can share a program running on any connected computer. This is similar to a remote access offered for many years by third-party vendors for use under MS-DOS, or various Windows versions. The person hosting the application on his computer can use the program to demonstrate features or offer help to users. Only the host computer needs to have the program installed for all to share in it.

To share an application with others, start that application, choose the menu options Tool Share Application, and then choose the specific application from the pop-up menu.

Chat

Chat can work similarly to other chats (such as IRC) or the so-called "CB simulators." It's a text-based application where people enter text in an entry place and users can see all people's comments in a common area next to their handles. Figure 17.16 shows a Chat dialog box offline. You start Chat by either choosing Tools Chat from the menu or pressing Ctrl+T.

FIGURE 17.16.

The Chat portion of NetMeeting has places to enter and see messages in a chat dialog.

The downside of Chat is that all users need to be proficient typists to have any significant conversational speed. To see the few options on the standard Chat tool, choose Options while within Chat itself.

Microsoft Chat

Microsoft offers an improved Chat tool where avatars add to the effect of (or distract from, if that's your view) a chat. An *avatar* is a character meant to represent you to the others in a multiuser session. Microsoft Chat doesn't require NetMeeting to run.

Figure 17.17 shows a Chat session with the improved tools with which users are all represented by avatars. Because the particular session caught included multinational participation, not all the comments are in English.

FIGURE 17.17.

You can put a lot of effort into and get a lot of effect from your Chat avatar.

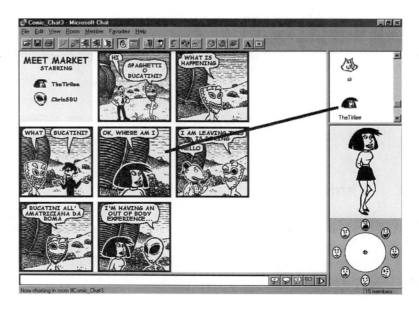

In Figure 17.17, the participant whose computer was used to shoot this screen (TheTirilee) has said, "OK, Where am I." You can see this in the second row, second panel from the left. You can see her name and her avatar at the top right.

 Tip

> The online world has many aspects. Before jumping in with both feet, lurk on the outside of any new type of group activity until you get a feel for the flow and culture of that activity. Trying to keep up with a group that has been online together for months and has developed relationships and conventions can be quite harrowing for the uninitiated.

You can choose your avatar and its aspect from many predefined types. In Figure 17.17, the local computer has the handle TheTirilee. The avatar for TheTirilee is shown in the middle right panel—the girl with short black hair and skirt. Her name is Anna. The bottom panel shows various facial expressions you can assign to your avatar, and the top panel shows the participants in this session.

To see the options for this chat, choose the menu choices View I Options. Figure 17.18 shows the Personal Info tab of the Microsoft Chat Options dialog box.

FIGURE 17.18.

The Personal Info tab allows you to enter information about how you appear to others in chats.

Here are the tabs for Microsoft Chat Options:

- Personal Info—This is where you enter what you want displayed to others about yourself when online.
- Settings—This is where you set what to send in the way of personal information, what actions you will allow, and whether you wish to censor content online. Figure 17.19 shows this tab with the Content Advisor (censor) opened. After you select one of the categories (Language, Nudity, Sex, or Violence), a slider will appear. You can set the slider to censor the content shown, choosing what you want to see or to allow others to see. For example, you can allow cartoon-type violence but disallow all sexual content.
- Comics View—Sets the actual display while online. Figure 17.20 shows this tab.
- Automation—Allows you to record macros and create an automated message to anyone who enters a room where you are. Greeting newcomers to a Chat session, especially if they are new to Chat, is a good way to make friends. The variables %NAME and %ROOM will substitute your name and the chat room's name where these placeholders exist in the message. Figure 17.21 shows the Automation tab.

17

FIGURE 17.19.

The Settings tab is the heart of Chat configuration.

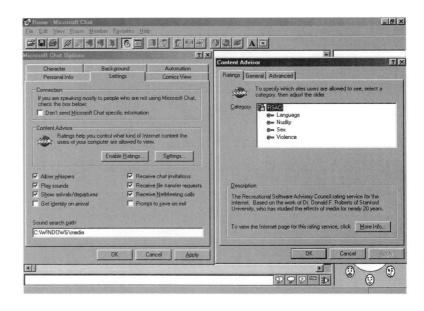

FIGURE 17.20.

Comics View will change how many panels you have displayed for chats.

- Background—Sets the background for your character. Figure 17.22 shows the Background tab along with a few backgrounds. You can acquire more backgrounds or make them up yourself.
- Character—This is where you choose your avatar and its default facial expression (see Figure 17.23). Note the facial expression on Anna has been changed to an angry aspect.

FIGURE 17.21.

You can automate greeting messages as well as create macros, using the Automation tab.

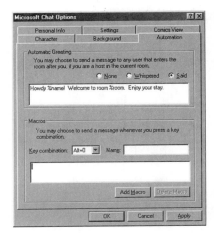

FIGURE 17.22.

Your characters need backgrounds; this is where they can get them.

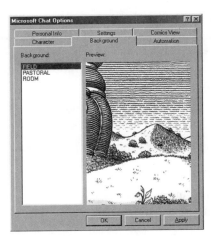

17

Editing or Creating Characters for Chat

Microsoft offers a character editor for Chat. This isn't part of the standard Windows 98 distribution CD-ROM or disk set. If you want to create or edit your own character, you need to download the Microsoft Chat Character Editor from Microsoft's Web site. The download page is http://www.microsoft.com/msdownload/ieplatform/chat.

You can use the editor to

- Create a new character using the editor-supplied sketching tools. These tools are somewhat, well, sketchy in capacity. Before you get good results, you'll need to practice. If you have experience icon editing, it will stand you in good stead here.

FIGURE 17.23.

Microsoft supplies some predefined avatars with Chat. You can get more predefined avatars or make them up yourself.

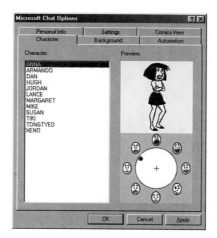

- Edit a previously drawn character if you have the source file. Such files bear the extension .avs by default. You can't edit created or compiled characters. Such files bearing the extension .avb can't be altered. Microsoft supplies at least one AVS file with the editor. Others are available from various download sources on the Internet and elsewhere.

- Create a new character from a graphics file using the editor's Import facility. The editor supports most standard Windows bitmap file formats.

Task 17.2 uses the editor to create a very simple avatar from an existing bitmap file.

Task 17.2. Making an Avatar

This exercise uses an existing bitmap for an avatar. The editor will enhance the existing file and add an icon for inclusion in NetMeeting:

1. If necessary, acquire the Microsoft Chat Character Editor from the Microsoft Web site or other location. Run its setup to install. Open the editor by choosing Microsoft Chat Character Editor from Start | Programs. The resulting dialog box is shown in Figure 17.24.

2. Choose File | New from the editor's menu to bring up a very simple wizard allowing you to specify some of the characteristics of your character. Fill in the blanks as you see fit. For this example, I name the character Marsha; the description is Marsha the Mediator, created by Tirilee Cassel. I use the wizard defaults for the rest of the run.

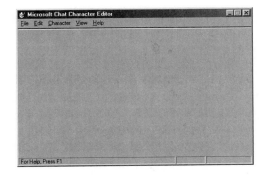

FIGURE 17.24.

Microsoft's Chat Character Editor starts with a blank screen.

3. Choose File I Import to import any bitmap into the editor. For the purposes of seeing how the editor works, any bitmap will do, although for the results to look somewhat like an avatar, you'll have to use an appropriate image. Figure 17.25 shows the editor with the import process finished. Naturally, your results will vary, depending on your bitmap. You might need to adjust the magnification of the image using the slider at the top of the Import dialog box. You will surely need to move the selection area (the dotted box) to capture the exact part of the image you want to make into an avatar. The reason for the selection box is to assure all avatars are the same size.

FIGURE 17.25.

The editor is adept at importing images created using different programs. This simple stick image was made using Paint Brush Pro 4.12.

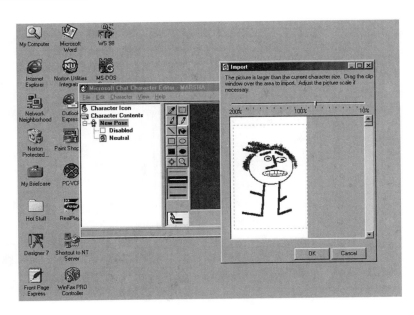

▼   4. Click OK after you've settled on your selection. This moves the image into the editor proper. Now that you're here, you can make any changes you want with the supplied tools. These tools are, for the most part, fairly standard bitmap editors. The flip tools, circled in Figure 17.26, are very handy for quick aspect changes of your character. Note that the image in Figure 17.26 has been flipped so it faces the opposite direction than it did in Figure 17.25. This flip can adjust your imported image to face the right way (screen right) for its default if it isn't so initially.

FIGURE 17.26.

The editor has the standard bitmap tools plus very handy flip tools.

5. Add new poses or new emotions by choosing the appropriate menu choices from the Character menu. Figure 17.27 shows the unflipped character from Figure 17.25 with a new angry emotion being created. Figure 17.27 also shows the zoom box active.

FIGURE 17.27.

A zoom box is almost mandatory for editing iconic bitmaps. The editor comes with a decent zoomer.

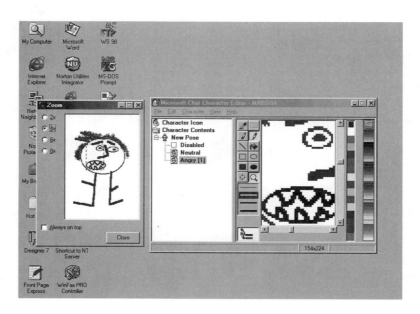

▼   6. After creating as many poses and emotions as you want, create an icon for your new avatar by clicking on the Character Icon entry in the left pane of the editor. You will likely want to zoom for making an icon. For this example, I use the letter *M* for an icon. You can activate the 8x zoomer by clicking on the magnifying glass editor tool and then choosing 8x from the option buttons. Figure 17.28 shows the icon under construction with the zoomer open. Tell the editor where the character's head center is (needed for dialog balloons) by clicking on that tool and placing it over your character's head center.

FIGURE 17.28.

The icon under construction with the zoomer open.

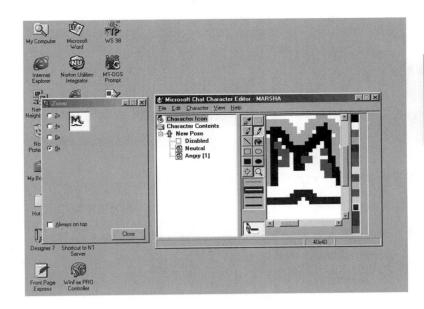

7. Finish the new avatar by choosing File | Make Character File (AVB) from the menu. Place the new character in whatever folder your Chat stores other avatars.

   Figure 17.29 shows the newly created Marsha character added to Chat as the
▼   default character.

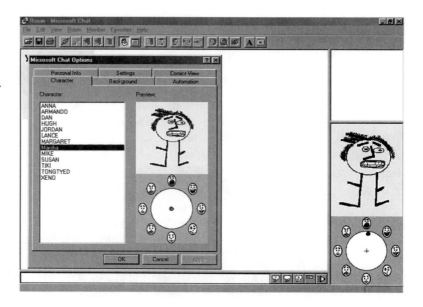

▼
FIGURE 17.29.

After you've finished the AVB, you're ready to use your new avatar in Chat.

▲

Summary

This chapter is a much-abbreviated tour of NetMeeting. This dynamic tool permits various forms of conferencing over networks. NetMeeting supplies the protocols and low-level tools. Its applets, such as Chat, Audio, Whiteboard, and Video, supply the actual interfaces for conferencing.

Conferences can be one-on-one or include many people. Local computers don't necessarily need to have applications or hardware to enjoy all potential facilities. For example, when you are sharing an application, only the host computer needs to have that application. Similarly, you don't need a video interface to receive video 'casts. You do need a camera and interface to send them, however.

Before going online, you need to tune some applets. This chapter covers the wizard for tuning audio so that you can hear and be heard if you have a sound-enabled computer and want it so.

Chat is a very popular medium for conferencing. You can use text-only chat or the enhanced chat that includes avatars. This type of chat was formerly called Comic Chat by Microsoft. Using this chat you can, with the aid of the free Microsoft Chat Character Editor, create or edit your own avatars.

The Whiteboard is another popular Chat tool. Using the Whiteboard is like having a whiteboard or chalkboard common to all participants in a conference.

As tools like NetMeeting increase in use, expect to see additional and enhanced applets and add-ons for them. We are now at the beginning of a brand new application of technology, and at this point nobody can predict how we'll be using such conferencing in the future.

Workshop

To wrap up the day, you can review terms from the chapter, see the answers to some commonly asked questions, and practice what you've learned. You can find the answers to the exercises in Appendix A, "Answers."

Terminology Review

avatar—A fictional character representing a conference member.

IRC (Internet Relay Chat)—A form of chat for use on the Web.

Microsoft Chat—A standalone product that optionally uses avatars for chat purposes.

NetMeeting—An optional part of Windows 98, useful for online conferencing.

whiteboarding—Using a drawing space for nontext conferencing.

`%windows%`—The path to Windows 98's folder.

Q&A

Q My NetMeeting drops so many video frames that it's almost useless. Will a faster modem help?

A You need faster throughput. If your bottleneck is your modem, that will surely help. Check with your ISP for a recommendation on a program to monitor your Internet transfer speed to determine where the bottlenecks exist.

Q Won't all this new traffic clog the Internet?

A The demise of the Internet due to more stuff being forced over the infrastructure has been forecast for many years. It hasn't happened yet. Several new initiatives will address the bandwidth problem. Nobody seems to know when the end will come or if it will come.

Q Can I use characters such as Charlie Brown or Lucy as my avatars?

A Doing so will violate copyrights. This isn't a technical issue, but a legal one.

Q Do I need a TV camera and a tuner card to receive NetMeeting video 'casts?

A You need neither. You'll need a TV camera and an interface card (not a tuner card) to send video 'casts. You need the tuner card only to receive cable or broadcast TV signals.

Exercises

1. Add yourself to the Four11 business directory for NetMeeting.

2. Use NetMeeting to connect with a business associate using a central business directory.

DAY 18

Creating a Web Presence with FrontPage Express

by Paul Cassel

To most people, the Internet means the World Wide Web, or just Web. The Web is, to put it simply, the graphical interface to the Internet. When people speak of sites or pages (such as home pages), they're talking about the Web.

Most independent users who sign up with an online service such as AOL, CompuServe, Prodigy, or MSN have contract space for their own Web pages as part of their service. Many ISPs (Internet service providers) such as Netcom, WorldNet, or Route 66 also have, as part of most service agreements, Web space for their subscribers. Corporate users tend not to have similar space but might need or want to create internal Web sites instead of personal ones. In those cases, the users go through their network administrator to get the space. The end effect is the same.

The problem many people have with making their own Web site is simply a lack of understanding about how to do it. This chapter addresses that problem by covering the following:

- The elements of a Web site
- Making Web pages, an introduction
- HTML, an introduction
- Making a simple Web site using Notepad
- Using FrontPage Express to make a complex site
- Editing a FrontPage Express framework
- Adding a graphic to a Web page
- Adding a hot link to a Web page

The Elements of a Web Site

Three steps to making a Web site are

1. Acquiring a site to host the page or pages
2. Creating the pages
3. Placing the created pages on the acquired site

Because acquiring a site is a business arrangement (not a computer issue) between a user and his service provider or network administrator, this chapter assumes that a site exists and that it is ready for a Web page post.

Creating the Web Pages

Today many different standards for creating Web pages exist, with more appearing at a distressingly rapid rate. This is because we're in the midst of a corporate struggle for de facto control of Web presentation. The players aren't interested in home pages but in other issues relating to their business models.

However, a basic standard underlies all Web work, and because this is a primer for new Web site makers, this book sticks to that standard. It's a simple computer language called Hypertext Markup Language (HTML).

When a browser or other HTML-enabled application, such as the later versions of Word or WordPerfect, encounters HTML, it interprets the language for presentation on a computer's console or monitor. Note that the interpretation is of the browser (Internet Explorer and Netscape Communicator are two browsers) and might vary for different machines.

> **Note**
>
> HTML isn't a page layout program. It is more like a hinting language; it directs by suggestion to the HTML interpreter (usually a browser) how to format a page. It can't force the browser to lay out a page in any particular manner. It also can't supply the fonts needed for an exact layout. A browser finding a call for a font unavailable to it will use the closest match. That match isn't necessarily a close match.

Defining an HTML Document with Tags

Tags are HTML commands. These tend to be mostly layout commands. Tags are alphanumerics within left and right angle brackets (< and >). HTML uses the slash (/) to end a command. The following line, appearing in an HTML document,

```
<B>This is bold</B>
```

will display the words This is bold in boldface, if possible, given the fonts on the client (browser) computer. The <B> starts the boldface and the </B> ends it. HTML tags can be nested. Make sure, when nesting, that you exit the tag commands in the same order you entered them, or be aware of the consequences if you intentionally choose not to; for example,

```
<tag1>
...some text here
<tag2>
...some text here
</tag1>
...some text here
</tag2>
```

will, in most cases, have very different results than the following:

```
<tag1>
...some text here
<tag2>
...some text here
</tag2>
...some text here
</tag1>
```

HTML text is the display text between these layout commands. There are also some commands that don't directly affect the layout of a page. This is a lot easier to see in action than envision from an abstract explanation, so off to an example.

18

Note

For more information on HTML, here are other sources: *Sams' Teach Yourself Web Publishing with HTML 4 in a Week* (Sams Publishing, ISBN 1-57521-336-2) and *Special Edition Using HTML 4* (Que Corporation, ISBN 0-7897-1449-3).

Task 18.1. Your First Web Page

In this example, you create a very simple Web page, using Notepad as an HTML editor:

1. Open Notepad or another pure ASCII editor. Notepad is available from the menu choices Start | Programs | Accessories | Notepad.
2. Enter the text shown in Figure 18.1. The editor in Figure 18.1 is different from the standard Windows 98 Notepad used to show entry detail.

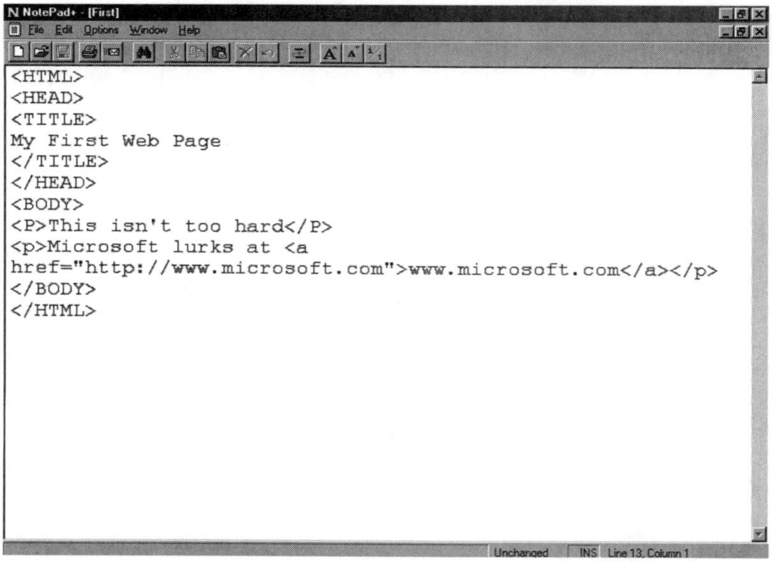

FIGURE 18.1.

You can use a simple editor to make Web pages.

```
N NotePad+ - [First]                                                    _ 8 x
 File  Edit  Options  Window  Help                                      _ 8 x
<HTML>
<HEAD>
<TITLE>
My First Web Page
</TITLE>
</HEAD>
<BODY>
<P>This isn't too hard</P>
<p>Microsoft lurks at <a
href="http://www.microsoft.com">www.microsoft.com</a></p>
</BODY>
</HTML>




                                              Unchanged    INS   Line 13, Column 1
```

This is the text to enter:
```
<HTML>
<HEAD>
<TITLE>
My First Web Page
</TITLE>
</HEAD>
<BODY>
<P>This isn't too hard</P>
```

```
<p>Microsoft lurks at <a
href="http://www.microsoft.com">www.microsoft.com</a></p>
</BODY>
</HTML>
```

3. Save your file, using a name such as `First.htm`. Make sure that the extension is either `.htm` or `.html`. That identifies it to Windows 98 as a Web-type document.

4. Using Windows Explorer, locate the file you just saved and double-click on it. This will load it into Internet Explorer or any other browser you have associated with the extension you used to save the file. Your screen will resemble Figure 18.2. Congratulations, you've just made your first Web document.

FIGURE 18.2.

Making Web pages without any tools except an editor is possible but very tedious.

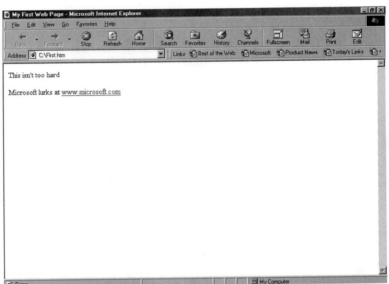

The Web page you made in Task 18.1 is a full, if simple, Web page. The Title instruction tells the browser what to put in the title bar; the link to Microsoft's site will work if you're online. The only complex line is

```
<p>Microsoft lurks at <a
href="http://www.microsoft.com">www.microsoft.com</a></p>
```

That's the link to Microsoft. The `<p>` and `</p>` tags are HTML for an explicit start and end to a paragraph. The `<a> href...</a>` tags are for a link reference. The first text after the tag is the link, and the second is how the link appears on the page.

If you choose to, you can construct an entire Web site by using an editor like Notepad and a reference work on the HTML language. Early Web publishers had nothing else to work with. Naturally, to construct and then include pictures or graphics, you also need a source for those pictures, such as drawing, painting, digitizing, or scanning software and hardware. There is more on this later in the chapter in the section "Pictures and Sound."

Today there are many tools for constructing Web sites using the familiar painting technique first pioneered by programs such as Visual Basic. These programs enable you to visually create your Web pages, and then they take your design specification and create the HTML (or other needed language) in support of your design.

Some of these programs are

- PageMill
- HotDog
- FrontPage 98
- Publisher 98 or Publisher 97

Windows 98 has a program called FrontPage Express as part of its standard components. This is an effective Web page designer suitable for those who are starting out or who don't want to incur any marginal costs for making their Web presentations. Just because this is part of Windows 98 doesn't mean it's a weak sister in any way. The FrontPage Express program with Windows 98 is more powerful than many dedicated Web page designers from only a generation back.

FrontPage Express is part of most standard Windows 98 setups, but not all. If you don't see it on the Start menu, open the Add/Remove Programs applet in Control Panel to the Windows Setup tab. FrontPage Express is under the Internet Tools entry, as you see in Figure 18.3.

FIGURE 18.3.

Most, but not all, Windows 98 setups have FrontPage Express installed by default.

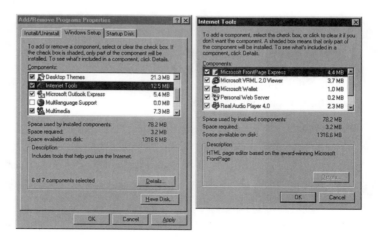

For Task 18.2, install FrontPage Express, if it's not part of your current setup. You can follow along well enough by reading alone if installing the program turns out to be a problem because of your company's policies.

Task 18.2. Making Your Personal Web Site

▼ TASK

This Task describes the initial steps for using FrontPage Express to create a personal Web site:

1. Launch FrontPage Express. Click File | New. Your screen will resemble Figure 18.4.

FIGURE 18.4.

FrontPage Express has a full selection of wizards to aid your page designs.

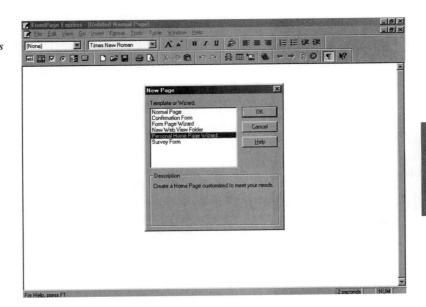

18

2. Choose the Personal Home Page Wizard from the New Page dialog box, as shown in Figure 18.4. Click OK. Your screen will now resemble Figure 18.5.

3. Here you can check off the templates that you want to include in the wizard-created section of the page creation process. The progress bar at the bottom of the dialog box graphically shows you how far you've progressed through the wizard.

   Select the first, third, fifth, and sixth templates, as shown in Figure 18.5. When following these wizards, you can select as many or as few templates as you want. Each template, as you'll soon see, results in a new page for your Web site. Click Next.

4. The next part of the wizard asks you to choose a filename (URL) and title for your site. Depending on your Web host, you might want to use a particular URL instead

▼

▼   of the wizard's default of home.htm. If in doubt, consult with your site administra-
          tor or use the default name. Add a title for your site. In the case of this site, I am
          using my name. Figure 18.6 shows this stage of the wizard. Click Next.

FIGURE 18.5.

*The first part of the
Personal Home Page
Wizard asks you to
select various sections.*

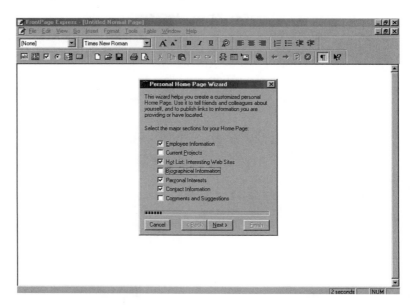

FIGURE 18.6.

*You can usually name
your home page any-
thing reasonable, but
check with your site
administrator if in
doubt.*

5. This wizard is heavily weighted toward making a personal Web site oriented toward
   your employment. Figure 18.7 shows the dialog box following Figure 18.6, which
   clearly indicates that. From here on, the next few dialog boxes ask you to specify
   options of what to include on each page you chose in step 3 and Figure 18.5.

6. Click through the next two dialog boxes, leaving the defaults, until you reach the
   box shown in Figure 18.8. This dialog box is different because it requests you to
   enter, rather than choose, information. Figure 18.8 shows my choices for Personal
▼ Interests. Use these or choose some of your own. Click Next.

▼

FIGURE 18.7.

Although business- or employment-oriented, the wizard can make a site of any nature.

FIGURE 18.8.

After many check boxes, you finally get to fill in some blanks.

18

7. Add whatever contact information is valid for you, or use the information for Tirilee, shown in Figure 18.9. Be careful posting personal contact information on public sites. You might end up with many junk contacts. Reflect long and hard before adding your address.

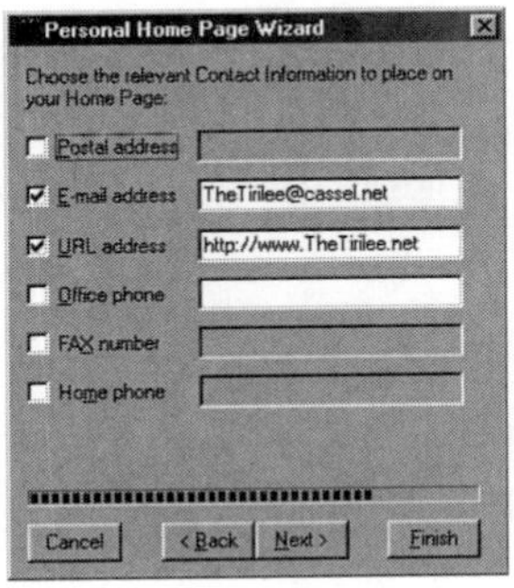

FIGURE 18.9.

Add your contact information in this dialog box.

▼

▼ 8. Click the Finish button or click Next and then the Finish button. That's all there is. The wizard will grind around a while, and when done, your screen will resemble Figure 18.10 (unless you didn't choose the exact same entries as the Task).

FIGURE 18.10.

The Finish button ends the wizard and generates the page, based on your chosen options.

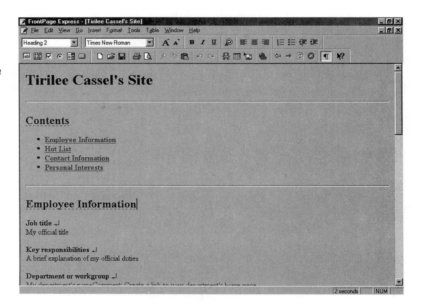

▲

If you choose File I New I Personal Home Page Wizard again, the wizard replays with your chosen information already entered. Thus, the wizard acts as an editor for settings, in addition to its role of creating new material.

It's a good idea to save your work at this point. Choose File I Save As, and in the resulting dialog box, choose to save your work as a file. Give the file any name or choose the default one, as shown in Figure 18.11.

FIGURE 18.11.

Save often or be ready to lose your work sometimes. Use an extension of .htm or .html when saving Web pages.

After saving your work as a file, locate it by using Windows Explorer and double-click on it. This will load your new page in your browser. Figure 18.12 shows the page loaded in Internet Explorer.

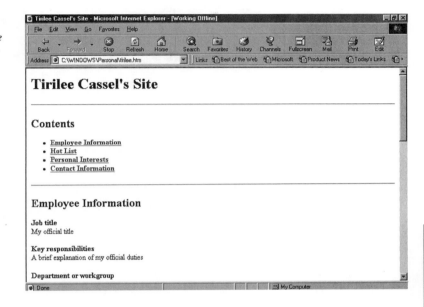

Try clicking the links, and you'll see that you jump to the proper anchor points. The only thing left to finish this simple site is to fill in the missing or placeholder text and then transfer (publish to the Web) the page or pages to your host site. The mechanism for site posting differs, depending on your host. Most public sites use simple FTP transfers. Check with your site administrator if you're unsure how to go about this.

Editing the Framework

FrontPage Express uses the familiar highlight-then-edit method to change text on a page. To add text, click at your desired insertion point and start typing. To change the font or font size, use the combo boxes on the toolbar.

If you've used modern word processors, you should be familiar with the method. For example, to edit the Personal Interests section of your page, scroll down to it (in FrontPage Express), highlight the section you want to replace, and type away. Figure 18.13 shows an edited section under Rock Climbing and another section, Volcano Exploration, ready for actual text entry.

FIGURE 18.13.

FrontPage Express edits work similarly to most modern word processors such as Notepad or WordPerfect.

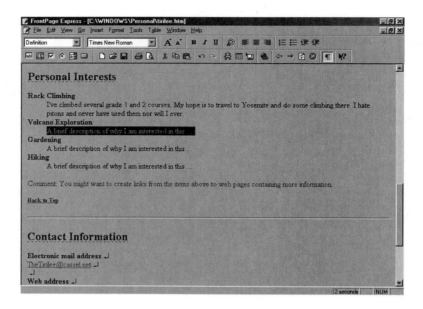

Although you can change the font to any typeface or size installed on your computer (or that your computer is capable of), be careful. If the same font or font size isn't available on the client computer (the one with the browser), that computer will use the closest approximation. Often this isn't a close approximation and can result in a very different display of your pages than you intended.

Make sure that you do your layouts using compromise fonts that you have good reason to expect are available on most computers. Exactly which fonts to use depends on the browsers your viewers will use and to what extent you want to accommodate them. For example, Macintosh computers often use different fonts and screen resolutions than IBM-style PCs. If you want to make your pages look good to Macs, you must consider these items.

If only a small or well-known group of computers, such as those on a company intranet, will access your Web page, you can use fonts more creatively.

Pictures and Sound

The Web is severely limited in how many colors it can display, compared to the variety that modern computers regularly display on their screens and printers. Rendering colors and scenes accurately over the Web is both a skill and an art. You'll need a Web-aware tool or painting program to reduce color depth to what the Web can host. This program should also have algorithms to optimize your reduced color images to show the closest color match to the original.

Not all paint programs can render to the Web successfully. Some that can, in the latest versions, are

- Micrografx's Picture Publisher
- Adobe's Photoshop
- MetaCreations' (Fractal Design) Painter
- JASC's PaintShop Pro
- Equilibrium Software's DeBabelizer
- Corel's PHOTO-PAINT

DeBabelizer is a highly specialized tool for Web graphics. The others are general-purpose image editors.

Of course, if you're not too meticulous, you can just insert your images in the page and let them be. If your color rendering doesn't have to be precise, this works fine. It seriously fails to please only in applications, such as catalogs, where accurate color balance is vital.

Task 18.3 shows the steps for inserting a graphic in the Web document begun in Task 18.2.

Task 18.3. Placing a Graphic in a Web Page

This Task inserts a graphic (picture) in the Web document from Task 18.2. You'll need a graphic image of some sort to follow along. Windows 98 comes with several BMP files that you can use. To locate these files, open Windows Explorer, choose Tools | Find, and enter *.BMP in the place for a file specification.

1. Open FrontPage Express with the file you made earlier. If you didn't do Task 18.2, choose File | New and run through a wizard, accepting all the defaults. This will give you a quick-and-dirty page with which to practice.

2. Place your cursor at the end of the placeholder text for the last entry in Personal Interests. If you're following the Tasks exactly, that entry is Hiking. Press Enter and enter the text **My Picture**. Highlight the text you just entered by dragging with the mouse, and make it bold 14-point type by using Format | Font. Click OK when you're done. Your screen will resemble Figure 18.14.

3. Click at the end of the text you just entered and press Enter twice to start a new paragraph and give yourself some working room. Choose Insert | Image and then browse for the file you want to insert. When you find the graphic you want to insert, select it and then click OK. Figure 18.15 shows the browsing process, and Figure 18.16 shows the picture inserted.

18

▲TASK

▼

▼

FIGURE 18.14.

You can change entered text by highlighting and then changing its font, font size, or font characteristics.

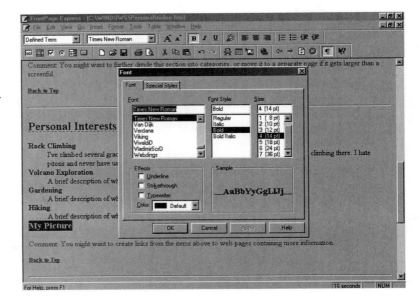

FIGURE 18.15.

You can browse for a graphic by using the typical Windows Explorer–type tools or by entering a URL.

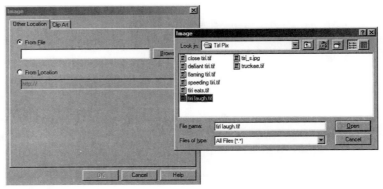

▼

FIGURE **18.16.**

When you find the image you want to insert, select it and then click OK to finish the placement.

That's it. You've now populated your Web page with a graphic. The Insert menu also has entries for inserting movies, WebBots, lines, breaks, background sounds, and several other useful or decorative components. Adding any of these is similar or identical to adding an image. Place your cursor where you want the insertion; then browse or specify the file or object you want inserted.

You might be a little confounded by the lack of fine control you have in file insertion and manipulation using FrontPage Express. Remember, this is a lighter duty version of FrontPage—a program that gives you much more control in these operations. Similarly, Microsoft Publisher and the other dedicated Web page composers offer you much more fine-tuned control.

Task 18.4. Adding a Hot Link

This Task shows you how to add a hot spot link to a Web page object:

1. Open FrontPage Express with the page from Tasks 18.2 and 18.3 loaded. If you don't have such a page, run through a File | New wizard to create a working example of a page.

2. Locate any text. If you're using the sample page, locate the Hot List section and highlight the text Sample Site 1. Enter **Microsoft**. Highlight the word you just entered. Click the Create or Edit Hyperlink button on the toolbar. That's the icon

▼ that looks like a globe behind a chain link. Enter **http://www.microsoft.com** in the space provided. Your screen will resemble Figure 18.17.

FIGURE 18.17.

You can add links as you want, but usually Web designers prefer to have text as the hot spot for a link.

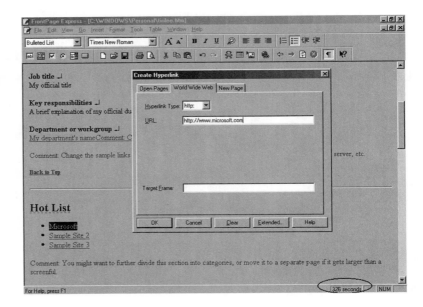

3. Click OK and you've just created a hyperlink to Microsoft's home page. Experiment with the Create Hyperlink dialog box. You'll see that it automates the hot link process not only to pages but also to email addresses, newsgroups, and files on your local computer or LAN.

▲

Load Time

The status bar on the lower right side gives you the estimated time to load your page. This area is circled in Figure 18.17. Keep in mind the types of connections your site will have. If people connect through a LAN, you can afford large, complex pages. If people are on modem dial-up, you might want to consider keeping the graphics to a minimum to speed up transmission times. In the example for this chapter, the load time increased dramatically after the large picture was added. When designing your Web pages, keep an eye on this metric to make sure you don't design yourself into an intolerably slow page. The fanciest page in the world isn't any good if people lack the patience to load it. If you have problems running any of your pages on your server, check with your administrator. Some oddball server setups don't fully support standard Web extensions such as active pages.

Summary

This chapter paints in broad strokes a description of publishing on the Web using FrontPage Express. Microsoft clearly wants to use FrontPage Express as a teaser application to get people to upgrade to its heavy-duty Web page designer, FrontPage.

This doesn't mean that FrontPage Express isn't capable of doing anything. You can make a serviceable Web page using it, although the fine control and Web site administration available in the full FrontPage isn't possible.

Workshop

To wrap up the day, you can review terms from the chapter, see the answers to some commonly asked questions, and practice what you've learned. You can find the answers to the exercises in Appendix A, "Answers."

Terminology Review

WebBot—A Web robot. An automated routine existing within a Web page.

Web—Short for the World Wide Web, which is a graphical interface for the Internet. The original intent of the Web was to be a way to publish hypertext on the Internet. It soon expanded to full multimedia.

HTML—A language for making pages on the Web.

server—For Web purposes, the physical place where your Web pages reside.

domain—The part of an Internet address to the right of the dot or @ sign. For example, in the address HELP@microsoft.com, the domain is microsoft.com.

FrontPage Express—A truncated version of the FrontPage program. Express comes bundled with Windows 98.

Q&A

Q Can I use FrontPage 98 to edit pages made in FrontPage Express?

A Yes. You should have no problem with this. However, if you're going to install FrontPage 98 anyway, there's no benefit to having FrontPage Express also installed.

Q How do I get my Web pages on the Web itself?

A You can create a folder structure locally and then FTP the structure to your server, or use your creation program (if it has the capability) to publish to the server directly.

18

Q How do I get my own domain?

A You need to apply to Network Solutions, Inc. Your ISP can handle this for you. There is a fee involved. You can't have a domain that already exists without buying it from the owner. For example, you can't buy the domains `ibm.com` or `microsoft.com`, for the same reason you can't manufacture a car and call it a Mercedes-Benz 300CE.

Exercises

1. The FrontPage Express Personal Home Page Wizard makes it very easy for you to create a home page, but the wizard creates your page with a boring gray background. Create a new home page and change the background to a light blue color.

2. Add links to Microsoft, Yahoo!, AltaVista, and MSNBC in the Hot List portion of your home page.

DAY 19

The Personal Web Server

by Michael Hart

A Web site without a Web is a waste of time, so now it's time to publish that great Web site you just created in FrontPage Express. Before you put it up for all the world to see, though, you want to make sure that the world sees what you intend it to. To do so, you'll learn about the Personal Web Server, included with Windows 98. This chapter covers

- Installing the Personal Web Server
- Creating your home page using the Home Page Wizard
- Publishing files and directories
- Publishing your own site
- Putting your site on the Web

It's important to put the role of the Personal Web Server (PWS) in the proper perspective; in other words, observe the *Personal* in PWS. This is not an industrial-class Web server—it's a personal server. This product is, however, appropriate for several uses: as a small office intranet, as a workgroup site, or for verifying a Web site before moving it to your Internet service provider (ISP). In fact, Microsoft has put a limit of 10 concurrent connections on the product. Because a single user might have more than one connection to a server at a time, this means that fewer than 10 users at a time can connect to the server. Having said that, PWS still stands ready as an easy, very affordable Web server for home, small offices, or workgroups.

Keeping in mind these limits, let's learn all about the PWS.

Installing the Personal Web Server

For a typical Windows 98 installation, you'll find an icon for PWS located in the Programs | Internet Explorer folder. Clicking it will produce the screen shown in Figure 19.1.

FIGURE 19.1.

This page tells you how to install the program.

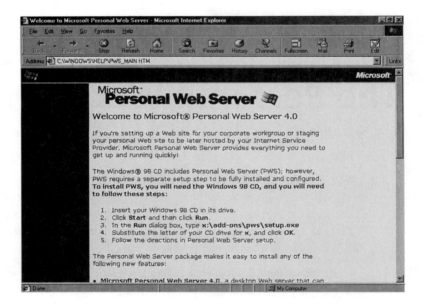

As you can see from Figure 19.1, you must install PWS separately. To do this, follow the steps in Task 19.1.

> PWS requires the installation of TCP/IP, the protocol of the Internet. You can install PWS without TCP/IP, but you won't be able to run it. If you don't have any networking protocols installed yet, you have two options at this point:
>
> - Wait until you've installed the networking components required.
>
> - Install the minimum necessary now.
>
> What you'll need is Dial-Up Networking (DUN) and one connection. Note that you don't have to connect to an Internet service provider, but you have to let Windows think you will.
>
> Day 20, "Windows 98 Networking," discusses the installation of Dial-Up Networking and DUN connections.

Task 19.1. Installing the Personal Web Server

This procedure helps you install and configure PWS in a typical installation configuration. You'll need access to your Windows 98 installation CD-ROM.

1. Using Windows Explorer, navigate to *(your CD-ROM drive letter)*:\add-ons\pws. Locate Setup and launch it. You'll see the Microsoft Personal Web Server Setup dialog, as shown in Figure 19.2.

FIGURE 19.2.

The Microsoft Personal Web Server Setup dialog.

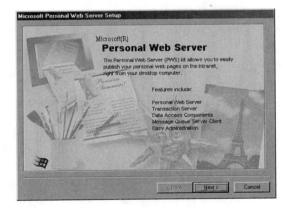

19

2. Clicking Next brings you to the license agreement, which you must, of course, accept before continuing. You'll then be presented with the choice of what type of installation you'd like to perform—Minimum, Typical, or Custom. Choose Typical and click Next.

▼   Selecting Custom enables you to choose exactly which additional components and
     documentation files you'd like installed. You can always come back later and rerun
     Setup to install any additional components.

3. A dialog box will be presented, showing the default WWW Server installation
   directory to be C:\Inetpub\wwwroot. Accept this default and click Next.

4. The installation will finish without any more intervention on your part, although it
   might be several minutes before it finishes. When it has completed, you'll be asked
▲   whether to reboot, which you should do.

Now that the installation is complete, you'll notice several changes. First, there will be a
new group, Microsoft Personal Web Server, under the Start | Programs menu, which con-
tains icons for related programs and documentation. You'll also notice that the icon for
PWS will be displayed on the System Tray. There will be a new icon on your desktop,
Publish, and lastly, there will be a new choice on the SendTo menu—Personal Web
Server.

When you installed PWS, the Personal Web Server started as you logged in to Windows.
To verify that the PWS is running, look at the System Tray; if you see a big red circle
with a white *X* in it over the PWS icon, the server isn't running. You can right-click it
and select Start Service to initiate it.

Open the Personal Web Manager (PWM), the control panel of the Personal Web Server,
by right-clicking the PWS icon in the System Tray and selecting Properties, by double-
clicking the PWS icon in the System Tray, or by selecting Start | Programs | Microsoft
Personal Web Server | Personal Web Manager. Figure 19.3 shows the main screen for
the Personal Web Manager.

FIGURE 19.3.

*The Personal Web
Manager controls all
aspects of your
Personal Web Server.*

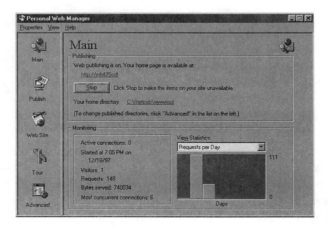

There are five tabs to the PWM:

- Main—Controls the basic operation of the PWS.
- Publish—Contains a wizard to assist you in publishing files and directories on your Web site for users to gain access to.
- Web Site—Contains a wizard to assist you in creating a home page. After you create the home page, it provides some links to help you edit the home page.
- Tour—Offers a short introduction to what the PWS can do.
- Advanced—Contains settings to control other aspects of the PWS, including the configuration of which directories actually contain your home page files.

Figure 19.3 shows the Main tab, which contains a lot of information. The top half displays basic configuration information about your Web server: its address, what its root directory is, and whether it's currently running. The bottom half of the Main tab shows statistical information about the Web server: how many users, bytes served up, concurrent connections, and so on. On the right is a bar graph that a user can select to see Requests (or visitors) per Hour or Day.

You can use the Stop button to halt the PWS service, making it unavailable to other users. If the PWS is currently stopped, the button will be a Start button. Clicking the blue line with the text Your Home Page Is Available At: launches Internet Explorer and takes you to your home page. If you haven't yet created a home page, you'll see the default home page shown in Figure 19.4.

FIGURE 19.4.

The home page you'll see in PWS until you create your own.

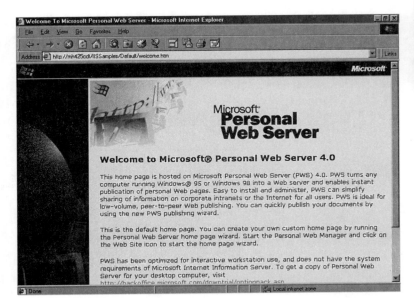

19

If you want additional help at any time, select Help from the menu in the Personal Web Manager; then select Personal Web Server Topics.

Creating Your Home Page with the Home Page Wizard

There are probably as many different ways to create home pages as there are people who want to create them. On Day 18, "Creating a Web Presence with FrontPage Express," you learned how to create a simple home page with FrontPage Express. One excellent feature of the Personal Web Server is the Home Page Wizard, which guides you through the process of creating a home page based on a template.

The wizard guides you through choosing a design for your page and gives you the option of including a guest book area where people can sign up and leave you a public message, like a graffiti area: Anyone can leave a message, and anyone can see it. The wizard also gives you the opportunity to add a drop box area—a place where visitors can leave a private message that only you can read.

The wizard provides three different style templates for your home page: Looseleaf, Journal, and Gunmetal. All three display the same information but in a different style. With the wizard, you can add links to other Web sites to your page. You also have the ability to publish documents or entire directories, but that will be covered later in the day in the section "Publishing Files and Directories."

Task 19.2. Creating a Home Page with the Home Page Wizard

In this Task, you'll use the Home Page Wizard in the Personal Web Server to create a home page:

1. Launch the Personal Web Manager either from the System Tray or from Start | Programs | Microsoft Personal Web Server | Personal Web Manager. Click the Web Site icon along the left edge, and you'll see the Home Page Wizard.

Note

Depending on your Internet Control Panel settings, you might see a Security Alert dialog box pop up; because you know that you're sending only to your own Personal Web Server, you can safely ignore this warning. If the dialog becomes annoying (because it continues to pop up), check the box labeled In the Future, Don't Show the Warning for This Zone.

▼ 2. On the next page of the wizard, you're asked to select a template style on which to base the design of your home page. Select any one of the three available (if you don't like it, you can easily change it later); then click the >> button.

3. The next two pages give you the opportunity to add a guest book and private message drop box to your page. Add both.

4. Finally, the construction phase is finished. After clicking the >> button, Internet Explorer will be launched, with your home page displayed, so you can enter additional information to further personalize your page. There are spaces to enter several headings and paragraphs of information, such as your address and email, your interests, the purpose of your Web page, or anything else you'd like. Fill in a couple of headings and put some text into the boxes.

5. Just below the text box area is a place where you add links to other Web sites. Type the URL, enter a description, and click Add Link. Now add a link to Microsoft. In the URL box, enter `http://www.microsoft.com`. Add some descriptive text, such as `Click to visit the Microsoft WWW site`. Click Add Link.

6. After you've finished adding text and links to your page, click the Enter New Changes button below the text boxes, and all your information will be posted to ▲ your Web site. You'll also see your page displayed as users will see it.

When your home page is complete, you can edit it at any time by clicking the Web Site icon in the Personal Web Manager. From now on, though, rather than see the Home Page Wizard, you'll see the choices shown in Figure 19.5: Edit Your Home Page, View Your Guest Book, and Open Your Drop Box. Note that you'll only see the guest book and drop box options if you select them while running the wizard or add them to your page later.

19

The available choices on the Web Site tab of the Personal Web Manager after using the Home Page Wizard.

When Web users visit your home page and choose to sign your guest book, they'll see
the screen shown in Figure 19.6. They can enter whatever comments and information
they like and post them to your book. Visitors can also view your guest book by clicking
the appropriate link, and they'll see a list of the other people who've signed your book,
as shown in Figure 19.7. By clicking the buttons, they can sort the list by date, author, or
subject.

FIGURE 19.6.

*The guest book feature
enables your site visi-
tors to leave public
messages when they
sign your guest book.*

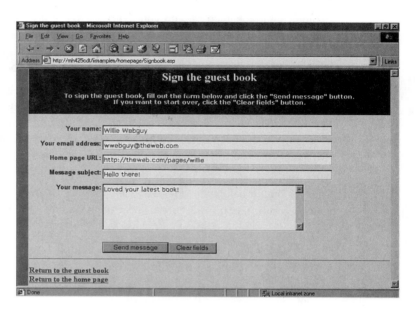

When you view your guest book by using the Home Page Wizard, it will appear very
similar to what your visitors will see, except that you can use simple queries to select
which messages you'd like to view. For example, you can search for messages by date,
author, or subject. You'll also have a button for deleting messages.

Managing your drop box is just as easy. You can read the private messages in your drop
box and either keep them or delete them.

Okay, now your home page is finished. Figure 19.8 shows what a home page will look
like, styled with the Looseleaf template.

FIGURE 19.7.

Site visitors can see and read all the messages in your guest book.

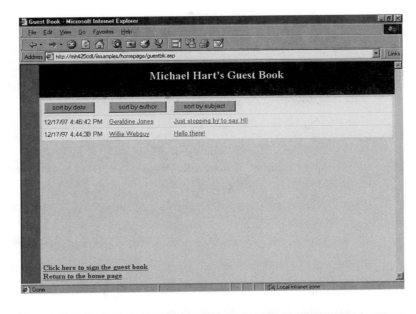

FIGURE 19.8.

A home page completed with the Home Page Wizard.

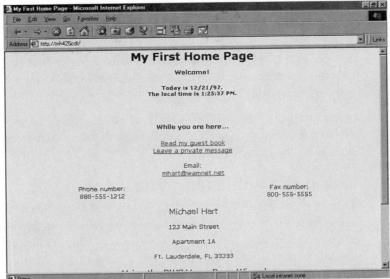

19

Publishing Files and Directories

Besides your home page, you'll probably want to publish other documents, either other pages that make up the rest of your site (larger Web sites can have hundreds or thousands of documents as part of the site) or something like a document repository that you want your site visitors to have access to.

The Personal Web Server provides several ways to publish documents:

- Using the Publishing Wizard in the Personal Web Manager
- Using the SendTo | Personal Web Server option on the context menu in Windows Explorer
- Dragging and dropping documents onto the Publish icon that the PWS setup placed on the desktop
- Using a virtual directory on the Advanced page of the Personal Web Manager

If you want to publish all the documents in a folder, choose the virtual directory method. I'll explain each publishing method in turn.

One primary application of publishing a directory with all the included files is when you have created a Web site using some other tool. On Day 18, you learned that you can use a multitude of programs to create a Web site, such as Hot Metal Pro or FrontPage Express, which is included with Windows 98. You even started a Web site in the Task sections in that chapter. If you've built a Web site using such tools, you can publish it by publishing a directory; that will be covered later in this chapter in the section "Publishing All the Documents in a Folder."

What specifically interests you now is how to use any of the previously mentioned methods of publishing documents to enable users to access them from the Web site you've built using the Home Page Wizard.

Using the Publishing Wizard

Using the Publishing Wizard is a quick, easy way to publish and link documents to your home page. Publishing documents on your wizard-created home page puts a new link on the home page, View My Published Documents. Clicking the link takes your visitor to the My Published Files page, which displays a listing of all your published files. There's a Home button conveniently displayed so that your site visitors can easily return from whence they came.

When you go to the Publishing Wizard page of the Personal Web Manager, you might see the message (in red) at the bottom of the window shown in Figure 19.9; if so, you'll have to first run the Home Page Wizard, as it says. Because the PWM is focused on serving up the Web pages that it generates, you must appease it by first running the Home Page Wizard. If you've previously run the wizard, you won't see the message in red.

FIGURE 19.9.

The message at the bottom appears in the Publishing Wizard if you have not yet run the Home Page Wizard.

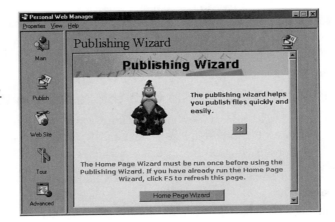

The Publishing Wizard screen shown in Figure 19.10 is where the work is accomplished. The Path box on the top is where you type the full path and filename of the file you want to publish. In the Description box, you type the text you'd like to appear next to the document icon. At the bottom of the page is a list of any files or folders already published. The Browse button opens a Java-based file browser window to enable you to easily select the file to publish.

19

FIGURE 19.10.

The section of the Publishing Wizard where you designate the file you want to publish.

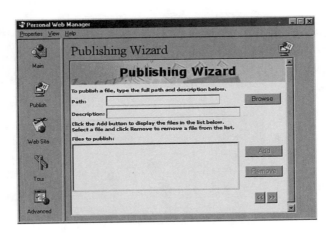

The Java browser is a neat idea. Depending on the machine and memory you have, you might quickly decide not to use it, though. I found it very slow. Instead, you'll find it much more effective to just type the path and filename in the Path box for the file you want to publish.

When your document links are placed on your My Published Documents page, you'll see both an icon representing the document and some descriptive text. Enter the description into the Description field; then click the Add button to add the file to your list of published documents.

Task 19.3. Publishing a File with the Publishing Wizard

Use this procedure to publish files on your wizard-generated home page. Before beginning, use Windows Explorer to locate a file in the C:\ directory of your PC; you can use AUTOEXEC.BAT or CONFIG.SYS (if they exist) or choose any other file.

1. Open the Personal Web Manager (PWM). Click the Publish icon on the left side of the dialog.
2. Click the >> button until you see the screen where you enter the filename and description, as shown in Figure 19.10.
3. In the Path box, type the filename of the file you found before starting this Task. Type a short description in the Description box; then click the Add button.
4. You'll see the filename and description moved to the list box at the bottom of the wizard, as shown in Figure 19.11.

FIGURE 19.11.

A file and its description have been added to the list to be published.

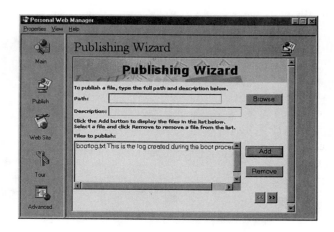

5. Click the >> button, and you'll see a celebratory message stating that your file has been added.

Use Internet Explorer to check your Web page, and you'll see a new link on your home page titled View My Published Documents. Clicking the link will take you to the My Published Documents page, where you'll see a document icon, your description, and the file size. Users clicking the link will then download the file.

PWS publishes your documents by creating a read-only copy of them and placing them in a special folder called WebPub (C:\InetPub\WebPub). If you were to change the original copy of the document after it's been published, the published copy would be out of date; it wouldn't include the latest changes. To update the Web documents, go to the Publish page of PWM, start the Publishing Wizard, and select Refresh Published Files from Their Originals.

Using SendTo | Personal Web Server

The Publishing Wizard is very handy if you have a bunch of files that you want to publish at one time. If you have only one to publish, though, typing the name or using the file browse button can be arduous. Naturally, there's another way to publish—with the new SendTo option, Personal Web Server.

You didn't see it when it happened, but during the setup procedure for PWS, a new menu item was added to your SendTo menu: Personal Web Server. Using the SendTo | PWS option as you would any other SendTo, open the Publishing Wizard with the selected filename already entered in the filename box. All you have to do to finish the publish process is to add a file description and then click the Add button.

Drag and Drop Documents onto the Publish Icon

Another side effect of the PWS setup that you might have noticed already is the addition of a Publish icon on your desktop. Double-clicking the Publish icon doesn't do what you might expect (launch the Publishing Wizard). Instead, it opens the Personal Web Manager.

If this is disappointing, take heart. Do you remember way back on Day 5, "Fonts and Printing in Windows 98," when you learned that you can print a file by dragging it onto the printer icon? Well, the same thing applies to the Publish icon. Just drag a document file onto the Publish icon, and the Publishing Wizard is launched, with the filename already entered in. Add a description, click Add, and your file is published.

You can use the SendTo or the drag-and-drop method to publish multiple documents. When the Publishing Wizard launches, you'll see all the filenames listed in the Path box, as shown in Figure 19.12. How do you add descriptions for the files? You can't. The solution is to add the files without descriptions by clicking the Add button. Come back later and add the descriptions to each file individually.

19

FIGURE **19.12.**

Publishing multiple files at a time.

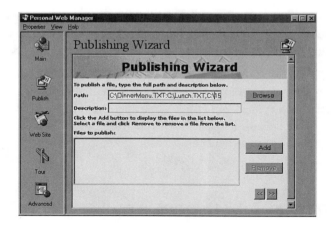

Publishing All the Documents in a Folder

There are two very common situations in which you might want to publish a folder (directory) of documents, instead of individual documents:

- To publish a Web site created by using something other than the Home Page Wizard
- To make all the documents in a directory available over the Web

In reality, these two things are exactly the same. How you go about them is going to be slightly different, for subtle reasons. When you have a folder or a directory of documents that make up your Web site, you generally want all those files, images, documents, HTML files, sounds, or whatever, available to the user, including any subdirectories. When you publish a directory full of documents that you want to add to your site, that document directory might not be a part of the directory tree that makes up your Web site.

A published directory of documents can appear one of two ways to a site visitor. You might choose to have a nice Web style page that lists all the documents and provides a link to them, similar to what you saw when you used the Publishing Wizard to publish a document. As you can imagine, though, publishing dozens or hundreds of documents with the Publishing Wizard or by manually creating links to documents is a tiresome task.

Instead, you can present your documents to your site visitors as a directory listing. By doing this, you don't have to maintain the links to your documents; your visitors just see a list of document names, as shown in Figure 19.13.

FIGURE 19.13.

When you have many documents to publish, a directory-style listing is quick and easy.

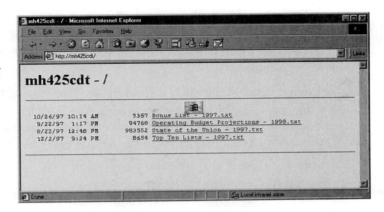

You learned earlier that PWS published documents by placing a read-only copy of them into the WebPub directory. WebPub is what's called a *virtual directory*. When you want to publish an entire directory, PWS makes a read-only copy of the entire directory and its contents, creating (you guessed it) a virtual directory. You might want to think of a virtual directory as a mirror image of the real directory.

Task 19.4. Publishing an Entire Directory

▼ TASK

To better understand the difference between publishing documents with the Publishing Wizard and publishing an entire directory, in this Task, you'll publish your Windows directory and then see what it looks like to a Web visitor:

1. Open the Personal Web Manager. On the Main tab, click the link to your home page to launch Internet Explorer.

2. After Internet Explorer has launched, go back to PWM and click the Advanced tab. Now you'll add a new virtual directory. Click the Add button. In the Add Directory dialog box, type the name of the directory to be published (or use the Browse button), C:\Windows for this Task. In the Alias field, type an alias for the directory, MyWindowsDirectory for now. The *alias* is the directory name visible to your site visitors. Leave the Read and Script check boxes checked.

3. Click OK. Switch back to Internet Explorer. In the Address box, add /MyWindowsDirectory to the end of your computer's name; then press Enter. You'll see an error message stating that directory browsing isn't allowed.

4. Switch back to PWM. At the bottom of the Advanced tab, find the Allow Directory Browsing option and check it. Now switch back to Internet Explorer and refresh the page. You will see a listing similar to that shown in Figure 19.13.

▼

19

▼   5. Your directory is now published. To unpublish the directory, go back to the
           Advanced tab of the Personal Web Manager. Find the virtual directory in the direc-
           tory tree at the top of the page and select it. Now click the Remove button. No
▲   more shared directory!

       Another handy method of publishing a directory is to Web share it. From Internet
       Explorer, right-click any folder and select Sharing. You'll see a new tab on the Properties
       box, Web Sharing. Click Share This Folder, enter an alias, and click OK. Figure 19.14
       shows the Windows directory, published with the alias MyWindowsDirectory (as in Task
       19.4).

FIGURE 19.14.

Publishing directories
with the Web sharing
method is even easier
than with the Personal
Web Manager.

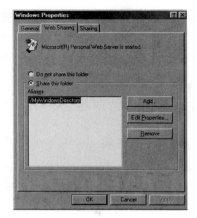

Publishing Your Own Site

The folder C:\Inetpub\wwwroot is the starting point, also called the *home directory*, for
all things you add to your Web site. Anything you want users to have access to should be
placed in the root or under it. For example, if my Web site is www.MichaelHart.net and
I use the default PWS setup, my home page would be stored in the directory
C:\Inetpub\wwwroot. Anyone visiting http://www.MichaelHart.net would actually see
the contents of C:\Inetpub\wwwroot.

Note

Before you delve deeply into developing your WWW site, make sure to
check with your ISP to see whether it has any particular naming standards
for files or directories.

You'll also want to consult your ISP before incorporating any Microsoft-
specific features, such as Active Server Pages.

What if you've built all the components of your Web site under a different directory structure and don't want to go back and change it? Not to worry; PWM lets you change your default home directory. By doing this, you can leave your Web stuff just as it is and publish it right from where it is.

Task 19.5. Changing Your Home Directory

In this Task, you'll change the PWS configuration to publish the home pages you created using FrontPage Express on Day 18. If you haven't yet finished that chapter, you can read through this now and do it later:

1. Open the Personal Web Manager by double-clicking the PWS icon on the System Tray or by selecting Start | Programs | Internet Explorer | Personal Web Server. Click the Advanced tab, shown in Figure 19.15.

FIGURE 19.15.

The Advanced tab of the Personal Web Manager contains the settings for virtual directories.

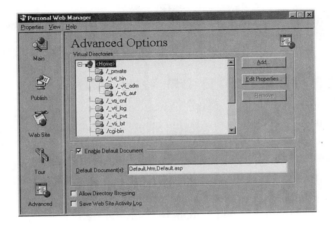

2. The virtual directory at the top of the directory tree is labeled <Home>. Double-click it or click it once and then click the Edit Properties button. The Edit Directory dialog box appears, listing C:\Inetpub\wwwroot as the directory name with its alias <Home> in the gray box below it. Because the Alias box is grayed out, you can't change it. This particular setting will always retain the alias of <Home>.

3. Click the Browse button. Navigate the Browse for Directory dialog until you find the folder C:\MyWebSite that you created on Day 18. Select it and click OK. Notice that the directory name now appears in the dialog box. Click OK again.

4. Click the Main tab of PWM; then click the link to your home page. When Internet Explorer launches to display your home page, you'll instead see a Server Application Error message. The reason for this is that you haven't told PWS which HTML document is your actual home page.

▼   5. Go back to PWM and click on the Advanced tab. Now look below the virtual directory listing at the Default Document(s) box. There are actually two settings there. The first is Enable Default Document, which is checked, and the second is Default Document(s). Leave Enable Default Document checked. In the Default Document(s) box, type the name of the home page you created in the Day 18 Task 18.2. (This will be your main page stored in the C:\MyWebSite folder.)

▲   6. Return to Internet Explorer and reload your home page by clicking the Reload icon or by pressing F5. Your home page now loads.

In step 5 of Task 19.5, you changed the default document name. The *default document* is the name of the document that the Web server will attempt to locate and display when the user switches to a new directory. If a document with the default name is found, it will be displayed. If no document with that name is displayed, the Web server will display the contents of the directory as a listing, as you saw earlier in Figure 19.13. You can enter several default document names in this setting box; the first document found with any of the listed names will be displayed.

Getting Your Site on the Web

Now that you've completed your Web site and tested it using PWS, you're ready for the big leagues—putting your site on the Internet. How exactly do you go about doing that? I have to tell you, in all honesty, that I don't know! It all depends on your ISP. Each provider has different procedures for publishing Web pages.

Many ISPs will limit the amount of storage you are given on their servers; 5MB is typical. This is enough for several pages, some documents, and some pictures. Some ISPs will also grant you a certain amount of bytes transferred per month. For example, one local ISP that I checked with allowed each user 5MB of storage room for his Web pages and up to 250MB per month in transfers. If you break that down and say your Web site consists of a total of 5MB worth of files, that means that 50 visitors per month could view every page of your Web site. After that, you might (with this particular ISP) incur additional charges. I checked with another ISP, a national one, and its accounts offer 7MB of storage space for Web pages and up to 250MB per month of transfer. Be sure to check with your ISP to see what its Web page policies are.

It's also likely that your ISP will have a slightly different process for getting your Web pages published. Let's assume that the name of my ISP is abcNet.net and my username is MichaelH. To get my Web pages on my ISP's server, I need to place the page files in the proper area, with the proper name. Every user account on an ISP's computer has a home directory (different meaning than the *home directory* talked about earlier in reference to your Web site structure). For my particular ISP, the procedure is to create a directory under my home directory, called `public_html`. Any Web pages I want published must be placed in that directory.

How do you place the files into the directory on the ISP's server? Using a program called FTP (File Transfer Protocol). (FTP is both a protocol and a program.) There are many freeware, shareware, and commercially available FTP programs. However, you don't need to buy one because an FTP is included with Windows 98. Using FTP, you simply transfer the files that make up your Web site from your computer to your ISP's computer, placing them in the proper directory—in my case, `public_html`.

One last detail. For people to see my Web site, they have to know how to find it. For my hypothetical ISP, my Web site address would be `http://www.abcNet.net/~michaelh`. Now, what will visitors see if they type that address? Do you remember what it looked like on the PWS when you published a directory and you browsed to the directory? You saw a file listing, like the one shown earlier in Figure 19.13. That's what you'd see at my site because I haven't given my home page the proper name. For my ISP, the home page is supposed to be called `index.htm` or `index.html`. Now, if I go in and rename my home page to `index.html`, visitors to my site will see my home page in all its glory.

Tip

Remember that changing the filename of any page might break some of your links. The best thing to do is to find out *before* you start building your pages what your ISP wants your home page filename to be. Use that name when building your pages, so you don't have problems later.

19

Task 19.6. FTPing Your Pages to Your ISP

Finally, you're going live with your site. After this, the world will have access to your Web pages, and you're off on your career to fame and fortune.

Okay, not really. Because your ISP will differ from mine, this Task is just an example. Use it as a guide when moving your pages to your ISP:

1. Open a DOS window by clicking Start | Programs | MS-DOS Prompt.

2. At the `C:\Windows` prompt, type `ftp`.

3. At the `FTP>` prompt, type `open ftp.abcNet.net`. You'll see some messages about connecting, and so on. When prompted, enter your username and password.

▼ 4. You'll be left in your Internet account home directory. Get a directory listing by typing `ls -laF` (uppercase and lowercase are important here—type it as shown). The directory listing, shown in Figure 19.16, shows you that you already have the required `public_html` directory. Directories are indicated by a / after their names.

FIGURE 19.16.

Using FTP to send your Web site files to your ISP server is easy after you do it once or twice.

>
> **Tip**
>
> If you're feeling that typing `ls -laF` is too nerdy, you can relax. Almost all FTP programs, including the one included with Windows 98, also allow you to type the familiar DOS command DIR to get a directory listing. However, the listing you get back might vary. Directories can either be marked with a d in the far left column of the listing or can be shown with a notation such as <DIR>.

> **Note**
>
> Sorry about the case sensitivity here, but most ISPs run UNIX servers, and UNIX machines are case sensitive.

> **Tip**
>
> If you need to create the directory, type `mkdir` *the_directory_name*.

5. Change to the proper remote directory by typing `cd public_html`. You should also change to the proper local (on your machine) directory by typing `lcd c:\MyWebSite`.

6. Now issue the `put` command to send your Web files to the server—for example, type `put index.html`. Be sure to also put up any other files that go to your site, such as pictures, documents, or other pages.

▼

▼ 7. When you've sent all your files, type bye, and FTP will automatically close the connection and exit.

> **Tip**
> If you remember from Day 18, Web pages are basically text. Images, though, are not; they're considered binary files. FTP transfers text and binary files differently. The default mode is text (actually, ASCII). Before you transfer any binary files, type bin at the ftp> prompt to change into binary mode. To change back to text mode, type asc at the ftp> prompt.

▲ 8. You can now fire up Internet Explorer and browse to your Web site.

Summary

In this chapter you learned how to use the Personal Web Server to publish a Web site. You used the Home Page and Publishing Wizards to create a home page and make documents available to your site visitors. You also found out how to make a large number of documents—a whole directory—available to Web users. You learned the process for putting your Web site on your ISP's Web server so that other Internet users can see your site.

Workshop

To wrap up the day, you can review terms from the chapter, see the answers to some commonly asked questions, and practice what you've learned. You can find the answers to the exercises in Appendix A, "Answers."

19

Terminology Review

drop box—An area on a Web site where visitors can leave private messages for the Webmaster or owner of the site.

FTP (File Transfer Protocol)—A protocol and a program used to transfer files between computers on a network.

guest book—An area on a Web site where visitors can sign in and leave public messages.

home page—The starting point for a Web site, usually the first or main page displayed upon visiting a site.

HTML (Hypertext Markup Language)—The formatting language used to produce Web pages.

Internet—A global network of interconnected computers and networks.

Internet service provider (ISP)—A company that provides individuals and companies with an account for accessing the Internet.

intranet—A network usually contained completely within an organization, company, or department, for use by only a limited set of people.

link (also called a *hypertext link*)—A hotspot that, when clicked, displays related pages of information.

protocol—A language spoken by computers to facilitate communication between each other.

publish—To make available to other users.

TCP/IP (Transmission Control Protocol/Internet Protocol)—The protocol used by all the computers on the Internet to talk to each other.

UNIX—The operating system used to run large multiuser computers, commonly used to run the majority of Web servers on the Internet.

URL (uniform resource locator)—An addressing standard for describing how to access a particular page located on a particular computer.

virtual directory—An alias to another directory, a mirror image of a directory and its contents.

Web server—A computer that responds to requests from browser clients to access Web pages.

Web site—A page or set of pages published to the Internet at large, accessible by anyone using a Web browser.

Q&A

Q I created a home page using FrontPage Express and then used the Publishing Wizard to publish some documents. When I view my home page, I don't see any links added for my published documents.

A The Publishing Wizard will add links only to a home page generated by the Home Page Wizard. Your documents were published, but you'll have to add the links to your home page by using FrontPage Express. To verify that your documents were published, browse to *(your Web site)*/webpub, or use Windows Explorer and see the files listed in the folder C:\InetPub\WebPub.

Q **I tested my Web site using PWS on my PC, and everything worked; all the links worked, all my images were displayed, everything. But after I transferred all the files to my ISP, I received 404 errors, and images don't display properly. What's the problem?**

A There could be several problems involved. Error 404 means that the item your browser told the server to provide couldn't be found. That could be caused by a misspelled URL link, or perhaps the page or object didn't actually transfer to your ISP. As far as the images not displaying, it's possible that when you transferred them via FTP, you didn't change the transfer mode to binary, which you must do before transferring any nontext file.

Q **I made up some spiffy Web pages using FrontPage Express, which I then published using PWS. But when I start the Home Page Wizard and then click Edit Home Page, I don't get to edit my real home page but, instead, the one that I created a long time ago using the Home Page Wizard.**

A Yes, that's the way it works. The Home Page Wizard is only smart enough (some wizard!) to edit the home page that it creates. To edit pages created in any other tool, you'll have to use the program you used to create the pages.

Exercises

1. Describe the steps necessary to create a home page using the wizard; then change the style to a different style template.

2. You've tired of the default home page you built using the wizard, so you've designed a much more elaborate one using FrontPage Express. You've designed everything in a directory called `C:\NewWebSite`. Your home page filename is `myhome.htm`. You now want to test your site by publishing it via PWS. Describe the steps necessary to do so.

19

WEEK 3

DAY 20

Windows 98 Networking

by Michael Hart

As powerful as personal computers can be, there comes a time when you need to hook up to something else—your LAN, the Internet and World Wide Web, an FTP site, or a bulletin board. All these different types of computer-to-computer connections are part of networking. Today you'll learn some networking concepts. You'll learn about configuring Windows to connect to a local area network (LAN) or wide area network (WAN); discover how to give others access to your computer's resources, such as disk drives or printers; learn how to access resources on other computers; use Dial-Up Networking to establish a connection to another network, such as the Internet; configure and use a terminal emulation program for accessing a bulletin board; and use direct cable connections to establish a mini-network between two computers.

If you're not a networking wizard, great! This is the chapter for you. I'm assuming you know little or nothing about networking. I'll be discussing a number of topics, from concepts to crawling around on your hands and knees hooking up LAN cables. By the time you're finished with this chapter, you'll be able to create your own LAN, astonishing your family and friends and making yourself feel pretty good about it. This chapter covers

- Networking concepts
- Setting up your own LAN
- Configuring your computer for the network
- Sharing resources
- The Dial-Up Server

 Note   Prices referenced in this chapter are current estimates at the time of publication. Actual prices of particular items might vary, depending on your vendor.

Networking Concepts

What is networking? In its simplest incarnation, it's the process of getting two computers, or a terminal and a computer, to talk to each other. This communication can be one-to-one—such as a fax modem talking to another fax modem, transmitting a fax document from one side to the other—or one-to-many—such as sitting at your computer listening to a live concert broadcast being transmitted over the Internet to thousands of listeners like you.

Whether you know it or not, you use networked computers almost every day of your modern life. Doubt me? Do you use an ATM money machine at your bank? Network. The ATM is a computer talking over a network to another computer to find out whether it should dispense money to you. Have you ever used a debit or credit card at the gas station or grocery store? Network. Inside the device where you swipe your card is a small computer connecting over a network (usually the phone system) to another computer, seeking authorization to allow the transaction. Drive a late model car? Ever notice how the dashboard performs a systems check? Network. Some cars have computers located throughout the vehicle, communicating with each other and a central computer via a network.

Do you get the idea? Networks are everywhere, in many different forms. The most ubiquitous of all networks I haven't even touched on yet. Can you guess what it is? Call someone and see whether you can guess.

Of course! The telephone! Telephone systems these days are just large (okay, really large) computer networks. You enter the code of the phone you want to connect to, and the computer in your local telephone central office (CO) figures out what remote CO to connect to over the telephone network. Together they set up a circuit for your call to travel over; then the remote CO rings your called party.

I hope that this discussion has helped demystify networks. Now let's see what these examples have in common and what makes up a network. In all the examples, there is some device, an endpoint, that transmits and receives information. There is another device, located elsewhere, that receives the information sent, relays it somewhere else, or sends back information. Finally, there is a communication channel of some sort.

There are other factors implied in the examples. For one device to connect to another, there has to be a means of specifying which other device to connect to, an address of some sort. When the devices are connected, you assume that they are speaking the same language so that they can exchange information. Lastly, you assume that some sort of security is in place so that only authorized devices can connect to each other.

So, what you have are clients, or nodes, talking through a network interface over some type of network media, using a common protocol to connect to a server, also called a *node*. There you have the basic network terms: *client*, *interface*, *media*, *protocol*, and *server*. Let's take a quick look at some of these.

A *node*, whether a client or server, is a device talking to another node. Your computer at work, which is logged on to the file server, for example, is a client node talking to a server node. For purposes of this discussion, a client (your PC) is a device requesting some type of service (Print This File) from a server (your file server). Sometimes clients can talk to other clients, such as when you print to a printer hooked up to your office mate's computer. Other times, a server might talk to another server.

The network *interface* is a device, usually installed inside the client computer, that enables the client to communicate over the network. In the case of your PC, the interface is usually a circuit board called an NIC (Network Interface Card) that connects your computer to the network. The NIC translates signals and voltage levels between those used inside your computer to those used on the network.

The *media* refers to the physical stuff of the network itself. There are many types of media, along with different network types and topologies. Network media or cabling can be coaxial cable, much like the coax cable that brings cable stations to your TV. It can be shielded or unshielded twisted pair (UTP) cabling, much like regular telephone wiring. It can also be fiber-optic cabling, which is an optical plastic, epoxy, or glass that carries information via light.

20

There are two main types of networks—token ring and ethernet. The type of network tends to determine the topology of the network. The *network topology* is the structure in which the network is laid out. A *ring* topology is usually used for a token-ring network. In a ring, each computer is hooked to only two others: the one in front of it and the one behind it. Information is transmitted from one computer to another until it reaches the destination. No particular computer can speak, or add something to the network, unless it is that computer's turn to speak. Ethernet networks are usually laid out in a *bus* or *star* topology, which is less structured. A computer trying to send information on an ethernet network is like people trying to hold a conversation in a large room. Whoever needs to speak, speaks. If two people talk at the same time, both quit speaking for a second, and then try again. If no one else is talking when you start, you continue talking. The type of network, token ring or ethernet, determines the type of NIC used.

The last term is the communications *protocol*. Think of it as the language. You might call someone on the phone, but if you're speaking French and the other person is speaking German, little communication is going to happen there. In networking, the common protocols are TCP/IP (the language of the Internet), Microsoft's NetBEUI, Novell's IPX/SPX, Banyan's VINES, and others. Nodes on both ends of the connection must be speaking the same protocol to communicate.

Building a Network

Putting together a small network in your home or office is simple. Notice that I said *small*. Lots of other issues become important when the size and complexity of the network grow beyond the basics. What I'll discuss is what's required for building, as I said, a small network for your home or office.

You might be asking, "Do I really need a network at home?" That depends. If you have two or more computers, you are certainly a candidate for a network. "But aren't networks expensive?" you ask. Not at all. A small network can be put together for as little as perhaps $100. What will having a network do for you? The same thing it does for the Fortune 100 companies that have those multimillion dollar networks run by legions of networking gurus: A network enables you to share information and resources. You might have a spiffy new color ink jet printer on your computer. What if your daughter wants to print a picture from her computer? Do you put the picture on a floppy and carry it over to your computer, only to discover that you don't use the same program, which now has to be installed on your machine, but you don't have enough disk space, and, besides, it would be illegal to install on your machine unless you bought another copy of the program, and…get the picture? With a LAN, you share your printer over the network and let her print from her program to your printer. Voilà!

Obviously, only you can decide what benefit you might derive from having a LAN. I will tell you that cost should be a mitigating factor. So, what do you need to put together a LAN? Assuming you are networking two computers together, using ethernet over UTP, Table 20.1 presents your shopping list. Take this with you to your local computer store, and you should be all set. Be aware that, although you might get away for as little as $100–150, you might also spend $500. Purchase only what you need now and add the frills later.

TABLE 20.1. SHOPPING LIST FOR YOUR LAN.

Item	Quantity	Cost	Comments
4–8 port TP hub	1	$50–100	Cheap hubs come in four to eight (twisted pair) ports. Get enough ports in case you might add a computer or two later.
TP network	2	$20–70	You need one per computer and you need the interface-proper bus type for your card's computer (ISA or PCI, typically, PCMCIA for laptops).
Cables	2	$5–15	UTP cables. These can be marked with RJ-45 connectors. Used between the NIC and the hub. Lengths of 5–25 feet—long enough to give you some room to move around in.

These are the specs on what type of LAN you'll build. You'll be putting together a 10Mbps ethernet LAN running over unshielded twisted pair cabling. You'll be configuring NetBEUI and TCP/IP protocols.

Building a 10Mbps ethernet network over UTP is easy and relatively cheap, but it's not the only alternative. Fast ethernet is becoming readily available. Fast ethernet is 100Mbps, ten times as fast. However, whereas ethernet hubs cost about $7–15 per port, fast ethernet hubs run about $50–150 per port. Likewise, an NIC that autosenses between 10Mbps and 100Mbps ethernet will run somewhat more than a standard 10Mbps NIC. If you can afford the dual mode cards, buying them gives you an upgrade path to fast ethernet, should you decide to upgrade in the future when the price of the fast ethernet hubs drops.

An alternative to UTP wiring is 10Base-T network media. The unshielded twisted pair cables have a connector on them that looks like a phone plug. This cabling is also

20

referred to as *10Base-2*. 10Base-T is based on a small, thin, coaxial cable, similar to your cable TV cabling. By buying NICs with BNC connectors (either instead of or in addition to the UTP connectors used for 10Base-2), you could hook all your computers together with 10Base-T and not even require a hub. I don't like the coaxial 10Base-T style as much as the UTP because you have to plan your cable runs so that the same cable run reaches all your computers. There are also cabling rules regarding how far apart the devices can be on the cable, how long the runs can be, and so on. With the UTP, you simply centrally locate your hub, and then each cable run is direct from the computer to the hub.

Building a token-ring network is, although technically possible, generally not a home office/small office solution. Token ring requires NICs and hubs that are more expensive and more complicated than ethernet equipment.

Although you probably want to install your network for as little as possible, don't be penny-wise and pound-foolish. Yes, you'll find NICs for as little as $15. You'll also see on the shelf the latest and greatest NICs by 3Com or Intel for upwards of $75. Your headache factor will probably be much greater with an NIC that is el cheapo than with a name brand. I suggest going with a midrange, name brand NIC for these reasons:

- Quality—The names didn't get to be names by selling substandard products.
- Warranty—What happens if your card dies nine months from now?
- Plug and Play (PnP)—The big boys all build Plug and Play compatible cards that really do plug and play. You don't want to fiddle with IRQ and I/O settings all afternoon, do you?
- Support—The name players all have WWW sites with tech bulletins, support notes, and updated drivers for download.

One last word on the NIC. Be sure to buy one for the proper bus. If your machine has a PCI bus, don't buy a 16-bit ISA card.

Hubs, on the other hand, are a different story. Remember where you're putting these? Your home, home office, or small business LAN—you definitely don't need lots of features in your hubs. These are essentially dumb devices; they just connect all the computers together. They either work or they don't. Here my advice is a little different than for the NICs—buy cheaper. You'll find 8-port hubs for $199 and for $49. Buy as much hub as you're comfortable with. Your main concerns should be the number of ports, the price, and the warranty.

After you bring everything home, you can start. Here's what you need to do to for each PC:

1. Install the NICs in the computers. For PCMCIA cards, just insert the card in the PCMCIA slot on the laptop. In most cases, you won't need to install any additional software. For the desktop PCs, turn off the power, open the case, and locate an empty slot. Be sure it's the right kind of slot (ISA, PCI, VLB).

2. Carefully remove the NIC from its box. Handle the card by the edges, not by the edge connector that plugs into the bus slot. Static electricity can damage the card, so ground yourself by frequently touching the frame of the computer. Make any jumper setting adjustments required. None will be required for a Plug and Play board.

3. With one hand touching the metal frame of the computer, remove the card from the antistatic bag and insert it in the slot in the PC.

4. Seat the card firmly. Secure the card with the mounting/hold down screw.

5. Close the case.

Here is what you need to do for the hub: Plug the hub's AC adapter into the hub and into an outlet. Turn on the power switch, if there is one.

For the network, plug one of the UTP cables into each PC, with the other end going into one of the ports on the hub.

Caution

If your computers are not close enough for you to easily collocate the hub conveniently between them and easily run a cable to the hub, you might consider running network cabling in the walls. That is beyond the scope of this book. There is potential danger of electrical shock if you start poking into the walls yourself. Seek professional help.

20

Power up the computers. When they boot up, Windows should recognize the new device and, if it's a PnP NIC, Windows will configure and install the card automatically. If not, you might have to configure the NIC into Windows yourself. The exact steps are beyond the scope of this book; however, the NIC documentation should be of assistance.

Your NIC manufacturer's instructions might make mention of 16-bit or real mode drivers. You want to avoid installing any 16-bit or real mode drivers for any device, if at all possible. You want to use the Windows built-in 32-bit protected mode drivers.

During this initial boot up, after installing the NIC, you'll likely be asked to insert your Windows 98 CD-ROM, also, so additional system software can be installed.

Your hub will probably have LEDs on it to indicate a connection. Generally, if there's a green LED glowing brightly on each hub port that you've plugged a computer into, everything is going right so far! Check the back of the NICs where the cables are plugged in; you'll often have an LED there that shows a connection. If the lights look good, you have yourself a network. If you have indications of a problem, perhaps no LEDs lit or an error light, double-check your connections; ensure that all cables are seated firmly, that there's power where there needs to be power, and so on.

Now, your network is up, but you haven't yet made the connection between the programs running on your computers and the network. Also, for this network, all the computers are considered peers; no one is more important than the rest. There are no labels to assign to specific computers, such as *host* or *client*; each machine is an equal, a peer.

Configuring Your Computer for the Network

The first thing to do is to verify that Windows knows your NIC is present, properly configured, and working. Then, you'll need to install, or verify that Windows has already installed, the remainder of the software components necessary for network operation.

Task 20.1. Verifying Proper Installation of the Network Interface Card

It doesn't pay to configure software to use an NIC that isn't itself properly installed, so before doing anything else, make sure that Windows recognizes your NIC hardware.

1. Go to the Control Panel and double-click on the System icon. Click the Device Manager tab.

2. Find the Network Adapters line. If the line is expanded, with a yellow exclamation mark or a red circle with a diagonal line through it next to your NIC, this is a problem. It indicates that something isn't right with your NIC installation. Refer to the installation directions from your NIC manufacturer and to Day 9, "Managing Hardware," for more information.

   If the Network Adapters line isn't present, click the Refresh button at the bottom of the window. If the Network Adapters line still doesn't show up, Windows isn't finding your NIC; again, refer to the installation directions from your NIC manufacturer and to Day 9 for more information.

   If the Network Adapters line has a plus sign next to it, click it to expand the section. Your NIC will be listed there. See Figure 20.1 for a screen shot showing a happy NIC listed in the Device Manager.

Figure 20.1.

The Device Manager, showing a network adapter installed and operating.

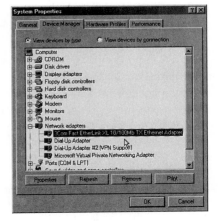

3. Double-click on your Adapter line if you want to see more information about the adapter or the drivers installed for it.

4. Click OK to close the Device Manager. You've just verified installation of the NIC. You can come back here in the future if you need to verify some other configuration or driver information.

Now let's get the software components installed and configured. You know that Windows already knows that there is a network interface device installed. To complete the software picture, you need to configure three additional pieces. You need to tell Windows what programs to use to connect to the network—the client, what kind of device you have—the adapter, and what language(s) to speak—the protocol(s).

The protocol is bound to both the client and the adapter. The client-to-protocol-to-adapter link must be in place before communication can occur. A protocol can be bound to more than one adapter or more than one client. Likewise, an adapter can have more than one protocol bound to it. The minimum requirement is to select one each from clients, adapters, and protocols. There are also some optional network services that you could choose to install.

The client is a set of drivers and programs specific to a type of network. Windows 98 ships with these kinds of clients:

- Banyan DOS/Windows 3.1
- Microsoft Client for Microsoft Networks
- Microsoft Client for NetWare Networks

20

- Microsoft Family Logon
- Novell NetWare (Workstation Shell 3.x [NETX])
- Novell NetWare (Workstation Shell 4.0 and above [VLM])

For your network, you'll choose the Microsoft Client for Microsoft Networks.

Next, you'll have to configure the protocols for the adapter. It might seem redundant because you already configured the adapter into the Device Manager. Nevertheless, it has to be done again. Windows 98 ships with configuration information for hundreds of different NICs from more than 75 vendors; the odds are good that your adapter will be supported.

The last required piece is the protocol. Windows supports most of the popular protocols in use today, including Banyan's VINES, Microsoft's NetBEUI, TCP/IP, and Novell's IPX/SPX, along with WAN (wide area network) and ATM (asynchronous transfer mode) support. For your small network, you'll choose NetBEUI and TCP/IP.

 Note

You might see references to NetBIOS and NetBEUI. Although technically not the same thing, for all intents and purposes they are synonymous. Both basically refer to the same protocol.

Last, you might be interested in installing some additional network services. The services available under Windows 98 include a couple backup agents, which enable you to connect your PC to a network server running a backup program, and, of greater interest, a File and Printer Sharing service, and a Personal Web Server. File and Printer Sharing, which you will configure later, enables you to make an entire disk, a subdirectory, or a printer available for others to use.

When you installed your network adapter card, Windows automatically installed some network components for you, shown in Figure 20.2. In preparation for the upcoming Tasks, in which you'll be configuring your PC and putting it on the network, you can either delete what Windows has already installed, before continuing, or add and change as you go along. I'm assuming for these Tasks that you have no installed components listed.

Let's get started.

Figure 20.2.

*The network compo-
nents automatically
installed by Windows
when the NIC was
installed.*

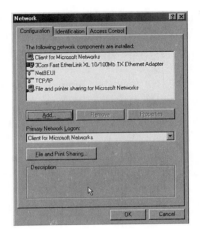

Task 20.2. Installing and Configuring the Network Software

Throughout the life of your LAN, you might be changing protocols or adapters or services. This Task guides you through making those changes. Before you begin the Task,
have your Windows 98 CD-ROM available—you'll need it. Also, if your NIC card came
with drivers on a floppy or CD-ROM, have that available—you might need it.

1. Open the Network applet from the Control Panel. There are three tabs on the
   Network dialog: Configuration, Identification, and Access Control. On the top of
   the Configuration tab is a box showing the components currently installed. Figure
   20.2 shows a client, an adapter, two protocols, and a service.

2. Click the Add button. The next dialog gives you a choice of adding a client, an
   adapter, a protocol, or a service. Click Client; then click Add.

3. On the left, under the Manufacturer column, is the list of vendors who've provided
   client software to Windows 98. Click on Microsoft, and under the right side you'll
   see a list displaying the three types of clients Microsoft provides. Click on Client
   for Microsoft Networks; then click OK.

   You'll be returned to the Select Network Component Type dialog. Windows has
   not only installed the selected client but also found and installed your adapter
   (NIC) and TCP/IP as the default protocol.

4. Click on the Microsoft Client line; then click Properties. The Logon Validation setting at the top is used when your PC is connected to a Windows NT network and
   authorization for your network logon comes from the NT server. Because you
   don't have an NT network, leave it unchecked.

▼TASK

20

▼   5. The Network logon options, at the bottom of the dialog, control the behavior of the network client when you log on to the network. If you select Quick Logon, your machine won't verify that any network drives you might have mounted to your machine are actually available until you go to use them. The Logon and Restore Network Connections option is the opposite: When you log on, Windows validates each network drive connection and alerts you if they aren't available. The main difference is in the time it takes to log on to the network—a nominal delay in most cases. I leave mine set at the Logon and Restore setting. Click OK.

   6. From the Network Properties dialog, click the Add button again; then click Adapter and then Add. If your adapter wasn't already listed on the Network Properties, you'd use this dialog to choose from the seventy-five-or-so manufacturers and hundreds of network adapter cards. Because your adapter is already installed, click Cancel and then click Cancel again to return to the Network properties dialog.

   7. Select the adapter line that has your NIC name in it; then click Properties. This dialog has three tabs: Driver Type, Bindings, and Advanced. Take a moment to explore each tab, and then go to the Bindings tab. Right now, TCP/IP is the only item listed in the white box, and it has a check mark next to it. This indicates that the TCP/IP protocol will be used to communicate through this adapter. Click OK.

   8. Click on the TCP/IP line; then click Properties. The TCP/IP Properties dialog will appear. Check out each of the tabs and investigate the settings available. Notice that the Bindings tab shows that the protocol has been bound to the Client for Microsoft Networks. This binding indicates that the client will use TCP/IP to communicate. Click Cancel.

   9. Back again at the Network Properties, you're ready to add some new components. Click Add, select Protocol, and then click Add again.

  10. Under the Manufacturers column, select Microsoft. In the Network Protocols column, scroll down the list to NetBEUI. Select it; then click OK. You'll see a dialog or two flash by as the software is installed from the CD-ROM. Then you'll be back at the Network Properties box.

  11. Click Add again, select Service, and then click Add. Select Microsoft again; then click on File and Printer Sharing for Microsoft Networks. Click OK. Your Network properties will now look like Figure 20.2, except your NIC will be listed in place of my 3Com adapter.

  12. Click on the NetBEUI protocol; then click Properties. Notice the Bindings tab shows that NetBEUI will be used by the Microsoft client, as is TCP/IP, and also
▼   used for file and printer sharing, as shown in Figure 20.3.

FIGURE 20.3.

NetBEUI Properties showing the NetBEUI protocol bindings.

13. Click the Advanced tab and select the option at the bottom—Set This Protocol to Be the Default Protocol. Click OK.

14. Select TCP/IP again; then view its properties. You can now see that File and Printer Sharing has been added to the Bindings tab for this protocol. Click Cancel to return to the Network properties tab.

15. Under Primary Network Logon, you have two choices: Client for Microsoft Networks and Windows Logon. The visible difference is in the appearance of the dialog box you'll see when logging on to Windows. Figure 20.4 shows the Windows logon box, and Figure 20.5 shows the Client for Microsoft Networks logon box. Behind the scenes, the difference is that if you select Windows Logon, you won't be notified at logon time if the network isn't available for use. My personal preference is Windows Logon.

FIGURE 20.4.

The Windows logon box.

20

FIGURE 20.5.

The Client for Microsoft Networks logon box.

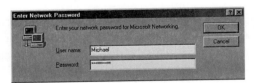

▼ 16. Click the File and Print Sharing button. The three options available are

   - I want to be able to give others access to my files.
   - I want to allow others to print to my printer(s).
   - I want to give others access to my files through the Internet.

   The third option relates to the Personal Web Server and is covered on Day 19, "The Personal Web Server." The other two options are what you've been trying to get to! Check both to enable these features; then click OK.

   That finishes the network component installation. A few more settings and you'll be through here.

17. Click the Identification tab. There are three settings for you to fill in:

   - Computer Name—This must be a unique name, 15 characters or fewer in length, with no spaces. No other computer on your LAN can have the same name, or you'll encounter problems.
   - Workgroup—This can be thought of as a group of computers. The default Workgroup name is *Workgroup* and can be left as that. Computers in the same workgroup can share resources.
   - Computer Description—This is descriptive text that users will see when browsing the network.

   When you've filled these in, click the Access Control tab.

18. The two options under Access Control determine how you control user access to the resources on this machine. Share-level access control means you'll give a password to each shared resource; if a user knows the password, he'll have access. User-level access control requires a Windows NT server. For your network, click Share-Level Access Control; then click back to the Configuration tab.

19. Click OK. Windows might again want the CD-ROM and then will display the message that you must reboot before changes can take effect. Reboot when ready.

20. After rebooting, open Windows Explorer. Navigate down to Network Neighborhood; click the plus sign next to it to expand the tree. Listed below it (and
▲ in the right pane) should be the other computers on your network.

Success! That finishes the installation and configuration of the networking components. Your computer is now merrily communicating on the LAN. If you have any difficulties, retrace your steps through this procedure. If that doesn't solve it, open the HelpDesk and use the Network Troubleshooter.

Note

Remember that the hardware and software installations you just performed need to be completed in order for each computer to be attached to the network.

Configuring TCP/IP on Your Network

So far on your network, you've installed and configured the required components, verified their operation, and shared resources over the wire. Because you configured NetBEUI as your default protocol, however, you've not yet used TCP/IP. This isn't by accident. Before TCP/IP can be used on the LAN, more configuration is required. Some background on the protocol will set the stage.

Note

If you don't intend to run TCP/IP on your private network, you can skip Tasks 20.3-20.5. You might still want to read these, though, because the background information will be useful later when I discuss using TCP/IP over a dial-up connection. For information on configuring TCP/IP over a dial-up connection, see the section "Connecting to the Internet" on Day 21, "Mobile Computing with Windows 98."

Just as every computer using the NetBEUI protocol must have a unique 15 character name, every computer running TCP/IP must have a unique address—its IP address. IP addresses are formatted in four segments, like this: *xxx.xxx.xxx.xxx*, where *xxx* is a decimal number between 0 and 255. If you do the arithmetic, you'll discover that more than 4 billion IP addresses are possible (256| 256| 256| 256). However, some IP addresses are reserved. For example, the address 127.0.0.1 is always used for the machine name localhost, which every TCP/IP running computer knows means *me*. Also, addresses ending with 0 or 1 are reserved for special use. Lastly, addresses ending in 255 are reserved as broadcast addresses.

If you're going to configure a TCP/IP network, you need a range of addresses for your computers. You could pick one out of thin air; certainly your computers wouldn't care. In fact, as long as you never connect to any other network, you'd be just fine. As you might guess, though, if your network connected to other networks, such as the Internet, you'd experience (or cause!) problems if you were using someone else's IP addresses. For this reason, the range of IP addresses from 192.168.0.0 through 192.168.0.255 is considered private IPs. The addresses in the 192.168.0.*xxx* range are reserved, and those addresses will never be issued to computers on the Internet. The intent is that this range can then be used for anyone's internal network.

20

Going back to the NetBEUI protocol, recall that you had to give each computer a unique name; that configuration task had to be done on the machine itself. Similarly, each computer must have some way of being given an IP address. In a large corporate network, the last thing you (as network administrator) would want to do is to run around to thousands of machines, configuring IP addresses. Not only would the initial task be difficult, if not impossible, but also the tracking would be a full-time job in itself.

To alleviate that problem, larger networks have a server or servers that run the Dynamic Host Configuration Protocol (DHCP) task. DHCP servers automatically assign an IP address, from a pool of addresses, to every workstation that requests one. Because the address assignment is automatic, a whole lot less administration is required. In your small network, though, you won't have a DHCP server.

As you know, computers like to deal with numbers like 192.168.0.145; humans much prefer to deal with names like EngServer1 or www.microsoft.com. Problem is, something is needed to translate between the two. For TCP/IP networks, one solution to the problem is called a HOSTS file—a text file that lists known IP addresses and the names that go with those addresses. A copy of the HOSTS file is needed on every TCP/IP machine.

Just as with the assigning of IP addresses, maintaining a copy of the HOSTS file on hundreds or thousands (or more) of computers is an impossible task. For larger networks, including the Internet, domain name service (DNS) servers perform the address translation tasks on request. Properly configured, a workstation that needs to know the IP address for www.microsoft.com will issue a DNS request; a DNS server will respond with the appropriate address—207.68.137.62.

For your small network, consisting of only a few machines, the HOSTS file will suit your needs just fine. For Windows 98 computers, the HOSTS file is stored in the C:\Windows directory. There is no HOSTS file by default, but there is a sample file to start from— HOSTS.SAM. Copy this file and save the copy as HOSTS. (with nothing after the period). The HOSTS file contains any number of lines describing IP addresses. The lines are in this format:

```
127.0.0.1   localhost       #local loopback address
```

The first part of every line is the IP address of the machine being described. Following the address, with at least one space between them, is the name or names of the computer. There could be one name or several, as aliases. For example, this line is a host entry for a computer with three names:

```
192.168.0.25   Blackjack  www.hart.com   HartServer1 #my server
```

In this example, the machine with the address 192.168.0.25 will answer to three names: Blackjack, www.hart.com, and HartServer1. Anything that appears after a # is a comment and is ignored. HOSTS files should always have the entry 127.0.0.1 localhost in them for loopback and testing purposes. After the files are created, they need to be distributed to each machine.

Now you must address these remaining requirements to enable TCP/IP on your network:

- Configuring the HOSTS file for each machine
- Setting the IP address for each machine
- Verifying connectivity

For your first task, you'll create the HOSTS file that will serve as a kind of telephone directory for your small network.

Task 20.3. Creating a HOSTS File for Your Network

As just discussed, you'll need a HOSTS file on each computer to do address translation between names and IP addresses.

1. On a piece of paper, write down a name for each of the computers on your network. The name must be unique; it doesn't need to be the same as the NetBEUI name you configured earlier, but it could be.

2. Now, create an IP address for each machine. The first machine gets 192.168.0.1, the second 192.168.0.2, the third 192.168.0.3, and so on. (If you have more than 254 machines, STOP NOW! Get a good book on TCP/IP networking, and install and configure DHCP and DNS!)

3. Using Notepad, create a text file and save it as C:\Windows\HOSTS.. Notice that there is no file extension. In the file, enter as the first line 127.0.0.1 localhost. Then, add all your machine addresses and names, one machine per line. Save the file and exit Notepad.

4. Use Windows Explorer to verify that the file was saved with the proper name: C:\Windows\HOSTS.. There must not be an extension; Notepad is very persistent about appending .txt to its files.

5. Copy this file to all the machines in your network.

▲ Done. Step one is completed—all machines now have a valid HOSTS file.

Now that each machine's IP address has been recorded in the phone book, you need to configure each machine with its IP address.

TASK ▼

20

Task 20.4. Setting IP Addresses

This Task needs to be performed for each machine in your network. Be sure to follow your list of machine addresses and names carefully.

1. Open the Network applet in the Control Panel.

2. Your TCP/IP protocol line can show up in one of two ways: It might just say TCP/IP, or it might say TCP/IP —> (your NIC name). Click the line; then click Properties.

3. Click the IP Address tab. Because you're manually configuring the IP addresses, select Specify an IP Address. Enter the Subnet Mask as 255.255.255.0, as shown in Figure 20.6. Click OK.

FIGURE 20.6.

The TCP/IP Properties box IP Address tab, showing a manually configured IP address and subnet address.

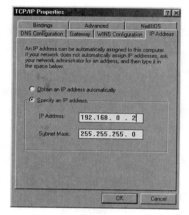

4. Click OK again and you'll get the by-now-familiar message that you must restart before the changes will take effect. Reboot when ready; then log on again.

5. If you receive an error message at boot time like that shown in Figure 20.7, you've used a duplicate IP address somewhere—either in the HOSTS file or when configuring the computers' addresses. Double-check the preceding steps and try again. The message in Figure 20.7 indicates that TCP/IP (the interface) is disabled for this machine until the problem is resolved.

FIGURE 20.7.

This error message indicates that the IP address configured for the machine is a duplicate.

Now that the configuration is complete, how can you test to ensure that TCP/IP connectivity is really functional? One of the utility programs that come with Windows 98 TCP/IP is the ping (Packet Internet Gopher) utility. Ping's purpose in life is to find the machine with the given address and report back on how long it took to get a message to it.

Task 20.5. Verifying TCP/IP Connectivity

Ping will attempt to translate a host name into an IP address, send a message to the destination machine, and time how long it takes the message to return, if it does.

1. Open a command prompt from Start | Programs | MS-DOS Command Prompt. At the C:\Windows prompt, type **ping 192.168.0.2**. Press Enter (assuming you've used this address as one of your addresses; if not, substitute one of your IP addresses). If this machine is .2, then ping another address.

2. You will see ping responding as shown in Figure 20.8. The lines that say Reply from 192.168.0.2 indicate that the other machine answered, which is a good thing!

FIGURE 20.8.

The ping utility, in an MS-DOS box, showing the results of a successful ping of address 192.168.0.2.

3. If you receive a message such as Destination Host Unreachable, you've likely mistyped the destination address.

   Issue another ping command, this time using the name of the other computer: ping Blackjack. Substitute your computer name for Blackjack. You will see a similar message, indicating not only that the host was reachable but also that ping was able to do the name translation to acquire the address.

4. If you receive a message like Unknown Host xxx, you've mistyped the destination host name either on the command line or in the HOSTS file. Double-check and try again.

▲

20

You should be able to ping every machine from every other machine and get a response.

You've just finished the configuration of TCP/IP on your network.

Sharing Resources

After your computer is configured and hooked up to the network, the real value of the network will become evident. Up to this point, you've set up this great communication pathway between two or more computers, but they're not doing anything yet. The two resources you'll be sharing over the network are printers and disk space. In both cases, you can assign a level of security to ensure that only authorized users are allowed to access the shared resource.

In Microsoft networking, a resource that's shared over the network is called a *share*. Every share has a share name, or network name, which might or might not be indicative of what its real name is. For example, the folder `C:\Windows\Program Files\WinZip` might be shared with the share name `Net WinZip`. My DeskJet 600 printer might be visible to network users as `Michael's DJ600`.

When sharing a resource, you can additionally configure access to the resource. Printers can be set up to require a password before allowing a user access. You might want to do this if you have a color laser printer that produces beautiful prints but at a cost of $3 per page; you wouldn't want someone printing out the Windows Help file there by accident!

With shared drives or folders, you can also determine what kind of access users will have: read-only or full (read/write). For each share, you can set both a read-only password and a full password. Which password users enter will determine what type of access they are granted. Passwords are not required, however. Therefore, you could put no password on read-only access but restrict full access to those who know the password.

Task 20.6. Sharing a Folder Across the Network

▼ TASK

In this Task, you'll finally put the network to use; you'll make a folder on one PC available over the network for access by a user on another PC. You'll also set the level of access to the folder:

1. On one computer, open Windows Explorer. Click on the drive icon for your C: drive. Create a new folder in C:\ called `Shared Documents`.

2. After the folder is created, right-click on it; then select Sharing.

3. On the Properties box, select Shared As. The Share Name box will already list a share name, with a maximum of 12 characters. You can leave the share name as is or enter a new one. The share name is the name that users will look for when trying to locate this resource. For this folder, enter **SharedDocs**.

▼

▼   4. Select the Access type: Read-Only, Full, or Depends on Password. For this folder,
          select Full. Don't enter a password. Click OK.

Okay, half the work is done. Now, test whether you can access the folder from elsewhere
on the LAN:

1. From a computer on your LAN other than the one where the shared resource is
    physically located, open Windows Explorer, and go to Network Neighborhood.
    Find the sharing computer; then click the plus sign next to it. If there's no plus,
    click View Refresh, or press F5. (Sometimes new shares take a minute to show
    up.) Under the computer's name, the folder SharedDocs should be visible in all its
    glory.

2. Drag a file from your C: drive into the SharedDocs folder. Because you shared it
    with Full access and no password, the file will copy right into the folder.

That's all there is to it. You've successfully used your network to share resources
▲ between two computers.

Having shared a folder, let's take a look at sharing a printer. In Task 20.7, you won't
install a printer; the printer must already be installed and configured. You learned about
installing printers on Day 5, "Fonts and Printing in Windows 98," which you can refer to
if you need to install a printer.

Task 20.7. Sharing a Local Printer for Network Use

This Task will enable you to give others the ability to print to your printer:

1. Using Windows Explorer, open the Printers folder.

2. Locate the printer you want to share, and right-click on it. The Properties box for
    the printer will open, with the Sharing tab displayed.

3. Click the Shared As option. Give the printer a share name; this is what users will
    see when browsing for the printer. Enter a comment to describe the printer, perhaps
    something like Diana's DeskJet—Room 4.

4. If you want to restrict use of this shared printer to users who have the password,
    enter a password. Leave the Password field blank to allow access to all users.

5. Click OK. In a few seconds, the sharing hand icon will appear under the printer to
    indicate that it's now available as a network printer.

6. To test network accessibility, click on Network Neighborhood in Explorer. Click
    on this PC under the Network Neighborhood. The shared printer, along with any
▲   shared folders, will appear in the right pane.

You've now also successfully shared a printer resource. Between sharing of folders and
printers, you'll be making maximum use of your network.

20

Configuring a Dial-Up Server

After you set it up, you might be thinking, "So, how do I dial in to my own network?" Actually, it's surprisingly easy. Included with Windows 98 is a Dial-Up Server (DUS) component. By configuring one of your machines with modems and phone lines, you can allow remote access to your own private network.

As discussed previously, questions of scale become important. If you're trying to provide dial-up access to a legion of remote users who need to get into your network, the Dial-Up Server included in Windows 98 isn't the answer. If your needs extend beyond a few users, say, four to eight, it will pay for you to investigate industrial-strength, enterprise-scale solutions. The specialized remote access products on the market provide higher performance, better security, and additional functionality not present in the DUS in Windows.

To set up DUS, you'll have to have your modem(s) already configured and installed, as covered on Day 9. You'll also need to have the DUS component installed. Use the procedures for installing optional Windows components from Day 2, "Installing Windows 98," to install it, if needed, before continuing.

Task 20.8. Configuring a Dial-Up Server

▼ TASK

If you need to provide remote access to your network, either to other users or for yourself, carry on. If the Dial-Up Server component has not yet been installed, install it by using the optional component installation procedure discussed on Day 2. The Dial-Up Server component is listed under the Communications section of the Windows Setup tab in the Add/Remove Programs Control Panel applet. To configure your DUS, complete the following steps:

1. Open the Dial-Up Networking folder.

2. Click on the Connections menu; then select Dial-Up Server.

3. The Dial-Up Server dialog appears. Figure 20.9 shows my Dial-Up Server dialog, with two tabs displayed. The Sportster shown on the front tab is configured to enable dial-up. Your Dial-Up Server dialog box will likely be different because you'll see a tab for each modem device that you have installed on your computer.

4. Each modem can be individually configured to allow or disallow dial-up connections. To enable dial-up, select Allow Caller Access.

5. If you want to require a password before callers are allowed in (highly recommended), click the Change Password button.

▼

FIGURE 20.9.

The Dial-Up Server status dialog, showing two modems configured.

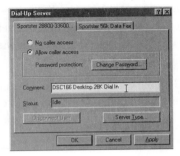

6. Enter a descriptive comment in the Comment field.

   Below the Comment field, the Status field displays the current status of this dial-up connection.

7. Click the Server Type button; the Server Types dialog, shown in Figure 20.10, is displayed. Just as you had to determine a server type when configuring a Dial-Up Networking connection, so, too, must you determine what kind of connection your Dial-Up Server will offer your dialers. Unless you have a specific reason to choose otherwise, select PPP: Windows 98, Windows NT 4.0, Internet.

FIGURE 20.10.

The Server Type dialog, showing the current port configured as a PPP dial-up.

8. Under Advanced Options, select Enable Software Compression for enhanced throughput and Require Encrypted Password for enhanced security. Remember to enable these options in the DUN connection when dialing in to your Dial-Up Server.

9. Click OK. Configure any additional DUS ports, as desired.

10. Click OK when all ports have been configured.

Look in the System Tray and you'll see that a new icon has appeared there—Dial-Up Server. Double-click it to bring the DUS dialog back up. For any modems that you enabled for dial-up, notice that the Status field now says Monitoring.

Your Dial-Up Server is ready for callers.

20

When you configure the *client side*—that is, the computer that will be dialing into the DUS—you have to be sure that your Dial-Up Connection specifies the same networking protocols that the DUS has bound to the Dial-Up Adapter. To check this, open the Network Neighborhood Properties on the Server machine; then check which protocols are bound to the Dial-Up Adapter(s).

To test your server, launch the DUN connection you created; then click Connect. You should be able to successfully connect and then browse the remote network, using Windows Explorer.

> **Tip**
>
> You might not immediately see the shared resources on the Dial-Up Server show up in your Windows Explorer; sometimes it takes quite a while before they do. To get to them, try using Windows Explorer Tools I Find I Computer tool. Type in the name of the computer you dialed in to, like this—**ComputerName**—and then click Find.

Summary

In today's chapter, you absorbed a lot of information about networking. Starting with a discussion of networking basics, you learned about network terminology, including nodes, adapters, protocols, services, network topologies, network types, and cabling. From there you moved on to what it takes to build your own LAN, using readily available, inexpensive network components from any respectable computer store. I covered everything from what to buy, and why, to how to hook it up. After the LAN setup, you learned how to install the networking software components on your networked PCs and then how to configure them for multiple protocols. You also learned about setting up and configuring TCP/IP on a private network and caught a glimpse of how large IP networks like the Internet work. After completing the network infrastructure, you learned how to share and access resources over the network, such as disks, folders, and printers. Lastly, you learned how to set up your PC as a Dial-Up Server to allow remote dial-in to your network.

Workshop

To wrap up the day, you can review terms from the chapter, see the answers to some commonly asked questions, and practice what you've learned. You can find the answers to the exercises in Appendix A, "Answers."

Terminology Review

broadcast—Sending the same information to all stations on a network.

client—A device (such as a computer) or a process (such as a program) that requests information or services from a server. A client might issue a request such as "Send me the list of part numbers between 1000 and 1100," which a server task or machine will respond to.

Dial-Up Server (DUS)—A machine that accepts dial-in connections. Windows 98 also includes software that enables a PC to be used as a Dial-Up Server so that others can connect to it and gain access to resources on the host.

domain name service (DNS)—A computer program that provides name resolution services to client computers to aid in their connecting to the desired named host computer.

ethernet—A common networking standard based on a CSMA/CD (Carrier Sense Multiple Access/Collision Detect) scheme.

fast ethernet—An ethernet protocol running at 100Mbps instead of the normal 10Mbps.

file server—A computer on a network that stores files for users and provides access to the files as requested.

hub—A device that creates a network for a group of nodes. Multiple devices, PCs, or printers can plug into the hub and then connect to each other.

IPX/SPX (Internet Packet Exchange/Sequenced Packet Exchange)—The standard protocol in Novell networks.

LAN (local area network)—The wiring, hardware, and software that connect a set of computers in the same general vicinity, such as within a building.

NetBEUI—A common, nonroutable protocol used in networks, also interchangeably called *NetBIOS*.

NetBIOS—See *NetBEUI*.

Network Interface Card (NIC)—A circuit card containing the interface circuitry needed to connect a computer to a network. The NIC converts the data from the computer into signals that can be transmitted across the network, much as a modem does for telephone communications.

node—A device on a network. A node can be a PC, a server, or a printer.

20

port—A connection between your computer and the outside world. Ports are typically serial ports for communication purposes or parallel ports for printers and other add-on devices. Universal Serial Bus ports are a new, emerging port type. Many ports have different subtypes; for instance, parallel ports come in standard, ECP, and EPP flavors.

protocol—The language spoken by devices on a network. As with people, two devices must speak the same protocol in order to communicate.

server—A device or process that responds to requests from clients.

TCP/IP—Transmission Control Protocol/Internet Protocol.

terminal—A display device with a keyboard and possibly a mouse, used to connect to a computer. Typically, the terminal is *dumb*, having little or no processing power of its own.

terminal emulator or *terminal program*—Software that makes a PC act like a dumb terminal for communicating with a host computer.

topology—The way a network is laid out. Common topologies include the star, the bus, and the ring.

unshielded twisted pair (UTP)—Network cabling utilizing inexpensive copper wiring composed of pairs of wires twisted together.

WAN (wide area network)—The wiring, hardware, and software that connect a set of computers not located in the same general vicinity, such as two networks in different cities.

Q&A

Q On my home network, I don't always see my other computer under Network Neighborhood. I've double-checked, and both computers have the NetBEUI protocol loaded, the LAN cables are plugged in, and the lights on the hub ports are lit. What's the problem?

A It sounds like all the network hardware and software is configured correctly. Under Windows networking, you won't see another computer listed under Network Neighborhood unless that other computer has some sort of shared resource, such as a disk drive or printer. You'll be able to see the computer in Windows Explorer after you share a resource.

Q **It seems awfully complicated to have to assign IP addresses for the 14 comput-ers on my small office network. Isn't there an easier way?**

A Yes! Use the NetBEUI protocol. Although certain characteristics of NetBEUI make it unfavorable in a large network environment, it's well suited to smaller networks. Using NetBEUI, you don't have to do any kind of address assignment or tracking. Just assign a unique network name to each machine (on the Identification tab of the Network Properties dialog) and you're set. You'll still be able to use TCP/IP for connecting to your ISP for Internet access.

Q **How do I configure TCP/IP to connect to my Internet service provider?**

A For detailed instructions, read Day 21.

Exercises

1. Several people want to use Jane's printer; there isn't a network installed. Describe, in brief, the major steps you take so that other people can use Jane's printer.

2. To connect your computer to the local area network in your office, your adminis-trator tells you that you must assign a static IP address to your computer. The address for your computer should be set to 145.241.0.45. Describe the steps nec-essary to make this setting.

20

DAY 21

Mobile Computing with Windows 98

by Michael Hart

Even if you don't use a laptop, there's a pretty good chance that you'll want to connect to the Internet either for World Wide Web access or just for email or news. Whether you are already an experienced Internet user or are just want to get connected, you'll find what you need to get online in this chapter. This chapter covers

- Dial-Up Networking
- Using HyperTerminal
- Using the Briefcase
- Power management
- Using PC cards
- Multiple hardware configurations

- Offline printing
- Dialing locations
- Road warrior tips and techniques

For those of us who use a laptop, the one thing constant in our day-to-day travels and travails is the number of different situations we find ourselves in. At home, the laptop might be securely nestled into a docking station or port replicator happily connected to who knows what manner of nontraveling peripherals. Yesterday, it was connected to a client's Ethernet network; today, dialed in to a server at a remote location; tomorrow, who knows.

Road warriors, mobile users who need to use a computer away from the comfortable environs of a desk, face numerous difficulties and configuration issues. Besides the obvious physical problems such as dropping a laptop, spilling some unfriendly liquid into it, having someone sit on it, or having it walk away while you turn you back on it for just a second, just using a laptop in an infinite variety of locations presents its own challenges.

Fortunately Windows 98 continues and enhances the features available to the traveling computer user. These features include

- The Briefcase
- Power management
- PC card (PCMCIA) support
- Multiple configurations
- The ability to print while offline

Dial-Up Networking

Sooner or later, you'll need to access a network that is somewhere other than where you are. The network you're seeking to gain access to might be your network, while you're away on travel; it might be the Internet. Either way, what you want to do is get connected so you can get access to the data and services available on the network.

Enter Dial-Up Networking, or DUN. DUN automates much of the hassle of establishing a modem connection to a remote computer and getting connected. Think carefully about the subject: Dial-Up *Networking*. I'm not discussing using a terminal program to access a bulletin board (although I do cover that type of dial-up later). What you're actually trying to establish is a network connection over a modem—a network connection which, once established, makes it appear as though your PC is actually on the destination network, albeit usually at a slower connection speed.

Although you might not have considered it in this light before, connecting to the Internet is really just your computer making a dial-up connection to a (really big) network—the Internet. So whether you're dialing into the small network in your office or connecting to the Internet, you'll be using the same tools.

In Windows, DUN is most often used to make a connection to the Internet and is also used to make connections to private networks. Both are discussed in this chapter. However, before going on, you'll have to install some software to enable DUN, if it's not already installed. To check to see if it's already installed, click Start | Programs | Accessories. If you don't have a Dial-Up Networking folder, it's not yet installed. Refer back to Day 2, "Installing Windows 98," for the procedure for installing optional Windows components.

The heart of DUN is the connection. Everything needed to get connected to the remote system is contained in the connection. As mentioned earlier, this chapter covers the two applications of DUN: connecting to the Internet and connecting to a private network.

Connecting to the Internet

The automation of a connection to the Internet is probably the most common and wide-spread use of DUN. Having DUN configured properly removes the step of manually initiating the connection, allowing the connection to happen on demand, unattended.

Before connecting to the Internet, you will need to set up an account with an Internet service provider (ISP). When you do so, the ISP will give you the information you need to properly connect through it to the Internet. To set up an ISP account, you need to know

- Your username
- Your password
- The type of dial-in connection
- Whether your ISP supports software compression
- Whether your ISP requires encrypted passwords
- The ISP's telephone access number(s)
- Any additional connection commands
- Whether the provider will dynamically assign you an IP address
- Whether the ISP's server will dynamically assign nameserver addresses
- Whether the ISP supports multilink dial-up

The username and password requirements should be obvious, as well as the telephone access numbers. The type of dial-up connection is important. There are two main types,

21

PPP (Point-to-Point Protocol) and SLIP (Serial Line Interface Protocol). Most ISPs today support the newer and somewhat faster PPP connections. For additional throughput, some ISPs support software compression. For additional security, some support the use of encrypted passwords.

You'll also need to ask your ISP if it requires any additional commands to be typed to establish the connection. Some ISPs require commands to be typed in after the modems have connected but before the Internet connection is actually established. If your ISP requires such commands, you'll be happy to know that DUN supports the automated entering of these commands via the scripting facility; scripting is covered briefly later in this chapter.

Your ISP should also tell you whether it will be assigning you a static IP (highly unlikely) or doing dynamic IP addressing. Remember when you learned about assigning IP addresses in the section "Configuring TCP/IP on Your Network" on Day 20, "Windows 98 Networking"? Same thing here. However, it's likely that your ISP has only a certain number of IP addresses; probably fewer than the number of people who subscribe to the ISP. Therefore, everyone can't have a personal IP; there aren't enough. So, every time someone dials into the ISP's system, he or she is given a new IP address on demand.

Remember, too, the DNS discussion from Day 20? DNS is the service that provides hostname to IP address translation. Your ISP will either tell you that it will configure you with the address of the name servers when you dial in, or it will give you one or two DNS server addresses, which you must configure into the connection before dialing in.

The last item on the list is a new technology, derived from Integrated Services Digital Network (ISDN) technology, and in Windows 98 called Multilink Channel Aggregation. The concept is that by using multiple dial-up channels (regular modems or ISDN connections) combined into a single channel, higher total throughput can be obtained. Your ISP must support the protocol before you can use it, however.

The entire process of finding an ISP in your area can be facilitated using the Internet Connection Wizard in the Start | Programs | Internet Explorer folder. If you already have an Internet account, you can skip the next section.

Using the Internet Connection Wizard to Get on the Internet

If you don't already have an Internet service provider, want to get on the Internet but aren't sure where to turn, and would just like someone to help you out, the Internet Connection Wizard (ICW) is here to help. The ICW will guide you through each step of the process, from getting the software configured that you need to connect, to getting you a list of ISPs in your area, and even getting you signed up.

You can launch the Internet Connection Wizard by clicking Start | Programs | Internet Explorer | Connection Wizard, or by opening the Internet applet in the Control Panel, clicking the Connection tab, and then clicking the Connect button at the top of the dialog.

 Note

> The list of ISPs that you'll get for your area code when you use the Internet Connection Wizard is not a complete list. You can find many other local ISPs by checking with local computer or electronics stores, checking your local newspaper advertisements, and looking in any local computer newspapers.

Configuring a Dial-Up Connection

Unlike configuration of the "wired" network, TCP/IP dial-up is configured for specific access points. In other words, when you configured NetBEUI or TCP/IP to run on the network, you configured it once, and it applied to the whole machine, no matter what machines you talked to over the network. When you are configuring TCP/IP dial-ups, however, each ISP can have its own configuration requirements, and you might need to connect to several ISPs. If there were only a single configuration for TCP/IP, you'd have to be changing the settings every time you connected to another ISP, which would take a reboot, and is just generally unacceptable. For that reason, there are two ways to apply TCP/IP settings to dial-up connections.

Task 21.1. Investigating Global Versus Specific TCP/IP Dial-Up Configuration Settings

In this Task you'll learn how and where to apply IP configuration changes to achieve the proper result:

1. Open the Network applet from the Control Panel.

2. In the installed components list, click the line that says TCP/IP -> Dial-Up Adapter (see Figure 21.1). Then select Properties.

3. The dialog shown in Figure 21.2 appears. Read it carefully. It's telling you that if you change the IP properties right here—that is, the properties for the TCP/IP protocol bound to the dial-up adapter—you'll be applying a *global* change; all dial-up TCP/IP connections will get the settings changes that you make here. This is most likely not what you want. Instead, as the dialog indicates, you should set the dial-up TCP/IP properties in each individual dial-up connection. That way, those changes will apply only to that connection.

21

FIGURE 21.1.

Selecting the TCP/IP entry bound to the dial-up adapter.

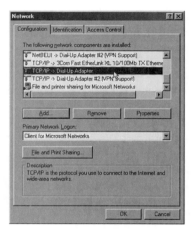

FIGURE 21.2.

Advisory dialog suggesting that perhaps you don't want to change global dial-up TCP/IP parameters.

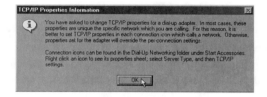

4. Click OK at the dialog box, Cancel at the IP Properties box, and Cancel at the Network Properties box.

You'll see the proper place to set TCP/IP configuration options in Task 21.2.

Before starting Task 21.2, you must already have a modem installed and configured. Installation of modems is covered on Day 9, "Managing Hardware."

Task 21.2. Creating a Dial-Up Networking Connection to the Internet

Using all the configuration information from your ISP, you'll configure a DUN connection for Internet access:

1. Be sure you have all the required information at hand.

2. Open the Dial-Up Networking folder. Double-click on the Make New Connection icon, or select Connections | Make New Connection.

3. The first field in the Make New Connection dialog box is for the name of the computer you are dialing. Make this an easy name for you to identify as your dial-up connection; I usually enter the name of my ISP in this box.

▼

▼   4. In the device field, select your modem from the list. Click the Connection button to bring up the properties for the modem. The settings on the General, Connection, and Options tabs were covered in more detail on Day 9. Click OK.

5. At the Make New Connection dialog, click Next.

6. Enter the area code and access phone number of your ISP. Select the country if different than United States. Click Next.

7. A summary page is displayed. Click Finish.

8. Open the Dial-Up Networking folder again. Locate the icon for the connection you just created. Right-click on it and then select Properties.

9. There are four tabs in this Properties box: General, Server Types, Scripting, and Multilink. On the General tab, the ISP phone number and your modem are displayed. If you don't need to dial the ISP's area code from your location, deselect the Use Area Code and Dialing Properties option.

10. The Configure button in the Connect Using section gives you access to the modem properties, which you've already set.

11. Click the Server Types tab. Under Type of Server, select the appropriate choice, as determined by the information your ISP provided you; most likely it'll be PPP: Windows 98, Windows NT 4.0, Internet.

12. Under Advanced Options, deselect Log on to Network; note that some ISPs do want this option on. Select Enable Software Compression and Require Encrypted Password if required by your ISP.

13. Under allowed protocols, deselect all but TCP/IP. Click the TCP/IP settings button.

14. If your ISP gave you a specific IP address to use, select Specify an IP Address; otherwise, leave Server Assigned IP Address selected. Likewise, leave Server Assigned Name Server Addresses selected, unless your ISP has given you DNS server addresses to enter. If so, select Specify Name Server Addresses and then enter the Primary DNS address and the Secondary DNS address if there is one.

15. Leave the Use IP Header Compression and Use Default Gateway on Remote Network checked, unless otherwise specifically instructed by your ISP. Click OK.

16. Click the Scripting tab. If your ISP requires additional commands between modem connection and session commencement, they can be incorporated into a script and set to automatically run.

17. Click the Multilink tab. If your ISP supports multilink connections and you have multiple modems, click Use Additional Devices, and select the other devices to use.

▲   18. Click OK to accept the changes you've made to this connection.

21

Great! You've completed this DUN connection.

When you're ready to access the Internet, double-click on the icon for this connection, or right-click and select Connect. The Connect To dialog box shown in Figure 21.3 will open. The username displayed might not be the correct one; the displayed name is drawn from your Windows logon. Change it to the correct username, and it will be remembered for the next time. Next, enter your password. If you don't want to be prompted to enter a password every time you use this connection, click the Save Password box. Click Connect and you're off.

FIGURE 21.3.

The Connect To box displayed when a Dial-Up Networking connection is launched.

Connecting to a Private Network

Using Dial-Up Networking to connect to a private network is virtually identical to connecting to the Internet. As expected, the primary differences will be the protocols you'll be using over the dial-up connection, and possibly some other configuration settings as well, such as the Log on to Network option.

You'll create a DUN connection in the same manner as you did in Task 21.2, using the settings that the administrator of the destination network gives you.

As an example, let's configure a DUN connection to the network. If you remember, you configured a Dial-Up Server on Day 20.

Task 21.3. Creating a DUN Connection to a Private Network

Use this same procedure whether connecting to your network or another:

1. Open the Dial-Up Networking folder.

2. Click Connections | Make New Connection, or double-click the Make New Connection icon.

3. Give a name to this connection, such as Dial My Network.

4. Select the modem you want to use to connect. Click the Connect button to view and/or change any modem properties.

▼   5. Click Next. Enter the area code and phone number of your dial-in server. Select the proper country.

6. Click Next and then click Finish.

7. Find your new connection in the Dial-Up Networking folder; right-click it and select Properties.

8. Deselect Use Area Code and Dialing Properties if it's not needed.

9. On the Server Types tab, select the PPP type. Check Log On to Network, Enable Software Compression, and Require Encrypted Passwords under the Advanced Options section.

10. Under Allowed Network Protocols, deselect all but NetBEUI.

11. No settings are required on the Scripting or Multilink tabs, so click OK.

▲   12. Verify that your Dial-Up Server is up and waiting for a connection.

Double-click the DUN connection you just completed.

Direct Cable Connections

LAN connections and dial-up connections are great; they allow access to local or remote resources easily and quickly. But what about those times when you can't connect via the LAN or a dial-up? Or you want to transfer some files between two nonconnected PCs, and don't want to bother with setting up LAN or dial-up connections?

Windows 98 provides another networking component called Direct Cable Connection (DCC). DCC uses your computer's serial, parallel, or infrared ports to connect to another computer. The end result is a network connection between the two, allowing sharing of files or printers. In fact, you could even gain access to a network using DCC.

In Direct Cable Connections, the machine being connected to is designated the host. The other machine, the one doing the connecting, is the guest. Access control can be configured to require a password. If the host is on a network, the guest will also have access to the network.

When running DCC, you connect one machine to another using a data transfer cable (except when using the infrared [IR] port). The machines are connected either parallel port to parallel port, serial port to serial port, or IR to IR port. With the Enhanced Capability Port (ECP), parallel ports installed on newer computers, or the FastIR ports on newer laptops, very high transfer rates can be achieved between computers.

Special cables are required for DCC. If you intend to use parallel port transfers, there are cables marketed as data transfer cables, or data link cables, available in computer stores.

21

Standard printer cables will not work. If you want to use the serial ports for DCC, you'll need a null modem cable, with appropriately gendered (usually f/f) and sized (usually DB-9, possibly DB-25) connectors on each end. Some manufacturers make a datalink cable with multiple connectors on each end of the cable, allowing maximum flexibility.

Of course, if you're using the IR ports, no cables are required. For IR transfers, you need each machine's IR port pointed in the general direction of the other, and approximately three to ten feet apart. Some IR ports will work at longer ranges.

Note

> You might have heard Direct Cable Connection cables referred to as *LapLink cables*. Although the concept is correct, LapLink is a trademark of Traveling Software and should only be used in conjunction with its product.

Before you can use DCC, you'll have to install the software. As before, you'll start from the Control Panel, the Add/Remove Programs applet, on the Windows Setup tab. Refer back to Day 2 for details on installing optional Windows components.

Also, here are the requirements for using DCC:

- Both computers must be running NetBEUI.
- Both computers must be in the same workgroup.
- The host must have file and printer sharing enabled.
- The host computer must have at least one disk or folder shared.

Task 21.4. Configuring a Direct Cable Connection Host

Have an appropriate data link cable ready for use before beginning the following steps:

1. Start Direct Cable Connection from Start | Programs | Accessories | Direct Cable Connection.

2. The first dialog asks if this computer is to be configured as the host or a guest. Select Host and then click Next.

3. Now you must select the port to be used for the connection. In the port list will be all the serial and parallel ports detected on this system. Select the appropriate port (probably LPT1).

4. If you haven't already done so, connect the cable to the selected port on both computers. Click Next.

5. If you want to require the guest computers to enter a password before accessing the host, click the Use Password Protection box and then click the Set Password button to enter a password. Click Finish.

6. You'll see a dialog indicating that DCC is initializing, and then the dialog shown in Figure 21.4 will appear, stating that the host is waiting for a guest computer connection on the port.

FIGURE 21.4.

Host computer waiting for a Direct Cable Connection guest to connect.

7. If no guest connection attempt is detected within fifteen seconds or so, you'll hear a beep and see a dialog asking if a guest computer is running; just leave the dialog box up because DCC is still listening for a connection.

Of course, no host configuration would be complete without a guest, so continue on with Task 21.5.

Task 21.5. Configuring a Direct Cable Connection Guest

1. On your guest computer, start DCC.

2. Set this computer to be a guest; click Next.

3. Select the same port that you selected when the host was configured. Click Finish.

4. You'll see the guest immediately begins the connection attempt to the host. The dialog will indicate Verifying Username and Password; if you've configured the host to require a password, a prompt box will appear. Enter your DCC password and then click OK. You don't have to enter anything into the Logon Domain field.

5. You should see a connected message, and it'll also say Looking for Shared Folders. DCC will then pop up an Explorer window showing the shared contents of the host computer.

6. Using the Explorer window, you can now browse the contents of the shares. Alternatively, you can use Windows Explorer to go to Network Neighborhood and browse for the name of the host computer. It might not show up right away; press F5 or click View|Refresh. After the host shows up in the list, you will be able to view any shared resources on the host.

7. When you're done using the host, bring up the DCC window again and click Close.

For quick and dirty and relatively fast connections, Direct Cable Connection is the right tool.

21

Infrared Configuration

If you have a laptop or desktop computer with an infrared port, you might have to perform a few extra steps to get the IR working. However, you'll find that when you need it, the IR is a very convenient tool for transferring files.

Now, besides being convenient, the IR stuff is just pretty cool. It's neat to be able to just point your laptop at someone and send him a file over the beam, so to speak. Your infrared port can be used to send files back and forth, as a link for a Direct Cable Connection, or to print to an infrared-equipped printer.

Like Direct Cable Connection and all the other optional Windows components that you've learned about in the last three weeks, infrared needs to be installed from the Add/Remove Software Control Panel applet's Windows Setup tab. Depending on your original installation, the IR stuff might have already been installed. When it's installed, you'll find a listing for an Infrared PnP Serial Port on the Device Manager tab of the System Properties dialog box. As shown in Figure 21.5, it's possible that the device will be listed but shown with a red X on the icon in front of the listing for the port, indicating that it's disabled.

FIGURE 21.5.

The Device Manager tab showing the infrared port installed; it's shown as having a problem of some sort.

Displaying the properties for the Infrared PnP Serial Port will show, as illustrated in Figure 21.6, that the device is installed but currently disabled. Click the button to enable the port. When you exit the Device Manager, you'll get a dialog box telling you that because you've made hardware changes, you should shut down and power off the computer and then turn it back on. When you do so, check Device Manager again, and you will see that the IR port is enabled.

FIGURE 21.6.

Pressing the Enable Device button will turn the device on; however, you'll have to shut down and restart your computer before the port is functional.

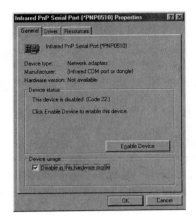

After the reboot, you'll notice a couple of changes to your system. The first one might not be too obvious; in Device Manager, you'll now see a new device line labeled Infrared Devices. If you view the contents of My Computer, either via Windows Explorer or by double-clicking on the My Computer icon on your desktop, you'll see a new icon labeled Infrared Recipient. If you check the Send To menu on the context menu (the right-click menu), you'll see Infrared Recipient there too. Lastly, you'll find a new icon on the System Tray on the taskbar—an icon for Infrared Monitor.

The Infrared Monitor, which can be opened by clicking on the IR icon on the System Tray or by double-clicking the Infrared applet on the Control Panel, is shown in Figure 21.7. The IR Monitor is where you can control all IR activity. The first time you launch the Infrared applet, you might get a wizard to assist in the configuration of your IR ports. There's not much to the wizard; simply accept the defaults through the process.

FIGURE 21.7.

The Infrared Monitor is used to get status on your IR communications and to configure and control your IR ports.

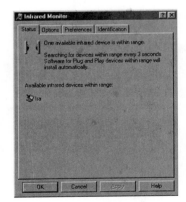

21

The Status tab of the IR Monitor displays the current status of your IR ports and any IR devices that are detected within range. The Options tab contains four settings, two of which are very important. The first, Enable Infrared Communication, determines whether or not your IR port will send or receive data at all. Below that will be displayed the serial and parallel ports that are supported by the IR port.

The last setting on the tab, Install Software for Plug and Play Devices Within Range, is the next important setting. When a device other than a laptop is detected, such as an IR-capable printer, this setting will allow Windows to automatically install any software needed to use those devices. So if you should walk into a room that contains an IR printer, Windows will detect this and then automatically install the software needed (a printer driver in this case) to utilize the device. You might be prompted for the Windows CD-ROM; however, after the first time the software is installed for a particular IR device, you won't have to reinstall the software again.

On the Preferences tab are three settings that control how IR Monitor works. The first, Display the Infrared Monitor Icon on the Taskbar, controls whether or not the IR icon is displayed in the System Tray. Remember that even if it's not, you can still get to IR Monitor via the Control Panel. Lastly, the Identification tab contains the name and description that other IR devices will see for your laptop.

You can keep IR Monitor open while doing IR communications, but it's not necessary.

Double-clicking the Infrared Recipient icon in My Computer will open the Infrared Transfer application window, shown in Figure 21.8. The Infrared Transfer application is how you send and receive files over your infrared port. The top half of the window shows a status message about what other infrared devices are within range and what their names are. These other IR devices are also shown as icons below the status line. If there were multiple IR devices within range, say a couple of other laptops and an IR printer, you'd click on the device you want to send information to.

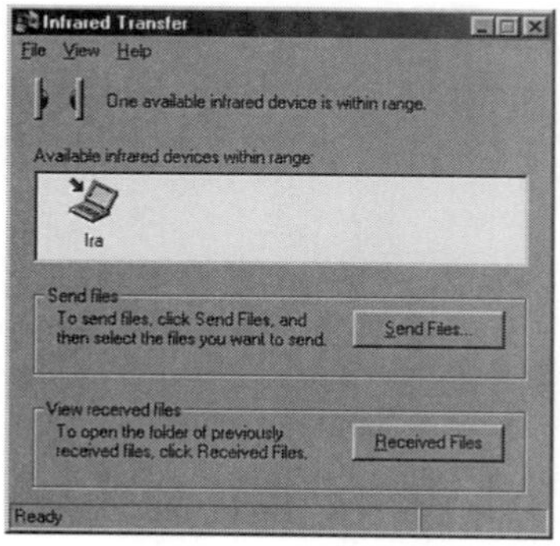

FIGURE 21.8.

The Infrared Transfer application is your IR window to send files to and receive files from other IR devices.

Below the IR devices section in Figure 21.8, you see a Send Files section and a View Received Files section. Clicking the Send Files button opens a standard File Browse dialog where you can select the files you want to send via IR to another IR device. Clicking the Received Files button opens a Windows Explorer window into the `C:\My Received Files` folder, a new folder on your C: drive where all IR-received files are placed.

Having IR capability is not a reason to fear attack by stealthy intruders, though. Another IR device cannot send you files unless your IR Transfer application is running. Also, any files you do receive are automatically placed into the `C:\My Received Files` folder. The IR Transfer application and the IR Monitor both have a number of sound effects for IR events, such as when another IR device is detected, when contact with an IR device is lost, when files are sent, and when they are received.

Using HyperTerminal

Sometimes, no matter how great all these networking tools and technologies might be, you still need to use a terminal emulation program and just plain dial into a bulletin board–type system. It's nothing to be ashamed of, either!

For those times when only a terminal emulator will do, Windows 98 comes to the rescue with HyperTerminal. HyperTerminal allows you to store the settings needed to connect to a dial-up system so you don't have to reenter the settings the next time. It also allows you to send and receive files and capture the screen to either a file or a printer.

HyperTerminal is nice for a terminal program because it will autodetect the type of terminal emulation the host expects, if possible. The shipped version of HyperTerminal is a smaller version of the full-featured HyperTerminal available from Hilgraeve, the producer of the program. Click Help | About HyperTerminal to display the About box; then click the Upgrade Info button.

The HyperTerminal folder comes with several preset connections. These connections are for AT&T Mail, MCI Mail, and CompuServe. If you use one of these accounts, most of the work of setting up the connection is already done for you.

When you start HyperTerminal by double-clicking on the program icon (rather than one of the preset connections), you'll get the dialog box shown in Figure 21.9. This dialog is asking you if you'd like to use HyperTerminal whenever a Telnet application is needed. (Telnet is a terminal program that runs over a TCP/IP connection. You might occasionally use Telnet, but it's probably not likely.) Choose Yes or No, as you like. If you choose Yes, you won't see the question again; choose No, and you'll see it every time you start the program, unless you also select Stop Asking Me This Question.

21

FIGURE 21.9.

*HyperTerminal dialog
asking if you'd like
HyperTerminal to
be invoked whenever
a Telnet session is
needed.*

When you need to dial into a remote system as a terminal, you'll need to know these configuration settings:

- The telephone access number
- The number of start, stop, parity, and data bits expected
- The terminal emulation expected

When you know these, you can set up your terminal session. Before beginning, you'll need to have your modem already installed and configured.

Task 21.6. Configuring a HyperTerminal Dial-Up Session

With Internet access ever more prevalent, you might not need this kind of dial-up connection very often, but it's still nice to know how to do it:

1. Open the HyperTerminal folder from Start | Programs | Accessories.

2. Double-click on the HyperTerminal program icon. The previously mentioned Telnet question will appear in a dialog; select No.

3. After the About box displays for a few seconds, you'll be left at a dialog box that gives you the opportunity to configure a new dial-up connection. Enter a name for this connection in the Name field and then select an icon to use for the connection. Click OK. The connection you are creating right now will show up with the selected icon in the HyperTerminal folder. The next time you need to use this connection, you can just double-click the connection icon.

4. At the Connect To dialog, you're asked to select the country you're in, enter the area code and telephone number of the system you're calling, and select the modem to use for the connection. Click OK.

5. Because the program assumes you want to make the connection, you're now at the Connect dialog box. The top half of the dialog shows the number to be called and includes a Modify button. In the center of the dialog are the dialing location settings. At the bottom are Dial and Cancel buttons.

6. Clicking the Modify button will bring you to the Properties box for the connection. The first tab, Connect To, is essentially the same settings you initially configured

▼   for the connection, with the addition of the Use Country Code and Area Code and Redial on Busy settings. Click them on as needed.

7. Click on the Settings tab to display the terminal property settings. The most important one is the Emulation field in the center of the page. Set it to the specific terminal type required by the called system, or leave it at AutoDetect.

8. Click OK and then click Dial to initiate the connection. After you've connected to the remote system, you'll be left at the main HyperTerminal window. Depending on the remote system, you might have to hit Enter once or twice to get a response.

9. When you've finished with the terminal session, click Call|Disconnect, or click the toolbar icon that shows the telephone handset suspended above the telephone.

10. If you quit HyperTerminal before saving the connection information, you'll be asked if you want to save it. If you ever intend to connect to this remote system again, you might as well save the connection, so as to not have to reenter the information in the future.

▲

Using the Briefcase

Has this ever happened to you? You have a bunch of important project files that you take home to work on. When you get back to the office, you plan to put your revised files up on the file server for everyone else to view/use. But you get distracted before updating them, and then don't remember exactly which ones you revised. Besides that, your associates indicate that they've also made some changes to some of the files. Now, how do you go about telling which files you've made changes to, and which they've changed? And how do you resolve the conflicts?

The Briefcase can help. This optional Windows component emulates an actual attaché case; put files into it, take them away, bring them back, take them out. The Briefcase also includes some smarts, though, that will help you track which files you've changed while you had them and which (original) files might have changed while you were away.

To make most efficient use of the Briefcase, just think of it as an actual briefcase. It's really just a regular folder with some special properties. However you care to think of it, using it is the same.

If you selected the Portable option when installing Windows 98, you already have the Briefcase installed. If you're not sure if you have a Briefcase (and you can have more than one), you can look for it in several ways. First, you can click the Desktop icon on the taskbar to minimize all open applications. You should be able to see a Briefcase on

21

your desktop. The second way is to open Windows Explorer and look in the left pane of the tree view, as shown in Figure 21.10. You'll see the Briefcase listed below all your disk drives, under My Computer. A third way is to right-click anywhere on your desktop or in Explorer where you can get a context menu with the New option. Select New, and if the Briefcase is installed, you'll have the option of creating a new Briefcase.

FIGURE 21.10.

Explorer and My Computer views showing My Briefcase.

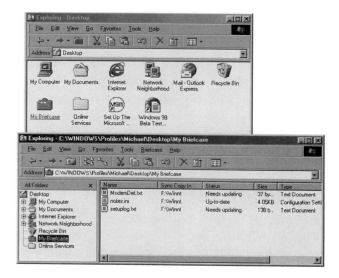

Working with the Briefcase is very simple. There are two variations on how you might use it; which you use depends on whether you're carrying the Briefcase with you or the computer. If you're working on a desktop computer and you want to take some files, either from the computer or from a LAN, with you when you leave, you'll be taking the Briefcase. The computer stays and you transport the Briefcase to another computer where you'll use the files.

If you are on a laptop hooked up to a LAN and want to take some files from the LAN with you, you'll use the Briefcase on your laptop. You'll be dragging files from some other computer on the LAN into the Briefcase on your laptop. In this case, you're putting files into the Briefcase and taking the Briefcase and the computer with you.

Tip

Remember, if the files you want to work with are already on your laptop, and nowhere else, you don't need to use the Briefcase—no one else will have access to the files, so you don't have any synchronization to worry about.

Taking Your Briefcase on a Floppy

When preparing to load your Briefcase up and depart, you'll follow one of the upcoming tasks in this section or the next section, "Taking Your Briefcase on a Laptop," depending on whether you're taking just the Briefcase with you (to another computer) or taking your laptop with you.

Task 21.7. Packing Your Briefcase Before Departure

1. Put the files you want to take with you into the Briefcase. You can click and drag them in, using Explorer, or you can right-click on files and select Send To I My Briefcase. (See the Technical Note about using Send To.)

2. After you've loaded up the files you want, open up the Briefcase. Click View I Refresh to refresh the folder contents. The files you just dragged in should show as Up-to-Date.

3. Insert a blank floppy into the drive. Be sure to label the floppy so you know it's your Briefcase! I like to include the date on the label. From Explorer or the My Computer window, either drag My Briefcase to the floppy drive or right-click and select Send To I Floppy.

> **Note**
>
> A blank (that is, empty) floppy is not technically required. The floppy must be formatted, though. A blank floppy just ensures that you have the maximum amount of free space for your Briefcase files.

4. The Briefcase will disappear from your desktop and appear on your floppy. Now you're all set.

> **Note**
>
> **Technical Note:** It's possible that the Send To I My Briefcase choice will not send files to your Briefcase. They'll go to a Briefcase, but it might not be yours! If your PC is not set up with multiple user logons, or you can't modify your own desktop settings, you can skip this.
>
> The Send To menu might point to `C:\Windows\Desktop\My Briefcase`, which is the default Briefcase. However, your Briefcase will be actually be `C:\Windows\Profiles\(your name)\Desktop\My Briefcase`. To check if the Send To menu is correct, use Explorer or My Computer to find the folder `C:\Windows\SendTo`. In there will be a shortcut labeled My Briefcase. Right-click on the shortcut and select Properties. In the Properties dialog, click the Shortcut tab. Listed in the Target box, as shown in Figure 21.11, will be the

▼TASK

21

target of this SendTo shortcut. If it doesn't list `C:\Windows\Profiles\`(*your name*)`\Desktop\My Briefcase`, you won't see files that you thought you put into your Briefcase; they'll wind up in the system Briefcase.

Windows 98 doesn't create separate Send To menus for each user, so you can't set up your own Send To options. What you can do, however, is create a shortcut on the Send To menu that points to your Briefcase. Take a look at Figure 21.12, and you'll see that I've added Michael's Briefcase to my Send To menu. To add your Briefcase to the Send To menu, display your `Desktop` folder (`C:\Windows\Profiles\`(*your name*)`\Desktop`). Right-click your Briefcase and then select Create Shortcut. You'll get a new shortcut called Shortcut to My Briefcase. Change the name of it to something like (*your name*)'s Briefcase. Now, drag the shortcut into the `C:\Windows\SendTo` folder. On your Send To menu, you now have your Briefcase as a destination.

FIGURE 21.11.

Shortcut properties that show the system Briefcase as the target.

FIGURE 21.12.

Send To menu after adding a shortcut to my personal Briefcase.

Task 21.8. Using the Files in the Briefcase

When you've arrived at your destination, you'll work on the files in the Briefcase. You have the option of either using the files in your Briefcase right off the floppy or copying the Briefcase onto the computer you'll be using. I prefer to copy the Briefcase because using files off the floppy is slower.

1. Insert your Briefcase floppy into the drive.

2. Using Explorer or the My Computer view, open the floppy drive.

3. Drag the icon for your Briefcase from the floppy to the desktop. The icon will no longer be visible on the floppy; you've just moved it.

4. When you want to open a file in your Briefcase, using whatever program, you'll just navigate to your Briefcase using the File Open dialog box, as shown in Figure 21.13.

FIGURE 21.13.

Locating the Briefcase in a standard file browse dialog box.

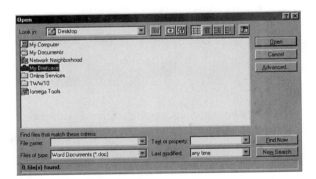

5. When you're finished working with your files, click File | Save from your application, and the file will be saved back into your Briefcase.

6. When you've finished working on this computer, use Explorer or My Computer to find your Briefcase. Move the Briefcase back onto your Briefcase floppy disk.

Task 21.9. Unpacking Your Briefcase

When you return home to your regular computer, you want to unpack your Briefcase. This updates the "home" copies of the files with any changes you made to the "away" copies that are now in your Briefcase.

1. Insert the Briefcase floppy. Use Explorer or My Computer to view the floppy drive.

2. Move the Briefcase on the floppy back onto your computer desktop.

21

3. Open the Briefcase. You should see the file listing that indicates the files in the Briefcase need updating. To unpack, or update, all the files, click on the Update All tool, or click Briefcase | Update All. You can also update only selected files by clicking on Update Selected.

4. When you click Update, you'll see a dialog similar to the one in Figure 21.14. This dialog gives you information about the files in your Briefcase and about the original files. The arrow shows you the recommended direction of the update; this should be from the Briefcase files to the original files.

FIGURE 21.14.

The Update dialog box from the Briefcase showing suggested update actions.

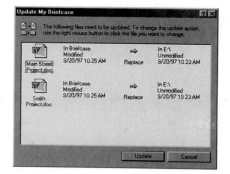

5. Click the Update button to update the originals with your changes.

6. After you've unpacked your Briefcase, you'll still have copies of the files in your Briefcase. I'll discuss what to do with these shortly.

Taking Your Briefcase on a Laptop

When preparing to load your Briefcase up and depart, you'll follow Task 21.10 if you're taking your laptop with you.

Task 21.10. Using Briefcase on a Laptop

1. Put the files you want to take with you into the Briefcase.

2. Open Briefcase, and all your files should be listed as Up-to-Date.

3. When you want to open a file in your Briefcase, just navigate to your Briefcase using the File Open dialog box, as shown earlier in Figure 21.13.

4. Click File | Save in your application when you want to save your work, and the file will be saved back into your Briefcase.

5. When you get back to home base, open the Briefcase. You should see the file listing that indicates the files in the Briefcase need updating. Click Briefcase | Update

▼   All or the Update All tool to synchronize your files. You can also update only
           selected files by clicking on Update Selected.

    6. When you click Update, you'll see the dialog that gives you information about the
       files in your Briefcase and about the original files. The direction of the recom-
       mended update is shown; again, this should be from the Briefcase files to the origi-
       nal files.

    7. Click the Update button to update the originals with your changes.

    8. After you've unpacked your Briefcase, you'll still have copies of the files in your
▲   Briefcase. I'll discuss how to get rid of these shortly.

Now that I've covered the operational differences in using the Briefcase, let's take a
closer look at it and see what it can do.

Looking at the Briefcase, as shown in Figure 21.15, you can see that there are some differences from looking at a normal folder. The first column shows the filename and the
icon for the file type. The Sync Copy In column shows the location of the original file—
the "home" copy, if you will. The Status column shows the status of the copy of the file
that's in the Briefcase. There are three possible statuses, as shown in Table 21.1.

FIGURE 21.15.

*When displayed in
Windows Explorer, the
Briefcase displays dif-
ferent columns than a
normal folder does.*

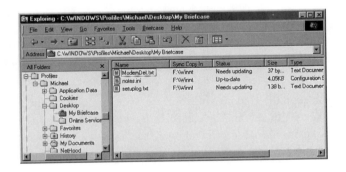

TABLE 21.1. BRIEFCASE FILE STATUS OPTIONS.

Status	Meaning
Up-to-Date	The Briefcase copy and the original copy are the same, based on file size, date, and time.
Needs Updating	Either the Briefcase copy has been changed since being put in the Briefcase, or the Briefcase copy and the original have different sizes, dates, or times.
Orphan	This file has no master or original.

21

When you click View | Refresh in Briefcase to update the view and status information, Briefcase attempts to find the originals of the files in the Briefcase, if it can. If it is able to locate them, it will get their file sizes, dates, and times and can then indicate to you whether your Briefcase files need to be updated from the originals.

What can happen sometimes is that your files are updated both by you, in your Briefcase, and by someone else working on the original file. Unfortunately, Briefcase cannot completely resolve this dilemma. It's not smart enough to combine the changes that two or more people have made to a single file. When this happens, as shown in the Update My Briefcase dialog in Figure 21.16, Briefcase suggests skipping the update action. If you chose to update, one person's changes would be overwritten by another's. This might be okay, but it's certainly something to consider on a file-by-file basis.

FIGURE 21.16.

The Update My Briefcase dialog box lists the suggested update actions for the files in the Briefcase.

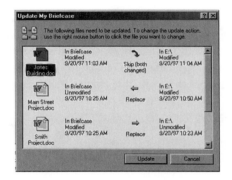

When you're in the Update My Briefcase dialog, you can right-click on any listed file to change the update action. You can force Briefcase to update in either direction—Briefcase over original or original over Briefcase—or to skip the update altogether.

When you no longer need a file in the Briefcase, getting it out needs to be done carefully. You can just delete it from the Briefcase, but you need to be alert to what happens the next time you update the Briefcase. When you next update the Briefcase, it will detect that you've deleted those files and suggest a course of action.

The suggestion will be to delete the original files, which probably isn't what you want to do! Likewise, if the original has been deleted, Briefcase will suggest deleting the Briefcase copy. Right-clicking on any deleted item will produce the context menu shown in Figure 21.17, which displays the delete options. The Delete option will delete the other copy of the file. Selecting Create will copy the existing file (Briefcase or original) to the other location. Selecting Don't Delete will leave the deleted file deleted and not touch the remaining file.

FIGURE 21.17.

When Briefcase files or the originals have been deleted, the Update options change to allow propagation of the deletes or recovery of the file.

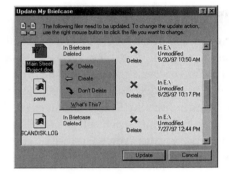

Another, slightly easier way to remove files from your Briefcase is to split them from the originals—in other words, create orphans out of them and then just delete them. Briefcase won't ever try to update them again. As a final option, you could just delete the entire Briefcase.

So, if you've just updated all the files in your Briefcase, use one of these methods to clean out your Briefcase.

Task 21.11. Removing Files from Your Briefcase

Use only one of these alternatives to clean out the Briefcase.

Option A

1. Delete the files you no longer need in the Briefcase. Either select them and click Edit | Delete, or drag them to the Recycle Bin.
2. Click the Update All tool.
3. For all the files that show deleted, right-click them and then select Don't Delete.
4. Click Update.

Option B

1. Select the files you want to remove from the Briefcase.
2. Click Briefcase | Split from Original. The status for each selected file will change to Orphan. Now delete these files.

Option C

1. Find your Briefcase in Windows Explorer or My Computer. If you have multiple usernames on your computer, it will be in `C:\Windows\Profiles\(your name)\Desktop`. If not, it will be in `C:\Windows\Desktop`.
2. Select the Briefcase and then delete it.

21

Power Management

Power management is the capability of the operating system and the computer to work together to conserve power by powering down devices that are not needed, and finally, by putting the entire machine into a sleep state. Power management is perhaps most important for laptop users trying to squeeze out every available second of precious battery life, but it's also valuable in conserving energy resources for the millions of desktop machines that are on all day and idle a great percentage of the time. As newer machines replace the older ones, the energy savings should increase even more.

Many laptops have their own power management settings, usually in BIOS, that control some aspects of the laptops' operation. A common one is to lower the CPU speed and dim the screen when running on battery.

Windows 98 carries the power management philosophy a bit further by allowing you to define a power scheme for your computer—be it desktop, server, or laptop—that controls the monitor and hard drives. Using power schemes, you can set your monitor (display panel) to turn off after three minutes of inactivity when running on battery and to spin down the hard disk after ten minutes of inactivity.

These settings allow you to tailor the power management to your style of working while conserving as much power as possible. Power management in Windows is controlled from the Power Management applet in the Control Panel.

On the Power Schemes tab, you'll find a drop-down list of preinstalled power schemes for your computer. These schemes can be altered and then saved under different names so you can switch back and forth between power schemes quickly and easily. For each scheme, you can control the time delay before Windows suspends your computer, shuts off the monitor, or powers down the disk drive(s). For each setting, the range of available options is from one minute to five hours, or never. Both settings indicate the time the computer is inactive before the setting kicks in. Inactivity is defined as the absence of mouse or keyboard activity. The settings on the Power Schemes tab apply to both desktop and laptop computers. If you are running on a laptop, though, you'll have two different sets of settings: one for when you're running on AC power and one for when you're on battery power.

On laptops, you'll find an Alarms tab and a Power Meter tab. On the Alarms tab, you can configure what notification you'll receive and what action Windows will take for a low battery alarm and for a critical battery alarm. The definitions of both are user configurable, to a percentage of battery power, also on the Alarms tab. Clicking the Alarm action button for either setting allows you to configure an audible and/or visible warning, and to define an action, if desired. The available actions are do nothing, go into Standby, or Shutdown.

On the Power Meter tab, Windows will display statistics that detail both the total best estimate of remaining battery power and time and statistics for each individual battery in the laptop. The enhanced power management also allows for tracking of individual batteries for historical information and tracking. Note that such smart batteries are not very widespread yet.

On the Advanced tab are some additional settings that only apply to laptops. Under the Options section is a setting to Show Power Meter on Taskbar. This will display either an AC plug when the computer is running on AC power or a battery icon when running on battery. The battery icon will also display a charge level, and holding the mouse over the battery will bring up a display of approximate percentage of power and time remaining.

On laptops, a second option will appear: Prompt for Password When Computer Goes off Standby. This will prompt you for your Windows password when the computer is turned back on. The third option (second if not on a laptop) is Turn on Computer to Phone Calls over the Modem. This will wake up the computer from a sleep state if the modem signals that a call is incoming. The computer will wake up, handle the call in whatever method it's set up to do, and then go back to sleep again.

The bottom section of the Advanced tab, Power Buttons, concerns laptops and newer PCs with motherboards that support the OnNow standard. The first setting is When I Close the Lid on My Portable Computer. Almost all laptops detect when the cover is closed and can act on it; usually the user can configure the laptop to either suspend or shut off when the user closes the lid. This setting tells Windows to take over control of the action that results from closing the lid.

The OnNow standard allows the computer to go to sleep when the power button is pressed instead of turning off. The idea is that if the computer is sleeping, it'll come up to a ready state much quicker than a computer that has to boot from a cold start. If your computer supports it, the option will be enabled. You can then determine the behavior of your PC when the power button is pushed—to either shut down or suspend.

Using PC Cards

Personal computers don't fit on your lap; that's why they're called desktops. Laptops (or notebook computers) do fit on your lap. And yes, that's why they're called laptops. One of the primary reasons laptops are so much smaller is that they don't have those bus slots that I talked about back on Day 9 to add expansion cards. Laptops generally come configured with most of what you'll need to have a nicely functional computer. The operative word here is *most*. Many laptops don't have built-in modems, and if there's any machine that needs a modem, it's a laptop. Many other devices are not included in most

21

laptops, such as network connections, CD-ROM drives, additional hard disks, or possibly video or sound devices.

To remedy the lack of expansion options, laptop manufacturers would have to include expansion slots. Including bus type slots like you learned about in Day 9, such as ISA, VLB, or PCI slots, would unacceptably increase the size of the laptops. Instead, the PC card (originally called PCMCIA) was invented. The PC card slot is a small slot into which a credit card size expansion card fits. There are three types of PC cards: Type I, Type II, and Type III. The different types relate to their thickness, not their length and width. Type I and II cards both fit into a single PC card slot.

A Type III card takes a double-high slot. Type III devices are typically PC card hard drives—hard drives, usually with capacities of between 40MB and 340MB, that are only about 3/4-inch tall. Most other PC card devices, like modems, SCSI controllers, sound cards, and network cards, plug into a single Type II slot. You won't usually find a Type I slot. Most laptops are configured with two Type II slots or one Type III slot. This means that there are actually two Type II slots, one on top of the other. You could fit a Type II card into either slot, or a Type III card (remember that it's twice as thick as a Type II) into the bottom slot only; the top slot would be unusable.

PC cards were, and are, a great idea. But back in the Windows 3.x days, using PC cards often meant shutting down your computer and then rebooting with a different configuration—not very convenient. So the PC card makers came up with Card Services software to ease the process. With the advent of Windows 95, many PC cards became hot-swappable and Plug and Play, meaning that you could add or remove cards with the machine on and running, and without rebooting. There were, of course, exceptions, but in general it worked. With Windows 98, that tradition continues with enhanced PC card support and support for the newer types of cards, the CardBus and the lower power consumption 3.3v cards.

The important thing to remember about PC card support is that Windows 98 supports them directly. What that means is that you should not be loading any additional software to support PC cards. If you buy a PC card and the instructions say that you should install any kind of Card Services software, don't. You most likely don't need it. You might need a driver, or an updated driver, but the chances are extremely high that you will not, and should not, install any other support software for the PC cards. If your software attempts to install (or insists on installing) PC card services, you should contact the manufacturer for an updated version.

When installing a new PC card, always install the card first and let Windows see if it recognizes it. Most of the time that's all that will be required. If Windows won't find the card and there's no other way to make Windows recognize the new card, then install the support software.

PC cards are usually truly Plug and Play. As an example, say you have a PC card modem that you've used on your laptop before, but it's not installed right now. In order for you to use it, all you have to do is plug it into the PC card slot. Windows will recognize that a card has been inserted, load the device drivers required, and make the new device available to the rest of the system, all within a few seconds, and without rebooting.

PC cards, while not fragile, should still be handled with care. Avoid water and moisture (as with all electronic equipment!). Don't bend or crush the cards, and avoid dropping them. For cards that have cables that plug into the cards, insert the cables carefully; don't force the connection. When the cable is properly aligned, it will plug in with little insertion force required, and should securely click into place. The cards are small, as are connectors; it's not difficult to break a card connector by trying to force a connection. Break a pin on a PC card cable connection, and the card is probably shot—there's no repairing it. For cards that have more than one cable connection, such as combination modem/LAN cards, make sure you plug the right cable into the right connection; they're not usually interchangeable. Check the markings before plugging in. Plugging the wrong cable into the wrong plug will probably kill the card (I've seen this several times) and could damage your laptop or worse.

If you have a laptop with PC card slots, open up Properties for My Computer or open the System applet in the Control Panel. Go to the Device Manager tab and you should see a PCMCIA socket listed as one of the devices in your computer. Expand it and you should find one (or more) PCIC or compatible PCMCIA controller devices and a PCMCIA Card Services device. These devices control the PC card and the interface between the card, the laptop, and Windows. Figure 21.18 shows the Device Manager tab.

FIGURE 21.18.

The Device Manager tab with the PC card controllers listed as well as two PC card devices: a modem and a network interface.

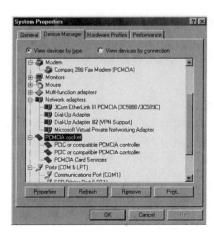

21

In Figure 21.18 you see that on my laptop there are two PCIC controllers listed. The reason is that my laptop sits attached to a port replicator. The laptop has two Type II slots, as does the port replicator. Both the laptop and the port replicator have a controller in them, so when the laptop is in the port replicator, Windows sees both controllers.

Also listed on the Device Manager tab in Figure 21.18 are a Compaq 288 Fax Modem, listed under Modem, and a 3Com EtherLink III card, listed under Network Adapters. Both of these devices are PC card devices. What I want to point out is that they are shown under their type, not under the PCMCIA socket device. Just to show that they really are controlled by the PCMCIA socket, though, look at Figure 21.19. The screenshot shows the Device Manager tab with View Devices by Connection selected. Here you can plainly see that the modem and network adapter are both controlled by PCMCIA controllers.

FIGURE 21.19.

The Device Manager tab with all devices shown by their connections. Here the modem and network adapter are shown under the PC card controller they are connected to.

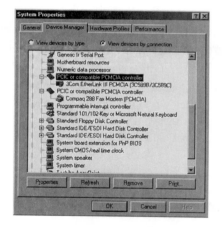

Installing a PC card is very easy, as detailed in Task 21.12. This example is generic, but the procedure would be nearly the same for most types of devices.

Task 21.12. Installing a PC Card

Many people are leery of inserting a card into a computer that's powered on. For a desktop computer, that's a wise precaution. For a PC card, however, it's perfectly acceptable. For this task, you can start with your laptop either on or off. I'm assuming that it's on.

1. Remove the PC card from its protective packaging. Inspect carefully for obstructions or coverings on the connector end of the card. If there are any shipping or protective coverings, remove them.

2. Insert the PC card into a slot. The card should insert straight and level. It will slide in very easily when installed correctly. Do not tilt the card front to back or side to

▼ side when inserting it. Push in until you feel resistance. At this point, you are just about to plug the card in.

3. Push firmly on the card; you should feel it seat. It might move in about one-quarter of an inch. Don't force it, though. It will feel very secure when properly seated.

   (If your computer is off, turn it on now.)

4. Windows will pop up a dialog saying it has found new hardware and is installing the software for it. If Windows can't determine the type of card, you'll be asked to pick from a list of devices.

5. You'll likely be asked for the Windows 98 CD-ROM, so insert it. If Windows can't find an appropriate driver for the PC card, you'll be asked to insert a disk with the driver on it. Your PC card will have come with some installation disks; insert the one specified as containing the drivers.

6. Windows will finish the installation. You might have to reboot, but usually not.

7. To verify that your PC card was recognized and installed properly, open the System applet on the Control Panel and click on the Device Manager tab. You should be able to find your new device listed under the appropriate type.

▲

From now on, whenever you insert this PC card, Windows will recognize it and enable it so that you can begin using it right away, without any manual reconfiguration or rebooting.

When removing PC card, you can do it the nice way or the not-so-nice way. The not-so-nice way is to just eject the card and pull it out. Amazingly, this actually works much of the time. You won't hurt anything by doing this, but it's just, well, not nice. You haven't informed any other hardware devices or software that might need to know about your intentions. When you remove a modem, for example, no other hardware in your laptop really cares. Some software might care, but it'll find out soon enough. But if the PC card you're removing is a SCSI controller with two external hard drives connected to it, the drives would like to be nicely shut down, and any programs that might be writing to the drives should be informed to stop writing to them, don't you think? Especially since you might be losing data by interrupting the its flow.

The nice way to remove a PC card is to stop it, via the PC Card Properties, first. There are two ways to get to the properties—either from the Control Panel (the PC Card applet) or from the PC Card icon on the System Tray. The PC Card Properties box is shown in Figure 21.20.

21

FIGURE 21.20.

The PC Card Properties box displays all PC card slots and the card resident there, along with controls to stop the cards.

The Socket Status tab displays the status of all the PC card slots and the name of whatever card might be currently inserted. There is also a Stop button which, when clicked, nicely informs the PC card that it's time to go to sleep. A dialog box will pop up when the card has been shut down. The Properties box will then display Empty for that slot, even though the card hasn't been removed. At this point, you can remove the card.

Also visible on the Socket Status tab are two check box options: Show Control on Taskbar and Display Warning If Card Is Removed Before It Is Stopped. The first controls whether or not you'll see the PC Card icon on the System Tray in the taskbar. The second option controls whether you'll see a warning dialog if you forget to stop a PC card before removing it.

On the Global Settings tab is a Card Services Shared Memory setting that should be left at Automatic. Below that is a check box, Disable PC Card Sound Effects. If checked, you'll get a very distinctive sound when Windows enables and removes a PC card. It's a nice confirmation that your card has been inserted/removed properly.

Multiple Hardware Configurations

With the increasingly able and agile laptops on the market today, the laptop is a serious contender for a desktop replacement. In fact a single laptop with suitable desktop accessories—such as a port replicator or docking station, monitor, mouse, and keyboard—makes practical and economical sense in many cases. This is even besides the convenience of not having to transfer files back and forth between multiple machines (the Briefcase and other mobile features notwithstanding!).

When Windows is configured, it expects to find the same equipment configuration every time it's started. When it doesn't, sometimes it complains, sometimes it silently sulks, and occasionally it'll even refuse to continue, although this is usually the fault of an ill-behaved peripheral device driver and not Windows itself.

Laptops are especially prone to having varying equipment configurations, so Windows supports the concept of multiple hardware configurations. As an example, sometimes you might have your laptop plugged into a docking station at work with a monitor, mouse, keyboard, a network card in the docking station, a SCSI controller, and an external SCSI tape drive. When out on the road, you have just the laptop with no extra goodies. When home, you might plug into a port replicator with a different monitor, a different keyboard, a trackball, and a parallel port Zip drive.

If you tried to configure your laptop to use all these devices at once, either you, Windows, or the laptop would just give up and go away! Using hardware profiles, though, you can just tell Windows which equipment profile to load, and presto, you've got all the right equipment at the right time, with no errors for missing equipment.

For laptops, Windows will automatically create a Dock1 or Undocked profile, depending on whether or not you originally installed Windows while in a port replicator or docking station. For desktops, you'll start with a single profile called Original Configuration. To view the profiles, open the System Properties dialog box and go to the Hardware Profiles tab, as shown in Figure 21.21; all your profiles will be listed there. Using the buttons, you can copy an existing profile to make a new one, rename an existing profile, or delete one.

FIGURE 21.21.

The Windows System Properties Hardware Profiles tab lists all the available hardware configuration profiles.

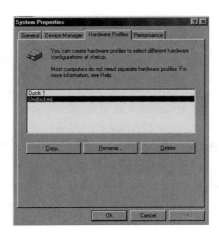

Because Windows deals pretty well with devices that are missing or unavailable at any particular time, chances are that you won't need to do anything regarding multiple profiles. If you happen to run across a device whose driver isn't very cooperative when the device is not available and insists on hanging up your system, you might consider creating a profile to alleviate the problem. To copy a profile that you can then modify, you'll need to perform the steps in Task 21.13.

21

Task 21.13. Creating a New Hardware Profile

▼ TASK

The first thing you'll do is create a copy of your existing profile, just in case.

1. Open the System Properties by right-clicking on My Computer or double-clicking on the System applet in the Control Panel.

2. Click the Hardware Profiles tab. Select your configuration, click Copy, and then enter a name such as Original Config.

3. Reboot your PC. When you reboot, you'll see a message indicating that Windows cannot determine what configuration your PC is in. All your configurations will be listed; enter the number for the configuration you want to use.

4. When it's finished rebooting, you can go into the Device Manager and disable any devices from the current hardware configuration by displaying the properties for the device and then selecting Disable in this hardware profile.

▲

Every time you boot using this hardware profile, the selected devices should be disabled. Note that if you were to choose Remove from all hardware profiles or just deleted it, the device, if still present, would be detected on the next boot and reenabled. The single biggest downside to having multiple configurations, beyond what Windows detects and creates, is that you have to tell Windows at boot time which configuration to use.

Offline Printing

Printing via Windows 98 was covered extensively on Day 5, "Fonts and Printing in Windows 98," but it's worth covering some specific topics as they apply to the road warrior. During the course of the day, there are often times when I print something out for someone else, intending to give it to them later. I'll usually print it out when asked, primarily because if I try to remember to do it later, I usually don't. It also happens fairly frequently that I'll be out on the Internet and see something that I want to print for someone.

None of this is unusual or exotic; everyone prints. But as a laptop user, what happens when you don't have your printer with you? You could make a note to print that file later, but what about a Web page? You could always dial in later from home base to print it, but what a pain. And, there's the chance that the information you want to print won't be available later.

Windows eases this problem by allowing you to print to a printer that's not currently available, a procedure called offline printing. When you print to a printer that's offline because it's turned off, or out of paper, or it's back at the office, Windows will queue up your print jobs, saving them until the printer is once again detected as being available.

When the printer is once again available, you'll be asked if you want to print the pending jobs, at which time you can print them, delete them, or save them for later.

Task 21.14. Using Offline Printing

There is no real preparation required to utilize offline printing, but you'll simulate conditions so that you can see what will happen when you use this feature.

Your printer needs to be unavailable for this task. Either disconnect from the network, if using a network printer, or turn off your printer if it's connected directly to your computer.

1. Open the print queue for your printer by going to the Printers folder (or Control Panel applet) and double-clicking on the icon for your printer.

2. Click on the Printer menu and make sure that Use Printer Offline is not checked. If it is, select the menu choice to uncheck it.

3. Open a file and print a page or so. You can use any application, such as Notepad, and print any file. You'll get an error similar to the one shown in Figure 21.22, depending on exactly how you made your printer unavailable. The message will ask/tell you that your work can be queued to a printer queue for later printing. Click OK to save the print job into the queue.

FIGURE 21.22.

When the printer you're trying to print to is unavailable, you'll see a dialog box such as this one.

4. Switch back to the print queue window (open your Printer icon if you closed it before). You'll now see that the title bar of the window should list not only the name of the printer, but also a message, User Intervention Required, and the status of the printer, Use Printer Offline.

5. If you made your printer unavailable by turning it off, turn it back on now. If you removed your computer from the network, plug back in and log in to the network again. (You might have to restart or log off/log on.)

6. When Windows detects that your printer is again available, it will prompt you, as shown in Figure 21.23, to choose whether to print the pending jobs, hold them, or delete them.

▼

FIGURE 21.23.

When your printer is again available, and print jobs are queued up for the printer, you're given the option of printing them now, holding them for later, or deleting them.

When you know your printer will be unavailable, you can head off the error message you received in step 3 by setting the printer to offline status manually. To do so, open the printer and then click Printer | Use Printer Offline. When the printer is set to offline, Windows automatically captures all print jobs into the queue and won't report any printer errors.

Dialing Locations

Using a laptop to dial out to other systems is very easy. Dial-Up Networking was covered already on Day 14, "The Internet and Internet Explorer 4." One thing not covered on Day 14 was the concept and usage of dialing locations.

Let's say you have an ISP with a local phone number. From home, you set up your Dial-Up Networking (DUN) connection to dial just the phone number. Now, you take your laptop to the next county and try to dial your ISP. What happens? You have to change the DUN connection to now dial the area code. Next, you check into a hotel. To get an outside line you must dial an 8 and then the number. Okay, so you change the DUN connection again to dial an 8 first and then the area code and number. The next hotel you're at requires a 9 for an outside line. Change the DUN connection again. It gets frustrating, making repeated changes like this.

Enter dialing locations. Remember that when you create a DUN connection, as shown in Figure 21.24, all you specify is the area code and phone number of the computer you're calling. There's no information about where you're calling from, or any other dialing parameters. A dialing location is a collection of all the settings required to correctly dial a phone number from your current location. So, you can have a dialing location called Office which dials a 9 for an outside number, but no area code for local numbers; and another location called NYC Hotel-8, which sets the local area code to 212, dials 9 for an outside line, and uses your company calling card for long distance calls.

FIGURE 21.24.

When creating a DUN connection, the area code and country should always be specified.

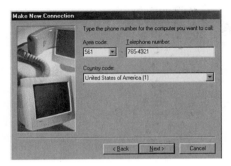

You can create any number of dialing locations you might need. If you frequently travel to the same locations and even the same hotels, you might want to create a location for each hotel or city. You can even create duplicate sets of dialing locations, one set for direct dial, another using a phone card. Whatever combination of settings you find beneficial can be accommodated.

Task 21.15. Creating a Dialing Location

For this task, you'll need to have Dial-Up Networking installed, and at least one DUN connection configured:

1. Call up the Properties for your DUN connection, as shown in Figure 21.25. If the Area Code and Country Code boxes are grayed out, click the Use Area Code and Dialing Properties option. Set the area code and country as appropriate. Close the DUN properties.

FIGURE 21.25.

The Use Area Code and Dialing Properties option on the DUN Connection Properties should be checked to enable the functionality of the dialing locations.

21

▼ 2. Now double-click on the DUN connection to get the Connect To box. Click on the Dial Properties box.

3. The Dialing Properties box, shown in Figure 21.26, contains all the settings for this dialing location. In the I Am Dialing From box, enter **Home**. Make sure the Area Code field is set properly. The center section of the dialog contains fields where you'd enter what you have to dial to get either a long distance or local line. Clear the boxes if they're not blank. If you have call waiting on your phone line, click the To Disable Call Waiting box, and enter or select the dialing code to disable it. All other options for this dialing location should be unchecked. Watch the Number to be dialed line just above the OK button, and you can see the effect that each dialing option has on the number that will be dialed for this DUN connection.

FIGURE 21.26.

Using Dialing Properties, a DUN connection can be dialed automatically from any location.

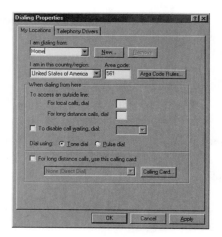

4. Click New, and the settings for the Home location will be saved and a new dialing location, called New Location, will be created. For this location, simulate a hotel in another city. Enter a name for this location, such as NYC Hotel. Enter an area code for the city, and configure a 9 for outside local calls, an 8 for outside long distance, and disable call waiting with a *70.

5. Click OK, and you will wind up back at the Connect To box for your DUN connection. The Dialing From field should say NYC Hotel; change it if it doesn't. In the phone number field, you'll see the entire number that Windows will be dialing to make the connection (*70, 9, 1 xxx yyy-zzzz).

▲ 6. Select the Home location now in the Dial From field, and the number will change to yyy-zzzz because the Home location doesn't specify any special dialing rules.

The Windows 98 dialing locations have been enhanced over those in Windows 95, with the addition of area code rules and much better calling card support.

Using area code rules, you can specify that Windows dial a 1 for certain prefixes (exchanges) within your area code, or to always use 10-digit dialing. You can also instruct Windows not to dial a 1 when dialing to particular area codes.

The calling card support really stands out. The configuration options should enable you to configure Windows to use almost any dialing sequence to use a phone card. Follow the steps in Task 21.16 to configure a dialing location to use a phone card.

Task 21.16. Configuring a Phone Calling Card

▼TASK

Open a DUN Connection and click Dial Properties. To enable a calling card from a dialing location, check the box labeled For Long Distance Calls, Use This Calling Card.

1. Select from the long list of major phone companies, both U.S. and international. To use any calling card not listed, select Calling Card via 0.

2. Click the Calling Card button to display the Calling Card dialog. To create a calling card with a custom name, click New and type a name in.

3. The rest of the dialog contains the section labeled Settings for This Calling Card. Enter your PIN (Personal Identification Number) for the card in the PIN field. In the Long Distance field, enter the number to dial when calling long distance, and right below that, the number to dial for international calls. If you selected a credit card in step 2, the access numbers will be shown in the Long Distance and International fields. Verify that they are correct.

4. Click the Long Distance Calls button to set the exact steps needed to use the calling card. The Calling Card Sequence dialog is shown in Figure 21.27 and displays the order of events Windows should observe when dialing this number. If you selected one of the predefined calling card types, this should already display a proper sequence. If you're creating a new calling card type, you'll have to use the different options to properly sequence the call. (The options available here are covered after this Task.)

5. Click OK until you get back to the Connect To box for the DUN connection. Here you'll see that all the numbers to be dialed, including the access number for the long distance carrier, are shown in the phone number field. Your PIN is not shown, for security reasons.

▼

21

FIGURE 21.27.

The dialing rules for using a calling card for Dial-Up Networking connections can handle the most complex dialing sequences.

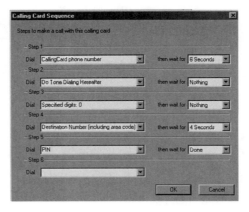

The Calling Card Sequence dialog displays the steps Windows must take to successfully dial using a calling card. These steps are configurable, in order to accommodate changes and calling cards from other carriers. Table 21.2 lists all the options and their meanings for the Dial field, and Table 21.3 lists the options for the Then Wait For field.

TABLE 21.2. OPTIONS AND ACTIONS FOR THE DIAL FIELDS.

Option	Action
CallingCard phone number	Dials the long distance access number for the long distance carrier.
Destination Number	Dials just the exchange and number (without area code) of the party you're trying to reach.
Destination Number (including area code)	Dials the entire number, including area code.
Destination Country/Region	For international calls, dials the country code.
PIN	Dials your Personal Identification Number.
Specified digits:	Allows you to enter a customized string of digits to be dialed.
Done	This sequence is complete.
Do Tone Dialing Hereafter	If doing pulse dialing before now, switches to tone dialing.

TABLE 21.3. OPTIONS AND ACTIONS FOR THE THEN WAIT FOR FIELDS.

Option	Action
Nothing	Don't wait, continue with the next step.
Tone	Wait until a tone is detected.
Done	This calling sequence is done.
2–46 seconds	Wait the specified amount of time and then continue with the next step.

Using the tables, let's analyze the sequence displayed in Figure 21.27. Step 1 tells Windows to dial the access number for the long distance service and then wait six seconds. Note that there is no condition checked for at the end of the six seconds; step 2 just commences then. This could have been set to Wait for Tone because this carrier gives an audible tone when it answers the phone. Step 2 says to switch to tone dialing for everything after this step. The reason for this step is that the connection could have been dialed using pulse dialing. Pulse dialing doesn't work with long distance access carriers; everything must be done from a touch tone phone. So step 2 switches to tone dialing just in case Windows originally dialed the phone using pulses.

Step 3 instructs that a 0 be dialed, followed immediately by step 4, which dials the destination phone number and area code. Remember that this number is the number of the computer being dialed in the DUN connection. Windows is instructed to wait four seconds before proceeding with step 5. At this point, many carriers present a signal tone indicating that you may enter your PIN. So, this could also have been set to Wait for Tone. Finally, in step 5 your PIN is entered as authorization, which finishes the dialing sequence.

Road Warrior Tips and Techniques

Being able to carry a computer with you during your travels—be they cross town, cross country, or international—is both a blessing and a curse. What follows are some tips and techniques, learned firsthand or contributed by other road warriors, that might help you avoid some pitfalls in your travels.

The Laptop

The decision about which laptop to buy is influenced by any number of factors ranging from corporate standards to features, price, or color. Get as much as you can afford. I've found three things to be very important to me: weight, screen, and power.

The difference between a seven-pound laptop and an eight-pound laptop seems pretty negligible in the store. It makes a difference when you're at Terminal B Gate 47 and you need to walk to Terminal D Gate 24. Lighter is better.

If you spend a lot of time on your laptop and can afford the extra expense, get an active matrix screen. They're much brighter and sharper. On the downside, they do run around $500–900 more, consume more battery power, and allow someone to read your screen from over your shoulder. If you work on very sensitive documents, the security aspect might convince you to go with a good dual scan or the new high contrast screens.

21

Power is the road warrior's friend; it's consumption that's the enemy. There's nothing worse than running out of battery an hour into a six-hour flight, with three hours of work to do before landing. I like laptops that have an internal AC adapter, which means there's no external brick power adapter to carry. Also, look for laptops with Lithium Ion (LiIon) batteries because they last longer per charge and have a longer service life than other battery types.

Accessories

Many laptops have both a CD-ROM drive and a floppy. Consider whether you need to carry both. Many times a floppy can be more critical than a CD-ROM. Almost all of the newer laptops also have IR (infrared) ports, so even a floppy can become optional; exchanging files can be done over the wireless IR ports.

Carrying an extra battery might be a good idea if you go long stretches between available outlets. There are even after market batteries for some laptops that will last twelve hours.

PC card modems and network adapters add little weight but bring their own baggage with them. Both require a cable adapter; without the cable adapter, the PC card is useless. Of course, the cables are specialized and only available from the manufacturer, and at a premium. Don't lose them. The exception are the modems with the built-in phone cord jacks such as the U.S. Robotics X-Jack or Simple Technologies' SimpleJack.

A good laptop bag is a requirement. It should be large enough to hold all your accessories, provide adequate protection for your laptop, have a comfortable padded carrying strap, and be lockable. If you can find one that doesn't look like a laptop case, all the better; this makes it less of a target to laptop thieves.

Security

Let's face it—your laptop is valuable. Somewhere, there's someone who is willing to go to a lot of effort to separate you from your laptop. Interestingly, a growing number of laptop thieves are less interested in the intrinsic monetary value of the laptop itself than in the data on the laptop—industrial espionage meets the computer age. There are actually two levels of security to be aware of: physical security and data security.

For physical security, the key is to be alert. All the obvious reminders should be in place: Don't leave your laptop (in the bag or not) unattended, EVEN FOR A MINUTE; don't turn your back on it—if you must, at least keep a hand on it; don't check your laptop as baggage, carry it. When going through the security points at airports, you can request that your computer bag be hand searched. Don't put your bag on the X-ray conveyor belt unless you can walk through at the same time; you want to be waiting when it comes out the other side.

Data security requires more vigilance and care, and some common sense. Don't tape your account passwords on the laptop; don't store them in a text file on your drive. For programs that support encryption, use the feature. Sure, it's a pain to have to enter passwords, but what's the cost if your competitor gets access to your confidential materials? If the data is encrypted, a thief won't be able to get at your data using a disk editor.

For your dial-up accounts, consider not storing your passwords in Windows; in other words, don't let Windows do automatic entry of passwords; enter them manually. That way if someone were to, ahem, inherit, your laptop, he wouldn't also be able to dial in to your corporate and/or Internet email accounts.

Any time passwords are involved, I feel compelled to give my standard passwords lecture. Don't use your name, your spouse's, significant other's, children's, or pets' names; don't use Social Security numbers, phone numbers, addresses, birthdates, or license plate numbers. Don't use easy stuff like `1234567890` or `abcdefg` or `password`. The best passwords are difficult, if not impossible, to guess; they're also impossible to remember.

If your programs support it, use upper- and lowercase letters, throw in a number or two, and even a special character such as an exclamation mark or a space. A password like `This is 3x better!` is infinitely harder to guess than `password`. Use a phrase or song lyrics; just use anything besides something related to you. The absolute best passwords are long, mix characters, numbers, and punctuation, and are randomly generated by programs. These will produce passwords such as `P8piKr.35d`. Although these might seem impossible to remember, after typing them a few times, you will start to remember them. You can also try making phrases out of them to help you remember. The preceding password might be phrased out as "pea ate piker. 35 days."

General

When traveling, if you have an hour or so between flights, look for an outlet to plug into and recharge. They are not always obvious, but they're around. Look behind poles, near water fountains and phones, and near service doors. You'll often find the floor outlets, which are under circular plates in the floor. All these locations are usually used by maintenance staff to plug in vacuums, and so on. Feel free to open the outlet covers on the floor plugs or use any outlet to juice up.

21

Don't leave PC cards plugged into your laptop unless you're using them. PC cards, even when not being used, still draw power. So remove them when not needed. The newest generation of PC cards just coming out are built so that Windows power management can put them to sleep, so they'll draw the absolute minimum amount of battery juice.

For maximum battery life, use your battery. Sounds strange, but it's true. If your laptop is plugged in for long periods, like days, every week or so, unplug it and let the battery run down; then recharge it. This is especially applicable if you have anything other than an LiIon battery, as other types suffer from the so-called "Memory Effect," where they begin holding less and less charge.

Be sure to utilize the power management settings under Windows, as they will help maximize your battery life. Slowing down the processor, spinning down the disk after a few minutes of non-use, and dimming the screen will all add precious minutes to your battery.

Summary

In this day's work, you learned about the Windows features that will help you in your PC travels. You discovered the Briefcase to help you keep copies of files in sync. You explored the ins and outs of power management and learned some tips and techniques for maximizing your battery life. Next was PC cards—their secrets laid bare. You learned about hardware configurations and using offline printing. The intricacies of fine-tuning the Dial-Up Networking dialer were explored, covering topics such as multiple locations and using calling cards. Finally, you received tips and techniques learned over the years by weary laptop travelers.

Workshop

To wrap up the day, you can review terms from the chapter, see the answers to some commonly asked questions, and practice what you've learned. You can find the answers to the exercises in Appendix A, "Answers."

Terminology Review

Direct Cable Connection—A networking connection between two computers connected with either a serial or parallel cable.

ISP (Internet service provider)—A service company that provides you with an account that you use to connect to the Internet.

modem—Short for modulator/demodulator. A device that converts the digital ones and zeros from a computer into tones that can be transmitted across a phone line to another modem, where the tones are converted back into ones and zeros and sent to the receiving computer.

PPP (Point-to-Point Protocol)—A commonly used protocol for networking over a serial communication line.

port—A connection between your computer and the outside world. Ports are typically serial ports, for communication purposes, or parallel ports for printers and other add-on devices. Universal Serial Bus ports are a new, emerging port type. Many ports have different subtypes; for example, parallel ports come in standard, ECP, and EPP flavors.

protocol—The "language" spoken between devices on a network. Just as with languages, such as English and Spanish, two devices must speak the same protocol before they can communicate.

server—A device or process that responds to requests from clients.

SLIP (Serial Line Interface Protocol)—Another common protocol used for networking over serial communications lines.

TCP/IP—The protocol of the Internet. TCP/IP is the acronym for Transmission Control Protocol/Internet Protocol.

terminal—A display device with a keyboard and possibly a mouse, used to connect to a computer. Typically the terminal will be *dumb*, having little or no processing power of its own.

terminal emulator or *terminal program*—Software that makes a PC act like a dumb terminal for communicating with a host computer.

Q&A

Q Do I need to use HyperTerminal when I connect to the Internet?

A Usually not. As mentioned, you can use HyperTerminal for a Telnet session over the Internet. Most Internet users will never have any use for a Telnet session, so they will probably never use HyperTerminal either. HyperTerminal will usually be used for connecting to a bulletin board–type system.

Q Can I have Dial-Up Networking connections to multiple Internet service providers?

A Of course! You can have unlimited DUN connections to any number of ISPs or other networks. One connection will be designated your default connection and will be used for all connection requests unless you specify another connection.

21

Q I've noticed that my laptop battery life is shorter if I leave my PC card modem plugged into the laptop when I'm not using the modem.

A Most PC card devices, such as modems, SCSI interfaces, network cards, and so on, will consume power when they're plugged in, even if you're not using them. Newer PC cards will put themselves into a low power mode when they aren't in use, extending your battery life. For maximum laptop battery life, remove any PC cards not in use.

Q Can PC cards be removed from my laptop with the power on?

A As a rule, yes. All newer laptops and PC cards support this hot plugging. Check the documentation that came with your laptop and with your PC card devices to be positive.

Q I have a 33.6Kbps modem, but I can never get a connection faster that 28.8Kbps to my ISP.

A For any dial-in connection, the fastest connection you'll ever get is the speed of the slowest communication device in the chain. If your ISP only supports dial-in speeds of 14.4Kbps, no matter how fast your laptop or your modem, you'll never get a connection faster than 14.4Kbps. If your ISP offers dial-in access at higher speeds, be sure your DUN connection is configured to dial the number for the higher-speed access lines.

Exercises

1. Configure a DUN connection for an imaginary ISP with the following connection information and configuration requirements:

    Name: Michael's ISP   Access Number: (800) 555-1234

    Connection Type: PPP   IP Addressing: Dynamically assigned

    DNS Addresses: 192.168.0.43   (Domain Name Server)
                     192.168.100.123

    Use IP Header compression and default gateway.

2. Create a custom Power Management profile with the name My Profile that never turns off the disk or display and never goes into standby when the laptop is plugged in. Set it so that when it's running on batteries, it goes into standby after twenty minutes, turns off the monitor after ten minutes, and turns off the disks after five minutes.

APPENDIX **A**

Answers

This appendix provides the answers to the exercise sections at the end of each chapter.

Day 1

1. Name three ways to display the contents of your C drive.

A Here are four ways: Use Windows Explorer, My Computer, File Manager (if you've upgraded from Windows 3.*x*), or the dir command in a DOS window:

- To use Windows Explorer, choose Start | Programs | Windows Explorer. Now click the icon for the C drive.
- Open the My Computer icon on the desktop; then open the icon for the C drive.
- Choose Start | Programs | Program Manager | File Manager. Then open the C drive.
- Open a DOS window by choosing Start | Programs | MS-DOS Prompt. At the C:\ prompt, type **dir**.

2. List three ways to run the Notepad program.

A Again, because there are always a number of different ways to accomplish the same task in Windows, here are four ways to launch Notepad. You'll probably find others, as well.

- Choose Start | Programs | Accessories | Notepad.
- Choose Start | Run. Type **notepad**; then click OK.
- From a DOS prompt, type **notepad**; then press Enter.
- From Windows Explorer (or File Manager), find the notepad.exe file in the C:\Windows directory and double-click it.

Day 2

1. Because you like playing FreeCell so much, you've decided to remove the game from your system so that you can actually get some work done. Describe two ways to remove the FreeCell game.

A To remove optional Windows components, use the Windows Setup tab of the Add/Remove Programs applet in the Control Panel. Doing so ensures a clean removal of all the associated files. In this case, you can also manually delete the program files:

- *The manual method*—Using Windows Explorer, navigate to the C:\Windows folder. Locate the file Freecell.exe and delete it. Now navigate to the folder C:\Windows\Help. There you'll find three files, Freecell.chm, Freecell.cnt, and Freecell.hlp, that you also need to delete.

At this point, you've deleted the program files for FreeCell. However, the icon for the game is still in your Start | Programs | Accessories | Games folder. To remove this icon, you can *(a)* right-click the Start button, open the Programs, Accessories, and Games folders, and then delete the FreeCell icon; *(b)* right-click the taskbar, select Properties, click the Start Menu Programs tab, click the Remove button, expand the Accessories and Games folders, select the FreeCell icon, and then click the Remove button; *(c)* click Start | Programs | Accessories | Games, right-click FreeCell, and select Delete; or *(d)* use Windows Explorer to navigate to your Start menu folders (C:\Windows\Start Menu\Programs\Accessories\Games if you are the only person to use the computer or C:\Windows\Profiles*your username*\Start Menu\Programs\Accessories\Games if there are multiple users of your computer) and then select and delete the FreeCell icon.

- *The Windows Setup tab method*—Using the Windows Setup tab is definitely the preferred method for adding or removing Windows components such as games. The only downside for this particular example is that all the Windows games will be removed instead of just FreeCell. Open the Add/Remove Programs applet in the Control Panel. Click the Windows Setup tab. After the Searching for Installed Components dialog goes away, click the Accessories line and then click the Details button. Clear the check mark on the Games line and then click OK. When it's finished, click OK again to close the Add/Remove Programs applet.

Day 3

1. Earlier in this chapter, you learned that the Control Panel uses Windows Explorer to present the tools that allow you to change the settings for your computer. The Control Panel is also included in the Windows Explorer that you launch from the Start menu. Use Windows Explorer to show the Control Panel.

A Complete the following steps:

   1. Open Windows Explorer. (Use Start | Programs | Windows Explorer.)
   2. Navigate down on the left side until you see the Control Panel folder.
   3. Click the Control Panel icon.
   4. Now you'll see the Control Panel icons on the right side of Explorer instead of files. You can use the icons to change settings by double-clicking on them.

2. Create a new toolbar that allows you to run the Windows Paintbrush program with one click. (Hint: First create a directory, put a shortcut in the directory, and then add the toolbar.)

A Complete the following steps:

   1. Open Windows Explorer.
   2. Make sure that you've selected your C drive in the left side; then click File | New | Folder. A new folder will be created; the name will be highlighted. Change the name to My Toolbar and then press Enter.
   3. The folder My Toolbar will be selected in the right side of the screen. Press Enter to go into the folder.
   4. Now create a shortcut to the Paintbrush program by clicking File | New | Shortcut. The Shortcut Wizard appears. Click the Browse button to display a file dialog; then go to the Windows directory and select the Pbrush.exe program. Click the Open button to return to the Shortcut Wizard.

5. Click the Next button to go to the second page of the Shortcut Wizard. Now select a name for the shortcut; enter the name **Paintbrush** and then click the Finish button.

   You're almost done! You've created a folder and a shortcut; now you just need to add it to the toolbars.

6. Right-click on the toolbar. Select Toolbars from the context menu and then select New Toolbar from the side menu that appears. The New Toolbar window appears and prompts you to choose a folder or select an Internet address.

7. In the directory listing, select the My Toolbar folder that you created in step 2. You'll find it if you expand the C drive.

8. With My Toolbar selected, click the OK button. You'll see your new toolbar appear with the Paintbrush icon!

Day 4

1. Having a folder named My Documents is useful, but there will probably be occasions when you waste time looking through all those files. You need a way to instantly locate your key documents. Create a new folder named Key Documents at the same directory level as My Documents and place a few files in it.

A Complete the following steps:

   1. Open Windows Explorer.
   2. Click once on C: (or whatever letter represents your hard drive).
   3. Click File | New | Folder.
   4. Find the new folder. (It should be at the bottom of the file listing in the right panel.) If the name of the folder is highlighted with a box around it, type in the name of your new folder—Key Documents. If the name isn't highlighted, click it once, pause, and click it again. (Don't double-click; you'll open it.) Then type the name.
   5. Find the folder that contains the key files you want to move.
   6. Find the file in the right panel. Click it and drag it to the directory tree on the right. When *Key Documents* is highlighted, let go. Repeat for each file to move.

2. Now that you've mastered file manipulation, take a good look at the way your files are organized. Are you happy with them? Is there a more intuitive way to organize things? Take a shot at a new organization method.

A I'm not going to provide you with a total answer here because you need to organize according to your preferences and to best suit the way you work. Here are a couple of tips, though:

- Don't go overboard with subdirectories within subdirectories. It gets pretty tiresome if you have to click more than 5 folders to get to your file.

- By the same token, you need some folders. Don't just put all your files in a single folder; you'll be searching forever.

- Take advantage of long filenames. Gone are the days of 8.3 names such as WORKFILE.DOC and WORKFIL2.DOC. The more descriptive you make the names of files and folders, the easier it will be to find a certain file 12 to 18 months after you create it.

Day 5

1. Take advantage of the powerful font support in Windows 98 and use the standard WordPad program to make a simple birthday banner. Give the banner a bold Happy Birthday title in a large font, and then put a personal message underneath it in a smaller font.

A Here's one way:

1. Launch the WordPad program by using Start | Programs | Accessories | WordPad.

2. Switch WordPad to landscape mode so that you can use some really big fonts. To do that, go to File | Page Setup. In the lower-left corner of the Page Setup dialog, select Landscape for the Orientation setting and then click OK.

3. Now select Arial by clicking the down arrow next to the box that contains *Times Roman*. When you click the down arrow, a list of available fonts will appear. Scroll until you see Arial and then click to select it.

4. Click the down arrow next to the box containing the number 10. This controls the font size for the text. Select 72 for the font size.

5. Click the center button on the WordPad toolbar to center the text that you'll enter. (The center button looks like small lines that are aligned through the middle. If you hover the mouse over any of the icons in the toolbar, a short description will appear.)

6. Now enter the text **Happy Birthday!!** and press Enter to go to a new line.

7. Change the font to Times Roman, size 24, and then enter the text **Best wishes from your pal!**. That's it; using the standard Windows fonts, you've created a simple but attractive birthday greeting.

2. Windows Explorer allows you to navigate to practically any part of your Windows system. Use it to quickly view the status of all your printers.

A   To check the status of your printers, follow these steps:

1. Open Windows Explorer from the Start menu by clicking Start | Programs | Windows Explorer.

2. Scroll down the left side until you see the Printers folder.

3. Click on the Printers folder to view the printers in your system.

4. Click View | Details on the Explorer menu. You'll notice that you'll see the name of the printer, the number of documents that are in the queue for the printer, the printer status, and comments for the printer. If you have multiple printers, this is a very convenient way to quickly view the status of all of them.

Day 6

1. For this exercise, suppose that you're tired of seeing unlabeled CDs and songs when you use the music CD Player. Take your favorite CD and play it on the computer. While you are enjoying the music, type in the name of the artist, the CD's title, and the titles of the songs. When you're done, exit the CD Player, eject the CD, and then reinsert the CD to make sure the information was saved.

A   Complete the following steps:

1. Open the CD Player. (Choose Start | Programs | Accessories | Multimedia | CD Player.)

2. After you insert the CD, click Disc | Edit Play List. Change each title in the appropriate box.

3. The titles will automatically save when you exit. If your changes do not save, look under Options | Preferences and make sure that the Save Settings on Exit option is checked.

2. Install NetShow.

A Complete the following steps:

   1. Click Control Panel | Add/Remove Programs.

   2. Click the Install Program button.

   3. You should be an old hat at this now, but even if you aren't, don't worry. The wizard will take you through each step, and then NetShow will be located in the Start menu under Programs | Accessories | Multimedia.

Day 7

1. As a Windows user, you should frequently back up your important data files to ensure that you don't lose any work in the event of a hardware malfunction. Windows Help provides information about backing up your files; use the Help Search to find out how to back up your files.

A Follow these steps:

   1. Run Windows Help from the Start menu by clicking Start | Help. The Windows Help screen will appear.

   2. Click on the tab marked Search. The left side of the screen will change to enable you to enter a keyword. Enter the keyword **file** and click the List Topics button.

   3. When you search for only the keyword file, you'll notice that you get many matches. To narrow down the list, enter **backup** next to file and then click the List Topics button.

   4. Double-click on the To Back Up Your Files entry and follow the directions.

2. Sometimes when you are troubleshooting a problem with your Windows system, it helps to know which programs are automatically started when you start up Windows. Display a list of all of the programs that are started automatically when Windows starts. (Note: The Startup folder in the Programs folder on the Start menu doesn't list all the Startup programs.)

A Follow these steps:

   1. Display the Run dialog by selecting Start | Run from the Windows Start menu.

   2. Type **msconfig** into the text box next to Open and click OK. The Microsoft System configuration utility will appear.

3. Click on the Startup tab to display the tasks that are run automatically by Windows. If you compare this list with the programs in the Startup subfolder of the Program Files folder, you'll notice that the list has several additional entries. Most of the entries are internal programs that are required by Windows.

Day 8

1. Try out some of the Display settings by changing the Windows background to a nice, partially cloudy sky. (Hint: Windows comes with a cloudy bitmap.)

A Follow these steps:

1. Show the Display settings by right-clicking on the desktop to show the context menu; then select Properties. (Note: You need to click the desktop; make sure that you don't click an icon or an application.)

2. Click the Background tab to show the Windows background settings.

3. In the Wallpaper section, find Clouds in the Select an HTML Document or a Picture list. When you select Clouds by clicking on it, you'll notice that a preview appears in the window above the list.

4. Click OK to change the Windows desktop.

2. It's very important to maintain an up-to-date Windows startup disk so that you can easily recover from problems that can occur. Make an updated startup disk.

A Complete the following:

1. Use the choices Start | Settings | Control Panel to launch the Control Panel.

2. Double-click the Add/Remove Programs icon.

3. Go to the Startup Disk tab. You'll see a Create Disk button and text that describes startup disks. Click Create Disk.

4. The Insert Disk dialog appears. Put a blank floppy in the disk drive and click OK.

5. After Windows is finished creating the startup disk, you will return to the Startup Disk tab. Click OK to close the window. Now you've finished creating a startup disk; remove the disk from the drive, label it and include a date so that you know when the startup disk was updated, and keep it someplace handy in case you run into a problem!

Day 9

1. Set your display adapter to display an 800×600 pixel desktop and a color depth of 16 bits (if your adapter will support these settings).

A Open the Display applet by right-clicking the desktop and selecting Properties or by double-clicking Display in the Control Panel. Click the Settings tab. Set the display resolution to 800×600 by clicking the slider control in the Screen Area section of the dialog box on the lower-right side. Set the color depth to 16 bits by clicking the drop-down list box under the Colors section and choosing High Color (16 bit). Click the Apply button. You might be asked to reboot. Otherwise, you'll be given a dialog box that says Windows will now change your settings; if the display becomes unusable, just wait 15 seconds and the original settings will be restored. If you can see the display correctly after Windows resizes the screen and want to keep the current settings, click OK. Otherwise, click No (or just wait 15 seconds) and your original settings will be restored.

2. Describe two different ways to access the System Properties dialog box (the one that displays all the devices configured in your system).

A Getting to the System Properties dialog box can be accomplished in at least three different ways:

- Right-click the My Computer icon on the desktop and select Properties.
- Click Start | Settings | Control Panel and then double-click the System icon.
- Using Windows Explorer, scroll down the left side of Explorer until you see Control Panel. Click once, and then find and launch System from the right pane of Explorer.

3. Describe how and where you would find the following information:

   a) Your registered username
   b) Your Windows license number
   c) How much memory is installed in your computer
   d) Whether or not your PC has a Plug and Play BIOS

A Open the System Properties box as described in exercise 2. Your name, your license number, and the amount of RAM on your computer will be displayed on the General tab. Click the Device Manager tab, find System Devices, click the + to expand it, and then look at the devices listed. If your BIOS is Plug and Play, it will indicate that by showing a Plug and Play BIOS line as a device.

Day 10

1. Use the Control Panel to determine whether or not you have the optional Windows Quick View utility installed.

A Follow these steps:

    1. Open the Control Panel by clicking Start | Settings | Control Panel.

    2. Run the Add/Remove Programs Control Panel applet.

    3. Click on the tab marked Windows Setup. The system will pause for a moment while Windows examines the installed software.

    4. Select Accessories in the Components list. Next click Details to see the specific accessories that are installed. An Accessories dialog will appear. Move through the Components list until you find the Quick View entry.

2. Display a list of all the currently running programs. (Note: Please be careful!)

A Follow these steps:

    1. Close any open files that you may have; then press Ctrl+Alt+Delete at the same time. Make sure that you only press them once! If you press them more than once, you may reboot your machine.

    2. The Close Program dialog will appear. You can use this dialog to forcefully close a program that may appear to be hung. To do so, select it from the list of programs and click the End Task button. However, you can also use it to simply get a quick listing of the programs that are currently running.

    3. Click Cancel to close the Close Program dialog.

Day 11

1. One of the most useful features of the DIR command is that it can be used to create a text file listing of a directory. Use DIR to create a listing of the files in your Windows directory, sorted by file size.

A Follow these steps:

    1. Use the Start menu to run the MS-DOS command prompt (Start | Programs | MS-DOS Prompt).

    2. Type **DIR /?** and then press Enter to get help on the directory command. You might notice that some of the information scrolls off the screen. Enter **DIR /? ¦ MORE** to pause the information as it scrolls. Take notice of the /O flag that enables you to change the sort order.

A

3. Change to your Windows directory by typing **CD** **\Windows** and pressing Enter. The prompt should now read C:\WINDOWS>. (Note: This can vary if Windows is not installed on your C: drive.)

4. Type **DIR** **/O-S > DIRLIST.TXT** and press Enter to create a DIRLIST.TXT file that contains a sorted listing of all the files in your Windows directory. (Note: The > listed here tells MS-DOS to take the output from the DIR command and insert it into a file.)

2. The DIR command is extremely powerful. You can use it to get a listing of all the files in a directory and its subdirectories. Use it to make a listing of all the files in your Windows directory and below.

A Follow these steps:

1. Use the Start menu to run the MS-DOS command prompt (Start | Programs | MS-DOS Prompt).

2. Type **CD** **\Windows** to switch to the Windows directory.

3. Type **DIR** **/S** to display a listing of all of the files in the Windows directory and below. If you want to capture the list in a file, type **DIR** **/S >** **MYFILE.TXT**. You can replace the name MYFILE.TXT with any name. You can use this technique in combination with the /O option to create sorted listings of your files.

Day 12

1. Create a scheduled task to run ScanDisk regularly.

A Open the Scheduled Tasks folder. Double-click Add Scheduled Task. Select ScanDisk from the task list. Give this task a name and select when it should run. Display the Properties for your new scheduled task and click the Settings button. Configure ScanDisk to run with the desired options.

2. Describe the Compression Agent settings that would give maximum performance of a compressed drive. Describe the settings that would provide maximum storage space on a compressed drive.

A For maximum performance, configure Compression Agent to not UltraPack any files, and to not HiPack the rest of your files. This will result in all files being stored using Standard Compression. Of course, absolute maximum performance would be obtained by not compressing your drive at all.

To obtain maximum storage space for a compressed drive, change the settings of Compression Agent to UltraPack all files.

3. Describe the procedure to create a compressed drive on your system using 25MB of free space on an existing hard disk.

A This procedure is not compressing an entire drive, but creating a drive from the free space on an existing drive. If DriveSpace is not listed in your System Tools folder, use the Add/Remove Programs applet in the Control Panel to install the compression software from your Windows distribution media. Then display the properties of the disk drive on which you want to create the new compressed drive. Click the Compression tab and then click the Create New Drive button. Select a drive letter for the new drive. Direct DriveSpace to use 25MB of the free space to create the new drive. Click Start. Reboot when directed.

Day 13

1. The people who share the computer with you don't want to have to type in their usernames; they'd rather pick them from a list. What would you do to accommodate them? How would you set it up?

A What your users are asking for is the Microsoft Family Logon. To install it, open the Network applet in the Control Panel. Click the Add button, select Client, and then click Add again. In the Select Network Client dialog box, select Microsoft in the left pane and Microsoft Family Logon in the right and then click OK. You might be prompted for the Windows 98 CD-ROM or a disk. When you return to the Network properties box, click the drop-down arrow under the Primary Network Logon setting and select Microsoft Family Logon. Click OK; you might once again be asked for the Windows 98 installation media. You'll then get a dialog that says you should reboot. You can reboot now or the next time it's convenient. From now on, your users will see the family logon, with a list of all the usernames registered on this computer.

2. Create an account for a new user that will allow users to customize their own Start menu settings, wallpaper, and Favorites lists, without interfering with anyone else's settings.

A For this one, you'll need to create a new user account, with the appropriate profile settings. To do this, you'll need to use both the Passwords Control Panel applet and the Users applet.

First, open the Passwords applet. On the User Profiles tab, select the Users Can Customize Their Preferences and Desktop Settings option at the top of the tab. This will take care of the requirement of saving the wallpaper, which is a desktop customization. This will also enable the bottom half of the tab, shown in the User Profile Settings section. The question didn't specify whether or not the Desktop

A

icons and Network Neighborhood settings needed to be kept for each user, so you can ignore that setting. The Start menu customization was a requirement, however, so you must check the bottom option, Include Start Menu and Program Groups in User Setting. Click OK to finish with the Passwords applet.

Next, open the Users applet. Click the New User button to launch the Add User dialog. Enter the user's name and a password if desired. On the next screen, check the Desktop Folder, Start Menu, and Favorites folder options, as required by the question. Using the bottom option on the dialog box, you can either copy the current settings or create the new user with blank settings—your choice. Click Next and then Finish, and the new user account will be added.

3. When setting up a computer for members of your family to share, you realize that everyone will need to use the same programs. What settings would you make or change so that whenever a new program is installed, everyone sees it on the Start menu?

A   In this case, the only thing we know for sure is that all users will share the same Start menu. There are two ways to accomplish this. The first would be not to allow any user to make changes to any settings, and the second would be to just make all users share the same Start menu. The procedures for setting up both methods follow.

To make all users use all the same settings, open the Passwords Control Panel applet. On the User Profiles tab, ensure that the top setting, All Users of This Computer Use the Same Preferences and Desktop Settings, is checked. Click OK; you might be told to restart. From now on, all users will share the same settings, desktop, and Start menu.

To allow users to customize their own settings but share the same Start menu, on the Passwords User Profiles tab, choose Users Can Customize Their Preferences and Desktop Settings. Then uncheck Include Start menu and Program groups. When you next log off or restart Windows, all users will share the default Start menu.

4. You, your spouse, and your two kids all share the same computer, but you each have different programs listed on your Start menu. Your daughter installs a nifty game that your spouse would also like to run, but it's not listed on your spouse's Start menu. You know that installing the game a second time would just be a waste of disk space. What would you do to put the icon for the game onto your spouse's Start menu?

A   As usual in Windows, there are a couple of ways to answer this question. I'll give what I consider to be the most complete one.

What you're going to do is copy the program group or icon from your daughter's Start menu to your spouse's. First, locate your daughter's profile settings. If her name were Jaimie, it would be in the folder `Windows\Profiles\Jaimie`. In that folder will be another folder named `Start Menu`, and in that will be one named `Programs`. Continue drilling down in her `Windows\Profiles\Jaimie\Start Menu\Programs` folder until you find the program icon or group that you want to add to your spouse's Start menu. When you've found it, select it and then copy it. Now, open your spouse's Start menu, which will be found in the folder `Windows\Profiles\`(*your spouse's name*)`\Start Menu\Programs`. Now paste the folder you copied here. If it doesn't show up immediately, have your spouse press the F5 key to refresh the view. The copied folder should now be visible, and should also appear on your spouse's Start menu. To verify, have your spouse click Start | Programs and look for the new folder or icon.

Day 14

1. Frequently, you'll find that a search on the Web returns lots of hits that don't necessarily make sense to you. Consequently, it can be useful to use a subject index. Yahoo! is one of the most popular subject indices. Use Yahoo! to find online tutorials for the Internet.

A Follow these steps:

1. Start Internet Explorer by clicking on the Internet Explorer icon in the Windows toolbar. If you're not sure which icon is the right one, hover the mouse over the icons to see a quick tip.

2. Enter **www.yahoo.com** in the Address bar for Internet Explorer and then press Enter.

3. You should now see the main Yahoo! page. Yahoo! begins with a series of subject links. Click on WWW underneath the heading Computers and Internet.

4. Now you should find yourself in the World Wide Web Yahoo! index. Find and click on the Information and Documentation link in the list of subjects.

   From here, you can navigate to a number of quick online tutorials about using the Internet.

A

2. Change your home page to MSNBC so that you get a news update each time you log in.

A Follow these steps:

1. Run Internet Explorer by clicking on the icon in the Windows toolbar.

2. Go to View | Internet Options.

3. In the address section, enter `www.msnbc.com` and then click OK. Next time you start Internet Explorer, you will see the front page for MSNBC. If you want to change back to your original page or to change to a different page, go back to the Internet Options and change the address.

Day 15

1. The MSNBC Web site has terrific news content covering a wide variety of topics. Add the MSNBC site to your desktop so that you can get updated headlines automatically. (Hint: The MSNBC site is `www.msnbc.com`.)

A Follow these steps:

1. Make sure that your desktop is set to view as a Web page. You can set it by clicking Start | Settings | Active Desktop | View as Web Page.

2. Open the properties for the desktop by right-clicking on the desktop and selecting Properties from the pop-up menu.

3. Click on the Web tab in the Desktop Properties box. The View My Active Desktop as a Web Page check box should be selected. Click New to add a Web page.

4. A dialog box may appear asking you if you want to go to the Microsoft gallery. Click No. The New Active Desktop Item dialog will appear. In the Location box, enter `www.msnbc.com` and then click OK.

5. A verification dialog will appear. Click OK to dismiss the dialog and update your new MSNBC desktop channel.

   When you return to the Display Properties dialog, click OK to save your changes. You should now see the MSNBC Web site on your desktop.

2. Windows Explorer is your gateway to almost anything on your Windows system. Use the Windows Explorer bar to view your current channel listing; then use it to view a helpful search guide.

A Follow these steps:

1. Start Windows Explorer by clicking Start | Programs | Windows Explorer from the Start menu.

2. Within Windows Explorer, click View | Explorer Bar | Channels. Instead of seeing the directory listing in the left side of the Explorer window, you should now see your channel listing. Click on a channel to view its contents in the right side of the screen.

3. Now switch to the Search view. To do so, click View | Explorer Bar | Search. Now you should see the Search bar in the left side of the screen.

4. If you want to return to the standard directory listing, click View | Explorer Bar | All Folders.

Day 16

1. Use Microsoft Outlook Express to create a birthday email using the standard birthday stationery.

A Complete these steps:

1. Run Microsoft Outlook Express. The quickest way to do this is using the Email icon on your toolbar.

2. From the main menu, select Compose | New Message Using | 1. Running Birthday.

   A formatted email message should appear with a birthday image. Make any changes that you want to the body of the message; then address it using the To: field. When you're finished, you can send it by clicking the Send button.

2. When you've received a lot of email, it can be very difficult to find individual messages. Keep yourself organized by creating a new folder called Work-Related.

A Follow these steps:

1. Run Microsoft Outlook Express.

2. When Outlook Express starts up, select Outlook Express in the left side of the screen (the portion that contains the folders). Right-click on Outlook Express.

3. From the context menu that appears, click New Folder. A Create Folder dialog will appear. Enter **Work-Related** in the Folder Name field and then click OK.

You're done; you should see a new folder in the left side of the screen. Now you can organize your messages by selectively dragging and dropping them from the Inbox to the Work-Related folder.

Day 17

1. Add yourself to the Four11 business directory for NetMeeting.

A Complete the following steps:

   1. Run NetMeeting from the Windows Start menu by clicking Start | Programs | Internet Explorer | Microsoft NetMeeting.

   2. Click Tools | Options from the NetMeeting Main Menu. The Options dialog will appear.

   3. Click the Calling tab. Select the Log On to the Directory Server When NetMeeting Starts box. Next, select ils.business.four11.com in the Server box. Make sure that Do Not List My Name in the Directory is not selected. Click OK to save your change and return to the main NetMeeting screen.

2. Use NetMeeting to connect with a business associate using a central business directory.

A Complete the following steps:

   1. Run NetMeeting from the Windows Start menu by clicking Start | Programs | Internet Explorer | Microsoft NetMeeting.

   2. Find the person you want to call in the list of people in one of the directories. If you want to use the ils.business.four11.com directory, help your associate to add his or her name to the directory by following the directions in exercise 1. Select the person's name, and then click the Call icon underneath the NetMeeting menu.

   3. A New Call dialog will appear. Verify that his or her ID shows up in the Address box. Click the Call button to connect to your associate. People should have NetMeeting open when you try to call them.

   4. Enjoy dynamic collaboration via the Internet! Try out the Whiteboard feature to share your ideas in a rich forum.

Day 18

1. The FrontPage Express Personal Home Page Wizard makes it very easy for you to create a home page, but the wizard creates your page with a boring gray background. Create a new home page and change the background to a light blue color.

A Here is one way:

1. Run FrontPage Express by clicking Start | Programs | Internet Explorer | FrontPage Express from the Windows Start menu.

2. In FrontPage Express, use File | New to display the New Page dialog. Select Personal Home Page Wizard and click OK.

3. In the Personal Home Page Wizard dialog, select the various options that you want and click Next. Repeat until the Next button grays out and then click Finish.

4. You will see your new home page with the boring background. Right-click the page and select Page Properties from the context menu. The Page Properties dialog box appears.

5. Switch to the Background tab. You'll see the Background list box with a gray rectangle with the word *Default*. Click the down arrow to display the list of available colors and select Aqua. Click OK to update your home page with the new background color.

2. Add links to Microsoft, Yahoo!, AltaVista, and MSNBC in the Hot List portion of your home page.

A Complete the following steps:

1. Create a home page using the FrontPage Express Personal Home Page Wizard. Use the defaults for the home page. For more details, see exercise 1.

2. Hit Page Down until you see the Hot List section.

3. Delete Sample Site 1 through Sample Site 3 and then enter **Microsoft**. Hit the Enter key to go to a new line and then enter **Yahoo!**. Repeat with **AltaVista** and **MSNBC**.

4. Use the mouse to select the word *Microsoft*. Now add a link to the Microsoft Web site by clicking Edit | Hyperlink. The Create Hyperlink dialog appears. In the URL field, enter **http://www.microsoft.com** and then click OK.

5. Repeat step 4 for the other links, but instead of entering **http://www.microsoft.com**, enter **http://www.yahoo.com**, **http://www.altavista.digital.com**, and **http://www.msnbc.com**, respectively.

Day 19

1. Describe the steps necessary to create a home page using the wizard; then change the style to a different style template.

A Assuming that the Personal Web Server is already installed, the steps are as follows:

1. Open the Personal Web Manager.
2. Click Web Site. Step through the wizard dialogs.
3. When Internet Explorer launches, fill in the fields on your Web page. Click Enter New Changes to commit your changes. Your Web page will be displayed as the user will see it.
4. Back in PWM, click again on the Web Site tab. Click Edit Your Home Page.
5. Internet Explorer will launch and display your page in edit mode. Select a different style from the three templates listed at the top of the form; then click Enter New Changes.

2. You've tired of the default home page you built using the wizard, so you've designed a much more elaborate one using FrontPage Express. You've designed everything in a directory called C:\NewWebSite. Your home page filename is myhome.htm. You now want to test your site by publishing it via PWS. Describe the steps necessary to do so.

A Remember that the following steps are always necessary when publishing a site via PWS:

1. Open PWM. Click the Advanced tab.
2. Click the <Home> virtual directory and click Edit.... Enter C:\NewWebSite in the directory box; then click OK.
3. Make sure that Enable Default Document is checked on the Advanced page.
4. Enter the name of your home page, myhome.htm, in the Default Document(s) field.
5. Verify that your site publishes properly by using Internet Explorer to browse your new site.

Day 20

1. Several people want to use Jane's printer; there isn't a network installed. Describe, in brief, the major steps you take so that other people can use Jane's printer.

A If all the people who want to use Jane's printer are close together, a printer sharing switch can be used. Whoever wants to print will just set the switch so that she has control of the printer. In most cases, a network is necessary. Each computer needs to have the following installed: a Network Interface Card, the networking protocols, and a hub. You need to run network cables, test network connectivity, share Jane's printer across the network, and add Jane's printer as a network printer to each computer.

2. To connect your computer to the local area network in your office, your administrator tells you that you must assign a static IP address to your computer. The address for your computer should be set to 145.241.0.45. Describe the steps necessary to make this setting.

A Several pieces actually need to be in place before the addressing can be set. First, the network interface card must be installed in the computer. The networking components of Windows and the TCP/IP protocol need to be installed. The setting of the static IP address is the last step.

To set the address, open the Network applet in the Control Panel. Find the Network Components line that shows TCP/IP —> (your network card). Click the line; then click Properties. On the Address tab, select Specify an IP Address; then enter the desired address, 145.241.0.45, in the IP address field. Click OK and again OK. You'll be prompted to reboot, after which your IP address will be set.

Day 21

1. Configure a DUN connection for an imaginary ISP with the following connection information and configuration requirements:

Name: Michael's ISP   Access Number: (800) 555-1234

Connection Type: PPP   IP Addressing: Dynamically assigned

DNS Addresses: 192.168.0.43   (Domain Name Server)
                     192.168.100.123

Use IP Header compression and default gateway.

A   After completing this exercise, you can delete the DUN connection you created. Open the Dial-Up Networking folder. Double-click on the Make New Connection icon. Enter a name for this connection; enter Michael's ISP or any other name that you'll remember. Select the proper modem. Click Next. Enter the area code (800) and the number (555-1234). Select United States under the Country setting. Click Next and then click Finish.

So far, you've completed the configuration for the dial-up connection. Now you must configure the TCP/IP settings for this particular ISP. Find your new DUN connection in the Dial-Up Networking folder; right-click it, and select Properties. The area code and telephone number are already set; click the Use Area Code and Dialing Properties setting so that it is checked.

Click on the Server Types tab. Select PPP:Internet, Windows NT Server, Windows 98 under Type of Dial-Up Server. Uncheck all the options under the Advanced Options section; if any of these were needed, the ISP would have told us. Under Allowed Network Protocols, make TCP/IP the only selected protocol. Click the TCP/IP Settings button. Ensure Server Assigned IP Address is selected at the top of the tab. The ISP gave us specific DNS addresses, so click on Specify Name Server Addresses. On the Primary DNS line, enter `192.168.000.43`. On the Secondary DNS line, enter `192.168.100.123`. Select Use IP Header Compression and Use Default Gateway on Remote Network.

Click OK. This ISP doesn't require entering any manual commands to log in, nor does it support multilink dialin, so no settings need to be changed on the Scripting or Multilink tabs. Click OK. You're finished!

2. Create a custom Power Management profile with the name My Profile that never turns off the disk or display and never goes into standby when the laptop is plugged in. Set it so that when it's running on batteries, it goes into standby after twenty minutes, turns off the monitor after ten minutes, and turns off the disks after five minutes.

A   Open the Power Management applet in the Control Panel. Click Save As and then type My Profile as the name. Click OK. Under the Plugged In column, select Never for all the settings. Under the Running on Batteries column, select 20 minutes for the System Standby setting, 10 minutes for the Turn Off Monitor setting, and 5 minutes for the Turn Off Hard Disks setting. Click OK.

APPENDIX B

Windows 98 Tips, Tricks, and Traps

by Paul Cassel

This appendix lists several tips, tricks, and traps for running Windows 98 faster, easier, or both, arranged by the following general topics: shortcuts and navigation, customization, tuning and maintenance, Registry, and DOS. Many of the items in this appendix apply to other versions of Windows such as Windows 95 and Windows NT. Many come from the public domain. Others are published for the first time in this book. In some cases, the same information appears in a different form in other locations in this book. These items are repeated here so that you can find them easily.

Shortcuts and Navigation

Trick: Fast Formatting   When in Windows Explorer, you can format any floppy or similar media by right-clicking on the drive and choosing Format from the context menu. Figure B.1 shows this context menu.

FIGURE B.1.

A context menu has the Format command added when Windows Explorer looks at a floppy drive.

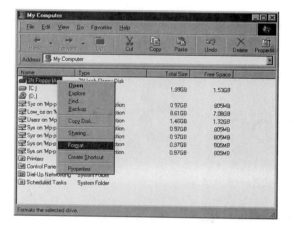

Tip: Fake Right Mouse Button   When dragging files, Ctrl+Shift+left-click drag functions the same as a right-click drag. Useful when your right button stops working or with some laptops.

Trick: Fast System Properties   Right-click on My Computer either in the Windows Explorer or the desktop and choose Properties from the context menu to take a fast trip, leaving you at the same place as the longer ride of Start I Settings I Control Panel I System.

Trick: Play the Cool Switch   The Cool Switch, Alt+Tab, was introduced in Windows 3.1 and remains active for all subsequent Microsoft operating systems. Using the Cool Switch, you can rotate through open programs and even dialog boxes that don't appear on the taskbar. Shift+Alt+Tab rotates backward through open programs. The Cool Switch packs some intelligence. If you switch between the same several programs, it will move those programs to the top of the queue.

Trick: Boots That Scoot   Hold down Shift while clicking OK with the Restart option button of Shutdown selected. Keep Shift held down until you see the Starting Windows message. This restarts Windows 98 without a full boot of your machine.

Tip: Avoiding the Desktop   Remember, you can access items such as the Control Panel, desktop folders, and Network Neighborhood from Windows Explorer. You don't need to use the Start menu or see the desktop for those or other items located, but usually overlooked, at the bottom of the left panel of Windows Explorer (see Figure B.2).

FIGURE B.2.

Windows Explorer has direct routes to often used areas such as the Control Panel.

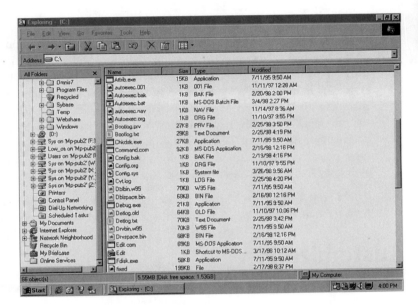

Tip: What's on Your Clipboard?   Windows 98 includes a little-known applet called the Clipboard Viewer. To view your current Clipboard, open this applet by choosing Start | Programs | Accessories | System Tools | Clipboard Viewer. You can use this viewer to delete the current contents of the Clipboard or to save them in a file format. Figure B.3 shows the Clipboard Viewer in action.

FIGURE B.3.

The Clipboard Viewer can display the Clipboard contents and save it as a file.

Tip: Keyboard Navigation in Folders   Windows 98 will jump to the first program or shortcut in a folder upon the pressing of the key with the same letter as the start of the program or shortcut's name. For example, if you open a folder with the application Bryce 3D in it and press the *b* key on your keyboard, you'll jump to that program, assuming it's the first program or shortcut starting with *b*. Press Enter and you'll launch the program. To see this in action, use Windows Explorer to open your Windows folder, and then press the *f* key. The focus will jump to the first file beginning with the letter *f*. Now press the *r* key to make the jump to the start of the *r* files. This works anywhere in Windows Explorer.

Trick: Fast Tab Moves   You can use the Ctrl+Tab key combo to move forward between dialog box tabs. Shift+Ctrl+Tab moves backwards through the tabs.

Customization

Trap: You Get Mystery UNIX Messages When Trying Newsgroups Posts   If you start getting messages from your ISP about not being able to locate a directory (usually ../Sendmail) when you're trying to post to public newsservers, try configuring your Outlook Express to send plain text only rather than HTML. To do this, open up Outlook Express, choose the menu items View | Options, and then go to the Send tab. Select the Plain Text option for Mail sending format. This will solve many mysterious posting problems but will disable your ability to post fancily formatted messages.

Trap: DUN Connects Sporadically or Gives Bizarre Messages About Protocols
If you can't get Dial-Up Networking (DUN) to connect, you might be asking it to connect using unsuitable protocols. If you're dialing the Internet, you probably need only the TCP/IP protocol. Any other protocols will at best delay your connections. At worst, they'll prevent them from occurring. To see what protocols you have for DUN, open

DUN by choosing Start | Programs | Accessories | Communications | Dial-Up Networking. Right-click on the troublesome connection and choose Properties from the context menu. Choose the Server Types tab and inspect the Allowed Network Protocols section shown in Figure B.4. Uncheck any unneeded protocols. If in doubt and your connection is to the Internet through an ISP, try leaving only TCP/IP checked.

Figure B.4.

The little-known allowed protocols section of DUN can create connection havoc if misconfigured.

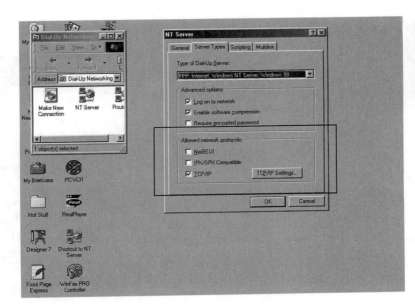

B

Trick: Start a Program Automatically on Windows 98 Startup   This trick is simple. To have a program launch upon Windows' start, right-click the Start button. Choose Open. Open the Programs folder. Open the Startup folder inside the Programs folder. Into this folder, drag or otherwise create a shortcut to the program you want to start automatically. Close things up. The next time you start Windows 98, the programs in Startup will launch automatically.

Tip: Really Delete Files   You can prevent a file or files from appearing in the Recycle Bin by pressing Shift as you drag them from Windows Explorer to the bin. If you don't want files to appear in the bin by default, right-click on the Recycle Bin. Choose Properties from the context menu; then locate the Do Not Move Files to the Recycle Bin check box on the Global tab. Check this box for permanent deletion of your files. Note that not moving files to the bin doesn't mean they're securely erased. Secure erase requires multiple overwrites of the file space. Windows 98 doesn't have a built-in facility for this chore. You'll need a third-party utility to do this.

Trick: Taskbar Travel   You can move the taskbar to any side of the screen you want. Some canny users like to move the taskbar to the left side of the screen, make it wide enough to show the full names of programs, and then set it to Autohide so that it gets out of the way when not in use. This keeps the taskbar out of sight when not in use but shows running programs with their full names. Figure B.5 shows this setup. If you choose to run this way, make sure to put the taskbar on the left side of the screen. If you place it on the right, you'll activate Autohide when you want to use the vertical scrollbar.

FIGURE B.5.

A taskbar placed on the left side is a much better taskbar.

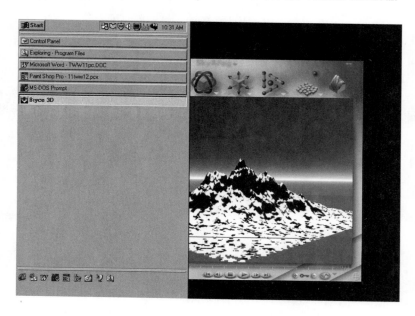

Trick: Any BMP File Is an Icon   You can use any BMP file for an icon. To do so, right-click on any shortcut or program, and choose Properties from the context menu. Select Change Icon and then Browse. Change the file selection from Icon Files to All Files. Browse for the BMP you want to use, select it, and then OK your way out. Figure B.6 shows the choosing process; Figure B.7 shows the result of the change.

FIGURE B.6.

Any BMP file makes a good icon for your programs or applications.

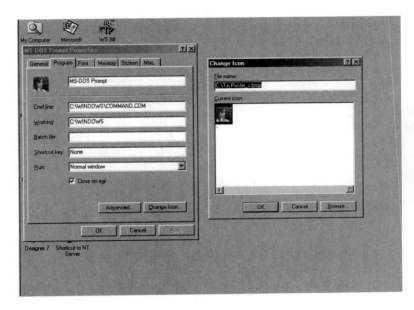

FIGURE B.7.

Here the MS-DOS Prompt icon has been created out of a large BMP file of a little girl. Windows 98 does a good job of "iconizing" the large file for use as an icon.

Trap: Get Out of My Documents   Windows 98's Setup will have many, if not all, applications placing their data files in My Documents. This works for most users, but some prefer to place their files in different locations. A proper Windows 98 or Windows NT program will allow you to specify where it saves its files by default. Finding that option isn't always easy, but if you press the issue, you can usually wrinkle it out. Figure B.8 shows the dialog box for this option in Microsoft Word.

FIGURE B.8.

You don't have to accept My Documents for your data files. Search out the way individual programs point to their save files to change this behavior.

Trick: Fonts and Colors in Start   You can change the fonts and colors for Start and the taskbar using the Display Properties dialog box. Choose the Appearance tab and Selected Items for category. Changes there will leak through to Start and the taskbar's menu (although not to the running programs boxes). The results of changing this parameter are far reaching. Be sure to save your current scheme before making any changes so that you can return to the way you were.

Trick: Tweaking for Twerps   Microsoft supplies an unofficial tool for tweaking Windows 98. Intended for the dweeb and twerp set, TWEAKUI is useful to everybody but must be used with caution because you can tweak yourself into an unusable operating system if you use it unwisely. A version of Tweak UI is in the TWEAKUI folder on most distribution CD-ROMs. If your CD-ROM doesn't have such a folder, you can download the utility from the usual suspects, including the Microsoft site. After you've located or downloaded it, right-click on the TWEAKUI.INF file and then choose Install from the context menu. This will create a Tweak UI applet in Control Panel. Figure B.9 shows this utility opened and ready to customize your Windows 98.

Tip: Fax Is In...for Some   Microsoft dropped the full version of Microsoft Fax somewhere in between when Windows 95 became Windows 98. If you have one of several programs (such as Exchange or Windows 95 fax) already installed, you can add fax to Windows 98 by looking in the FAX folder on the distribution CD-ROM. The exact location and even the existence of the folder varies, depending on the distribution version of Windows 98 you have.

FIGURE B.9.

The once secret tool of the dweeb and twerp set, Tweak UI is something everybody can use to make his Windows 98 act just as he prefers it.

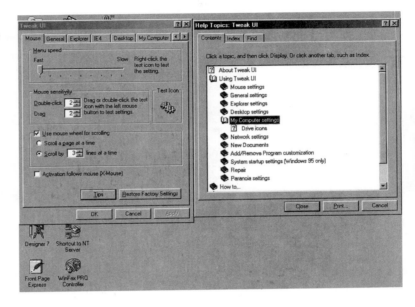

Maintenance and Tuning

Trick: Tune Your Machine   Windows NT system administrators use the Performance Monitor to tune their systems. A smaller version of this tool is part of the Windows 98. It is called System Monitor. If you don't see it as part of Start | Programs | Accessories | System Tools, you can install it using the Windows Setup tab of Control Panel | Add/Remove Programs applet. Launch the System Monitor and add what systems you want to monitor. Just like the Performance Monitor in Windows NT, the System Monitor can log its findings for later analysis. Figure B.10 shows the System Monitor chugging along, tracking CPU usage, threads, and virtual machines.

Trap: Beware of WordPad   Many will tell you that WordPad is just a large Notepad with some formatting. There is another big difference. A Notepad file is pure ASCII, whereas a WordPad file is in a binary format. That makes Notepad suitable for editing batch (BAT) and INI files, whereas WordPad isn't. There are several free Notepad replacements available that have much of WordPad's function (such as capacity of larger file sizes) while still using the pure ASCII file format of Notepad. An Internet Explorer search of the Internet will reveal these programs located in the usual download sites. Figure B.11 shows one such program, written by RogSoft, at `http://www.xs4all.nl/ ~theroge/`. It is also freely available on the Internet at various download sites.

FIGURE B.10.

Windows 98 has a version of Windows NT's Performance Monitor as part of its standard tools.

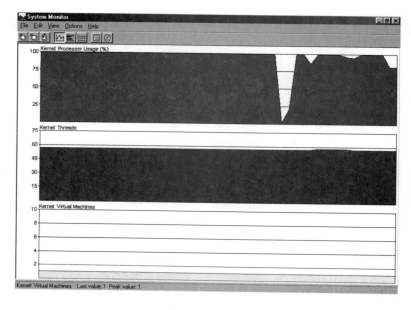

FIGURE B.11.

You don't have to be saddled with Notepad's limitations or WordPad's file formats. RogSoft's Notepad+ is one of several free programs that do the job of both.

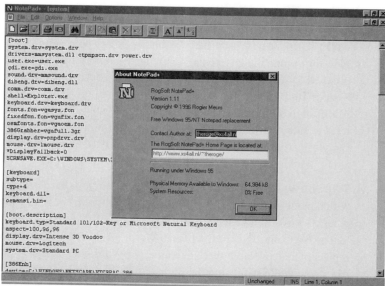

Trap: Internet Explorer Will Eat Your Disk   Internet Explorer will, by default, take up 10% of your disk space for its temporary files. This is a decent percentage for FAT16 volumes that rarely exceed 500MB. However, new, larger volumes are part of the game with volumes of several gigabytes, and that 10% no longer makes sense. Open Internet Explorer, choose View | Internet Options from the menu, and then click the Settings button in the middle section of the tabbed dialog box. This will reveal a slider allowing you to adjust the size and location of your temporary files to suit your needs. Figure B.12 shows the series of relevant dialog boxes. You can also use this series of dialog boxes to view your temporary files or to move them permanently to another volume. If you find you're running out of room on your %windows% volume (usually C:\Windows), look here first. Most people need no more than 10MB of temporary files. On a 4GB volume, IE will, if left alone, eat up 400MB!

FIGURE B.12.

Internet Explorer will go berserk eating up your disk space unless you bring it to heel.

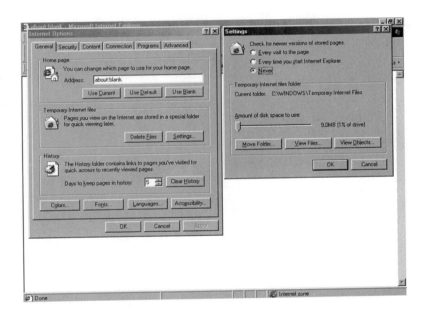

Trap: Autorun Runs Automatically   Most people like the Autorun feature of the CD-ROM drive. A few, especially those who want to access only a few files on a CD-ROM, consider it a pain. To disable this feature on a disc-by-disc basis, hold down the Shift key while inserting a CD-ROM. To disable it for good, right-click on My Computer to open the Device Manager. Choose Properties from the context menu; then choose the Device Manager tab. Locate your CD-ROM drive, right-click on the drive, and choose Properties from that context menu. Choose the Settings tab. Locate the Auto Insert Notification check box and clear it. That will do it.

Tip: Tune Windows 3.1 Applications Windows 98 comes with an undocumented utility to tune Windows 3.x (16-bit) programs. It's called MAKE COMPATIBLE. To run this utility, use the menu choices Start | Run and then enter MKCOMPAT on the command line. This will bring up the dialog box shown in Figure B.13. Choose the program you want to apply the changes to from the File menu. These options are advanced and technical in nature. With luck, the 16-bit application itself will, through error messages, give you some hints as to what it needs.

FIGURE B.13.

The Advanced list of options from the MAKE COMPATIBLE utility.

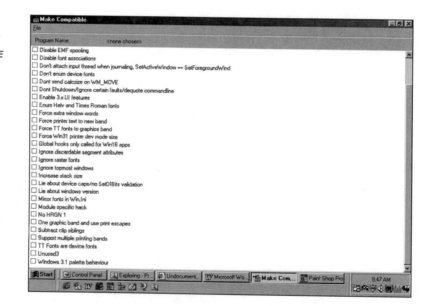

Tip: Run Tune-Ups in Order To get the most out of Windows 98 tuning, run Disk Cleanup before running Disk Defragmenter. Running the two in the opposite order reduces the effectiveness of the Defragmenter.

Tip: Swapfile Moves to Speed Up Windows 98 You can give a real performance boost to Windows 98 by locating its swapfile on its own physical disk. If that's impossible, locate it on its own volume to prevent any fragmentation of the swapfile that occurs if it shares space with regular files. To move the swapfile, choose Control Panel | System | Performance | Virtual Memory. If necessary, create a volume (partition) especially to host the swapfile if you want Windows 98 to run at its top speed.

Registry

Some of the hints in this section require you to edit the Registry. This isn't terribly difficult, but a mistake can have disastrous consequences, even to the point of making Windows 98 fail to run again. Before tackling Registry editing, you should have an up-to-date ESD (emergency startup disk), and you should back up the Registry before making any modifications.

One further thing: Make changes to the Registry singly. Test to make sure Windows 98 is working properly and then make the next modification. This way, if you need to roll back a change, you'll know specifically what must be rolled back.

The Registry is the heart of Windows 98. There is no such thing as too much caution when doing heart surgery. If you are in any doubt about how to back up and restore a Registry in case of a problem, leave the surgeries until you have lost that doubt.

Trick: Arghhhh! It Won't Die! Some programs don't uninstall properly. These often will be removed, or you will remove them manually, but they'll still appear on the Installed Programs section of Control Panel | Add/Remove Programs. To excise these programs manually, open up your Registry using REGEDIT (Start | Run | Regedit). Locate the branch HKEY_LOCAL_MACHINE\Software\Microsoft\Windows\ CurrentVersion\Uninstall and manually remove the offending entry. Those uncomfortable with REGEDIT should approach this operation with some caution. All should back up their Registry by using the REGEDIT menu choices Registry | Export Registry before attempting any Registry edits. Figure B.14 shows this branch of the Registry along with the Add/Remove Programs applet. As you can see, the Registry contains a superset of what appears in the applications list section of the applet. Remove items with care!

Trick: Hey! My Name Isn't I. MIUEU!EY#** If Windows 98 has your name spelled wrong as part of its registration information, you can change your registered name by searching for the current string in REGEDIT. Use the menu choices Edit | Find or press Ctrl+F. When you find the misspelled string under the key HKEY_LOCAL_MACHINE\ Software\Microsoft\Windows\CurrentVersion, just replace the data with the correct one. This also works for your company name. Beware of messing with this key of the

Registry. The entries here are vital for proper Windows 98 functioning. Use the usual cautions for playing with the Registry. Note that this change will not necessarily be reflected in currently registered programs. You'll need to hunt out all wrong data entries for all applications to see this rippled throughout your Windows 98 setup. A better solution is to make sure you enter your name correctly during the initial setup.

FIGURE B.14.

You can wrestle control of your Add/Remove Programs applet away from Windows 98 by manually editing the Registry.

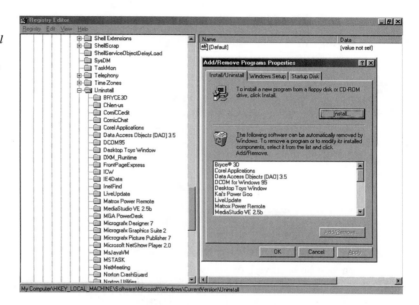

Trap: A Program Starts Automatically with Windows 98, and You Don't Want It To   If the program isn't in Startup or in the Run line in Win.ini, look at the Registry key HKEY_LOCAL_MACHINE\Software\Microsoft\Windows\CurrentVersion\RUN.

That's where many of these pesky items lurk.

DOS

Trap: MS-DOS Delete Does Not Use the Recycle Bin   Files deleted in the command-line interface (CLI) will not be moved to the Recycle Bin. They cannot be undeleted using the tools supplied by Windows 98. Third-party utilities do perform this trick, however.

Tip: Don't Forget DOSKEY The program DOSKEY enjoyed a short but popular life at the end of the MS-DOS era. Its existence lives on in Windows 98, although Microsoft is quiet about any command-line features of its latest GUI operating systems. Introduced in MS-DOS version 5, this utility buffered and then allowed the user to recall a series of commands. This is extremely useful for most CLI sessions. Many experienced users run DOSKEY right after launching an MS-DOS shell.

Trick: Long Filenames Live Under MS-DOS You can use long filenames at the command-line interface (CLI) or the DOS prompt. To do so, you only need to enclose the long filename in double quotes. So, for example, the command

```
CD program files
```

is invalid due to the space and the length. However, the command modified to read

```
CD "program files"
```

will change the directory to Program Files. Note: The MS-DOS CLI is not case sensitive for long filenames, too. Most people feel that using long filenames with quotes is a lot easier than hunting for the tilde to use the 8.3 file equivalent name. The MS-DOS dir command will show long filenames as well as the 8.3 name. See Figure B.15 for an example of the dir command and using long filenames at the CLI.

FIGURE B.15.

MS-DOS is 90% ready for long filenames. If you know a trick or two, you can up that another 10%.

Trick: Document-Centered MS-DOS Starts You can launch documents using their associated programs from the command line. Just enter the word Start and the document name on the command line and then let the magic occur. For example, to launch Word (if it's associated with the .doc extension), enter **start myfile.doc** at the command line. myfile.doc must be in the local path, of course.

Summary

This is an unusual element in this book because it's not so much a tutorial, as is the rest of the book, but a miscellaneous bunch of ideas to make Windows 98 work better or more to your liking.

Each of these tips, tricks, or traps was figured out by typical users like you. Feel free to experiment with Windows 98 to invent some of these types of items yourself. Just be careful when editing the Registry—especially if you're flying without a guide wire. Every Registry tip cost some user or users about 10 Registries. Be backed up and be safe.

INDEX

Symbols

< > (angle brackets), 449
* (asterisk), 284
/ (forward slash), 449
? (question mark), 272
10BASE-2, 494
10BASE-T, 493
404 error messages, 487

A

<A> HTML tag, 451
Access Control tab
  (Network dialog box),
  502
Accessibility options, 12,
  178-180
    Automatic Reset, 182
    display options, 181
    keyboard options, 180

mouse options, 182
Notification, 182
SerialKey device sup-
  port, 182
sound options, 180
Accessibility Properties
  dialog box
    Display tab, 181
    General tab, 182
    Keyboard tab, 180
    Sound tab, 180
accessing
  MS-DOS, 268
  multiple user accounts,
    344
  newsgroups, 409-412
accounts (multiple user)
  access control, 344
  creating, 345-346
  duplicating, 346
  individualized desktops,
    337-342
  Microsoft Family Logon,
    342-344

passwords, 348-349
removing, 346
restoring, 347
switching between, 347
Accounts tool (Address
  Book), 407
activating spooler, 111
Active Desktop
  channels
    adding, 389
    channel bar, 385
  configuring, 49-53
  customizing, 156-157
    color depth, 165-166
    colors, 158, 161-162
    icons, 157-158
    imitating Windows
      95, 168-169
    multiple user
      accounts, 338-342
    resolution, 163-165
    wallpaper, 166-168
  definition of, 392
  icons, 26

Q-R